The Complete Idiot's Referenc

The Seven Best Places to

On this page and throughout this book, you'll find some handy r
ghost expedition. For more detail, you'll find the essentials for yo
explained in Chapter 11. In Part 4 you'll read about hundreds of
out card lists seven broad categories of sites where you might be l
page makes your fingers itchy to work a Ouija board, you'll find the spirit-channeling device described in
Chapter 8. Happy hunting!

1. **Old houses.** Those rundown mansions might just be haunted, especially if a death occurred inside. The Borley Rectory was once said to be the most haunted house in England.

2. **Castles.** Dungeons, drafty rooms, and dark corridors are pretty enticing to spirits of the night. Glamis Castle, the traditional (though not historical) site of Macbeth's murder of King Duncan, is a perfect example.

3. **Churches, monasteries, and abbeys.** For whom do the bells toll? Ghostly monks and nuns, especially those of martyrs, have been sighted throughout the world. Glastonbury Abbey, England's first Christian Church, was excavated in the 20th century with the assistance of spirit monks.

4. **Cemeteries.** This is a no-brainer. The ghosts don't even travel far from home. Bachelor Grove and Resurrection cemeteries outside Chicago are two of the most famously haunted.

5. **Theaters.** Many actors just never want to leave the stage. They linger on long after the spotlight has faded. Hundreds have sighted the spectre of Man in Grey in London's Drury Lane Theatre.

6. **Battlefields.** Sites of tragedy and loss, such as those seen during the horrors of war, are often haunted. Two of the most famous battlegrounds are at Gettysburg and outside Fort Ticonderoga.

7. **Death sites.** Sometimes the spirits stay behind because they don't know they're dead. Some can't break free from the trauma surrounding their death. Others just to revisit the sites of their demise.

Twelve Essentials for Your Ghost-Hunter Field Trip

1. **Food and water.** You may be waiting for a long time. If you get hungry or thirsty, who ya gonna call?

2. **Wristwatch.** You should record what time the ghost appears … and know what time to go home.

3. **A 35 mm camera with several rolls of high-speed film.** You don't want to be caught with an empty camera if a ghost does show up.

4. **Video camera and videotape.** When ghosts are on the move, you'll want to catch them in action.

5. **Audio recorder and audiotape.** Tape sounds you hear (and possibly noises you don't hear) to analyze when you get home.

6. **Flashlight.** Maybe ghosts can find their way in the dark, but you probably can't.

7. **First aid kit.** Be prepared. Enough said.

8. **Notebook, with pens and/or pencils.** Record everything you even *think* you see, hear, or feel.

9. **Plastic bags or clean containers.** Keep that evidence untainted. You don't want your proof thrown out of court for being contaminated.

10. **Chalk.** Outline objects to prove, later, how much they've been moved by ghosts or poltergeists.

11. **Compass.** You can use it to chart the direction in which ghosts and flying objects move … and to find your way home.

12. **Thermometer.** You'll want to record the sudden temperature swings that often signal the presence of spirits.

tear here

alpha
books

Try the Ouija Board for Yourself!

You'll find a miniature Ouija board printed below. Lay the Ouija board out flat in front of you on a table. Lightly rest the fingertips of one of your hands on the board, with the fore-finger pointing forward. Think of a question that you want the spirits to answer, or ask the question out loud. If you feel your hand wanting to move, let it. Record the sequence of letters and numbers your forefinger points to or goes near. If the spirits are with you, they'll spell out words or give numerical answers to your questions.

1 2 3 4 5 6 7 8 9

OUIJA

A B C D E F G H I
J K L M N O P Q
R S T U V W Y Z

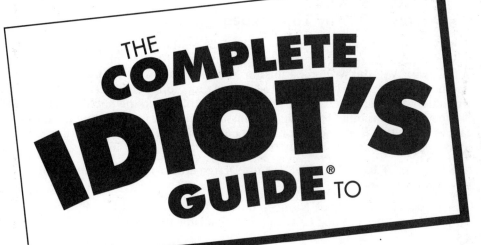

THE COMPLETE IDIOT'S GUIDE® TO

Ghosts and Hauntings

by Tom Ogden

alpha books

Macmillan USA, Inc.
201 West 103rd Street
Indianapolis, IN 46290

A Pearson Education Company

To Mom, Dad, Jeanne, Wayne, and all my other family spirits

Copyright © 1999 by Tom Ogden

THE COMPLETE IDIOT'S GUIDE TO and Design are registered trademarks of Macmillan USA, Inc.

International Standard Book Number: 0-02-863659-7
Library of Congress Catalog Card Number: Available upon request.

01 00 99   8 7 6 5 4 3 2 1

Interpretation of the printing code: The rightmost number of the first series of numbers is the year of the book's printing; the rightmost number of the second series of numbers is the number of the book's printing. For example, a printing code of 99-1 shows that the first printing occurred in 1999.

Printed in the United States of America

Contents at a Glance

Contents

Foreword

"They're here!"

When I was asked to create the role of Tangina Barrons, the medium who's able to contact and exorcise the evil spirits in the movie *Poltergeist,* I became very excited. It was a dream role for an actress: She's a colorful character who seems just this side of crazy, but she's completely committed to what she knows is true.

And what Tangina knew was this: Ghosts and poltergeist *can* and *do* exist, and, if they want to, they can *find* you!

Up until the time I was cast as "ghostbuster," I'd given very little thought as to whether poltergeists, much less ghosts or other spirit entities, actually exist.

I had heard the stories—they were in all the tabloids—that poltergeist phenomena and other odd events had occurred on the sets of other high-profile supernatural thrillers such as *The Exorcist* and *The Amityville Horror.*

But I guess we were the lucky ones: Nothing of that sort took place during the shooting of the three *Poltergeist* movies. Fortunately, all those animated skeletons and spirited spooks you saw in our films were special effects for the screen.

The book you hold in your hands isn't exactly spooky, but some of stories do get pretty scary! It's a fun and sometimes frightening read.

Tom Ogden's spent a lifetime studying magic and the supernatural, so you're really in for a treat. He's collected some of the most famous ghost stories of all times. You'll see how ghosts have haunted people throughout history and how we of the living have tried to communicate with those on the Other Side. (Having portrayed a medium myself in several films and TV shows, I felt right at home with the chapters on séances!) And, this book tells you how to become a ghost hunter yourself. That is, if you dare!

Do I believe in ghosts? I'm not sure. But I'll tell you what: *They* believe in *you.*

Happy hauntings,

Zelda Rubinstein

ZELDA RUBINSTEIN

Zelda Rubinstein is probably best known for her portrayal of the medium in *Poltergeist, Poltergeist II: The Other Side,* and *Poltergeist III,* as well as her recurring role as Ginny Weedon on the television series *Picket Fences.* Her other film credits include *Lover's Knot, Little Witches, Timemaster, Teen Witch, Guilty as Charged, Anguish,* and *16 Candles.* She has also guest starred on such television shows as *Caroline in the City, Martin, Sable, Whiz Kids, Poltergeist: The Legacy,* and many others.

Introduction

When my friends heard I was writing a book about ghosts and hauntings, they all asked the same question: Do I believe that ghosts exist?

Well, yes, I believe it's *possible* that they do. But then, for almost all of my life, I've been a professional magician. And in Magic 101 we're taught to believe that *anything* is possible. (In fact, that's what we magicians do for a living: We make the impossible possible.)

Have I ever seen a ghost?

Well, no, not that I know of. But I've heard strange, unexplained noises at the other end of the house. Have I ever experienced a chill as I walked beside a cemetery at night? Sure. Have I ever felt someone—some invisible presence—standing in the room with me, even though I knew I was all alone? Well, yes again. What were these experiences? Were they ghosts? Or was it just my medication kicking in?

The answer I give my friends is very simple: I don't have to *see* something to know it exists. I've never seen an atom but I know they're there. (Well, that is, they are if I trust Mr. Clark of my seventh-grade science class.)

Who hasn't been fascinated with what—if anything—lies beyond this life of ours? And is it ever possible to return, in any form, to the world of the living? These are the questions of which ghost stories are made.

Throughout the centuries, too many people have reported too many things for us to ignore them or to say with certainty, that ghosts don't exist. They saw, heard, or felt *something*. What could their experiences have been? Spirits? Ghosts? And if not, what?

How to Use This Book

The Complete Idiot's Guide to Ghosts and Hauntings is divided into five parts, each of which examines some segment of the world of ghosts.

Part 1, "The Great Beyond," takes us back to when humankind first started to question the mysteries of life and the afterlife. We'll trace Western beliefs in ghosts through the eyes of the Egyptians, the ancient Greeks and Romans, and the early Christian Church. Then we'll take a look at the pesky folkloric household spirits and demons, followed by a walk on the wild side with the poltergeists.

Part 2, "Don't Call Us, We'll Call You," traces the rise and fall of the spiritualism movement in America and abroad. Sitting with a medium around a séance table served an important purpose for some: If the ghost wouldn't come to you, maybe you could go to it! We'll meet some of the stars of spiritualism and follow along into the séance room to find out what goes on when the lights go down.

Part 3, "Who Ya Gonna Call?" may be where you want to turn first if you think you've seen a ghost. This section of the book introduces some famous skeptics, psychic societies, and paranormal investigators. We'll look at their methods and learn for ourselves how to become ghost hunters and ghostbusters!

Part 4, "Make Yourself at Home: The Hauntings," is my favorite part of the book, because it's filled with scary stories from the literally thousands of legends, case histories, and reports of sightings. Just for the fun of it, I've broken the chapters down into what or where the spirit haunts: a house, cemetery, castle, theater—you name it!

Part 5, "We Are Not Alone," looks at some of the ways ghosts and spirit phenomena have been reflected in popular culture. First, you'll discover the magic connection— how illusionists have used their secret art to seemingly create ghosts and phantoms, sometimes for fun, sometimes for profit. Then we'll review some of the more popular books, plays, and movies that have featured ghosts and ghost stories.

On top of all that, I've added four appendixes. For the serious student, I think it's important information and worth a read.

Appendix A, "Phantom Phrases," collects all the definitions and jargon terms that have been introduced through *The Complete Idiot's Guide to Ghosts and Hauntings.*

Appendix B, "Continuing the Ghost Hunt," is a collection of the names and addresses of the major psychical societies and paranormal investigators. Some of the more popular Internet Web sites, set up by professional ghost hunters or aficionados, and ghost tours are listed here.

Appendix C, "Boo-Boo-Boo, Books!" is a list of recommended reading about ghosts, spirits, and hauntings. Bear in mind that, at any given time, there are hundreds of books in print about ghosts. These are a few that have stood the test of time, are readily available, or that highlight a particular area of interest.

Appendix D, "Haunted Places in the U.S. and Great Britain," gives the addresses, phone numbers, or directions to all of the major haunted sites mentioned in this book that are open for tourism, are public properties, or welcome your business patronage.

Spooky Boxes

Throughout this book, I've added four types of boxes that give you extra information:

Ghostly Pursuits

These little side stories and colorful anecdotes give you background information or provide a different point of view to our tales of ghostly terror.

Ghostbusting

Here are some special hints and tips to help you contact the spirit world, see a ghost, or even get rid of a pesky phantom.

Boo!

Do you want to wind up being a ghost yourself? Here's what to avoid when you're out there in the dark looking for spooks.

Phantom Phrases

These are the special words—and some common words with really weird meanings—as used by ghost hunters, ghostbusters, and people involved in the paranormal.

Acknowledgments

There are many people I have to credit for putting me in touch with the spirit world. My special thanks goes out to Marcello Trucci, Michael Kurland, Max Maven, Eugene Burger, Gordon Bean (librarian at the Magic Castle, Hollywood), and Lilly Walters for their advice and research assistance.

Thank you to all those who made my quest for photographs much easier: Patrice Keane and the American Society for Psychical Research (ASPR); Gill Crawford and The Strathmore Estates (Scotland); Betty Jean Morris and Peggy Ebright of the Pasadena Playhouse; Pamela Young for the excellent spirit photo of Invisible Irma; the Magic Castle; Mark Willoughby of Collectors Book Store in Hollywood (CA); Mel Pierce Camera (especially Bob Ross); Norman Deery; *Country Life* magazine; Major Kearn Malin RMP; Greg Bordner and Abbott's Magic Manufacturing Company of Colon (MI); Dave Ngan and Van Tran at Davco Printing; and Richard Kaufman. A special thanks goes out to my patient and understanding editors Gary Krebs, Lynn Northrup, and Robyn Burnett. And, finally, thanks to all of you who shared with me the stories of your own personal ghost encounters. I hope you're happy: Those stories are the reason I now can't sleep at night.

Trademarks

All terms mentioned in this book that are known to be or are suspected of being trademarks or service marks have been appropriately capitalized. Alpha Books and Macmillan USA, Inc. cannot attest to the accuracy of this information. Use of a term in this book should not be regarded as affecting the validity of any trademark or service mark.

The following trademarks have been mentioned in this book:

Haunted Mansion®

Magic Castle™

Invisible Irma™

GOOSEBUMPS®

Oscar®

OUIJA®

Disneyland®

Casper™

The Ghostly Trio™

OUIJA®

Mention and illustrations of ouija or Ouija boards throughout *The Complete Idiot's Guide to Ghosts and Hauntings* are not intended to, nor should they be, confused with the OUIJA® game and its distinctive elements, which are the trademarked property of Hasbro, Inc.

Reality and Proof Disclaimer

Finally, because there is no definitive proof that ghosts or other spirits actually exist, all of the many sightings and hauntings described in this book should be considered accounts of *alleged* occurrences of paranormal activity.

Part 1
The Great Beyond

I know what you want: "Tell us some ghost stories! Please?"

Don't worry, there are plenty of spooky tales coming up. But, first, we should put the whole realm of ghostdom in context against the background in which these legends have evolved. In this section we'll take a peek into the distant past to find out what ancient civilizations thought about survival after death and what they believed happens to us after we, well, bite the dust. And, if we do come back, in what form do we return?

Then we'll look at some of the first recorded ghost stories in Western culture and how they were reinterpreted by the early Christian Church. That's not to ignore the old wives' tales, superstitions, and friendly folklore that have grown up about phantoms. They're here, too—including that pesky prankster, the poltergeist.

So don't be frightened—turn the page!

Chapter 1

Let's Enter the Spirit World

In This Chapter

➤ Ghosts vs. apparitions

➤ Survival after death

➤ The destination of the soul

➤ Festivals of the dead

There are ghosts among us! At least, that's what people have claimed since the earliest of times. Ghost stories filled folklore long before the written word. Animistic societies saw the ghosts of their ancestors. To foretell the future, ancient seers called up spirits (at least they "looked" like spirits). By the 1st century A.D., historians were beginning to write down popular ghost tales and legends.

Two thousand years later, our quandary continues. There've been too many reports of spectres and ghostly phenomena to be ignored: Something must be out there! But—and here's the big but—what is it that everyone's seeing and hearing and experiencing?

Hopefully, by the end of this book, you'll have some answers.

Before we plunge into case histories (sorry, *ghost stories*), we have to make sure we're all speaking the same language. Let's take a look at some of the simple, yet sometimes misunderstood vocabulary that's specific to the study of ghostly phenomena.

It's a Bird, It's a Plane, But Is It Supernatural?

Most researchers and theorists of spirit sightings tend to shun the word *supernatural*. I'm not sure why. It's a perfectly fine word with a very clear meaning: "existing or occurring through some agency beyond the known forces of nature." The word comes from the Latin *super,* meaning "above," and *nasci,* meaning "to be born." In other words, it was created; we just don't know how. It's beyond anything we know or understand.

Yet, the study of ghosts is a quirky and questionable subject to begin with. And for investigators who wanted to be taken seriously, perhaps the word "supernatural" carried too many divine, occult, or even Satanic connotations. So, they prefer to use a related word: *paranormal.*

Many people who are interested in ghosts have a general interest in all psychic phenomena. The related field of parapsychology looks for evidence of phenomena caused by the mind but can't be explained. In layperson's terms, it's the study of ESP (extrasensory perception). There are many categories of psychic phenomena, including, but not limited to:

➤ **Telepathy.** Communication through means other than the five senses, normally referred to as mind-reading

➤ **Clairvoyance.** Seeing objects or events that no one knows and cannot be perceived by the five senses; for example, foretelling the future

➤ **Psychokinesis.** Making objects move through mind power alone

Phantom Phrases

Something that's **supernatural** cannot be explained by any known means or force of nature. It is above or beyond natural explanation. The word generally carries the suggestion that some divine, demonic, or Higher Power is involved in making the event occur. To avoid this mystical connotation, researchers prefer to use the term **paranormal,** which also means something beyond the range of normal human experiences or scientific explanation.

Phantom Phrases

A **ghost,** as the word is used by most people, is the visual appearance of a deceased human being's spirit, life force, essence, or soul. In more general terms, an **apparition** is the visual appearance of any spirit phenomenon. Laypeople use the words interchangeably; paranormal investigators prefer to use the word apparition. To them, a ghost is only one kind of apparition.

Is It a Ghost or an Apparition?

Most people use the word *ghost* to mean any phantom object when what they really mean is the spirit of a deceased human being. In this book, I'll concentrate on ghost sightings.

But much of the reported phenomena over the centuries have involved objects that are or were never human. For example, people have reported seeing phantom animals and phantom trains. But they weren't human, and they certainly didn't have (as usually defined) a soul or spirit that could return from the dead.

So, to avoid any confusion, paranormal investigators prefer to use the more general word *apparition* to mean the visual appearance of a disembodied spirit. This encompasses all types of phantoms, human or otherwise. For example, the appearance of an angel by your beside would be an apparition, but you'd never call it a ghost.

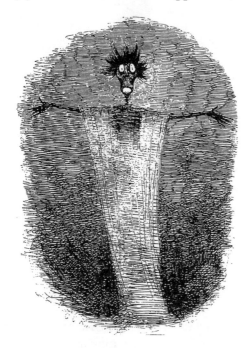

An apparition. (Engraving by George Cruikshank)

Think of this way: All ghosts are apparitions, but not all apparitions are ghosts.

To add to the confusion, here are just a few more synonyms for an apparition, all used colloquially to mean "ghost":

➤ Nightshade

➤ Phantasm

➤ Phantom

➤ Shade

➤ Shadow

➤ Spectre or specter

➤ Spook

➤ Vision

➤ Wraith

And poltergeists are another thing altogether. We'll take a special look at them in Chapter 5, "Poltergeists: They're Here!"

Now I realize that these are distinctions not normally made by people on the street. But to avoid confusion as to what claims are actually being made, investigators feel it's best to stick to the word "apparition" unless you specifically mean a ghost.

There are all sorts of ghosts, and they keep all sorts of schedules.

➤ Some have been sighted only once. There's a well-documented case of the luminous ghost of a boy appearing in Corby Castle in Cumberland, England, on the night of September 8, 1824—only.

➤ They appear at a certain date or time of night. You'll read in Chapter 21, "School Daze: America's Most Haunted Schools," about a female ghost who appears at midnight on every Friday the 13th at Simpson College in Indianola, Iowa.

➤ Some mark the anniversary of an event. A phantom hitchhiker most often appears on the anniversary of his or her death (see Chapter 13, "Urban Legends").

➤ Many—the focus of this book—tend to take up residence at a particular place and are seen there with some frequency. They haunt a specific location.

Phantom Phrases

The person who sees an apparition is called the **percipient**. An apparition seen by a percipient, especially one that wills itself into visibility, is the **agent** of a paranormal sighting.

In paranormal parlance, the person who sees the apparition is called the *percipient*. The apparition that's seen is called the *agent*. (The term "agent" is especially used when referring to an apparition that deliberately makes itself visible, that wants to be seen, so that it can deliver some sort of message.)

Do You Believe?

Do ghosts exist? *Can* they exist? For those who say, absolutely not, no way, to both questions, consider these things everyone once knew to be absolutely, uncontrovertibly true:

➤ The world is flat.

➤ The sun and stars revolve around the earth.

➤ The moon is made of green cheese.

Yet, all three have since been proven false. (Well, we haven't explored the entire moon yet, but the chances of finding any Gruyère or Brie aren't very promising.)

Can we ever really know for certain that ghosts exist?

A good researcher carries a healthy dose of skepticism, but not cynicism. Perhaps all that's required is to be open to the possibility.

It's been said that those who believe ghosts exist don't need hard evidence to prove it. Conversely, no amount of evidence would ever be enough to convince those who don't believe in ghosts.

But it's not a black-and-white issue. It's hard to separate the believers from the non-believers. Much of it's tied up with whether you believe that there's life, or any type of survival, after death.

For example, there are those who:

➤ Don't believe in survival after death. Therefore, the deceased couldn't possibly return as ghosts.

➤ Believe in survival after death, but they don't think the deceased can return to the world of the living in the form of ghosts.

➤ Believe in survival after death, and in the possibility that the deceased can return as ghosts.

And it's not even that simple. Many people who may or may not believe in life, or survival, after death believe in other spirits, such as angels and demons, that can make themselves look like humans, but are not the ghosts of human beings.

Then there are apparitions of the living (people who are currently alive but not physically present). In other words, while a person is still alive his or her "ghost double" appears to someone else. But more about that in Chapter 3, "Do the Dead Return?"

And, of course, there are those literal folks who don't believe in anything: life after death, ghosts, heavenly spirits, or demons. They may see or experience something paranormal, but they insist there must be a logical, natural explanation for it.

After Life, Then What?

The belief in ghosts is necessarily tied to a belief in an afterlife. If nothing survives death, there can't be such a thing as a ghost. There would be nothing to come back.

Since the beginning of recorded time, and no doubt eons before that, people have wondered what happens to us when we die. Don't you? Unless you subscribe without argument to a particular philosophy or religion, any and all answers to that eternal question are theoretical at best. Why? Because no human being has ever died and returned to this mortal world with the memory to tell us, conclusively, what was on the other side—unless you know something I don't.

But there's been lots of conjecture as to what does happen when we bite the dust.

Is That All There Is?

Few people want to believe that this life—whatever time's allotted to us right now—is all there is. There's got to be something else, something more. Doesn't there?

Almost every recorded culture in history has believed in some form of life after death. As you might expect, beliefs in what happens to the soul, or life force, after death vary greatly from one society to another. Among the many theories, some say:

➤ The spirit continues a similar existence, but in another realm.

➤ The spirit is judged and assigned to "heaven" or "hell," based on one's deeds during life.

➤ The spirit undergoes a series of rebirths or reincarnations, trying to improve toward a higher spiritual plane.

➤ The spirit waits for an eventual rebirth or resurrection.

Almost every society has had a class of people who could communicate with spirits of the deceased. In tribal societies this is the *shaman,* who acts as an intermediary for messages between the worlds of the living and the dead. In classical times, oracles and priests related messages and warnings from the deceased to the living. *Necromancers* were seers and prophets who contacted the dead to obtain information about the future. In some faiths, priests can accept alms and penance from the living to lighten the punishment of the deceased. In spiritualism, a faith we'll examine in some detail in Part 2, "Don't Call Us, We'll Call You," mediums acted as a go-between to the worlds of the living and the dead, especially in contacting the spirits of the dearly departed sitting at séances.

Phantom Phrases

The **shaman,** considered a wizard in tribal societies, acts as an intermediary between humans, the dead, and the gods. His duties usually include rainmaking (and similar magical feats), healing, and transmitting messages from the Beyond. A **necromancer** is a wizard-seer who calls up ghosts of the dead (**necromancy**) to forecast the future.

Ghostly Pursuits

E.B. Tylor, the founder of modern anthropology, called animism—in simplest terms, the belief that souls may exist apart from human bodies—the world's first religion. He published his theories about the belief system of souls and spirits found in the many tribal societies he studied in *Primitive Culture* (1871). He defined two types of spirits: those that came from deceased humans, and those that had a life of their own, independent of humans. Although many of his ideas have since been dismissed, the importance of his basic finding remains: Even the most primitive of societies seem to believe in some sort of survival of a soul or spirit after death and a means for the living to contact the dearly departed.

A shaman, or witch doctor, from Zimbabwe in Africa.
(Photo by author)

Which Way Do We Go?

So, if the soul survives death, where does the spirit go? Belief in the location of the spirit realm varied tremendously from one society to the next.

➤ Ancient Greeks wrote of an underworld found literally beneath the earth. Caves, crevices, and cracks in the earth's surface acted as doorways to Hades.

➤ Animistic societies believe that spirits of their deceased ancestors exist side by side with them, but unseen.

➤ Occultists and cabalists described concentric outer layers or plateaus around the earth, each inhabited by different types of spirits.

➤ Most Christians think of heaven, the afterworld reserved for the good, as being skyward; hell, the realm of eternal damnation, is thought of as being downward, though not necessarily literally underground.

➤ Some cultures put the deceased on "hold," assigning them to an invisible nether world or dimension while they wait for judgement or rebirth.

How the spirits got to the Other World was another problem. In Egypt during the time of the Pharaohs, the walls of the tombs and the sarcophagi were decorated with hiero-glyphs (collectively known today as the *Book of the Dead*), which instructed the dead on how to proceed to be judged, then be reborn in the Other World. It was the job of the wizard-priests, through ritual prayers and mummification of the corpse, to ease this passage. Even so, the ancient Egyptians believed that the soul had *two* parts, the *ba* and the *ka,* both of which were able to leave the tomb and walk among the living at night. The ba held the characteristics, traits, and personality of the human; the ka was the life force. I wouldn't want to run into either of them in a darkened pyramid.

A tomb in the Valley of the Kings, in Luxor, Egypt, decorated with hieroglyphs from the Book of the Dead.
(Photo by author)

The myth that the soul had to travel over a river to judgement actually began in Egypt at the time of the Pharaohs. Classical Greece expanded the belief, teaching that the soul had to cross the River Styx into Hades on a small boat piloted by the ferryman Charon. The legend was adopted and adapted into the Roman mythology.

One of the big "selling points" of early Christianity was St. Augustine's declaration that there wasn't any River Styx or Charon that you had to pass to reach the Kingdom of God. In the next chapter, we'll learn the path that most modern Western civilizations (well, at least those since the 10th century or so) believe the soul takes after death.

Celebrate the Soul

Festivals to honor and ward off the dead date back thousands of years. Ancient Greeks held the Anthesteria in late February or early March. You invited the spirits of your ancestors into your home to eat, but afterward you politely asked to them leave for a full year. The hope was that by throwing them a party once a year, the ghosts would remain contented and non-malicious.

The ancient Romans believed in all sorts of different types of spirits of the dead. Lares were good spirits, welcomed into people's homes and towns, where they acted sort of like guardian angels. Many families had their own individual lares (usually a deceased relative); but there were also lares for the public at large.

On the other side of the coin, larvae were evil spirits, who tried to scare or even harm others. Lemures, ghosts of people who died without any surviving family, were thought to be larvae. So, too, were the ghosts of those who died prematurely, violently, or by murder or drowning. These evil spirits were thrown a three-day party every year in early May. If they went away happy, maybe they'd just stay away.

Today, many cultures hold an annual Day of the Dead to honor the deceased. Usually, the festivals involve parties and feasts. The Chinese, who are known throughout the world for honoring their ancestors, hold three special rituals to honor the souls of all humankind. Hindu *sraddhas,* rites to honor the ancestors, last for 10 days. The Hungary Ghost Festival is two weeks of feasts and parties; even the spirits of those who died without descendants are specially remembered.

The most impressive Day of the Dead festival probably takes place in Mexico, where *El Dia de los Muertes* is celebrated on November 2. Preparations and parties often begin on Halloween. The Mexican Day of the Dead is a time for family reunions and feasts. Decorations include graphic and macabre depictions of skeletons, especially skulls. (Can you believe? Until the 20th century, actual skulls were sometimes dug up for the big event!) Often, families hold picnics on the gravesites of their relatives who have passed to the Great Beyond. The parties, prayers, and meals are all intended to calm the dead and allow them to rest comfortably for another year.

Treat or treat! Halloween, or All Hallows Eve, is probably the best-known festival of the dead. It started as a pagan ritual in Celtic lands, celebrated on October 31 to mark the end of the autumn harvest and the onset of winter. Meanwhile, down at the Vatican, Pope Boniface IV introduced All Saint's Day in the 7th century to replace the Roman Feralia, yet another pagan festival intended to give peace the dead. Later, Boniface moved the date of the festival from February 21 to November 1, and over the years the Celtic, pagan, and Christian festivals somehow merged into one big celebration: Halloween.

Today, it's primarily celebrated, at least in the United States, as a night of costumed trick-or-treating and partying.

Ghostly Pursuits

What the heck do Halloween costumes and bags of candy have to do with Celts and Christians? The candy—a bounty by any kid's standards—probably comes from the celebration of a plentiful harvest. The costumes, however, come from folklore about demons and the dead. Many believed that the barrier between the worlds of the living and the dead was thinnest on All Hallows Eve, and on that night spirits of the dead could cross over on their own. Other, scarier legends said that it's also the night when Satan, witches, and all other demons are free to walk the earth. In a famous European story, witches and devils dance 'til dawn on the top of Walpurgis Mountain in Germany. This tale served as an inspiration for the famous music composition, "The Night on Bald Mountain." So, to make a long story even longer, *that's* why kids dress up in scary costumes: to imitate the demonic spirits who travel far and wide on Halloween Eve.

Now it's time to take a look at some of the earliest recorded ghost stories, starting back in ancient Greece. Then we'll see how those tales of terror were first embraced, then adapted by the Christian Church.

The Least You Need to Know

➤ Since the beginning of recorded time, humans have contemplated the possibility of life after death.

➤ All ghosts are apparitions, but not all apparitions are ghosts.

➤ Paranormal research is the investigation of experiences beyond the range of normal human or scientific explanation.

➤ Belief systems on ghosts and the afterlife vary enormously from one civilization to the next.

➤ Most cultures have celebrated some form of a festival or rites honoring the dead, especially the spirits of family ancestors.

Chapter 2

In the Beginning: The First Famous Phantoms

In This Chapter

➤ Necromancy and the Witch of Endor

➤ The first ghost stories

➤ Ghost beliefs of ancient Greece and Rome

➤ Ghost beliefs of the early Christian Church

Some of the first records we have of living people trying to contact the ghosts of the dead date back to early Hebrew scriptures.

As you learned in Chapter 1, "Let's Enter the Spirit World," almost all civilizations have believed that there's some form of existence after death. Many have taught that the soul, or essence, of the departed "lives" in some ethereal plane where the spirits there aren't circumscribed by the earthly laws of time. Thus, their ancestors were beyond, or above, time and should be able to see the past, the present, *and* the future. (If you want to find out what's going to happen tomorrow, who better to ask than those who really know?)

Fortunately, there were specialists who could help people contact the spirits: wizards, sorcerers, and enchantresses. They conversed with the dead using a specific type of divination or fortune-telling known as necromancy.

Voices from the Grave

Today the word *necromancy* is used interchangeably with "magic," although with a slight occult or nefarious connotation. Originally, however, the term simply referred to the art of being able to call on the spirits of the dead to foretell the future.

Necromancy was considered to be an essential skill for all true fortune-tellers, wizards, and (especially) sorcerers. Summoning a spirit involved great preparations and pains on the part of the sorcerer, often including fasting, arcane secret rituals (usually including the drawing of a magic circle), and the recitation of secret incantations.

Which Witch Was Which?

The most famous recorded case of necromancy is that of Saul consulting the Witch of Endor, told in the book of I Samuel: 28:7–16 in the Old Testament of the Holy Bible.

Phantom Phrases

Necromancy is a form of divination, or foretelling of the future, by calling up and consulting with the spirits of the dead. The word "necromancy" is derived from the Greek word *nekromantia,* which in turn came from the two roots *nekros* ("a dead person") and *manteia* ("divination").

Phantom Phrases

The **oracle** of classical Greece received messages from the gods (and sometimes from the deceased) concerning the future. Usually female, the prophetess-priestess would be set up in a temple dedicated to a particular god.

The Law of Moses strictly forbade the use of necromancy and witchcraft:

➤ "Thou shalt not suffer a witch to live." (Exodus 22:18)

➤ "A man or woman that hath a familiar spirit or that is a wizard shall be stoned to death." (Leviticus 20:27)

➤ "There shall not be found among you … any one who practices divination, a soothsayer, or an augur, or a sorcerer, or a charmer, or a medium, or a wizard, or a necromancer. For whoever does these things is an abomination to the Lord." (Deuteronomy 18:10–13)

Saul himself had outlawed sorcery among the Israelites, banishing "those that have familiar spirits, and the wizards." Nevertheless, the beleaguered king felt the need to seek out just such a necromancer.

Why? The Lord had anointed David as Saul's successor, and David collected an army against the ruling monarch. Saul needed advice, and fast. He decided to seek out the help of a necromancer—even though he had just outlawed them—in order to call up the ghost of Samuel to get guidance. Saul asked around and found out there was a medium living in the town of Endor who might be able to perform the forbidden deed.

So that he wouldn't be recognized, Saul disguised himself and visited the so-called Witch of Endor. She conjured up Samuel, but the deceased king was so infuriated at being "disquieted" that he refused to help or counsel Saul. Saul, of course, was soon defeated by David.

King Saul consults with the Witch of Endor, who conjures the spirit of Samuel.
(Joseph Glanvil, Saducismus Triumphatus, *1681 ed.)*

Current scholars suggest that the Witch of Endor was probably not a witch or sorceress in the modern sense of the word, but closer to our conception of the *oracle* in ancient Greece.

The Oracle of Apollo at Delphi was the most famous of numerous seers (almost all of whom were female situated at temples throughout ancient Greece). To consult an oracle, a supplicant would first make sufficient offerings, then ask a question concerning future events. The oracle would enter a trance to consult the gods and, if necessary, the spirits dwelling in the underworld. The oracle always delivered her answer in cryptic phrases, often requiring the recipient to decipher or interpret the true meaning of the message.

Modern Biblical scholars have pointed out that the Greek Septuagint translation of the Hebrew texts refers to the necromancer as a "belly-talker" rather than a "witch." This suggests that the Witch of Endor created the voices herself by practicing *gastromancy*— the art of lowering one's voice in tone and volume to make it appear as if it were coming from underground. It this is true, the Witch of Endor was not an enchantress but one of the world's first ventriloquists!

The temple of the Oracle of Apollo at Delphi. (Photo by author)

Ghostly Pursuits

Reginald Scot, author of *The Discoverie of Witchcraft* (1584), was one of the first to point out that the Witch of Endor was probably not a witch, not even a true necromancer at all. He noted the differences in the Hebrew and Greek renderings of the sacred texts, then suggested that:

Samuel was not raised from the dead, but ... it was an illusion or cozenage ...

Then, how did a run-of-the-mill fortune-teller/ventriloquist (albeit, one who created the illusion that she could talk to the dead) come to be branded as a witch? In 1604, King James convened a conference at Hampton Court to prepare an authorized version of the Holy Bible in English. It was well known that King James was a fervent believer in (and crusader against) witchcraft. It seems likely that, given the King's prejudice, the 47 revisers working on the new edition would have been much more likely to translate the Hebrew as "witch" rather than as "oracle" or "ventriloquist."

It's All Greek to Me

It's difficult to tell, thousands of years after they were written, whether the earliest records of ghosts were literary inventions or whether apparitions had, indeed, been observed.

In the *Iliad,* traditionally attributed to the 9th-century Greek epic poet Homer, ghosts are benign, passive spirits. They didn't bother the living, and the living didn't particularly worry about them. Once the proper burial and rituals were performed for the deceased, the dead were pretty much left to fend for themselves.

After death, the spirit of the deceased departed for Hades, a nether region below the earth's surface ruled by the god Hades. Certain cracks and fissures in the earth's surface, as well as some caves and grottoes, were believed to be entrances to the underworld. (Modern-day spelunkers—cave explorers—have pretty much discounted this theory.) These locations were often attended by a priest, priestesses, or an oracle.

In the *Odyssey,* also traditionally attributed to Homer, the enchantress Circe instructed the hero Odysseus how to travel to Hades to consult with the spirit of the long-dead prophet Tiresias. Circe told Odysseus that, after crossing the waters of Oceanus, he must make several offerings and sacrifices, including digging a trench and filling it with a mixture of honey, milk, wine, water, barley, and the blood of sheep. The spirits of the dead would be drawn to the trench, hoping to drink, but Odysseus should scare them off with his sword until Tiresias appeared. (Why ghosts, who have no physical body, would be afraid of a sword, is never explained.)

Odysseus followed the instructions to the letter. After Tiresias drank and made his revelations, Odysseus also spoke with the ghosts of his mother, Achilles, Agamemnon, the wife/mother of Oedipus, and Leda. (Leda mated with Zeus when he appeared to her in the form of a swan. The result of their union was Helen of Troy.) Ulysses also met Hercules, but he presumed it to be a phantom double (*eidolon*), since the actual Hercules had been accepted onto Mount Olympus with the gods.

The spirits in Hades were restless and constantly screaming; but otherwise, they were harmless. They also had no substance: When Ulysses attempted to hug his mother, for example, his arms passed right through her.

There was a great change in belief about ghosts and their nature between the times of Homer (8th century B.C.) and the Greek philosopher Socrates (469?–399 B.C.). Ghosts could be helpful and

Ghostbusting

The belief that a living being and its phantom double can exist simultaneously (as in the case of Hercules being in both Hades and on Mount Olympus at the same time) is reflected in the modern concept of the astral body or spirit double (see Chapter 3). If you're fascinated by the legends and lore from ancient Greek and Rome, check out *The Complete Idiot's Guide to Classical Mythology* (Alpha Books, 1998).

consoling, but they could just as easily be threatening. Ghosts were thought to be noisy, restless beings that might hurt or kill those who upset them or who wandered too close. For centuries, seers had called up spirits to do their bidding; now, ghosts sometimes made demands of the living! The ghosts of those who died prematurely or violently were thought to be especially dangerous.

It was thought that the spirit of a deceased person sometimes hovered near its grave, especially in the case of a suicide or a violent or premature death. Writing in his *Phaedo*, the Greek philosopher Plato (427–347 B.C.) warned against "prowling about tombs and sepulchres, near which, as they tell us, are seen certain ghostly apparitions of souls which have not departed pure."

Which Way Do I Go?

Whether people believed that ghosts existed and could interact with the material world was directly related to their belief of what happened to the spirit or soul after death.

Here are just a few of the beliefs in classical Greece of where the spirit or soul went after you died:

➤ The corpse and spirit remained unified and intact in the tomb. Some tombs even had tubes built into them so that those offering sacrifices could pour nourishing liquids into the graves. The spirit was also accessible by prayer or necromancy.

Boo!

It was believed that if your soul wasn't pure enough to immediately rise to the ethereal plane, it had to undergo—ouch!—purging and cleansing before being admitted to this heavenly sphere. If you wanted to avoid all that pain after death, you had to lead a particularly virtuous life. Many early Christian writers, including Augustine (d. 430), were greatly influenced by this point of view. It's also easy to see the beginnings of the Christian concept in Purgatory.

➤ The spirit left the corpse and traveled by a torturous, circuitous path to Hades. By the 3rd century B.C., it was thought that there were two different regions inhabited in the afterlife: a happy, pleasant area (sometimes called Elysium) populated by the souls of the righteous; or Tartarus (a name also used in the New Testament), a place of pain and suffering populated by the souls of the wicked. (This belief was mirrored in the Christian canon of a heaven and a hell.)

➤ The spirit left the body and rose to a spiritual realm, an ethereal plane above the earth, possibly merging with a Creator or ultimate Being.

➤ The soul could be sent back to Earth and into some non-human life form as punishment.

➤ The spirit died with the corporeal being. This was, perhaps, the least popular belief, espoused by the Epicureans, among others.

First Phantoms

Ghost stories dating from ancient Greek and Roman periods must be taken with a grain of salt. Such tales were often apocryphal or literary in nature. *Marchen* stories, as they were called, were the least reliable: They were generally assumed to be fictional. *Sagen* legends were based (as least supposedly) on fact with literary embellishments.

Perhaps the first extant report of a haunted house comes from a letter written by Roman author, statesman, and orator Pliny the Younger (A.D. 62?–c.113). He wrote his patron, Lucias Sura, about a villa in Athens that no one would rent because it had a resident ghost. At the dead of night, horrid noises were heard in the villa: the clanking of chains, which grew louder and louder. Suddenly, the hideous phantom of an old man appeared, who seemed the very picture of abject filth and misery. His beard was long and matted, his white hair disheveled. His thick legs were loaded down by heavy irons that he dragged wearily along with a painful moaning; his wrists were shackled by long, cruel links. Every so often he raised his arms and shook his shackles in a kind of impotent fury. Once, a few mocking skeptics who were bold enough to stay all night in the villa were almost scared senseless at the sight of the apparition. Worse, disease and even death came to those who ventured inside those cursed walls after dusk.

The notorious reputation of the villa did not stop another Athenian philosopher, Athenodorus, from leasing it. Short on money, he found the inexpensive rent too attractive to turn down.

According to Pliny, Athenodorus met the ghost his first night at the villa. The philosopher heard the faint rattle of chains, and the spectre appeared. The ghost silently motioned for the philosopher to follow him. When Athenodorus refused, the old man loudly clanked his chains, until the philosopher agreed to come along. The phantom floated into the garden, where he pointed to a spot on the ground, then vanished.

The next day, Athenodorus told his story to the local authorities, who dug up the garden. At the very spot indicated by the ghost, a human skeleton, bound in chains, was uncovered. The bones were properly buried, the house was ceremoniously purified, and the ghost, apparently finished with his earthly business, never returned.

Come Back and What For?

The appearance of ghosts demanding proper burial rites is a recurrent theme in classic Greek and Roman literature. Here are just three examples:

➤ During the war at Troy, the spectre of Patroclus appeared to his comrade Achilles, asking to be properly cremated. (The ghost also delivered the bad news that Achilles, too, would be killed in battle at Troy.)

➤ Elpenor, one of Ulysses's crew members, fell to his death on Circe's island. His spirit returned, asking his leader go back to suitably bury him.

➤ The ghost of the Roman emperor Caligula, who had been assassinated and quickly cremated, haunted the Lamian Gardens where his ashes were entombed until rites befitting an emperor were held. (He, or some other ghost, also haunted the theater where Caligula was murdered up until the structure was destroyed by fire.)

Quite often ghosts were invoked or returned on their own to offer advice or repay debts of gratitude. Still other ghosts returned to repay debts. Roman statesman and author Cicero (106–43 B.C.), told of Simonides, who buried the body of a stranger. The man's ghost appeared to Simonides, advising him not to board a ship on which he intended to sail. Simonides followed his warning, and later learned that the ship had been lost at sea.

Though some spirits weren't aware of current events, they were fully aware of the past. According to the 5th-century B.C. Greek historian Herodotus, Periander, a 5th-century B.C. tyrant in Corinth, Greece, was visited by his wife. She returned from the dead to help Periander find a precious object that he had lost.

Not all ghosts could foretell the future. In fact, it was only after the end of the classical period and the collapse of many oracular sites that more and more ghosts seemed to develop the ability to predict future events.

Ghostly Pursuits

Lucan, writing in the 1st century A.D., told one of the more gruesome stories of necromancy. A Thessalian witch was anxious to find out the final outcome of the battles between Caesar and Pompey in 49 or 48 B.C. She combed a recent battlefield until she found a corpse with undamaged lungs and reanimated him. She assailed him with spells and oaths and whipped him with snakes until he told her what she wanted to know. The reanimation of corpses in ancient Grecian and Roman legend perhaps led to the later tales of vampires and zombies.

Ghosts also returned to console the bereaved. The ghost of Aeneas's wife, who was burned during the sacking of Troy, returned to comfort her husband.

Still others who had met violent ends returned as ghosts to help the living find their murderers. Roman poet Ovid (43 B.C.–A.D. 18) wrote about the spectre of Remus returning to name his assailant. In *De divinatione,* Cicero describes two men staying at a tavern. The innkeeper murders one of the men; his ghost returns to help his friend find the corpse and to request a proper burial.

Ghosts could be disruptive creatures. In the 2nd century A.D., the Greek author Pausanias described the ghostly nighttime sounds of men in combat near the grave mounds on the field where the battle of Marathon had taken place more than 600 years earlier. As you'll discover in Chapter 18, "That These Honored Dead," haunted armies form an entire genre of ghost phenomenon.

In his *Life of Cimon,* the Greek biographer Plutarch (A.D. 46?–120?) writes that the baths at Chaeronea were haunted, reportedly by the ghost of Damon, a violent man who was murdered there. The spectral occurrences, including moans and other noises (though apparently no sighting of an actual ghost), became so disturbing that nearby residents sealed up the baths.

Some ghosts didn't wait for intermediaries to do their bidding. There are dozens of legends of spirits returning to harm their murderers or assailants. Although ghosts were usually thought of as insubstantial, in some cases they were able to physically assault their offenders. Many of these wronged spirits had also been deprived of proper burials.

Throw Them to the Lions

By the 3rd century, Christianity was making strong footholds in ancient Greece and Rome. To make conversion attractive to pagans, the early Christian Church had to adopt (or adapt) many of the prevalent popular religious beliefs, especially those concerning ghosts and the afterlife.

Early Christian writers such as Justin Martyr verified that this new faith acknowledged life after death. He pointed to the Old Testament story of Saul as one proof that Christians believed the ghost of Samuel (mentioned earlier in this chapter) demonstrated Christian belief in the existence of a soul after death.

The first Christian thinkers also argued that ghosts existed in spirit form only. Therefore, after death, all people would be social equals. This concept must have been mighty attractive and persuasive to the masses.

The big decision the Christian Church had to make, though, was difficult: Just where did the soul go after a person died? You might ask, why did it matter? Because where the spirit went might make a difference whether it could ever make it back to Earth in the form of a ghost.

All early Christian theorists and writers agreed that the soul traveled *somewhere* and stayed there while awaiting judgment. They narrowed the location down to three possible places:

➤ An "unseen region reserved by God"

➤ The so-called "Bosom of Abraham" (although no one seemed to know what or where that was)

➤ An intermediate region of punishment or comfort in the underworld

Purgatory: Neither Heaven Nor Hell

Even the great Christian theorist Saint Augustine didn't want to commit as to exactly where the soul went immediately after death. But by the 12th century, as the Middle Ages were drawing to a close, the concept of purgatory had been firmly established by the Catholic Church. An ethereal realm somewhere between heaven and hell, *purgatory* was where souls lingered, undergoing punishment as penance for their sins, while awaiting the Second Coming.

Phantom Phrases

Purgatory, in Roman Catholic theology, is an ethereal state or place, often thought to be "be-tween" heaven and hell, in which the souls of people who have died in grace must suffer while being cleansed of or atoning for their venial (or pardonable) sins before being admitted into heaven.

The word "purgatory" may have had its first "official" use in an ecclesiastical letter written to Pope Innocent IV in 1254. Purgatory was discussed at the Council of Lyons in 1274 and again at the Council of Florence (1438–1443). The Councils declared that communication to the dead (in the form of alms, for example) and messages to and from the dead (say, in the form of miracles) were a reality. The Church also established indulgences or performing good deeds or service on behalf of the dead as a means to lessen the number of years a spirit would have to spend in purgatory.

Apparitional sightings continued throughout the Dark and Middle Ages. Many visions of ghosts also appeared in the form of dreams. According to most descriptions from the time, ghosts in human form were pale and wore sad expressions. They usually showed the marks (such as burns and scars) from the suffering they were enduring in purgatory. Sometimes, a ghost might appear in a non-human form, such as a ball of light or a dove.

The Christian dead returned for any number of reasons—often, to make a confession and beg the pardon of those sinned against and to atone for their sins. But almost all ghosts of the era warned the living of the need to obey the sacraments and laws of the Church.

But the winds of change were in the air. In Part 2, "Don't Call Us, We'll Call You," we'll see how in the 16th century, Protestant writers and thinkers of the Reformation began to question the nature—even the existence—of ghosts.

But first, let's take a breather from theorists and thinkers. What have people actually *experienced* over the centuries that has convinced them there must be life after death? In the next chapter we take a closer look at the nature of ghosts themselves. If they do exist, what might they be made of?

The Least You Need to Know

➤ Seers tried to foretell the future with necromancy—consulting the spirits of the dead.

➤ The Biblical Witch of Endor, used for centuries by Judeo-Christian writers as proof of an afterlife, was more likely a ventriloquist than an enchantress.

➤ Ghosts have appeared in even the earliest Greek and Roman literature.

➤ The early Christian Church accepted many pagan beliefs about ghosts, then codified through its Councils where and in what condition spirits survived death.

Chapter 3

Do the Dead Return?

In This Chapter

➤ The connection between the body and the soul

➤ The search for the soul by Edison and other scientists

➤ Out of this world: the astral body and astral projection

➤ Out-of-body and near-death experiences

➤ Deathbed visitations

Let's say, just for sake of argument, that ghosts are real, that some part of us is able to return to visit the world of the living after we die. Is there any proof that some part of us—*something*—survives death?

For those who have seen and recognize the ghost of someone who's deceased, perhaps no other proof is necessary. But science can only believe in the soul if it can take quantitative measurements. Some researchers, not wanting to define the soul in religious terms, characterize it as some elemental force, such as energy.

Still others believe in the soul because of personal, otherwise-unexplainable paranormal experiences. These include cross correspondences, out-of-body experiences, crisis apparitions, and near-death experiences.

Do you need proof? Read on. Maybe one of these stories will make you believe.

You Gotta Have Soul

First of all, what would we name that surviving spirit? The *soul?*

The concept of the soul is hard to define because it means so many things to different cultures and civilizations. The very existence of the soul and it's nature are two of the fundamental theological and philosophical questions that humankind has pondered for thousands of years, and any definitive answer for the mystery is certainly far beyond the scope of this book.

In almost all of the world's religions, it's believed that the soul is eternal and survives the death of the body. According to Judeo-Christian thought, for example, the soul is a God-given spirit, bestowed at the beginning of life. When the body dies, the soul continues to live. It leaves the body and moves to an afterworld to await judgment and resurrection.

Phantom Phrases

The **soul** is the life force that distinguishes one person from another. It is a spiritual essence, separate and distinct from the physical body.

Many paranormal believers think that the soul or spirit can separate from and return to the body even while a person is alive, allowing an out-of-body experience (OBE) or a near-death experience (NDE). (We'll take a closer look at these phenomena in a moment.) Paranormal hair-splitters suggest that what actually departs from the physical body during an OBE or NDE is an *astral body,* which acts a vehicle and carries the soul on its journeys.

For some, this is an important distinction, because they claim that a ghost or apparition is not a returning soul: It's the astral body doing the traveling. The actual soul stays behind where it's supposed to be, either in the still-living person or in whatever afterworld it has traveled to after death.

Phantom Phrases

The **astral body** is a spiritual life force that's sometimes able to separate from and return to the corporeal, living body. Some paranormal experts use the term synonymously with the soul; others think of them as two distinct entities.

A Weighty Matter

Scientists have long wondered whether there might be a controllable, objective way to observe the soul.

Some attempted to detect or prove the existence of the soul by comparing a person's body just immediately prior to and after death. One famous experiment involved the weight of the soul ... yes, the actual pounds and ounces that a soul might weigh. If there were any observable, measurable weight difference within those few moments, is it possible that the difference—the thing that changed—could have been caused by the soul having departed from the body?

In one very limited 1907 study, researcher Duncan McDougall attempted to measure the soul by weighing five patients as they died. In two of the patients, there was a sudden weight loss of a half-ounce, followed by another sudden one-ounce weight loss within three minutes of the time of death. A third patient's weight fluctuated just after death, first dropping a bit, followed by an abrupt large weight gain (!), then another loss. There was no discernable change on the other patients. Needless to say, the results were inconclusive.

Link by Link

In the 1800s, many people believed that spiritualism provided proof of the soul and life after death, particularly with the phenomena known as *cross correspondences*. Cross correspondences are interrelated bits of information received from the spirit world by different mediums at different times and locations. These partial messages must be joined together to form the complete communication from the spirit(s). It's New Math: The whole message is greater than the sum of the two parts.

There are three types of cross correspondences:

- ➤ **Simple.** Two or more mediums independently produce identical or very similar words, or they independently receive phrases that are obviously related.

- ➤ **Complex.** It's not immediately obvious that the words or phrases received separately by the mediums connect or interrelate.

- ➤ **Ideal.** Mediums independently receive phrases or words that must be linked together, like pieces of a jigsaw puzzle, to complete a full sentence or message.

So far, there has never been a definitive explanation for the cross correspondence phenomenon. Those who believe the information is coming from the deceased claim cross correspondences are proof of survival after death. Other paranormal thinkers suggest that the mediums may possess some form of super-ESP (see Chapter 12, "If Not a Ghost, Then What?") which would allow them to unconsciously communicate with each other.

Ghostbusting

Want to become a star in the paranormal world? All you have to do is come up with a test that proves the soul exists. If the soul leaves the body at death, can we measure that departure? Duncan McDougall experimented with body weight. What else might change in a person's body at the moment of death? How could it be measured? Could that measurement be evidence of a soul?

Phantom Phrases

Cross correspondences are interrelated bits of information received from the spirit world by different mediums at different times and locations. They must be joined together to form a complete message from the spirit(s).

Edison's Search for the Soul

Albert Einstein (1879–1955), the great U.S. physicist born in Germany, taught that energy, like matter, could be neither created nor destroyed. It could merely be converted or transformed, from one state to another.

Perhaps this was also the thinking of inventor Thomas Edison (1847–1931) when, late in his career, he began work on a device to detect and communicate with the soul. Edison, of course, was born during the heyday of the spiritualism movement. In his youth, he was undoubtedly aware of mediums trying to contact spirits of the dead.

Edison believed that the soul, or whatever survived death, was comprised of what he called "life units." According to Edison:

> ➤ Humans—indeed, all life forms—are made up of microscopic life units that could arrange themselves in any variety of forms, from a starfish to a human.

> ➤ The life units had a memory. (Edison used this argument to explain skin regeneration, for example.)

> ➤ If the life units had a strong enough memory to remain together after the death of the body, perhaps the person's personality would remain intact. (But, Edison was quick to caution, he didn't think that the survival of an actual personality had been proved—as yet.)

> ➤ If the life units were not strong enough to stay together, they would disperse and reformulate into other beings.

> ➤ There's a fixed quantity of life units on this planet, and the number could never be increased or decreased.

> ➤ Life units are indestructible, so they definitely survived the death of the body.

Edison worked for years to create a piece of scientific apparatus that could detect these life units and act as a sort of megaphone or amplifier. Used correctly, the machine would register even the most minute life unit, even after the death of the body.

Edison worked on the presumption that the personality did exist after death. Because of his disbelief in the work of mediums, he wanted to create a scientific machine that would allow the spirits of the deceased to communicate with the living. After all, he pointed out that it was only reasonable to conclude that those who leave this earth would like to communicate with those they have left here. Accordingly, the thing to do is to furnish the best conceivable means to make it easy for them to open up communication with us, and then see what happens.

During his lifetime, Edison received hundreds of patents, and his laboratories created the first commercially viable electric light bulb, phonograph, and motion-picture projector. Unfortunately, Edison's life-unit detector and his ghost communication device remained uncompleted at the time of his death.

Do you think that this same genius, given enough resources and time, might have been able to provide us with the first positive proof of life after death, as well as a way for us to communicate with those on the Other Side? Only the spirits know.

Look at All the Pretty Colors

In 1937, Russian electrician Semyon Kirlian used the properties of electricity to create a series of stunning photographs. Kirlian set a piece of unexposed photographic film on a metal plate, then rested a small object on the film. Next, he grounded a high-voltage, high-frequency generator to the plate, and touched the other end of the wire to the object to be "photographed." As the film was exposed, a natural electrical discharge created a stunning, iridescent halo or corona on the photographic paper around the object, which appeared in silhouette. (The most famous example of these photographs is the oft-seen picture of a hand, with fingers extended and rays shooting out in all directions.)

Paranormal believers immediately claimed that Kirlian photography, as this phenomenon became known, was scientific proof that the soul exists and manifests itself in the form of an aura surrounding the body. Although amused by the photographs' novelty, scientists denied there was any connection whatsoever between the Kirlian photography and an aura or the soul.

Boo!

Do not—repeat, do not!—rig up electric wires to a metal plate, place your hand on it, and take a photograph. You'll knock out a few fuses, burn down the house, and electrocute yourself. That's not how Kirlian photographs work. If you must have one done to see your aura, seek out a professional.

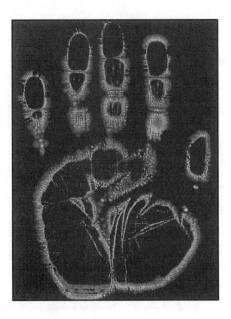

Even reproduced in black and white, this Kirlian photograph seems to reveal an aura surrounding the palm.

Leaving Your Body Behind

An *out-of-body experience* or *OBE* (also known as astral projection, bi-location, and, sometimes, ESP projection) is a paranormal phenomenon in which a spirit double (or astral body) of a person separates from the physical body.

OBE is actually the same paranormal phenomenon as astral projection, and the terms are often used interchangeably. If there is a difference, it's in connotation: Astral projection seems to indicate traveling a distance; out-of-body experience creates the image of hovering over or near the body.

Remember, in OBE, the actual person doesn't physically travel or transport through space to another location. Rather, a spirit double called an astral body makes the journey.

Sometimes the astral projection hovers near its human source; often it travels to and/or appears in a faraway location. Some astral projectors report having been transported to a different "world" similar to our own. Most of those who travel to such a dimension find it to be superior to ours in beauty and comfort. They also often report seeing friends and relatives who have died.

Phantom Phrases

An **out-of-body experience (OBE)**, or astral projection, is a paranormal phenomenon in which a spirit double (or astral body) leaves the body and travels to another location.

Sometimes, the astral body is able to bring back memories of the trip; on examination, this is often information that the person otherwise would not have known. This last sort of OBE, with experiences that can be verified, is the most valuable and most credible in psychic research.

On occasion, the double appears to another person. It might appear to the percipient as an apparition, ghostlike, or might appear to be solid flesh and blood. In his 1956 study "Six Theories About Apparitions," psychic researcher Hornell Norris Hart (1888–1967) concluded that astral projections and apparitions of the dead are essentially the same in character and substance.

Ghostly Pursuits

Stories of astral projection appear throughout history and folklore. Even the Puritan minister Increase Mather (1639–1723) chronicled the appearance of living persons in one location when, it was later discovered, they were actually in their homes at the time. His explanation, of course, was that Satan had created the doubles.

There have been some experiments in deliberately induced astral projection; that is, a person trying to send a duplicate astral self to another place or to a particular percipient. Although there have been some limited claims of success, paranormal literature does not boast many case histories.

Like most paranormal activity, out-of-body experiences weren't seriously examined until the 19th century. Dr. Robert Crookall, one of the earliest paranormal investigators, dedicated most of his paranormal research to the OBE, and he wrote more than 10 books on the subject. Unfortunately, through no fault of his own, most of his examples couldn't be independently verified. The cases he examined were once-in-a-lifetime events, and the OBEs couldn't be corroborated by any outside observers. It's a problem with the phenomenon itself: Most reports of astral projection are documented as first-person case histories.

Increase Mather believed that apparitions, poltergeist activity, and other spectral activity were, indeed, real. He detailed his observances of paranormal phenomena in the immensely popular *An Essay for the Recording of Illustrious Providences* (1684). His son, the Rev. Cotton Mather, became a major figure in the Salem witchcraft trials of 1692.

The Wilmot Apparition

The so-called Wilmot Apparition is one of the most fascinating case histories of astral projection in the annals of paranormal research. In 1889 and 1890, the case was thoroughly examined by the Society for Psychical Research, a British paranormal society, and was the first of its kind. The case remains a riddle.

The Wilmot case is notable because it involves both collective and reciprocal apparitions. A *collective apparition* is one in which more than one person sees the same spirit or ghost. Collective apparitions are quite unusual. A *reciprocal apparition*, in which both the agent (the visitor) and the percipient (the visited) see each other, is exceedingly rare.

S.R. Wilmot, a manufacturer from Bridgeport, Connecticut, sailed from England to New York on the *City of Limerick* steamship on October 3, 1863. A storm lashed the ship for nine days of the crossing. On the eighth day out, Wilmot dreamed that his wife (who was back in the United States) came to his berth and kissed him as he slept. The next morning, before Wilmot told him of the dream, Wilmot's roommate, William J. Tait, kidded him about having had a lady visitor the night before. When they compared stories, they realized that Tait had been awake and had actually seen the astral body of Wilmot's wife!

Phantom Phrases

In the case of a **collective apparition,** more than one person sees the same spirit phenomenon. In a **reciprocal apparition,** the agent and percipient see and respond to each other.

Wilmot arrived in Connecticut, and before he could tell his wife about the strange experience, she asked him whether he had seen a vision of her at sea. News of the storm at sea had reached her, and she had become alarmed. That night, she dreamed that she actually visited the ship to comfort her husband. The dream remained so vivid in her memory that, the next morning, she could swear she had actually been on board the ship.

If I Knew You Were Coming, I'd Have Baked a Cake

One of the more unusual types of OBE are "arrival cases," in which an apparition of a person shows up at a destination before the actual person gets there. The apparition appears in the same clothing that the person is wearing during travel. The ghost looks just like the real person; percipients often talk to the phantom. Sometimes, the ghost even answers back. The apparition always excuses itself and is gone by the time the real person shows up.

Mark Twain recalled having once experienced an arrival case while attending a large reception. He spotted a female acquaintance across the room, then met her later that evening at dinner. As it turned out, she had never been at the reception. She was still on a train at the time, heading toward the town where the dinner was held.

Your Friend in a Crisis

A *crisis apparition* is a specific type of astral projection in which the astral body is released or sent by the agent at the time of illness, trauma, accidents, or impending death to warn or inform another person, usually a loved one. Many times, the agent is not conscious, in a coma, or heavily medicated.

There is continuing study and controversy concerning crisis apparitions, which appear to the percipient at the time of the agent's death. Because the exact moment of death is hard to pinpoint, there is debate about whether the apparition actually appears just *before* or immediately *after* death occurs. The difference, of course, is whether the person is seeing a ghost (of someone's who's dead) or an astral body (of a living person). Regardless, the phenomenon itself is well documented, with hundreds of case histories.

Here are just three of the hundreds of crisis apparitions recorded by the Society for Psychical Research (a group of paranormal investigators that you'll read about in Chapter 10, "Ghost Hunters and Ghostbusters"):

Phantom Phrases

A **crisis apparition** is an out-of-body experience in which the agent projects his or her astral body at a time of crisis or death to some other person, usually a loved one.

➤ On March 19, 1917, Captain Eldred Bowyer-Bower, a British aviator, was shot down and killed over France. At the time of his death, he appeared simultaneously to his half-sister in Calcutta and to his niece in England. He was clearly recognized by both and disappeared after only a few moments.

➤ On the evening of January 3, 1840, Mrs. Sabine Baring-Gould of Exeter, England, was sitting at the dining room reading her Bible when her seaman brother Henry appeared across from her. After a few minutes, he faded from sight. Knowing that he was serving the Royal Navy in the South Atlantic, Mrs. Baring-Gould noted the time and date: A month later she found out that her brother had died at sea at that exact time.

➤ On January 3, 1856, Mrs. Anne Collyer of Camden, New Jersey, awoke to see her son Joseph standing in her bedroom doorway, his face battered and bandaged. She was surprised because he was supposed to be a thousand miles away, the captain of a steamboat on the Mississippi River. Soon, his image slipped from sight. Two weeks later, she learned that her son had died in a steamboat collision at the very moment she had seen his apparition.

Wow! That Was Close!

A *near-death experience* (*NDE*), is undergone by a person who clinically dies (or comes very close to actual death) and is revived. Often, the person recalls extraordinary, even paranormal, visions of an afterlife. The phrase "near-death experience" was coined in the 1970s by an American physician, Dr. Raymond Moody, to describe the phenomena that his patients said they had experienced while "dead."

Many people who have had an NDE describe the same experiences, including:

➤ A realization that he or she is undergoing an out-of-body experience.

➤ The sensation of floating above one's own body and looking down at it.

➤ An unconcerned and objective, almost detached, view of the situation.

➤ An end of pain.

➤ A feeling of happiness.

➤ The sensation of passing down a long, lighted tunnel or pathway.

➤ Meeting apparitions (sometimes deceased friends or relatives, unrecognized individuals, or spiritual entities) that are often glowing and dressed in white.

➤ Hearing a voice from the spirit world tell them that it's not their time yet, that they must return to the world of the living.

Phantom Phrases

A **near-death experience**, or **NDE**, is when a person dies (or comes very close to actual death) and is revived. Many people who have had NDEs have vivid memories of their approach to the other side. Dr. Raymond Moody coined the term in the 1970s.

Boo!

Okay, this shouldn't have to be said, but as neat as a near-death experience might be to undergo, it's not worth trying to induce one just to see what it's like. What if you got to the end of the long, white tunnel and no one tells you to turn back? Wait your turn: It'll come soon enough all on its own without any help from you.

About 97 percent of those surveyed who have had an NDE said that it was a positive and life-affirming experience. Most lose their fear of death and develop a belief in survival after death. Many become more religious or have a stronger belief in God.

Of course, there is no corroborative evidence to prove what a person who has undergone an NDE actually experienced. The scientific explanation most often proffered for NDE is that it's all a hallucination caused by an increase in natural or medicinal drugs or, more often, a lack of oxygen to the brain.

But this scientific theory doesn't explain why so many who have had an NDE see the same things, such as white lights and the long tunnel. Until someone actually dies and returns from the dead, the NDE phenomenon will probably remain an unsolved mystery.

Ghostly Pursuits

Perhaps the most famous person to relate her near-death experience is Elizabeth Taylor, who fell ill from pneumonia during a break in filming *Cleopatra* in March of 1961. Her health deteriorated, and she slipped in and out of a coma. At one point, her heart stopped, and for a brief time she was clinically dead. Fortunately, doctors were able to revive her. When she later spoke about her NDE at a fundraiser for the hospital, Taylor described the sensation of hovering over her bed, then going down a long tunnel with a light at the end, and then voices urging her to return to her body. Other celebrities who have reported similar NDE experiences include Peter Sellers and Erik Estrada.

As I Lay Dying

There are thousands of reports of people who have seen apparitions leading up to or at the moment of their deaths. It stands to reason, too, that the phenomenon occurs much more often than is reported: After all, many times the person who sees the ghost dies before being able to point out or describe the visitation.

In *Deathbed Visions* (1926), Sir William Barrett described case after case in which the dying seemed to see dead relatives who came to greet them and help them on their passage to the next world. Needless to say, if these visions were what the percipients claimed, it would be remarkable proof of survival after death.

To prepare his study *Deathbed Observations by Physicians and Nurses* (Parapsychology Foundation, 1951), Dr. Karlis Osis surveyed 5,000 doctors and 5,000 nurses about their experiences regarding apparitions that appeared to their dying patients. He concluded that dying persons in full possession of their faculties and in normal consciousness *frequently* "see" apparitions of the dead, including:

➤ Friends

➤ Relatives

➤ People who they didn't know had already died

This last phenomenon is an especially convincing proof of survival after death.

Sometimes, it's not only the person who's dying who sees the ghosts. There have been numerous instances reported of spectral entities being seen at the deathbed by those other than the person who was dying.

Whether they are seen at the end of a lighted tunnel during a near-death experience, or whether they materialize in the window frame of a haunted house, apparitions serve as possible proof for survival after death. People will continue to debate the existence of the soul forever. But, all the while, people will keep seeing ghosts.

Ghost legends have been with us for thousands of years and will continue for thousands more. In the next chapter we'll look at some of the ghosts that inhabit our folklore and tradition.

The Least You Need to Know

➤ The existence of ghosts is linked to the belief in the existence of the soul, or the survival of something after death.

➤ Scientists have tried to detect, measure, and communicate with the soul; so far, they have been unsuccessful.

➤ Out-of-body and near-death experiences seem to offer proof of survival after death and, therefore, the possibility that ghosts might exist.

➤ People near death, though still conscious, often have visions of deceased friends and relatives.

Something Wicked This Way Comes

People were seeing ghosts and spirits long before religions came along and told them what they were—or weren't—seeing. While many of the spirits were benign or, at worst, playful, there were many, many spirits that no one wanted to see!

It became alarmingly obvious that some of these spirit creatures only appeared just before someone died. Some resembled humans, some were mere specks of light. More often, the ominous vision looked like common animals, only somehow more sinister and foreboding. Many times, the doomed individual was the person who actually saw the spectral beast. Is it any wonder that their appearance wasn't welcome news?

Death and what—if anything—follows it is, of course, the ultimate mystery. It's only logical that traditions have grown up surrounding unusual events that more than coincidentally occur at the precise moment of death. Too, almost every culture has developed charms and lucky amulets against evil spirits and harbingers of doom.

Are You Dead Certain About That?

Every culture and folklore tradition has its death omens—spirits that portend disaster and tragedy. Trust me, when any of this gang shows up, nobody's happy.

The Cry of the Banshee

Everyone's heard of the "cry of the banshee." According to ancient Irish and Scottish tradition, a banshee is a female death spirit that appears to a household just before someone in the family is about to die. Oftentimes, her singing or crying is heard, but no apparition appears. There have been many descriptions of what she looks like. Folklore gives us several types of banshees. The Irish banshee known as Bean Si has long hair and is dressed in green or white. Sometimes she's wearing a veil or shroud; other times she's spotted as she flies across the sky in the bright moonlight. Regardless, it's her distinct, mournful cry that cuts to the heart and soul of all who hear it.

Boo!

Contrary to popular opinion, banshees do not wail. The sound is not a high-pitched scream or shrieking. Rather, it's that of mournful crying, as if the female spirit is weeping in inconsolable sorrow. If the ghost is screeching at you, it's probably something, or someone, else.

Ghostbusting

Feel lucky? Irish and Scottish folklore suggests that if you can bring yourself to suck a bit at the breast of a Bean-Nighe, she'll grant you a wish. (I wonder who found this out? And how?) Oh, and as a bonus, she also makes you her foster child—although it's unclear what benefits you'll receive from the adoption.

In the Scottish Highlands, but also in parts of Ireland, there's another kind of banshee called the Bean-Nighe or Little-Washer-by-the-Ford. It's supposedly the ghost of a woman who has died young during childbirth and is doomed to wash clothes in a stream until the time she would otherwise have died. Legend suggests that she's a death omen because the bloody clothes she is seen to be washing may be the burial clothes of the soon-to-be departed. Unlike the beautiful though baleful Bean Si, the Bean-Nighe is hideously ugly, with only one nostril, a single front tooth, long sagging breasts, and webbed feet.

The banshee legend never became very popular in the United States, despite the influx of Irish and Scottish immigrants to American shores. One banshee story that's still told today, however, dates to Revolutionary times. It seems a section of the Tar River near Tarboro in Edgecombe County, North Carolina, was haunted by a banshee. David Warner ran mill grinding corn and wheat on the river. He bitterly opposed British occupation, and when he refused to turn over any goods to some British soldiers, three of them bound him up, weighted him down with rocks, and threw him into the river.

The banshee awoke and let out a dreadful cry. Nevertheless, the soldiers' commanding officer ordered them to work the mill. The cries continued every night, until, finally, two of the men were lured by its sound to the riverbank. They fell in and drowned. The leader of the three murderers was driven insane and also eventually drowned in the river. His body was discovered floating in the exact spot where the trio had dumped David Warner.

It's said that the banshee still lives on the Tar River and can be heard crying on muggy August nights during a new moon.

The Ghosts of Murdered Boys

Radiant boys are the ghosts of boys who have been murdered by their mothers. As their name suggests, they glow in the darkness. The sighting of a radiant boy is an omen of a violent death (like his), or, in some traditions, very bad luck.

A medieval engraving of a radiant boy.

There are legends of radiant boys throughout Europe and England. This superstition's origin is uncertain, but some of the first European tales of children murdered by their mothers were the *Kindermorderinn* of Germany.

One of the most famous radiant boy sightings was in 1803 at Corby Castle, the ancestral home of the Howards in Cumberland, England. Apparently, a radiant boy had haunted a part of the house adjacent to an old Roman-era tower for some time. On the night of September 8, the rector of Greystoke and his wife were overnight guests. According to an account given by Howard in 1824, the rector had this experience:

> *Between one and two in the morning … I saw a glimmer in the middle of the room, which suddenly increased to a bright flame. … I beheld a beautiful boy clothed in white, with bright locks resembling gold, standing by my bedside. … He then glided gently toward the side of the chimney … and entirely disappeared.*

Fortunately for the rector, this radiant boy brought no ill tidings. It was also, apparently, a unique experience. The boy, whose ghost it was has never been identified, and it has never appeared to haunt Corby Castle since.

Winged Messengers of Death

Birds have been associated with death and the spirit world for centuries. In Egyptian hieroglyphics, the hawk was the primary representation of the ba, or soul. He was depicted with the god Horus and had the body of a man and the head of a hawk. In ancient Greece and Rome, birds acted as messengers for the gods, and carriers of the souls of the deceased.

Ghostly Pursuits

Birds have also played a large part in prophecy. Many cultures, dating back at least 3,500 years, have tried to interpret the flight patterns of birds. An early term for this practice was orniscopy (from the Greek *ornis*, meaning "bird"). In classical Rome, orniscopy was practiced by experts called Augers (from the Latin *avis*, meaning "bird," and *garrire*, meaning "to chatter"). Centuries later, Germans and Scots forecast their luck by counting magpies. In colonial America, the tradition changed to the counting of crows. In modern times, the term "augury" has become synonymous with fortune-telling in general.

Many folkloric traditions say that a bird trapped inside a house is a signal of important news, disaster, or death. An especially strong death omen is a bird that accidentally kills itself by flying into a glass window. Even a bird trying unsuccessfully to escape from a house by beating its wings against the window pane is a dangerous sign. And let's not even talk about birds flying down a chimney and into a house! If that happens, just start measuring yourself for a coffin.

Perhaps because they're the color of the night, black birds are particularly suspect—especially ravens. In fact, all nocturnal birds are considered questionable in some lore. Few things can cause more creeps and goosebumps than the lonely hooting of a barn owl bathed in the light of a full moon.

Edgar Allen Poe knew this was true: He wrote "The Raven" in 1845.

Aw, Shucks: Hounds from Hell

There are a variety of canine death omens, especially in Great Britain. The best known is the Black Shuck, also called Old Shuck or Galleytrot (among many other colloquial names). The tradition is especially strong in Norfolk, East Anglia, and Devon. The creature gets its name from *scucca* or *sceocca*, which are Anglo-Saxon words meaning "Satan" or "demon." The fact that the death omen is seen in the shape of a dog is attributed to an old Norse myth: Old Shuck is supposedly descended from the black Hound of Odin (or Woden) that accompanied the Vikings when they invaded the British Isles.

Black Shucks are usually, well, black and gigantic, about the size of a colt or calf. Their yellow, red, or green eyes (depending on who's doing the telling) glow or burn in the dark. Sometimes, the Black Shuck is headless; still the eyes burn like fire in the empty darkness where the head should be.

His walk makes no sound. He leaves no paw prints behind. Travelers in the dark sometimes feel his cold breath on their necks. His howl, usually heard on stormy nights, is blood-curdling. He haunts back roads, bogs, hillsides, and cemeteries.

If you see a Black Shuck, it means death (most likely yours) within a year.

There are other phantom or spectral dogs that appear in ghost and occult legends. Black dogs in general are associated with Satan and witches. The devil can supposedly take the shape of a black dog, and witches keep them as their familiars.

In another British tradition, the barghest (or barguest) is a spectral hound that roams Cornwall and northern England. When it comes to announce a death, it appears as an enormous dog or, sometimes, a bear. In Lancashire, it's called the Shriker, because it shrieks rather than barks; or Trash.

Yet another type of spectral hell-hound are the Whisht hounds that haunt the forests and vicinity of Devon, England. They take their name from *whist*, a slang word from the western region of England meaning "spooky." The term is further derived from *Wisc*, another name for the Norse god of war Woden (Odin).

Ghostbusting

In some traditions, the Black Shuck won't harm you if you ignore or don't disturb him. Some people think it's bad news even to mention his name or talk about him.

Other Denizens of Doom

Radiant boys, banshees, black birds, and horrible hounds are only a few of the dozens of death omens passed down through the centuries in old wives' tales. Most of them, like hideous cronies and monstrous demon dogs, are frightening in their own right. But others, at first, are not so terrifying.

Here are just a few more spirits that have been identified as death omens over the ages. In each case, their original association with the dying is long forgotten.

> ➤ Originating in British folklore, the *Seven Whistlers* are seven spirits that fly together like a pack of swallows. They whistle or sing to let you know death is in the air.

➤ The *deathwatch beetle* is a small insect found in the United States, the British Isles, and Europe. It makes knocking or ticking sounds as it bores into wood. The sound of the deathwatch beetle means a death in the family. Why the knocking noise became associated with impending death is uncertain, but belief is recorded in England back to the 17th century.

➤ A *kelpie* is a Scottish water spirit that lives in rivers and streams. It can take the form of a horse or a bedraggled man. According to tradition, if you see a kelpie, you will die by drowning.

Let There Be Light

Ghost lights have been seen and recorded in every country and civilization. The mysterious lights are usually seen as blue balls or yellow spheres (though occasionally as bobbing candle flames) glowing in the darkness. Although some scientists have suggested that the lights are caused by swamp gas, electricity, magnetism, or some phosphorescent material, so far no definitive natural source has ever been discovered for the sightings.

There have been attempts, of course, to trap a ghost light for examination, but pursued, they always seem to be just out of reach. At some point, they acquired the Latin name *ignis fatuus,* meaning "foolish fire," because it's considered foolish to try to follow or capture such a phantom light.

Perhaps because the appearance of spectral lights is so mysterious, folklore has traditionally suggested that ghost lights are souls of the dead. The appearance of the lights usually often signals death or disaster.

Ghostly Pursuits

The legend of the jack-o'-lantern and other ghost lights is celebrated on Halloween by carving out vegetables and using candles to make them into lanterns. In Ireland, beets and turnips are commonly used. In the United States, the pumpkin has been the vegetable of choice for jack-o'-lanterns since the latter half of the 19th century.

According to some legends, the light of an ignis fatuus is the ghost of a sinner who is condemned to wander the world for eternity. There are, as always, many variations to the tale. In German folklore, the *Irrlicht* is a forest spirit or a soul following a funeral procession. In Sweden, it's the soul of an unbaptized baby roaming the earth in search of water. In Finland, the *liekko* (literally "flaming one") is the soul of a child who was buried in the woods. In parts of Britain, it's sometimes called the will-o'-the-wisp and is a death omen. The ignis fatuus sightings and traditions are also recorded in Africa and among Native Americans.

Sometimes the lights are playful beings, trying to lure travelers to follow them to get them lost in the dark. This type of ignis fatuus is often known, especially in Britain, as the jack-o'-lantern. Legend has it that the light is the soul of a person who's been shut out of both heaven and hell and must roam the earth endlessly. According to the British folk tale about the jack-o'-lantern, Jack was a man so ornery and mean in life that heaven wouldn't take him and the devil didn't want him.

Phantom Phrases

Literally meaning "foolish fire," **ignis fatuus** are ghost or spectral lights. According to most folkloric traditions, the lights are souls of the dead.

Ghostly Pursuits

Sometimes people see floating candles, which have long been associated with death. In ancient Egypt and Crete, lit candles were used to ward off evil spirits. Lights have always been a part of Judeo-Christian death customs. They are lit near the dying, in the room of the dead (perhaps, at first, to help purify the air), and, later, in remembrance of the dead. In early America it was believed that leaving a candle lit in an empty room would cause death. (Of course, this superstition may have had a logical source. An unattended candle could easily lead to a fire.) By Shakespeare's time, it was a well-established fact in folklore and tradition that a flickering candle indicated the presence of a ghost.

There are a number of locations where there are regular sightings of ghost lights, some of which have created their own local stories. We'll take another look at these in Chapter 13, "Urban Legends."

The Moment of Death

Folklore links some events to the moment of death. A meteor or shooting star, for example, is traditionally believed to be the soul of someone who has just died. This belief probably goes back to classical Roman times when it was thought that every person had a star in the heavens, and when that person died the star fell from the sky.

Pictures sometimes fall from the wall—especially a portrait of the deceased—when someone dies. An object, especially one associated with the person who dies, may break or shatter without being touched. Clocks have been known to stop at the precise time of death.

Ghostbusting

Tired? Worn out? Looking hag-ridden these days? The name "Old Hag syndrome" comes from the folkloric belief that demonic night spirit or witch (an "old hag") would straddle a victim's chest while the person was asleep and "ride" to a nighttime sabbat. This gave rise to the phrase "hag-ridden" for someone who appears exhausted or run-down.

Boo!

If you persistently feel the symptoms of Old Hag syndrome, don't wait for the *spirit demon* to show up. Hurry to a doctor! Recent surveys have discovered that 15 percent of adults worldwide have experienced at least one incidence of the syndrome. In the 2nd century A.D., the Greek physician Galen diagnosed Old Hag syndrome as simple indigestion. Modern doctors know no definite cause: They agree that it might be common indigestion, but it could also be narcolepsy or other sleep disorders, stress, sexual anxiety, or any number of other medical or psychological disorders.

Some people have heard a disembodied cry or wail when someone they know dies. Others have reported hearing an unexplained knocking. If asleep, a loved one or relative often wakes with a telepathic jolt or a presentiment of the death.

Bad to the Bone

There's no getting around it. Some ghosts and spirits are just plain evil. They're always bad news. Here's a fast survey of some of the baddest cats from all over the world:

➤ In India, an *acheri* is the ghost of a little girl who causes disease, especially to other children. It can spread the disease simply by casting its shadow over the victim.

➤ In Arab legends, the *afrit* is the spirit of a murdered man who aimlessly seeks revenge by killing the living.

➤ In India, the *bhut* (or *bhuta*) is the ghost of a man who has died by suicide, accident, or execution. Just as nasty is the *airi,* the ghost of a man who was killed during a hunt.

➤ Again in India, a *churl* is the ghost of a (typically lower-caste) woman who died in childbirth or in some impure ritual. They have no mouth and their feet face the wrong direction.

➤ In ancient Assyria, an *ekimmu* is the ghost of a man who died a violent or unpleasant death. The spirit was denied entrance to the underworld and therefore had to haunt the earth.

➤ In Ireland, a *fetch* (called a "co-walker" in England) is an astral double or apparition of a living person. Generally, seeing one means bad luck; when seen at night, it's a death omen.

➤ Among Native Americans, *whirlwinds* are sometimes thought to be evil spirits of the dead.

➤ The Old Hag syndrome is an unexplained nighttime phenomenon in which a person suddenly awakens feeling suffocated, paralyzed, or weighted down in bed by some invisible force. The victim is unable to move or scream, and odd smells or even apparitions sometimes accompany the attack. The attack always subsides just before the individual loses consciousness.

➤ In medieval Europe, an *incubus* was a demon spirit that assumed the shape of a man who sexually attacked women in their sleep. A *succubus* took the shape of a woman who molested men in their sleep.

Charmed, I'm Sure

Every culture has had *amulets* or charms thought to have the power to ward off evil ghosts and spirits. Pure, natural objects, such as crystals and gemstones, were believed to be especially effective. Salt, carried in the pocket or sewn in the lining of one's clothes, helped keep away ghosts.

Certain metals have always been associated with the occult. Silver, best known in mystic circles for its ability (when made into a bullet) to kill were-wolves, was thought to have magical powers against all sorts of supernatural creatures, including ghosts. Using silver nails to close a coffin, for example, would prevent the spirit of the dead from getting out.

The ancient Egyptians used chalcedony, a type of quartz, to scare away ghosts and nighttime visions as well as to relieve sorrow. Usually cloudy blue, yellow, or white in color, this mineral was most often used to coat scarabs (beetle-shaped amulets), protective amulets that were carried and placed in tombs.

Several tribal cultures have carved or sculpted amulets as protection from the spirit world. For example, the Arawaks of the Caribbean carved wood and stone idols called *zemi*, which they believed could protect themselves, their families, homes, and villages from evil spirits of the dead. Some were small enough to be worn or carried. The charms took their name from Zemi, the Arawak god of death.

Ghostbusting

Legends of incubi and succubi grew out of medieval morality. If an unchaste woman was caught in a compromising position with a man—or worse yet, became pregnant—she could claim that an incubus had attacked her. Likewise, a man could deny all knowledge of a mistress by saying she was a succubus. So, now, the next time you get caught red-handed, you'll know what to say.

Phantom Phrases

An **amulet** is any object, natural or man-made, that's believed to be endowed with supernatural powers allowing it to fend off ghosts and evil spirits or to bring good luck.

*Scarabs—small, beetle-
shaped, carved, and
coated stones—were used
in ancient Egypt to ward
off evil spirits.
(Photo by author)*

*A small zemi amulet,
meant to be worn or
carried.
(Photo by author)*

In classical Greece, it was believed that sharp or pointed objects, such as knives, swords, or even thorns, could frighten away ghosts.

Many times a ritual object or act could be employed to fend off offending phantoms. A well-known Christian example would be crossing oneself. Many laypeople believed that stepping over a broomstick, laying a broom across the threshold, or even placing it under the pillow at night will do the same trick. Building a cairn (a pyramid or pile of rocks) over a grave was thought to keep the ghosts in the grave.

One of the most common folkloric traditions is a belief in the evil eye, being cursed by the glare of a witch, sorcerer, or other enchanter. Even today, the fear of "being eyed" is especially strong in southern Europe and in Mediterranean cultures. Various amulets have been fashioned to ward off the evil eye, and it's believed that they are just as powerful against ghosts and evil spirits. Most incorporate some stylized rendering of an eye.

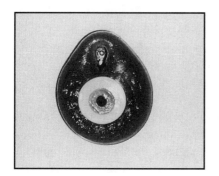 

Two versions of amulets able to protect against the evil eye. They are also thought to ward off ghosts and spirits. (Photos by author)

When you think of evil ghosts and spirits, ya gotta think poltergeists. There are so many poltergeist stories and legends, I've saved them for a chapter all their own, and it's coming up next.

The Least You Need to Know

➤ Every culture has legends about evil ghosts and spirits that are able to injure or kill the living.

➤ There are many ghosts and spirits whose appearances are thought to be death omens. Among them are banshees, radiant boys, spectral hounds, and ignis fatuus.

➤ Some folkloric traditions link certain events to the moment of death, such as a clock stopping or a shooting star.

➤ Every civilization has had its amulets and charms to ward off evil sorcery, ghosts, or other harmful phenomena.

Poltergeists: They're Here!

Any examination of ghost phenomena must include a discussion of poltergeists. For many, poltergeists are proof of a non-physical or non-material world, a realm occupied by spirits.

Poltergeists are not ghosts, at least not as we commonly use the word "ghost," because a poltergeist is not an apparition of a dead human being. Poltergeists are usually described as invisible spirits that are playful, simple, fun, mischievous, and teasing. But, at times, they can also be malicious, malevolent, dangerous, vicious, or merely annoying. On very rare occasions, poltergeists have appeared as apparitions.

In his 1945 book, *Poltergeist over England,* paranormal investigator Harry Price variously calls a poltergeist a presumed spirit, an entity, and a secondary personality. He notes that it is usually cruel, destructive, purposeless, and has noisy behavior, among other undesirable traits. But he never calls it a ghost.

What's the Difference?

Sometimes it's hard to tell whether a ghost or a poltergeist is haunting you because many of their activities are so similar. For example, both ghosts and poltergeists are known for their thumping and rappings. Indeed, the word *poltergeist,* from its Greek roots, literally means "noisy ghost."

Poltergeists tend to be more destructive in their behavior than ghosts. They're especially known for throwing stones (or making them rain from the air) and for starting spontaneous fires. Ghosts are not known for either.

Secret Identity

Since poltergeist activity doesn't usually seem to originate from any specific event or deceased person, the identity of the poltergeist is unknown. It's an unexplained force, possibly of pure disembodied energy, which plants itself in a particular place.

Why a poltergeist chooses to haunt a particular location or person, and why it will often start and cease activity quite suddenly, are mysteries as well.

Phantom Phrases

A **poltergeist** is a non-human spirit or entity, usually more malicious and destructive than the traditional ghost. The word, based on Greek roots, literally means "noisy ghost." Common poltergeist activities include thumpings and bangings, moving objects, stone-throwing, and starting fires.

Ghostbusting

If a baseball comes through your window, it's probably from the kids playing in the sandlot next door. But if stones start materializing above you in a closed room and drop to the floor, or if your wooden rocking chair suddenly bursts into flames all on its own, chances are you're dealing with a poltergeist—not pranksters, not the kids down the street. And almost *definitely* not a ghost.

Quiet Down!

Nandor Fodor and Hereward Carrington were two of the most active paranormal investigations in the first half of the 20th century. In their 1951 book *Haunted People* (published in 1953 in the United Kingdom as *The Story of Poltergeist Down the Centuries*), they define poltergeists by the stereotypically violent type of activity they produce. Carrington also points out a seeming connection between the poltergeist and a psychical energy emanating from a human's body at the time of puberty. Among the activities produced by poltergeists, Carrington noted:

➤ Kitchenware being smashed

➤ Bells ringing

➤ Various loud noises, including footsteps, knocks, raps, and crashes

➤ Objects tossed about by unseen forces

➤ Objects levitated or moving slowly through the air

➤ Tossed objects changing course in midair (not traveling in a straight line)

➤ Thrown objects that are sometimes unusually warm

➤ Spontaneous fires

➤ Stone-throwing

➤ Passage of solid objects through a wall or closed door

➤ Sprinkling or falling water

➤ Voices

➤ On rare occasions, visible apparitions

Likewise, Raymond Bayless, in *The Enigma of the Poltergeist* (Parker Publishing Co., 1967), lists the activities that he found most characteristic of the poltergeist:

➤ Falling or throwing of stones, sometimes in slow motion

➤ Unexplained fires, sometimes harmless, others destructive in nature

➤ Odd odors, sometimes sweet, othertimes repulsive

➤ Objects appearing and disappearing

➤ Objects moving seemingly without assistance

➤ Rappings and tappings, from light bumps to violent, house-rattling jolts

➤ Other unexplained sounds of all types: whispers, cries, shrieks, moans, explosions, crashes, even recognizable and understandable speech

➤ Rare but occasional apparitions

What Causes Poltergeists?

Currently, a very popular explanation for poltergeist activity suggests that it's actually caused by a secondary personality or agent (in other words, a human being) who is unknowingly using paranormal abilities to produce the phenomena.

Ghostly Pursuits

The concept of a female adolescent's repressed trauma exploding into psychokinetic, poltergeist-like activity formed the premise of Stephen King's 1975 novel, *Carrie*. It later serves as the basis for the 1976 MGM film, directed by Brian de Palma and starring Sissy Spacek as the traumatized girl and Piper Laurie as her possessive fanatical mother. Both women received Oscar nominations. In supporting roles, Amy Irving portrayed Carrie's one true friend, and William Katt and John Travolta played fellow classmates. *Carrie* also served as the basis of a major 1988 Broadway musical flop of the same name. In the story, Carrie, a shy and awkward girl just entering puberty, is taunted by her fellow students. At home, her domineering, fundamentalist mother pronounces Carrie's budding sexuality as sinful. The young teenager discovers that her inner hostility allows her to amplify an innate telekinetic power. In the tale's stunning finale, she uses her powers to kill her mother (by mentally flinging knives through the air and stabbing her to death) and wrecking destruction and death on the high school prom and those who tormented her.

It's been noted that many instances of poltergeist activity occur in households in which there is a child, especially ones in which a female is just entering puberty. Some researchers have advanced theories suggesting that, if the adolescent is undergoing mental or physical trauma, it might somehow unconsciously reveal itself in the guise of bombastic poltergeist behavior.

Interesting as this theory may be, there is a notable absence of children in many well-documented cases of poltergeist disturbances. Therefore, the theory is certainly no catch-all explanation.

Sticks and Stones May Break My Bones

Stone-throwing and falling stones are probably the single type of activity most associated with poltergeists. They're usually noted for their severity, their sudden appearance, and abrupt cessation. They're also distinguished by the seemingly impossible nature of the phenomena: Sometimes the stones seem to float or drop slowly down rather than dropping naturally by gravity or being propelled; often they appear and fall within a closed room, without coming through a window or hole in the ceiling.

The first recorded case of unexplained rocks hailing from the skies was in A.D. 335. Other early accounts date back to ancient Egypt, Greece, and Rome. Early Christian saints and writers also experienced paranormal stone-throwing; for example, in A.D. 1170 when the hermitage of St. Godric was inundated with falling rocks.

Unfortunately, most occurrences are isolated incidents and, therefore, can't be investigated. For example, for one night only in 1903, W.D. Grottendieck of Dordrecht, Holland, was attacked by a stone-thrower in his hut on the island of Sumatra. He woke around 1 A.M. to see stones slowly dropping to the floor around his bed, even though there were no holes in the thatched roof of his hut. He even caught one of the rocks, but it rose and floated out of his hand. He woke his young male servant to help him check all around the hut to make sure it wasn't the mischievous work of his laborers. Panicked, the boy fled; and soon after, the stone-throwing suddenly stopped. Most investigators of the incident point to the boy, even though he appeared to be sleeping through most of the event. The case remained unsolved.

A half century later, beginning on April 12, 1959, a well-documented poltergeist stone-thrower attacked the family and home of Don Cid de Ulhoa Centro in São Paulo, Brazil. The first volley consisted of only two stones, which fell into a hallway where three of Don Cid's children were playing. Soon, dozens of rocks were falling within rooms all over the hacienda. As is often the case with such disturbances, no one was hit by any of the stones.

Boo!

There have been few recorded instances when poltergeists deliberately seek to hurt or kill an individual. Nevertheless, if you ever suspect you're the target or victim of a poltergeist (rather than, say, a ghost) get away from the surroundings immediately! Even if you aren't directly harmed by the poltergeist, you might be hurt from ricocheting rocks, flying objects, fires, or other activity.

Over the next 48 hours, several neighbors witnessed the activity. In addition to the stones, other household objects such as pots, pans, eating utensils, and food began levitating, flying, and crashing about the kitchen and dining room. Finally, Don Cid called in a priest, Father Henrique de Morais Matos, to perform an exorcism of the spirit. Three exorcisms slowed but failed to end the poltergeist activity.

The rain of terror continued for 40 days and 40 nights, then suddenly stopped. Immediately, suspicion shifted from the supernatural to the natural. Even though she was never seen throwing any objects, a teenage maid named Francesca was accused of causing the stone-throwing by somehow attracting the pesky entity to the house. Paranormal investigators who later reviewed the case agreed that, indeed, she may have had latent mediumistic abilities, or she may have unconsciously released what is sometimes referred to as *repressed psychokinetic energy* to cause the activity.

Phantom Phrases

Some paranormals theorize that a person undergoing physical or mental trauma may unconsciously produce a force called **repressed psychokinetic energy**. This power, if released, might cause paranormal happenings such as poltergeist activity.

The Little Drummer Boy

Another form of poltergeist infestation is that of phantom drummers. Perhaps the most famous case is the Drummer of Tedworth, who appeared in Tedworth, England, in 1661. The incident was touched off when a real drummer (whose name is unknown) presented the town bailiff with a suspicious promissory note supposedly signed by a Colonel Ayliff. The drummer banged on his instrument non-stop and threatened to continue until he was paid. Although everyone in the town was annoyed, it wasn't until John Mompesson, an important and well-respected resident, complained that the drummer was arrested and his drum confiscated.

The drummer was soon released, but the drum was given to Mompesson. Within days, almost incomprehensible poltergeist activity began to occur at Mompesson's house. It started with the spectral sound of loud drumming, but soon more extraordinary phenomena erupted:

➤ Rude animal noises and unintelligible human voices were heard.

➤ Objects levitated and flew about the rooms.

➤ The children sometimes floated off their beds.

➤ Doors opened and shut by themselves.

➤ Chamberpots overturned onto beds.

➤ An unidentifiable apparition with glowing red eyes appeared to a servant and in the children's bedroom.

A rendering of a ghostly drummer by artist George Cruikshank, from Barham's Ingoldsby Legends.

And, through it all, the drum beating continued. The poltergeist activity continued for two years.

Occurring as it did while the witchcraft hysteria was in full swing in England, most locals believed that the events were the work of the devil. Some people blamed the Mompessons, saying that they must have been sinful and brought the curse upon themselves. The poltergeist case was personally investigated by one of the first paranormal researchers, the Reverend Joseph Glanvil, who you'll read more about in the next chapter.

The drummer was arrested elsewhere for similar fraud and disturbing the peace. While jailed in Gloucester Goal, he confessed, "Do you not hear of the drumming at gentleman's house in Tedworth? That I do enough, I have plagued him … and he shall never be quiet, 'til he hath made me satisfaction for taking away my drum." His words were used against him in court, and he was "condemned to transportation" (that is, exiled) from the area. The drummer returned to the region from time to time, however, and it was noted that during the periods he was nearby—and *only* then—the poltergeist activity started up again at the Mompessons'.

The Drummer of Tedworth, from Joseph Glanvil's Sadiucismus Triumphatus *(1661).*

Some Things Never Change

There have been so many reports of poltergeists over the past few centuries that it would be impossible to list them all. Some have been unusual enough to warrant special attention, including the next few examples.

Epworth Rectory

For about two months in the early 18th century, Epworth Rectory in Lincolnshire, England, was the site of daily poltergeist disruption. The Queen Mary gave over the rectory to the Reverend Samuel Wesley, but his family (especially his daughter Hetty) was not happy with the move into the faraway rural village. The local townsfolk were not particularly welcoming to the stern and severe new clergyman either: They set fire to the rectory in 1709 and injured the pastor's cattle. Wesley decided to rebuild the rectory, however, and stay on.

On December 1, 1719 (although some accounts say 1716), poltergeist activity started at the Epworth Rectory. Groans, knockings, and foot-stomping on the floorboards over-head, as well as other noises, were heard. The sounds of bottles smashing and pewter plates crashing could be heard in adjoining rooms; but when the rooms were checked, nothing had been disturbed. On at least one occasion, the bed of a daughter, Nancy, levitated with her on it.

Poltergeist activity became a nightly event, usually starting about 9:45 P.M. Once, Mrs. Wesley tried to scare the ghost away by blowing a loud horn throughout the house. The poltergeist responded by doubling its efforts to both day and night.

The Reverend Samuel Wesley.

The children blamed the manifestations on an invisible spirit whom they nicknamed "Old Jeffrey." Some people believed the culprit to be the ghost of "Old Ferries," which was the name of someone who had died in the rectory. No apparitions were ever seen, but some thought that a rabbit-like creature seen one night, and a badger spotted on another evening, were actually spirits in animal form. Also, no real communication was ever established with the poltergeist; it would repeat raps but would never use them to answer questions.

As suddenly as the poltergeist activity started, it abruptly stopped at the end of January 1720.

Paranormal experts suggest that the poltergeist phenomena were actually caused by the unleashing of pent-up psychokinetic activity, either on the part of the frustrated Mrs. Wesley (who was kept in an almost constant state of pregnancy—19 births in 20 years, only five children of which lived past infancy), or of the daughter Hetty (who hated the rectory and was at that poltergeist-triggering age somewhere between 14 and 19 years old). There is also the possibility that villagers who wanted to drive the rector and his family out of town perpetrated some of the activity.

Boo!

If you're a teenager reading this book, or can remember back to when you were a teenager, you know how difficult those years can be—mentally, physically, and emotionally. If you're a parent, friend, or adult caregiver, give special love and care to those who may need your attention most. And who knows? In the process, you may prevent poltergeist activity (caused by all that otherwise-repressed psychokinetic energy) from breaking out in your own home.

Ham House

In 1857, Mathias Ham, a well-to-do businessman, built a 23-room Victorian mansion overlooking the Mississippi River in Dubuque, Iowa. Shortly after the Dubuque Historical Society turned the house into a museum in 1964, seemingly paranormal (but not scientifically investigated) activity began to occur. Visitors have felt cold spots and breezes; a hallway light comes on and off by itself; an upstairs window locked at night is found open in the morning. Employees have heard unaccountable women's voices, footsteps, and organ music. To date, no apparitions have been spotted.

Real Poltergeists in the Movie Reels

Some of the most recent outbreaks of poltergeist activity have resulted in enormous press, especially in popular tabloid journals. Not surprisingly, the notoriety has often resulted in book deals and movie offers.

The Smurl Haunting

In a spectacular case history, the home of Jack and Janet Smurl in West Pittston, Pennsylvania, was purportedly haunted by poltergeists or possibly demons from 1974 to 1989. Over the course of a decade, the spirit activity escalated from minor annoyance to life-threatening.

The Smurls contacted two well-respected paranormal researchers from Connecticut, Ed and Lorraine Warren. (See the New England Society for Psychic Research listing in Appendix B, "Continuing the Ghost Hunt.") With the help of Rosemary Frueh, a nurse and psychic, they identified four evil spirits, one of which was probably a demon. The investigators decided that the entities had probably been in the house for years (it was built in 1896) but was psychically spurred into action by the onset of puberty in the daughters.

The Warrens brought in an exorcist, Father (later Bishop) Robert F. McKenna, but the poltergeist activity continued. In all, McKenna eventually performed three full exorcisms to no avail. The Smurls decided to go public with their appeal for help, appearing on a talk show and in the newspapers.

Paul Kurtz, chairman of the Committee for the Scientific Investigation of Claims of the Paranormal (CSICOP) asked to look into the hauntings, but the Smurls and the Warrens refused, claiming that CSICOP, a skeptic society, was too prejudiced to make a fair assessment.

Ghostbusting

If you've eliminated all other possibilities and still suspect that it's poltergeists or ghosts that are haunting your house, you'll probably want to call in a professional ghost investigator. Check out Appendix B for the names and addresses of the most respected paranormal researchers in the United States.

Indeed, without inspecting the premises, Kurtz published an article in CSICOP's journal, *Skeptical Inquirer,* musing on some of the possible causes of the Smurl haunting. He cited:

➤ Ground settling over the underground coal mines

➤ Leaky sewer pipes

➤ Antics by local teenagers

➤ Fanciful imagination, even delusion

Kurtz pointed out discrepancies in several of the Smurls' accounts and pondered their motivation in going public.

Press coverage picked up, prompting the Catholic diocese to take over the case. Shortly after the Smurls moved to a new town, Robert Curran's book about their ordeal, *The Haunted: One Family's Nightmare* (St. Martin's Press, 1988), was published. A film version of the book came out in 1991. A final exorcism by the Catholic Church in 1989 seemed to put the house's poltergeists or demons to rest.

The Mount Ranier Poltergeist

In January 1949, when he was almost 14, poltergeist activity started in the home of a young boy (noted in case histories as "Roland") in Mount Ranier, a Maryland suburb of Washington, D.C. At first, overhead scratching noises were heard in the boy's bedroom at night. Later, the boy's bed shook, and his bedclothes were torn off. Soon, activity was occurring day and night. Other noises, such as invisible squeaky shoes, were heard, and dishes and furniture sometimes moved on their own.

The parents, convinced that the boy was possessed by an evil spirit, called in their Lutheran minister, Luther Schulze, who prayed over the boy and commanded the demon to leave.

The activity worsened. Messages in scratched letters appeared on the boy's skin. A mental examination was considered, but instead, the parents moved the boy to a hospital. The scratchings continued to appear, and the boy began to spit up phlegm. For 35 days, a team including a Lutheran minister, an Episcopal priest, and some Jesuit priests took turns performing at least 20 exorcisms over the boy. Soon, the activity slowed. By April, the attacks had ended completely, and the boy returned home.

If this story sounds somewhat familiar, it's because author William Peter Blatty used the incident as the basis and inspiration for his 1969 book (and later the film) *The Exorcist*. He was a student at Georgetown University in August 1949 when he read a newspaper report on the events.

The Amityville Horror

Perhaps the most famous poltergeist "haunting" of them all—the Amityville Horror—led to an investigation which showed that most, if not all, of the alleged incidents never occurred.

On December 18, 1975, Daniel and Kathleen Lutz and their three children moved into a large house in Amityville on Long Island, New York. The enormous house was priced exceedingly low because it had been the site of an infamous murder the year before: 23-year-old Ronnie DeFeo had murdered his father, mother, and four younger siblings on November 13, 1974. Legend had it that the house was also sitting on an area that the Shinnecock Indians believed was beset by evil spirits.

By January 14, 1976, the Lutz family had left their new home, leaving all of their possessions behind. George and Kathleen Lutz claimed that they had been the victims of unnatural and severe poltergeist and ghost activity for 28 consecutive days. They said that they had seen hooded apparitions, and swarms of flies had attacked them in the children's room. There were wide temperature shifts, green goo appearing on the stairs, scratches on Kathleen's body, objects floating, and the sounds of a marching band. The Lutzes claimed that even people who visited the house later had troubles befall them, including a local priest, Father Ralph Pecararo, whom they had asked to bless the house before they moved in. Supposedly, he fell deathly ill and eventually had to be moved to another parish.

In 1976, *The Amityville Horror,* a non-fiction book by Jay Anson, became a best-seller. There was a successful 1979 film based on the book, and there were two sequel movies based on books by John G. Jones that supposedly told of the further adventures of the Lutzes.

Does success breed contempt, or was it all truly just a hoax? In January 1976, George Lutz contacted Jerry Solfvin of the Psychical Research Foundation to investigate the activity. Solfvin found no definite proof that poltergeist activity had occurred, so he brought in members of the American Society for Psychical Research. All were skeptical. Besides, there were some major discrepancies between actual occurrences, such as events in the weather, and those chronicled in what was supposed to be a non-fictional account. Anson had written the book in three or four months entirely from taped telephone interviews with the Lutzes.

Then, in 1979, William Weber, Ronnie DeFeo's lawyer, claimed that he and the Lutzes had

Boo!

Remember, not everything you read or see on TV or in the movies is true. Sometimes it's all just a big, fat story. It's especially difficult to separate fact from fiction these days when so-called docu-dramas and re-creations of historical events sprinkle actual truths among half-truths and lies. Even the most convincing tale should be taken with a grain of salt, and require extraordinary proof, if it's asking you to believe unbelievable events.

co-conceived the idea of inventing a story about poltergeist activity in the house in order to obtain book and movie deals. He sued for part of the profits. The Lutzes counter-sued.

But the lawsuits didn't stop there. The owners who followed the Lutzes into the house experienced no demonic activity, but they, too, sued the Lutzes, the author Jay Anson, and the book's publisher, because of their problems caused by curious thrill-seekers who constantly overran their property. Even Father Pecararo sued the Lutzes and the publisher for invasion of privacy and for making false claims about him.

The new residents of the house and Pecararo prevailed in their suits. As for Weber, the judge stated while hearing his suit that "the evidence shows fairly clearly that the Lutzes during this entire period were considering and acting with the thought of having a book published."

So there you have it, some of the best-known ghosts and poltergeists in legend and folklore. But so far, we've only looked at what happens when ghosts comes to haunt you. What do you do if you want to go to them?

The Least You Need to Know

➤ Poltergeists are not ghosts. They are non-human entities, not the returned spirits of the deceased.

➤ Ghosts and poltergeists are often confused or misidentified because they both produce phenomena such as unidentifiable rapping, footsteps, voices, and levitating objects.

➤ In general, poltergeists tend to be more malicious and destructive than ghosts.

➤ Poltergeist activity has been recorded since at least A.D. 335, but some of the more spectacular 20th-century accounts have been transformed into popular books and films.

Part 2
Don't Call Us, We'll Call You

Let's say you want to talk to the dearly departed. You can't just pick up a phone. Well, maybe you could, but chances are no one from the sprit world would answer.

If the ghosts won't come to you, maybe you could go to them.

Communication with the Beyond had always been the dominion of priests and oracles. It was sort of a religious monopoly of the highway to heaven—or wherever the spirit called home. But with the advent of spiritualism, mediums and séances changed all that!

In these chapters I'll tell you what takes place behind those closed doors, and—if you dare—how you can try to contact the spirits for yourself!

Chapter 6

Over My Dead Body!

In This Chapter

➤ Ghost beliefs of Catholics and Protestants

➤ How folks in the 16th, 17th, and 18th centuries felt about ghosts and apparitions

➤ Friedrich Anton Mesmer discovers the trance state

➤ Emanuel Swedenborg and Andrew Jackson Davis lay the groundwork for the arrival of spiritualism

Way back in Part 1, "The Great Beyond," we saw how Western civilization's ideas about ghosts and spirits changed between the Classical Ages of Greece and Rome and the Middle Ages. Ready for some more time travel? Catholics, Protestant reformers, scientists, and philosophers changed all those beliefs about ghosts once again, beginning in the 16th century.

This is going to be a whirlwind trip, because we're going to cover 300 years of ghost sightings, roughly from 1550 to 1850, in just a few pages. But, believe it or not, it's possible to trace almost a straight line from the church's teachings about ghosts in the 1500s to the birth of spiritualism in 1848.

Along the way, we'll look at witchcraft burnings, necromancy, psychic visions, and hypnosis. Look into my eyes: You're going back, back into time. When I snap my fingers, it's 1554, and you're at the Council of Trent.

Ghostly Reforms

By the time of the Reformation, Catholics and Protestants explained ghostly phenomena quite differently. In the most general terms, Catholics believed that ghosts were human souls coming back from the dead. In fact, at the Council of Trent (1545–1563) the Catholic Church confirmed its belief in a spirit-inhabited purgatory. Protestants, on the other hand, believed that ghostly apparitions were illusionary and caused by angels or, more likely, demons; likewise, they disavowed the existence of purgatory as a spirit-filled domain.

When Good Ghosts Go Bad

Catholic writers such as N. Taillepied (d. 1589), a Capuchin monk and a Doctor of Theology, suggested that, in addition to the ghosts of the dead, satanic spirits also existed, and they could take the form of loved ones. He listed several ways to tell if you were dealing with a demon ghost, as opposed to a good or neutral spirit. According to Taillepied, an evil phantom was more likely to:

➤ Hurt you (e.g., bite, pinch) or cause physical damage to your house or belongings.

➤ Flatter or tempt you. (Angelic spirits don't bother or need to do so.)

➤ Appear as a lion, bear, black dog, toad, snake, or cat. (Good ghosts manifest themselves as doves, lambs, handsome men with halos, or people dressed all in white.)

➤ Have loud, harsh voices, speaking heresy and with conceit. (Good spirits have soothing, musical voices, and they admit to their sins in groans and tears.)

Also, if a ghost says anything bad about the Catholic Church or contrary to its teachings, the spirit is evil. It *must* be.

Fortunately, Taillepied offered several practical suggestions for what to do if you saw an evil ghost. As a practical matter, he explained that swordplay would be useless: The sword would have no more effect than a pin in a pincushion. Instead, you should pray, say the Lord's name, make the sign of the cross on your forehead, and avoid speaking any blasphemy (which the demon could use as an excuse to take you away). Then, just to be safe, you should spend the rest of your life obeying and taking part in the sacraments of the Church. That oughta do it.

And what did the Protestants have to say? One of the best-known early Protestant books on ghosts was *De Spectris* (1570) by the Swiss reformer Louis Lavatar. In 1572 it was published in English as *Of ghostes and spirites walking by nyght, and of strange noyses, crackes, and sundry*

Ghostbusting

In the early days of spiritualism, unseen spirits would often announce their presence by knocking or tapping on a table or other solid object. But this was nothing new. Similar spirit rappings were described in Christian writings by the beginning of the 16th century. Sorcerers of the period also often asked spirits to knock to make themselves known. So who are we to disagree? If you hear a tapping noise, but no one's around, look out: You might have a ghost on your hands.

forewarnynges. Now there's a title! Lavatar explained that there were two popular opposing beliefs at the time, neither completely correct: "some thinking every small motion and noise to be spirits" and others "persuaded that there are no spirits."

Lavatar thought that most Catholic ghost sightings could be explained away as trickery, human error, or natural causes. Also, he dismissed all reports from women because they were, for the most part, "given to fear more than men" and think that they see and hear things that aren't really there. He did concede that "drunken men see strange things" that they mistakenly report as being ghosts.

Despite the Protestant church's official position, most 16th-century followers *did* believe in ghosts. There were just too many sightings, and the concept of apparitions was just too culturally ingrained for people to truly deny their existence. Likewise, not all Protestants believed that Satan was the cause for all ghosts.

Great Scot! It's King James!

The end of the 16th century wasn't a good time to be a witch. King James I (1566–1625), who had ruled Scotland, came to the throne in England at the beginning of the 17th century. The wrath of the Inquisition was winding down. Nevertheless, it was estimated that between 1450 and 1600, the Inquisition tried, convicted, and burned more than 30,000 "witches" in Europe. James was a fervent enemy of sorcery and penned the anti-witchcraft book, *Demonologie* (1597).

In it, James suggested that neither the spirits of the dead nor angels appeared as ghosts in this world. Satan was the source for all apparitions. James believed that the devil could assume the form of a deceased person or could reanimate the actual corpse—whether or not the individual had been good or bad while alive. (This, by the way, was James's explanation for how ghosts got into a house to haunt it. The demon spirit could produce a solid body out of the deceased person's spirit.)

In 1584, Reginald Scot wrote *The Discoverie of Witchcraft,* one of the first books to dispute the existence of witchcraft—at least to the extent that it was being punished by the Inquisition. Scot addressed the subject of ghosts in just one chapter. An avowed Protestant, Scot argued against purgatory, and he believed that the dead do not return to the material world from there or any other place. Demons might appear in the form of a dead person, but because the hellish creatures are merely ghosts rather than flesh and blood, they can't physically hurt living beings. The only true, worthy apparitions came from God, Jesus, or the heavenly hosts (angels), such as appearances of the Virgin Mary (see Chapter 13, "Urban Legends").

The Age of Alchemy

During the anti-witchcraft crusade of the Inquisition, the practice of necromancy did not disappear: It just went underground (if you'll pardon the pun).

Ghostbusting

Although the Kabbalah has its roots in ancient Hebrew mysticism, cabalistic teachings and principles are still popular today. Its teachings have many celebrity adherents, such as Roseanne. Check out the New Age section of any major bookstore; you'll find plenty of books on the Kabbalah.

A series of metaphysical thinkers in the 16th through 18th centuries embraced the Kabbalah, a collection of mystical Jewish writings, in their search for eternal truths and unlimited knowledge. They felt that the keys to unlock all of life's (and the afterlife's) secrets could be found in the books' deliberately obscure texts.

The practice of necromancy among these occultists was almost commonplace. Often the secret rituals took place at night in the local cemeteries. A famous 18th-century engraving by Ames, made from a drawing by Sibly, shows a successful necromantic churchyard ritual being conducted in England by the wizard John Dee (1527–1608), and his partner, medium Edward Kelly (1555–1595). A new rendering of the illustration was published by Mathieu Giraldo in Paris in 1846.

Spain was considered the capital of necromancy during the Middle Ages. The nefarious craft was actually taught in Toledo, Seville, and Salamanca, deep in caves outside the cities. When rumors started to circulate that witches were seen eating human flesh, Queen Isabella, a fervent Catholic, sealed up the caverns.

John Dee and Edward Kelly performing necromancy in a churchyard around 1582. (Mathieu Giraldo, Histaire curieuse et pittoresue des sorciers, *Paris, 1846)*

Ghost Stories of the 17th Century

Following the Restoration in 17th-century England, several important collections of ghost stories were assembled, including one by Joseph Glanvill (1636–1680), an Anglican minister and chaplain to Charles II. His stories were published the year after his death under the title *Saducismus Triumphatus; or a full and plain evidence concerning Witches and Apparitions*. Glanvill had a hands-on approach to the paranormal; in 1661, he investigated the site haunted by the famous poltergeist, the Drummer of Tedworth (see Chapter 5, "Poltergeists: They're Here!").

Glanvill believed that there were two "aspects," or parts, of the soul. At death, what he called the so-called "astral body"—the higher aspect—returned to its heavenly home, this different than the astral body. The "aerial body"—the lower aspect—sometimes remained as a spirit here on Earth.

In the ghost stories of the 17th century, the phantoms most often returned to Earth to:

➤ Give a warning, or to help, advise, or haunt mortals.

➤ Confess their guilt or sins.

➤ Provide for their heirs (especially if there was a large inheritance) by telling where treasure was hidden.

➤ Seek revenge, right a wrong, or obtain justice (especially if the deceased had been murdered).

Two thirds of the ghosts could be recognized by the people they were haunting. The ghosts of the Restoration period also tended to share certain attributes:

➤ They didn't materialize suddenly, float, or pass through solid objects, such as walls. They would open and shut doors, sometimes being polite enough to knock first.

➤ They appeared "normal" in voice and behavior.

➤ They resembled the corpse at the time of death. Thus, the ghost of a murder victim might show a slit throat or bullet wounds, or an accident victim might be disfigured.

➤ They showed no sign of having been in purgatory—no blackened faces, no singed clothing.

➤ They were aware of goings-on on Earth, especially of events in their own family and society.

Ghostbusting

Be precise when talking about ghosts. Many times the same word can mean two completely different things, depending which paranormal expert's doing the talking. Glanvil thought the astral body was only half of a soul or spirit—the part that, after death, ascended to a higher plane. In an out-of-body experience (see Chapter 3, "Do the Dead Return?"), the astral body is a whole spirit: It simply leaves a still-living body to take a short vacation.

From Enlightenment to Romance

The Enlightenment of the 18th century led to a rise in skepticism and disbelief in ghosts. After all, it was a time of science, discovery, and practicality. Charles Darwin's *Origin of Species* (1859) and *Descent of Man* (1871) questioned the creation of man. Free-thinkers openly debated and discussed religious doctrine the various possibilities of an afterlife.

During the Romantic era of the late 18th and early 19th centuries, society embraced the emotional and the spiritual. In *The Golden Bough* (1890), Scottish anthropologist Sir James George Frazer (1854–1941), for example, explored the role of myth and magic in early civilizations.

As humanity's beliefs about science and religion changed, so, too, did their beliefs about the soul, the possibility of survival after death, the existence of ghosts, and the ability to communicate with the dead.

Mystical Visions

It was against this backdrop that Emanuel Swedenborg (1688–1722) was born in Sweden. A scientist and scholar, he did believe in the existence of the soul. Swedenborg had no particular interest in the paranormal, but in 1743, when he was 56, all that changed.

Swedenborg had a series of dreams and trances in which he claimed he experienced visions of an Unseen World. He said that he was shown the nature and order of the universe during conversations with Jesus and God. Swedenborg also spoke with "angels," which is what he called the spirits of the dead. Among those Swedenborg said he talked with were Aristotle, Plato, and Napoleon.

Thinking that he was selected as a messenger for these divine revelations, Swedenborg began to tell others of his visions. He soon became a hermit and learned to place himself into a trance state. He began to deliver messages from the dead by *automatic writing*, a technique in which a person holds a pencil to paper and allows the "spirits" to move your hand.

Automatic writing is a form of *automatism,* which is any unconscious and spontaneous muscular movement caused by the spirits. Automatisms are especially impressive if they're skills such as painting, creative writing, singing, or the playing of a musical instrument, especially if it's not an activity normally practiced by the medium.

Phantom Phrases

Automatic writing is a technique used by mediums, usually while in a trance state, to deliver messages from the dead. The medium holds a pencil or pen to paper and allows the spirit to take possession or control of the hand, which then moves under impulses delivered by the spirit. It's a specific type of **automation,** which is any bodily movements caused by the spirit. Automatic writing was a great improvement over the old method of spirit communication: tedious rappings to indicate "yes," "no," or the letters of the alphabet.

Among his many teachings, Swedenborg proclaimed that a person exists simultaneously in the physical and the spirit worlds. The spirit survives death intact, with complete knowledge of its life on Earth. After death, the soul, enters an astral plane where the dead meets deceased friends and relatives. Then, after a period of reflection, the soul moves onto a sort of heaven or hell, an afterworld created by the soul's own memories from Earth. (Swedenborg didn't believe in redemption through Christ, nor did he believe in Satan.)

Ghostly Pursuits

Swedenborg's mystical teachings and revelations had gained a foothold, during his lifetime, but the Swedenborgian movement, based on his writings, started up after his death. It evolved into a religion still practiced today. Its first churches were established in England in 1778, and its first in America followed in 1792. In 1810, the Swedenborg Society was formed to publish the mystic's many writings, including his best-known book, *Heaven and Hell*.

Needless to say, Swedenborg's announcements didn't endear him to the Christian Church. Even many of Swedenborg's friends and colleagues thought that he was insane. Eventually, Swedenborg moved to London, where he died in 1772.

But what does Swedenborg have to do with ghosts? Well, his teachings would have a great impact on the soon-to-be-born spiritualism movement. Many of his ideas, such as the belief that the spirit (along with all its earthly memories) survives death intact, were wholeheartedly embraced by spiritualists.

Mesmerize Me

Today, we take it for granted that at a séance, before the spirits can be contacted, the medium has to go into a deep, deep sleep. Well, the trance state wasn't always taken for granted.

Its "discovery" and acceptance by the public can be traced back to Austrian-born Friedrich (sometimes seen as Franz) Anton Mesmer (1734–1815). (And yes, you're getting ahead of me. This is where the words "mesmerize" and "mesmerism" come from.) Mesmer's work proved to be the next big step among modern attempts to communicate with the Other World.

Phantom Phrases

Mesmerism, later called hypnotism, is the induction of a sleep-like or trance state by another person. Its discovery came as an outgrowth of therapeutic work by students of Friedrich Anton Mesmer, from whose name the word is derived.

Although a trained physician, Mesmer believed that the planets affected the human body with a power resembling magnetism. He treated his patients by setting magnets on the affected parts of their bodies. Over time, he also came to believe that a physician can heal with "animal magnetism" by discharging a curative force from his nervous system and out through the hands. During treatment, his patients often experienced physical convulsions, which Mesmer identified as the "crisis" period of the cure.

Traditional medicine was quick to dismiss Mesmer as a quack, resulting in at least three official investigations of his work. However, one of Mesmer's students, the Marquis de Puységur (1751–1825) discovered that patients didn't have to undergo convulsions to be cured. They could be put into a trance or sleep "mesmerized" state, in which, many times, they could diagnose and heal themselves.

Boo!

Kids, don't try this at home! Although it's not really dangerous *per se,* you shouldn't try to hypnotize someone until you've studied and read extensively on the subject. What could go wrong? As a quick example, if a hypnotist allows a subject to recall painful past and doesn't suggest that they be forgotten, the memories could remain resurfaced, fresh in the person's mind after waking up.

Look into My Eyes

Before long, physicians across Europe were experimenting with patients in mesmerized states. A French doctor, Alexandre Bertrand, suggested in *Treatise on Somnabulism* (1823), that the key to Mesmer's cures lay in the subject's sleep or "somnambulistic state." In the 1840s, British surgeon James Braid (1795–1860), coined a new term for the induction of a trance state: hypnotism (from the Greek *hypnos,* meaning "sleep"). Braid discovered that under a hypnotic state, the subject was especially responsive to suggestion.

Some of the other phenomena exhibited by hypnotized subjects included induced amnesia, the willingness to perform silly and sometimes seemingly impossible physical feats, the ability of withstanding pain, sensory hallucination, heightened powers of attention, extraordinary recall of past events, and the induction of extreme emotional states. Rumors soon surfaced that some mesmerized people showed telepathic or other extrasensory powers.

These fanciful engravings show subjects being hypnotized. Sleep rays don't come out of a hypnotist's fingers during induction, of course. However, Mesmer, from whose name we get "mesmerize," believed he could cure people by passing "animal magnetism" out through his hands.

Ghostly Pursuits

Around 1838, P.P. Quimby (1802–1866), an American clock-maker from Maine, became interested in mesmerism. He began to treat diseases by hypnotizing a young man, Lucius Burkmar, who was then introduced to the patient suffering from the disease. Burkmar was able to diagnose ailments and prescribe remedies through seeming clairvoyance (the extra-sensory power to mentally "see" things or events unknown to anyone). Quimby soon discovered that he, too, had the gift of clairvoyance and, when mesmerized, was able to read the patient's mind (telepathy). He believed that most patients' ailments were caused by unhealthy thinking, and that, if he could remove those diseased thoughts using mesmerism, the physical complaints would be cured. He variously called his methods "the Science of Health" and "Christian Science." Quimby's most famous patient was Mary Patterson, later Mary Baker Eddy, who founded the religion of Christian Science.

Lasting Contributions

In his 1986 book *Spirit Theater,* Eugene Burger identifies three important contributions that Mesmer and his followers made to the rise of the spiritualist movement:

➤ A ready-made audience for séances. People who had gathered to see demonstrations by Mesmer and his followers were even more astounded—and entertained—by séances.

➤ Demonstrations of mesmerism psychologically prepared audiences to accept fantastic, even spooky, entertainment.

➤ Mesmerism provided spiritualism with its most important asset: ready-made performers in the guise of mediums. Successful mesmerists could use many of their same demonstrations as supposed proof of spirit contact rather than magnetism.

Ghostbusting

Hypnotism is a fascinating subject, and the induction technique can be learned by almost anyone. Your eyelids are getting heavy! Sleep! Sleep! See how easy that was? If you want to learn more about how to hypnotize and otherwise mesmerize, check out *The Complete Idiot's Guide to Hypnosis* (Alpha Books, 1999).

Mesmerists, for example, had discovered that if two or more people sat with their fingers lightly resting on a tabletop, the table would often begin to move or tilt. They explained that "table tipping," as this phenomenon became known, was caused by magnetism (even if the table were made of wood, a non-metallic substance). Working as mediums, mesmerists claimed that spirits, not the human participants, were actually moving the table.

Ghostly Pursuits

In 1853, the English chemist and physicist Michael Faraday (1791–1867) dismissed the "magnetic" explanation. And Faraday should know: He discovered the properties of electromagnetism. Rather, Faraday suggested that the expectations of the sitters grouped around the table produced unconscious muscular pressures that moved the table.

A Deep Sleep Window to the Spirit World

For some, Mesmer's work made it "scientifically" acceptable to attempt to contact spirits while in a trance state. In his "Essay Upon the Ghost-Beliefs in Shakespeare,"

Alfred Roffe wrote that ghosts could see the material world through the eyes of a mesmerized person. It wasn't long before occultists began to speculate whether putting a "sensitive" person into trance would allow them to see into the spirit world—or whether the spirits could use someone in a trance as a way back to this world.

Before long, there were numerous reports of people who had been able to contact the spirit world while mesmerized. For example, two books appeared in the mid-19th century in which the authors told about what they had seen on the Other Side while hypnotized:

➤ *Arcanes de la vie future devoilés,* by A. Cahagnet (France, 1847 or 1848)

➤ *Somnolism and Psycheism,* by British physician Dr. J. Haddock (England, 1849)

Both men were heavily influenced by the teachings of Swedenborg, and the afterlife depicted in their books was strikingly similar to the one described by the Swedish visionary.

It all comes around, doesn't it? Like a Circle of Life thing.

Ghostbusting

Try table tipping for yourself! Seat two to four people in chairs around a card table. Lightly rest your fingertips on the tabletop, as if ready to play the piano. Concentrate, mentally commanding the table to move. Before long, the table will probably begin to shift, vibrate, or tilt. If all participants stand simultaneously, it's sometimes possible to make the table levitate, as if it were clinging to the fingers.

Ghostly Pursuits

There are many misconceptions about hypnosis: It can't change a person's basic personality. You can't make a person do anything they wouldn't while they're completely awake. (Of course, that does vary greatly among people, doesn't it?) It's not a truth serum: People can (and do) lie under hypnosis. (In fact, they often say what they think the hypnotist wants to hear.) The person who is "under" doesn't black out: Rather, the subject is completely aware of everything that's going on in the room and often remembers most of what went on (although hypnotists can often suppress these memories by suggestion).

The Poughkeepsie Seer

Andrew Jackson Davis (1826–1910), who was born in upstate New York, is remembered for helping to bridge the gap between mesmerism and spiritualism. In the autumn of 1843, Davis attended a performance in Poughkeepsie by J. Stanley Grimes, a magnetist, mesmerist, and phrenologist (someone who, it was thought, could tell a person's character and mental capacity by reading the shape of and bumps on the skull). Davis was fascinated. Davis was put into a trance for the first time in December 1843 by a local tailor named William Levingston, who had begun to dabble in mesmerism after Grimes' appearance in town. Davis showed ability at diagnosing illnesses while entranced, and he became known as the Poughkeepsie Seer.

In March 1844, Davis experienced a series of life-transforming visions. He claimed that while walking in the Catskills Mountains in a semi-trance-like state, he ran into Christ, the Greek physician Galen, and Emanuel Swedenborg. Successive visions convinced Davis that he had been selected to deliver some sort of sacred declaration.

Davis convinced S. Silas Lyon, an herbalist doctor he met in Bridgeport, Connecticut, to move to New York City with him to act as his mesmerist. Davis's visions were published as *The Principles of Nature, Her Divine Revelations, and a Voice to Mankind, By and Through Andrew Jackson Davis, the "Poughkeepsie Seer" and Clairvoyant,* more simply known as *The Divine Revelations*. According to Davis, spirits of the deceased resided in a realm called the Summer-Land. He wrote:

> *It is a truth that spirits commune with one another while one is in the body and the other is in the higher spheres ... and this truth will ere long present itself in the form of a living demonstration. And the world will hail with delight the ushering in of that era when the interiors of men will be opened, and the spiritual communion will be established ...*

Did I read that right? "This truth will ere long present itself in the form of a living demonstration"? Perhaps without even knowing it, Davis had predicted the arrival of spiritualism!

Soon, the lights would be lowered. Wait a second! Did you hear something? What's that knocking in the dark? Did you feel the table move? The spiritualist movement was about to be born!

The Least You Need to Know

➤ During the Reformation, Catholics and Protestants were split in their beliefs about ghosts, with the latter denying their existence.

➤ Both King James (*Demonologie*) and Reginald Scot (*The Discoverie of Witch-craft*) denied that apparitions were ghosts of the deceased. King James claimed that all spirits were demonic.

➤ Necromancy was still widely practiced throughout the 16th century, with Spain being a center for the occult arts.

➤ Several important collections of ghost stories were assembled in the 17th century, including those by Joseph Glanvill.

➤ Belief in ghosts waned during the Enlightenment of the 18th century.

➤ The work of Friedrich Anton Mesmer and his followers, along with mystics such as Emanuel Swedenborg and Andrew Jackson Davis, laid the path for the spiritualism movement.

Chapter 7

Spirit, Move Me: The Birth of Spiritualism

In This Chapter

➤ How spiritualism got its start

➤ The Fox sisters, spiritualism's first mediums

➤ The rising popularity of séances in the United States and England

➤ The Browning and Goligher home circles

People have been trying to communicate with the dead since ancient times. As we've seen, necromancers and early wizards claimed that they could raise the spirits of the dead as part of their stock in trades. It was still an age of wonders in the mid-1800s when spiritualism began. People were performing impossible feats while mesmerized or entranced. Tables miraculously tipped by pure magnetism. Visionaries, such as Swedenborg, claimed that a "living demonstration" of the spirit world was at hand.

The climate was ripe for a new "religion"—spiritualism—to be born. It would all start with two young girls in a remote, rural village, but by the end of the 19th century belief in the controversial faith would spread to England and much of the Western world. Journey with me now to another time, a step back, as we take a look at the humble beginnings of the spiritualism movement.

The Stage Is Set for Spiritualism

In 1848, two sisters in upstate New York began receiving spirit messages. The Fox sisters were proclaimed *mediums,* and the spiritualist movement was born.

It all started in a small wood-frame house in Hydesville, New York—a tiny town of no more than three or four dozen homes, just southwest of Rochester.

John D. and Margaret Fox moved into their one-and-half-story house on December 11, 1847. Two of their four children, the youngest, Catherine (Kate) and Margaretta (Margaret), lived at home. (There is some discrepancy as to the girls' ages. Reports have them as young as six-and-a-half and eight, respectively; Rochester records show them as having been 12 and 14.) An older daughter, Leah Fox Fish, whom Margaret later said was 30 at the time, had been recently widowed and was supporting herself as a music teacher in Rochester. A son, David, lived on a farm in nearby Auburn.

Almost as soon as the Fox family moved into their home in Hydesville, they began hearing unusual rappings and thumping sounds. When Mr. Fox could find no natural source for the noises, neighbors confided that the cottage had a reputation for being haunted prior to the Foxes moving in. Similar noises as well as footsteps had been heard by a former resident, John Bell, as well as by his employee, Lucretia Pulver, in 1843 and 1844. Michael and Hannah Weekman lived there for the two years before the Fox family and often heard knockings at the front door: When the door was opened, no one was ever there!

Phantom Phrases

A **medium** is someone who can communicate with spirits on behalf of another living being. The word suggests that the "medium" acts at a midway point, halfway between the worlds of the living and the dead.

One evening, on March 31, 1848, young Kate responded to the tappings by snapping her fingers and asking "Mr. Splitfoot" (a common nickname for the Devil) to repeat her actions. To the amazement of her mother, an identical number of raps was heard. Kate asked the invisible spirit to try again, but this time she only mimed the action of snapping her fingers. The correct number of taps were heard, and Kate delightedly informed her mother that the spirit must be able to *see* as well as *hear!* Within two days, the thumpings were appearing during the day as well as the night.

Boo!

Be careful what you wish for, they say: It may come true. The Fox sisters supposedly asked "Mr. Splitfoot" to answer them. Next thing they knew, the devil (or so some people thought) was at their door. If you start calling on spirits, be careful: You never know who might answer!

As word spread among the neighbors that an intelligent spectral presence was haunting the Fox house, the girls worked out a tapping code to communicate with the spirit. It supposedly told them that he was the ghost of Charles B. Rosma, a peddler, who had been murdered some years before and buried in the basement of the house. This prompted a lot of discussion but no agreement over whether a traveling salesman had ever vanished from the area. Nor were any human remains found in the Fox cellar. Nevertheless, some people claimed that John Bell must have been a murderer, though no charges were ever filed.

Imagine the sensation these events caused! Proof had been established that there was life after death, and that the living can communicate with the spirits—perhaps even with loved ones, the dearly departed!

Soon crowds were descending on Hydesville to hear the sounds for themselves. To restore some semblance of order to their lives, the Fox parents decided to send Kate to live with her brother, David; young Margaret moved in with her sister, Leah. Interestingly, the sounds stopped in Hydesville, but started up in Rochester and Auburn where David and Leah lived!

Taking Their Show on the Road

The girls began to invite visitors to experience the phenomena for themselves. Kate conducted "sittings," as she called her gatherings in Auburn, until the early 1890s. Margaret often referred to her get-togethers as "spirit circles." In time, such assemblies came to be known as *séances.*

In November 1849, Margaret received a spectral message that she was to provide a large public demonstration. Her sister Leah rented the Corinthian auditorium, the largest in Rochester, and spectators paid one dollar apiece to see and hear a spirit visitation. It was during these profitable exhibitions that Leah discovered that she, too, was a medium.

On three separate nights during Margaret's Rochester presentations, committees selected by the audience took part in the sittings on stage. None was able to detect any fraud.

With Leah as their manager, Kate and Margaret went on tour across the United States. In the spring of 1850, Horace Greeley, the powerful owner and publisher of the *New York Tribune,* invited the three sisters to his home in New York City, where they met and held sittings for his society friends and celebrities. Many were converted to this new belief called *spiritualism.* The Fox sisters' lifelong careers as mediums were launched.

Ghostbusting

Ghosts don't generally follow people from one location to another. They haunt a specific location. It would be very unusual for a murder victim to move on to not one, but two, new haunts. That being said, a medium can be located anywhere when calling up a spirit. It just seems odd that, once the girls left Hydesville, there was no more ghost activity there. Then, the rappings suddenly appeared at their new homes. Now I'm not going to tell you what *I* think was going on. (But then, I know how the story ends.) I'll let you decide for yourself.

Phantom Phrases

A **séance** (also known as a "sitting," "spirit circle," or "circle") is a gathering of individuals, usually led by a medium, for the purpose of receiving spirit manifestations or communication with the dead. The word "séance" is derived from the Old French *seoir* and Latin *sedere,* meaning "to sit." (Séances performed in a person's house, with or without the assistance of a medium, are known as home circles or home sittings, which I'll discuss later in this chapter.)

The Best of Times, the Worst of Times

During their heyday, the Fox sisters held séances for the great and the near-great. Kate held at least one séance for Mary Todd Lincoln, who wanted to contact her late husband, President Abraham Lincoln. There's no proof that contact was ever made.

Margaret's clients included William Cullen Bryant, James Fenimore Cooper, and Harriet Beecher Stowe.

Ironically, many attendees were convinced that the Fox demonstrations validated rather than opposed their Christian beliefs—that there was, indeed, a resurrection after death. More conservative Christians, however, thought that the work of the Fox sisters was demonic. Some participants were merely amused and dismissed it all as pure theatrical entertainment. Still others considered it to be deliberate fraud.

There were two early accusations of trickery. In January 1850, a committee of doctors investigating Margaret Fox discovered that spirit sounds wouldn't appear as long as they held tightly onto her legs during the sitting. Then, on April 17, 1851, Mrs. Norman Culver, a relative by marriage of the Fox sisters, told the *New York Tribune* that Kate had confessed that she secretly produced the snapping sounds by cracking the joints of her toes. Despite these semi-exposures, spiritualists refused to believe that they were being duped.

In the end, life was not terribly kind to the Fox sisters. In 1852, Margaret Fox became involved with a surgeon and Arctic explorer, Dr. Elisha Kent Kane. He departed on an expedition in 1856, and died unexpectedly in Cuba on February 16, 1857. During settlement of the estate, Margaret claimed that she and Kane had a common-law marriage. (To the end of her life, she frequently called herself Margaret Fox Kane.) Dr. Kane's brother challenged her in court. A financial agreement was reached, but the brother defaulted on the payments. Margaret, by necessity, returned to her life as a medium.

Boo!

It's amazing what people will say and do when there's money involved. Always be wary of people who profit in some way by their claims of seeing ghosts or experiencing other paranormal activity. The most reliable sources are those who have nothing to gain, and perhaps even something to lose (such as reputation), by the telling.

Phantom Phrases

Spiritualism is the belief system that spirits of the dead can (and do) communicate with living humans in the material world. Usually this contact is made through a medium.

At first, Kate fared better. In 1854, the Society for the Diffusion of Spiritual Knowledge engaged her for a full year to conduct free public séances. She perfected the art of producing automatic writing (see Chapter 6, "Over My Dead Body!") that was also mirror-writing; that is, backward script that had to be held up to a mirror to be read. And in 1861, Kate Fox became the first spiritualist medium to produce a *materialization*—a physical manifestation of a spirit.

From 1861 to 1866, Kate was hired by New York banker Charles F. Livermore to hold private séances for him in an attempt to contact his recently deceased wife, Estelle. In 1871, Livermore sent her to London, where she sat for physicist William Crookes and held séances with fellow mediums D.D. Home and Mrs. Agnes Guppy. (You'll be hearing a lot more about these two in the coming chapters.)

While in London, Kate married Henry Jencken in 1872. They had two sons. The first, Ferdinand, born in 1873, was proclaimed a medium by the age of three. Mr. Jencken died of a stroke in 1885, and Kate returned to the United States with her sons.

By the 1880s, both Margaret and Kate Fox were drinking heavily. Relations between them and Leah deteriorated. It's speculated that Leah feared her younger sisters would reveal their deceptions. In January 1888, the Society for the Prevention of Cruelty to Children had Kate's young sons taken from her because of her alcoholism, and Kate apparently suspected that Leah was somehow to blame. With Margaret's help, Kate obtained the release of the boys, and mother and sons departed for England.

Phantom Phrases

A **materialization** is the manifestation or production of some physical object or person from the spirit world. The most difficult and impressive materialization was all or part of a human being.

So That's How It's Done!

On September 24, 1888, Margaret Fox admitted in an interview published in the *New York Herald* that "every effect produced by us was absolute fraud." Just a month later, on October 21, 1888, she confessed in the *New York World* that she was eight and her sister nine-and-a-half years old when they started the rappings as a game to terrify their mother.

They produced the first thumps while in bed at night by tying an apple to a string and bumping it on the floor. When people began to flock to the house to see the children and hear the knockings, the girls became frightened that they would be punished and kept up the ruse for "self-preservation." Margaret explained that Kate first discovered that she could produce noises with her knuckles and joints "by swishing her fingers … and that the same sound could be made with the toes."

Margaret went on to implicate Leah, claiming the elder sister had secretly fed the young mediums information about the people who participated in the séances. Margaret said that she believed Leah wanted to use the girls to help found a new religion; she was making her belated confession in an attempt to save her soul, as well as that of her sisters. Leah, happily married for the third time to a wealthy husband, dismissed Margaret's claims. Kate, in England, at first made no response.

On October 21, 1888, the same day that Margaret's *New York Word* interview was printed, Margaret and Kate took the stage of the New York Academy of Music and showed how they produced their spirit rappings. (Kate returned from England for the occasion but did not speak at the demonstration.) Their confession did not change many people's opinions.

Spiritualists came up with many possible explanations for the confessions:

➤ The sisters had been coerced by the Catholic Church.

➤ They had been bribed by newspapers.

➤ The confession was incoherent or delusional because of the sisters' alcoholism.

➤ The Fox sisters were *real* mediums and didn't even know it! (The famed writer Sir Arthur Conan Doyle believed this about Houdini! See Chapter 24, "The Magic Connection.")

Indeed, many spiritualists who reluctantly accepted the Fox sisters' confessions argued that just because *they* were fakes, that didn't mean that *all* mediums were fakes.

The sisters set out on an exposé tour, but it soon faltered. Kate recanted her testimony and continued to perform séances. In 1891, penniless and abandoned by her wealthy and celebrity clients, Margaret also withdrew her confession and returned to the séance table.

Ghostly Pursuits

Located in Chautauqua County on the shore of Cassadaga Lake in upstate New York, Lily Dale is only 123 miles from Hydesville, where the Fox sisters made their first contact with the spirit world. Lily Dale was founded as a spiritualist retreat in 1879, and in the last century the village has played host to a diverse group of guests including Sir Arthur Conan Doyle, Mae West, Mahatma Gandhi, Franklin and Eleanor Roosevelt, and Susan B. Anthony. Visitors enter the town by passing under a large sign proclaiming Lily Dale to be "The Largest Center for the Religion of Spiritualism in America." Lily Dale still thrives as a haven for spiritualism and has daily activities from late June through Labor Day. For more information, contact Lily Dale Spiritualist Center, 5 Melrose Park, Lily Dale, NY 14752; phone: 716-595-8721; fax: 719-595-2442; Web site: http://www.geocities.com/SiliconValley/1591/lilydale.html.

How was this possible? Well, some spiritualists were more willing to accept the Fox sisters' retraction of their earlier confession. Perhaps they just didn't want to admit they'd been duped. People believe what they want to believe. Still, neither sister ever again enjoyed great success.

Leah Fox Fish Brown Underhill died in 1890. Kate Fox Jencken died on July 2, 1892, and Margaret Fox Kane died in poverty in a rooming house on March 8, 1893.

The original Fox house where it all began was moved from Hydesville to a spiritualists' retreat in Lily Dale, New York, in 1915. The camp is still there today, but a fire destroyed the cottage in the 1950s.

There's No Place Like Home: Home Circles

By the end of the 1850s, spiritualism had taken on a successful life of its own, independent of the Fox sisters, with hundreds of mediums sprouting up all across the United States and England. It was discovered that spirit contact could be made in any number of situations, but the most common was during a séance. People everywhere seemed to be meeting informally in their homes, trying to contact spirits for themselves. Home circles—séances conducted in one's home—reached their peak in popularity in the late 19th and early 20th centuries.

Ghostly Pursuits

The Spiritualist Church is still an active religion, with churches and congregations worldwide. Its beliefs encompass much more than mediums and séances. Many of churches in the United States are members of the National Spiritualist Association of Churches (N.S.A.C.), the oldest and founding organization for the science, philosophy, and religion of modern spiritualism. For more information on the Spiritualist church in America, contact the National Spiritualist Association of Churches, P.O. Box 217, Lily Dale, NY 14752; phone: 716-595-2000; fax: 716-595-2020; Web site: http://www.nsac.org. There's also an International Spiritualist Federation.

The Browning Circle

One of the most famous home circles of the 19th century was the so-called Browning circle, led by famed medium D.D. Home (pronounced *Hume*) in the London residence of John S. Rymer, a well-to-do solicitor, and his wife in 1855. Among the 14 sitters were the poets Robert and Elizabeth Barrett Browning. Home was one of the popular mediums of his age due to the many extraordinary manifestations that he produced during his sessions.

During the Browning séance, the sitters gathered around a large table in a room lit only by a dim lamp. After a series of raps, taps, and table-tilts, the Rymers's deceased son Wat spoke to his parents, then disappeared. (Home had made the ghost of their son materialize at previous private séances for the Tymers with whom he was staying.) Home asked five uncooperative sitters to leave the room. Then the séance resumed: The table tilted, and the ghost of Wat Rymer touched his parents. The spirit seemed especially interested in Elizabeth Browning, rustling her dress and placing a wreath on her head. Even the skeptical Robert Browning felt a spectral hand on his knees. Finally, ghostly hands played an accordion—this last bit being a trademark of sorts for Home.

Elizabeth Browning was convinced of Home's genuine powers. Her husband found Home "smarmy" and effeminate. (The medium had a reputation for consorting with young men, despite his two marriages.) Browning also variously called Home a sot, braggart, leech, toady, fraud, and "Dungball" (a wordplay on Home's middle name, Dunglas). Although he could not prove any specific trickery, Robert Browning pointed out that Home wore loose clothes that could conceal strings and mock appendages. The argument over Home was the poets' only public disagreement, and Elizabeth soon dropped all discussion and patronage of Home. For his part, Robert Browning became such an anti-spiritualist that he wrote a lengthy poem, "Mr. Sludge, the Medium," in which he attacked all mediums, but especially D.D. Home.

The Goligher Circle

An Irish family consisting of a father, four daughters, son, and a son-in-law led another famous home circle, the Goligher circle. Although all the daughters were mediums, one daughter, Kathleen, seemed to be particularly adept. Although standard activity, such as rappings and tilting tables, occurred at their family séances, Kathleen was the only one who could go into a trance and communicate with the spirits.

Their séances were usually private, but the family's reputation became well known among spiritualists. In 1914, William Jackson Crawford (1881–1920), a paranormal investigator and mechanical engineer from Queens University in Belfast, heard about the Goligher circle, and he got permission from the family to study them.

From the outset, Crawford accepted the ghostly phenomena, such as tappings and table tippings, as genuine. But Crawford wanted to measure the physical attributes of the spirit activity. For example, he ran tests to determine Kathleen's weight in relation to that of the floating table. He used an instrument that measures the elasticity of gases to discover the direction from which Kathleen's telekinetic forces seemed to emanate.

Crawford recorded all the spirit activity that he saw at the Goligher circle, and he wrote about his experiences in three books: *The Reality of Psychic Phenomena* (1916), *Experiments in Psychic Science* (1919), and *Psychic Structures of the Goligher Circle* (1921). In all of them, he pronounced Kathleen, the Goligher circle, and the spirit phenomena they produced as genuine.

The books sparked controversy among paranormal researchers. William Jackson Crawford committed suicide in 1920, but investigation of the Goligher circle continued. W.W. Carrington, a member of the Society of Psychical Research (SPR) had observed the Golighers several times in 1916, but he revisited the circle in 1920. He concluded that Kathleen's earlier manifestations were real but that she (or the entire family) used trickery to produce the 1920 phenomena.

E.E. Fournier d'Albe, another psychic researcher, had 20 sittings with Kathleen after Crawford's death. Little ghostly phenomena appeared, and he concluded that what he did see was fraudulent.

Kathleen Goligher married S.G. Donaldson in 1926. Seven years later, Donaldson conducted five sittings with his wife, in which he tried to capture spirit activity in the dark using the new technology of infrared photography. In a 1934 report in *Psychic Science* magazine, Donaldson claimed to have produced photographs of spirit phenomena in all five sittings. Unfortunately, the photos were accidentally destroyed during World War II, so no physical proof exists today. Kathleen Goligher was last seen publicly by the spiritualist community in 1962. It's not known if she still survives—as least, in *this* life.

So that's how spiritualism all began. Now let's go inside a séance room to see what really goes on. While we're there, we'll meet some of spiritualism's most famous mediums, along with their contacts in the spirit world. Most of the séance activity you'll be reading about normally takes place with the lights out, so I hope you're not scared of the dark. If you are, bring along a night-light.

Ghostbusting

If you're thinking of trying your luck as a medium, start today, before you age another minute! It's been observed that the psychic powers of mediums, both female and male, seem to wane as they grow older. This might explain why Kathleen Goligher's abilities lessened between Crawford's first test in 1914 (when she was 16) and Carrington's visit in 1920.

The Least You Need to Know

➤ In 1848, the Fox sisters, Kate and Margaret, triggered the movement known as spiritualism by claiming they could receive messages from the dead.

➤ Mediums act as intermediaries between the material and spirit worlds, usually in a setting known as a séance.

➤ Home circles—séances that were held in homes—became a craze in the United States and England.

➤ Some mediums impressed (and entertained) the participants at their séances by materializing ghosts and other phantom phenomena.

Chapter 8

BUMP!

Things That Go Bump in the Night

In This Chapter

➤ The spooky goings-on at séances

➤ Controls: spirits returning from the Other Side

➤ The Ouija board: the first form of spirit communications?

➤ Disembodied voices speak in the dark

➤ Ectoplasm appears as gooey, ghostly slime

➤ Spirit handwriting appears on slates

So, what actually happens at a séance? Do people just sit around in the dark, hoping to be grabbed by a ghost? Well, not exactly, but pretty close!

Over the years, mediums discovered some pretty amazing ways to talk with spirits. Sure, they still used Ouija boards, but before long the ghostly gang was writing notes, talking away, and, eventually, appearing right in front of the sitters' eyes. Let's take a peek for ourselves.

Getting the Most Out of Your Séance

As a result of the Fox sisters' demonstrations that you read about in Chapter 7, "Spirit Move Me: The Birth of Spiritualism," dozens—perhaps hundreds—of mediums in the United States, Great Britain, and, to a lesser extent, Europe began holding séances, often in peoples' homes.

Not everyone felt the need to engage a professional medium. Conducting or attending home circles became such a popular pastime in the 1870s that *The Spiritualist,* a weekly magazine in England, actually published suggestions on how to set up a proper home sitting, including:

➤ There is at least one person in every household who has the talent to be a medium.

➤ The best mediums are persons who are genial, impulsive, and affectionate.

➤ Never invite people who don't like each other to take part in the same sitting: The bad vibrations inhibit spirit materialization.

➤ Spirits most often appear in rooms that are kept cool.

Mediums offered their own tips for successful séances. Some mediums believed that if repeated sittings were going to be held in a home that the same room should be used every time. That way the spirits would get to know their way around and "feel at home." (Paranormal skeptics would point out, "Not to mention the mediums," who might have skullduggery on their minds.) Many mediums thought that there should be an equal number of men and women present, alternated in their seating around the circle. Also, they felt the number of participants should be strictly limited (usually to a maximum of 10 or so). Mediums claimed that spirits preferred dark rooms; needless to say, that's where the best results were always produced.

Usually séances were held at night. The lights were extinguished or dimmed; sometimes the séance was conducted by candlelight or by moonlight streaming through a window.

The parties would gather around a table holding hands or by placing their palms on the tabletop. Many groups simply sat in chairs that had been arranged in a circle.

Phantom Phrases

A **spirit cabinet,** or **cabinet,** is a solid or curtained enclosure within which the medium sat to allow the spirits to appear unimpeded in darkness. The first spirit cabinet was introduced in New York City by the Davenport brothers, and its use was quickly adopted by many of the leading mediums of the day.

Trusted or cooperative sitters were placed to the immediate left and right of the medium. To prevent dishonesty, they were often invited to hold the medium's hands, to place their hands on the medium's legs or in the medium's lap, and to rest their feet on top of the medium's shoes. In later years, some mediums had themselves tied up to prove that they were not using their own hands and feet to produce the spirit activity.

In the latter 1850s, the Davenport brothers (who were actually stage magicians working as mediums) introduced the *spirit cabinet,* an enclosed box in which the medium sat while entranced (see Chapter 24, "The Magic Connection"). Many mediums welcomed this new tool as a means to prove that they were totally removed from the phenomenon. Unfortunately, dishonest mediums also embraced the new technology: They realized that once they were hidden away in a cabinet, away from the prying eyes of the audience, they could get away with just about anything!

In the early years, some mediums began their sittings with the singing of hymns or the recitation of prayers. Besides having a calming effect on the attendees, it also reassured them that attending a séance was a perfectly acceptable activity for a Christian.

After the hymns or prayers, the fun could begin. The medium began to call on spirits to show themselves or give a sign that they were present.

Take Control

Almost every medium worked through a spirit, called a *control,* which acted as a guide or intermediary to the Other World. Some controls became as famous in the spiritualist world as their mediums.

Phantom Phrases

A **control** is a spirit of the dead who acts as a medium's guide or intermediary to the Other World. The control can take possession of the medium, at least enough to communicate through script (automatic writing or Ouija boards) or speech (direct voice phenomenon).

Ghostly Pursuits

Probably the hardest-working control in the business (if you can say such a thing about a spirit) was John King. First materialized by the Davenport brothers, King was supposedly a 17th-century pirate in his earthly life. Maybe it was the mystery and romance of his buccaneer background, but King proved to be a popular control for more than a half dozen of the 19th century's top mediums.

For a time, the famous medium Florence Cook (see Chapter 9, "Striking a Happy Medium") also worked through John King. Before long, however, she came in contact with John's daughter, Katie King, who was also in the spirit world. Katie worked as Cook's primary control for most of the medium's career.

Mediums usually employed one control repeatedly, although some had many controls. Spiritualists pointed to the existence of controls as proof of survival after death, although some mediums thought their controls were actually produced from their own subconscious minds. Regardless, controls always seemed to have unique personalities, separate and distinct from those of their mediums.

Drop by Sometime

An unexpected phenomenon at some séances was the *drop-in communicator,* a spirit or entity that suddenly made itself known, uninvited by the medium. As opposed to a control, the identity of the drop-in communicator was usually unknown to the medium or any of the sitters.

Because the spirit was usually a stranger to the participants, it would often communicate information that wasn't known to anyone in the room, occasionally it spoke in a foreign language. Sometimes the drop-in communicator would no ulterior motive; it simply may have been lonely, or have been unaware that it was in the spirit world. Other times, the spirit would arrive with a purpose or to convey a message. Usually the spirit departed as quickly as it came. Few drop-in communicators returned, so it was particularly difficult for paranormal researchers to investigate them.

Phantom Phrases

A **drop-in communicator** is an uninvited spirit that suddenly makes its presence known at a séance. Its identity is almost always unknown to the medium and the sitters.

Ghostly Pursuits

One of the oddest cases of a drop-in communicator involved the spirit of Runolfur Runolfsson, who barged into a series of séances conducted by Iceland's most famous medium, Hafsteinn Bjornsson, between 1937 and 1940. Runolfsson wanted his leg back! The spirit claimed to have died in October 1879: He had gotten drunk, passed out on a beach, and was swept out to sea and drowned. His decomposed remains finally washed ashore a year later; they were buried, but the thighbone was missing.

Runolfsson claimed that a local fish merchant named Ludvik Gudmundsson had the bone at his house. Upon inquiry, Gudmundsson discovered that the carpenter who built his house had placed a bone between two of the walls—why, no one knows. The wall was torn open, the leg bone was found, and it was given a proper burial. Runolfsson later "dropped in" to a séance to express his thanks, and eventually he became a regular control for Bjornsson.

Up to Code

Back in the séance room, table tipping (fresh from the mesmerists' bag of tricks), became standard fare. Spiritualists, of course, claimed that ghosts moved the table.

But it wasn't enough for the table to move. People wanted the spirits to talk to them. To keep one step ahead of the competition, mediums had to devise more and more ingenious ways to keep the lines of spirit communication open. Each new method marked one small step for a medium, one giant leap for mediumkind.

Knock Once for "Yes": Tapping at the Table

In Hydesville, the Fox sisters had worked out a rapping code for the spirit to communicate with them. No raps meant "no," one rap meant "yes," and a series of raps indicated that a numerical answer was coming. Five quick raps meant the spirit wanted to answer in alphabetic letters. The medium would call out the letters one at a time, A to Z, and the spirit would rap again when the medium reached the correct letter.

Needless to say, this was tedious going. By the time of Margaret Fox's demonstrations in Rochester, a streamlined code had been devised. One rap indicated "no," three raps meant "yes," and two raps meant the question couldn't be answered. But the biggest improvement was Margaret's introduction of automatic writing into the séance room (see Chapter 6, "Over My Dead Body!"). She would hold a pencil in her hand, and the spirits would "take possession" of her hand to write their answers to questions. This was spookier, and certainly much quicker, than the old rapping alphabet code!

The Ouija Board

Sometimes, in lieu of automatic writing, the medium would receive answers to questions through the use a board preprinted with letters and words. The earliest board of this type dates to ancient China, and a similar board was used in the 6th century B.C. by the Greek philosopher Pythagoras and his followers. Today, this device is commonly known as a *Ouija board*. Its name is derived from *oui* and *ja,* the words for "yes" in French and German, respectively.

Phantom Phrases

A **Ouija board** is a small piece of wood or card pre-printed with letters, numerals, and words, used by mediums to receive spirit communications. Usually a **planchette,** a small pointer held at the fingertips, is used to spell out words or point to numbers or words.

Boo!

Some warn that playing with a Ouija board is dangerous when used by someone who isn't experienced in dealing with spirits. Some people can become dependent on the board for answers and advice. But the real danger, according to some occultists, comes when a neophyte asks a spirit to provide physical proof of its existence. This request may "open a doorway," allowing a violent or physically destructive spirit to enter the material world.

Ghostly Pursuits

Early versions of a planchette date back to at least the 6th century B.C., when Pythagoras led séances using a wheeled table that moved across a stone slab engraved with mystic symbols. The modern planchette (and its name) dates to 1853, however, when it was created by a French spiritualist whose name was M. Planchette. By 1868, the planchette (which means "little board" in French) was a popular mass-marketed "toy" in the United States.

American Elija J. Bond invented the modern Ouija Board as a fortune-telling game in 1892. In 1966, Parker Brothers marketed OUIJA as a game for entertainment purposes only. Today, their design board is distributed by Hasbro.

Most modern Ouija boards include the letters of the alphabet, the numerals zero through nine, and the words "yes" and "no." A small instrument called a *planchette*— a palm-sized, triangular-shaped wooden platform—is set on the board.

One or more people rest their fingertips on the planchette, and someone asks a question. Usually, the planchette—supposedly animated by spirit impulses—begins to move from letter to letter (or perhaps to a numeral or word), to spell out a message.

Ghostly Pursuits

Katy D., a family friend, tells about a time she stayed overnight at her grandmother's and decided to play with a Ouija board. She tried to contact her late grandfather and asked for a sign of his presence. At first, she was disappointed. The only word that the planchette spelled out was "candles," but she decided that her own subconscious hand motion might have written the word. After all, she had started her Ouija "ceremony" by lighting candles at the four corners of the board.

Katy, finished with the spirit world for the evening (or so she thought!), blew out the candles (as she had promised her grandmother she would), and went to sleep. The next morning Katy awoke to find all four candles burning brightly. Her grandmother hadn't lit them. Had the grandfather told Katy through the Ouija board the night before that he'd use the candles to give her a sign? Only the spirits know for sure.

Spiritualists claim that spirits move the planchette, but most skeptics dismiss Ouija-board phenomena with scientist Michael Faraday's explanation for table tipping: Unconscious muscular motion moves the planchette. The direction of the movement and the answers, they contend, are supplied subliminally by the sitters themselves.

Ghostly Pursuits

Try a Ouija board for yourself! You'll find a miniature Ouija board printed on the tearout card at the front of this book. Lay it out flat on the table in front of you. You can use your hand as the planchette: Lightly rest the fingertips of one of your hands on the board, with the forefinger pointing slightly outward. Think of a question or ask it out loud. If you feel your arm wanting to move, let it. Record what letters your forefinger nears or points to. If the spirits are with you, they'll spell out words to answer your question.

The Spirit Writes; and Having Writ, Moves On

Direct writing was an even greater step forward than rapping, automatic writing, or Ouija boards. With direct writing, the script simply appeared on the paper or other surface without the use of the medium's hand. Long messages could appear quite quickly. Needless to say, direct writing became an important tool among mediums.

Of course, direct writing by the spirits could appear on any surface. But, perhaps because they were so common and seemingly free of trickery, small chalkboards (or slates) such as those used by schoolchildren became the most popular surface for direct writing to appear on during séances. In fact, William E. Robinson wrote in his book, *Spirit Slate Writing and Kindred Phenomena* (Munn and Company, 1898), that nothing converted more people to spiritualism in the 19th century than the direct writing that appeared during séances on slates.

Phantom Phrases

Direct writing is a paranormal phenomenon, usually seen in a séance, in which spirit handwriting (without the use of the medium's hand) appears directly on a previously unmarked surface.

Although a single slate was sometimes used, usually two were employed. All sides of the slates would be shown free of writing. They would be strapped together, sometimes with a small piece of chalk between. Later, when the slates were inspected, there would be a message in "spirit" handwriting on one or more sides of the slates.

Ghostly Pursuits

Slate writing is credited to the medium "Dr." Henry Slade (1825–1905), who claimed to have discovered slate writing in the 1860s. Slade's new way to communicate with spirits was an immediate success, and mediums everywhere soon adopted the method. Perhaps Slade did produce real spirit phenomenon on occasion, but he was also exposed regularly for trickery. (It turns out Slade was able to secretly write with extremely small pieces of chalk held in his mouth, in either hand, or between the toes of either foot.) In 1876, for example, he fled London after a court found him guilty of fraud. By 1892, with his reputation and clients gone, Slade's career was finished. Reports of his last years vary, but the true end of the man who gave spiritualism slate writing, one of its most valuable tools, are unknown.

Talk to Me

It was only a matter of time before mediums discovered that they could speed up communications as well as captivate the audience if the spirits were to speak instead of having to write everything down.

At first, mediums allowed their controls to speak *through* them. The spirit took possession of the medium—or, at least, of the medium's vocal chords. Then the spirit talked through the medium's mouth, almost always sounding different, or altered, from the medium's own voice.

This was fine, if the control had a lot to say. But if the medium wanted to have a conversation with the spirit, well, you can imagine it sounded somewhat schizophrenic when the voice started switching back and forth between the spirit and the medium.

That's when mediums began to produce *direct voice phenomenon* (DVP), speech from a spirit without the apparent use of the medium's mouth or vocal cords. Usually, the ghost's voice would seem to come from a point slightly above or to the side of the medium's head. This so-called "independent direct voice" phenomenon was possible, according to mediums, because the phantom had somehow constructed and spoken through an invisible, artificial larynx. Skeptics dismissed the stunt as mere ventriloquism.

Phantom Phrases

In **direct voice phenomenon (DVP)**, heard most often in a séance, a spirit speaks directly to the sitters, not through the voice of the medium. Usually the sound appears to come from some point near the medium (usually above or to one side), or possibly from a spirit horn or trumpet, but not from the medium's mouth.

Sometimes, especially in the early days of séances, mediums introduced a megaphone-shaped horn known as a spirit trumpet. During the séance, the spirit would levitate the trumpet and speak through it as the horn floated about the room. Supposedly, the spirit needed the trumpet to condense its vocal energy and amplify its sound.

DVP was introduced in the 1850s in séances led by an Ohio farmer/medium, Jonathan Koons. Although other unintelligible spectral voices were heard at Koon's sittings, his primary control, John King (yes, him again), was quite articulate—and loud: King spoke through a floating tin horn. (Koon's séances were also musical events. During a sitting, Koons and his wife filled the room with musical instruments. Once the lights were dimmed, the instruments flew about the room while being played by invisible spirits.)

Whatever Possessed You?

People have believed since ancient times that a person's mind, body, and soul can be taken over—possessed—by a spirit, god, or demon.

Many mediums actually wanted to have the spirits take possession of their hands (for automatic writing), or even their whole bodies. The spirits of mediums usually seemed quite willing to cooperative. And, unlike demons, they would depart on command.

Don't Try My Patience

On rare occasions, drop-in communicators take possession of a medium. Such was the case with the spirit Patience Worth, who first took possession of Pearl Curran on July 8, 1913, while the St. Louis housewife was playing with a Ouija board. The spirit (Worth) claimed to have been born in 1649 in Dorsetshire, England, to a poor family. Unmarried, she traveled to the American colonies, where she was killed by Indians. From 1913 until around 1922, Worth, through Curran, dictated poems, plays, epigrams, allegories, short stories, and historical novels—more than four million words in 29 volumes. Literary experts who have examined the writings are divided in their opinions of whether Curran, who left school at 14 years of age, could have produced the works on her own.

But Is It Art?

In late 1905, Frederic L. Thompson, then a 39-year-old metalworker and amateur artist, developed an overwhelming need to paint. His new works bore an uncanny resemblance to those of the noted landscape painter R. Swain Gifford. Thompson had once met Gifford briefly, and had written him once for a recommendation, but they barely knew each other. In fact, Thompson didn't know that Gifford had died about six months before he developed his new obsession to paint seascapes.

In January 1907, Thompson visited James H. Hyslop, a paranormal investigator and one-time president of the American Society for Psychical Research, with the claim that he was possessed by Gifford's spirit. To test Thompson's theory, Hyslop took him to a well-known Boston medium, Minnie M. Soule (also known as Mrs. Chenoweth). She agreed that she felt Gifford's presence near Thompson. In later séances with the two men, she claimed to contact Gifford, who gave his approval of Thompson's work.

In a December 9, 1908, séance with the medium Mrs. Willis M. Cleaveland, Gifford's spirit asked Thompson to carry on his work, then said good-bye, scrawling "R.S.G." through Cleaveland's automatic writing. Hyslop believed he had observed a true case of spirit possession. As for Thompson, he devoted his life full-time to his art. He prospered, moved to Miami in the 1920s, and probably died there around 1927.

What Possessed You to Do That? The Insanity Plea

Hyslop also worked on the Doris Fischer case from 1914 to 1918. Doris Fischer had experienced multiple personalities since she was three years old in 1892. Hyslop was convinced that spirit possession rather than schizophrenia caused her problems. In séances arranged by Hyslop and led by Minnie Soule, Fischer was confronted by the spirits of her mother, Count Cagliostro (an 18th-century Italian mystic and reputed necromancer), Richard Hodgson (a deceased leader of the American Society for Psychical Research), and Longfellow's literary character Minnehaha. Hyslop conducted a psychic exorcism of Cagliostro, whose presence troubled him most, and for a while Fischer seemed cured. In 1918, Hyslop wrote a book (*Life After Death*) about the case, which was his last major investigation. Doris Fischer moved with her adoptive family to California. Her illness returned and plagued her for years. Eventually, she died in a mental hospital.

Phantom Phrases

An **apport** is a solid object, which seemingly appears from nowhere in the presence of a medium or other "sensitive" individual. Spirits supposedly assembled some apports from invisible matter; other apports are simply teleported from another location. The opposite of an apport—something that disappears or is teleported to another location—is called an **asport.**

Appearing out of Thin Air

But written words and voices in the dark weren't enough for sitters at séances. They wanted more! To stay one step ahead of the competition, mediums began to manifest or materialize real, solid objects. At first, the spirits didn't personally appear. Instead, they produced spectral gifts, such as flowers or fruit, which they dropped into the laps of the surprised and delighted sitters.

An object that appears from nowhere in the presence of a medium is called an *apport,* from the French word *apporter,* meaning "to bring." Two 19th-century mediums who were especially known for their ability at producing apports were Agnes Guppy and Eusapia Palladino. Not all apports were pleasant: Palladino sometimes produced repulsive objects such as dead rats.

Ghostly Pursuits

Mrs. Agnes Guppy herself became an apport at one of the most celebrated spiritualist events of the 19th century. Frank Herne and his partner Charles Williams, two popular British mediums and protégés of Mrs. Guppy, were conducting a séance in their home in London in July 1871 when one of the sitters, Mr. W.H. Harrison, jokingly challenged them to teleport Mrs. Guppy to their séance room. Before three minutes had passed, the lights came up. There, sitting in the center of the séance table, was a seemingly surprised Mrs. Guppy, dressed only in her night robe and holding her pen and account books. The very large Mrs. Guppy had apparently teleported from her own home, two or three miles away, into the center of their circle.

There are two ways that an apport can be produced: The spirits form some from invisible matter, or, more often, the apport is said to travel from another location, sometimes through solid matter (such as a wall), and into the medium's presence. This form of paranormal transportation is commonly known as *teleportation*.

The opposite of an apport—that is, an object that is made to vanish or is teleported to another location—was known as an *asport*. Needless to say, asports were not as popular as apports. After all, who wants to see their presents disappear?

Spiritualists had various theories about what apports were and where they came from:

➤ The spirits brought them from another dimension.

➤ The medium used magnetism and psychic power to bring them from another dimension.

➤ Apports were previously existing objects that the spirit or medium disintegrated, teleported, then reassembled in the presence of the medium.

➤ Apports were created from the material matter called ectoplasm excreted from the medium (more about that coming up).

Phantom Phrases

Teleportation is a kind of paranormal transportation in which an object is moved from one location to another, sometimes through a solid object such as a door, wall, or closed window.

Ghostly Pursuits

Some of the most unusual asports were produced by the Australian medium Charles Bailey (c. 1870–1947). He was first sewn into a canvas bag, with only his neck and arms extending out through holes in the sack. Then, all of the lights in the room were turned out. In the dark, Bailey produced such varied asports as dripping wet stones from the ocean, live birds with their nests and eggs, live fish, crabs, turtles, antiques, human skulls, clay tablets bearing supposedly Babylonian script, gemstones, and so on. When the lights were turned back on, there was Bailey, still securely tied up inside the bag, surrounded by his mysterious productions and the baffled and astounded sitters.

"I've Been Slimed!"

Remember that phrase from the movie *Ghostbusters?* In the jargon of the medium, the icky, green goo that covered the ghost hunter in the film is called *ectoplasm*—a materialization of spirit essence or matter. It appeared as a fluid but shapeless, gelatin-like material oozing from one or more of the medium's orifices (usually the mouth, nose, or ears). The production of ectoplasm was pretty impressive stuff, especially if it formed into a pseudopod, such as an ectoplasmic hand or arm.

Phantom Phrases

Ectoplasm is spirit substance or matter which exuded from the body (usually one of the facial orifices) of a medium. Ectoplasm was usually dense but liquid and milky white, with the scent of ozone. Although fluid and shapeless at first, ectoplasm often molded itself into spirit limbs, faces, or entire bodies.

The word ectoplasm was coined in 1894 by French physiologist Charles Richet to describe the third "arm" (actually a false limb, or pseudopod) that sometimes emerged from medium Eusapia Palladino during her séances. The word comes from the Greek *ektos*, meaning "exteriorized," and *plasma*, meaning "substance."

Was ectoplasm a true manifestation of a spirit's essence? Sitters weren't allowed to touch or examine it too closely—if at all—at the time, and no samples have been preserved to look at today. And, even though séances are still carried on today, the vogue for the production of ectoplasm has passed. Perhaps we'll never know.

But we *do* know *fraudulent* mediums produced phony ectoplasm. Constructed in advance from cheesecloth or netting, the fake ectoplasm was often covered with luminous paint so that it would glow in the dark.

Hidden assistants revealed the "ectoplasm" by lowering it from above by strings or by lifting it up from below the table. How did ectoplasm come out of a medium's nose? Well, maybe it wasn't a trick. But, having written *The Complete Idiot's Guide to Magic Tricks* (Alpha Books, 1999), I know that even the worst magicians can pull off miracles in the dark.

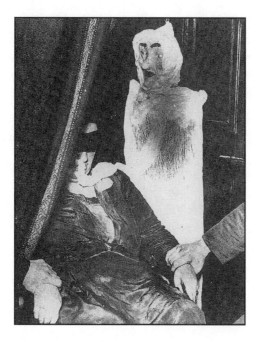

A spirit is captured on film standing beside medium Mrs. Duncan, as ectoplasm oozes from the spiritualist's nose.

Ectoplasm was exciting, but soon came the *pièce de résistance*. Sitters actually got to *see* the spirits! At first, only the spirits' faces appeared, but, before long, "full-form" (complete head-to-toe) materializations of spirits were becoming common at séances everywhere. After all, what could be more exciting than the materialization of an actual, entire ghost? What indeed?! The first medium to regularly produce full-form spirits was Florence Cook, and it made her a star! (You'll read about it in the next chapter.)

As the séance field became saturated with mediums, only those with the best "shows" drew large followings, and found fame and fortune. In our next chapter, we'll take a look at some more of the more successful mediums in the history of spiritualism.

The Least You Need to Know

➤ Mediums often drew up their own rules of engagement to maximize their chances to produce spirit phenomena.

➤ A medium usually established a relationship with one particular spirit, called a control, who acted as a guide and intermediary into the Other World.

➤ Mediums developed a variety of ways to allow a spirit to communicate with them, including table tipping, rapping codes, automatic writing, slate writing, Ouija boards, and direct voice phenomenon (DVP).

➤ Other proof that spirits were present at séances included teleportation, apports and asports, levitation, the production of ectoplasm, and materializations.

Striking a Happy Medium

Who could follow an act like the Fox Sisters? Who indeed?

Several important mediums, many of whom created sensations in England and Europe, gained a large following. Some, like D.D. Home and Florence Cook, made significant additions to the repertoire of the craft. Another important development was the discovery that spirits could be photographed! And the medium mania hasn't died—it's just changed names. Today there are channelers and people like James Van Praagh, who claims to be able to talk to the dead.

You might want to dim the lights while you read this chapter. Spirits prefer the dark.

The Amazing Physical Feats of D.D. Home

D.D. Home (1833–1886), already mentioned as the leader of the Browning circle (see Chapter 7, "Spirit Move Me: The Birth of Spiritualism"), was a Scottish medium who performed physical feats at his séances. Home (pronounced *Hume*) usually materialized spirits, sometimes levitated or elongated and shrank his body, and made inanimate objects move (such as the obligatory tipping table) without touching them.

A Young Medium Emerges

Home was born in Edinburgh, Scotland, and supposedly showed paranormal abilities from an early age:

➤ His cradle rocked without assistance.

➤ At four years of age, he predicted a cousin's death.

➤ He later claimed to have known three days in advance that his mother would die.

➤ At 13, he had a vision as his boyhood friend died in a faraway location.

Home was adopted by his mother's sister, Mary Cook, when he was still a baby, and they moved to the United States when Home was nine years old. Home was 15, living with his aunt in Connecticut, when the rapping of the Fox sisters began. Soon, similar sounds began to manifest themselves for Home. His aunt asked local preachers to help rid the house (and the boy) of demons. When, in 1850, the lad told his aunt that he had seen a vision of his dead mother, kindly Mary Cook tossed the boy out.

Trademarks and Trickery

Home attended séances, although he was usually unimpressed and considered most to be frauds. He began to hold his own séances—usually in dimly lit rooms, rather than in the customary dark chambers. He often asked sitters to hold his hands and feet to prove that he wasn't using trickery.

Home quickly impressed his sitters with the physical manifestations he was able to produce: ghost lights and knockings, disembodied ghost hands that shook hands with those present, and phantom guitars that played music. He received messages from spirits, which he delivered by pointing at letters on alphabet cards. Home claimed the spectral assistance of different controls, the most common being a spirit named Bryan.

Ghostbusting

Learn from the best. Build on their success, and eliminate their mistakes. D.D. Home was a quick study and learned how to perform a more entertaining yet still-deceptive séance. You can take the tips of early ghost investigators to hone your skills as a ghost hunter.

But Home had three signature pieces that really put him on the map:

➤ **A spirit-played accordion.** Home would hold an accordion, opposite the keyboard end, under the table, and before long, the music began, apparently played by phantom fingers.

➤ **His stretching and shrinking body.** Home had the ability to stretch—sometimes as much as 11 inches—to 6^1/$_2$ feet in height; or shrink as much as seven inches to five feet tall.

➤ **Levitation.** Home would levitate séance-goers as they sat in their chairs, and he would also occasionally float himself! His first self-levitation occurred spontaneously during a Connecticut séance when Home was 19 years old. He appeared to rise up about a foot and hover, before rising all the way to the ceiling. In later séances, he was reportedly able to fly about the room.

Although often accused of trickery, D.D. Home was never actually caught in the act of fraud. Two of the most famous magicians of the era, John Nevil Maskelyne and Harry Houdini, swore that Home was little more than a very clever illusionist. Houdini probably best expressed the reasons why Home was never exposed: He pointed out that, although some of Home's individual manifestations had been discovered to be fakes and that all of his effects could be reproduced by conjurers if given the same performance conditions, the medium never gave public demonstrations. Home led séances in people's homes, where it would have been exceedingly impolite, if not downright rude, to suggest that their house guest was cheating.

Behind Every Good Man ...

For the next decade, Home was in his heyday. His séances caused a sensation in England. It was during this period, in 1855, that Home conducted the famous séance for the Browning circle (see Chapter 7). He held séances for European nobility such as Napoleon II and Empress Eugenie (for whom he manifested the ghost of Napoleon I). He married Alexandria, a wealthy Russian noblewoman; she soon died, but the courts cut Home off from the estate.

Then, in 1866, Home became the spiritual advisor to a 75-year old widow, a Mrs. Lyon. Two years later, she became disenchanted with Home after her romantic advances were rejected and demanded the return of about £30,000, which she claimed she loaned him while under his spell. Despite her rambling and raving during the trial, the court found in her favor and denounced spiritualism as "mischievous nonsense, well calculated on the one hand to delude the vain, the weak, the foolish, and the superstitious."

The Ashley Place Levitation

Interestingly, the trial seemed to spur Home on to new heights, figuratively and literally. In 1867, Home performed several stunts to prove that he was impervious to fire: He stuck his head into a lit fireplace without even singeing his hair, and handled hot coals. He also enabled others to handle the burning embers.

Then, in December 1868, came the famous Ashley Place Levitation. Three sitters at a séance held in a London manor claimed that, while in a trance, Home rose, walked into the next room, opened the window, levitated up and out the window, then

Boo!

Here's a double whammy: Don't jump to conclusions, and don't believe everything you hear. Home's Ashley Place Levitation became accepted as fact even though no one really saw him do it. But because three reputable people gave the account, their illogical explanation was accepted as the truth. Check out all ghost claims for yourself before blindly believing.

floated back through the window of the room in which they sat. The three witnesses (the Master of Lindsay, later the Earl of Crawford; Viscount Adare, later the Earl of Dunraven; and Captain Charles Wynne, a cousin to Adare) gave varying accounts. None of them claimed to have actually seen Home open the window in the next room, nor float out; even the circumstances of Home's reentry were reported inconsistently. Nevertheless, the levitation resulted in a media frenzy.

Ghostly Pursuits

Although the feat is seldom part of his repertoire these days, motivational speaker Anthony (Tony) Robbins first made a name for himself by his ability to walk barefoot over a path of red-hot coals and empowering others to do the same. Robbins's demonstration was designed as proof that the mind is capable of miraculous things and can meet impossible challenges. Although Home's technique probably differed, his ability to withstand flames had the same powerful effect on his audiences.

D.D. Home and the Ashley Place Levitation.

The End Games

In 1871, Home was subjected to a number of scientific tests devised by Sir William Crookes (1832–1919), a brilliant 19th-century chemist, physicist, and investigator of mediums. (Medium Florence Cook would also later sit for Crookes.) Home passed the tests with flying colors, making an untouched accordion play, despite its being surrounded with an electrified cage. (Crookes had hypothesized that Home used some sort of electromagnetic force to move the instrument.)

In October 1871, Home was back in Russia, where he married the wealthy Julie de Gloumeline. Home retired in 1873. He died that year of tuberculosis in Auteuil, France, and was buried at St. Germain-en-Laye. His widow wrote two biographies about him, augmenting Home's two autobiographies: *Incidents in My Life* (1862) and *Incidents in My Life, 2nd Series* (1872).

Florence Cook Meets Katie King

British medium Florence Cook (1856–1904) was renowned for the number and variety of spirits that she materialized at her séances, especially full-form figures. Born in London, Cook discovered her powers to tip tables at an early age. Her family introduced her to a local spiritualist group, the Dalston Association, in 1871. The following year, she drew the attention of Frank Herne and his partner Charles Williams, the British mediums famed for teleporting their mentor, Mrs. Guppy, across London. Herne's spirit guide was John King (see Chapter 8, "Things That Go Bump in the Night"), and it was during her apprenticeship with Herne that Cook discovered her own control: King's daughter, Katie.

Katie King, Cook's most frequent control and the daughter of spirit control John King, materialized at a séance.

Let the (Spirit) Show Begin!

Cook was young, beautiful, and talented, so she drew a large, dedicated following. In 1873, Mr. Charles Blackburn, a wealthy spiritualist from Manchester, became her patron.

From her earliest séances, Cook specialized in materializations. At first, she only produced spirit faces. They would appear in a window cut out of the door of a large cupboard that she used as her spirit cabinet. Before long, Cook was manifesting the full bodies of spirits, rather than just a ghostly face or hand.

Cook's standard séance began with her being placed in the cupboard with a rope draped across her lap. The door to the cabinet was closed, then immediately reopened. Cook was found tied to the chair at her neck, waist, and wrists. The door would be closed, lights would be dimmed, and spirit faces would appear in a window in the door. (Detractors claimed the face always seemed to resemble Cook draped in white gauze.)

Later in the séance, the cabinet door would be flung open wide, and Katie (bearing an amazing resemblance to Cook) emerged. Cook would be heard moaning, hidden behind a curtain. At first Katie only smiled and nodded; before long, she was walking among the sitters, shaking her solid hand with theirs, and answering questions. Katie would return to the cabinet, the doors would be reopened, and Cook, still bound and exhausted, was released.

Crookes Checks out Cook

During a Cook séance in December 1873, one participant, Mr. William Volckman, grabbed Katie King's arm. Some sitters restrained Volckman, while others helped Katie back into the cabinet. When the doors were reopened, Florence Cook was still bound. Nevertheless, Volckman swore that Katie King had actually been Cook in disguise. (Interestingly, Volckman later married Mrs. Agnes Guppy.)

Boo!

Never grab a ghost. You never know what kind of spirit you might be capturing. Volckman's behavior at the Cook séance was considered a real no-no: It was considered impolite for sitters to hang onto mediums or their controls in the dark.

British scientist and paranormal investigator Sir William Crookes publicly defended Cook. She subsequently allowed herself to be investigated and tested by British scientist Sir William Crookes, starting in December 1873. In his preliminary report, issued in February 1874, Crookes endorsed Cook, although he admitted that the only way to prove that the manifestation of King was genuine was to have both ladies appear together. Cook soon moved into the home of Crookes and his wife to continue being tested. Crookes was allowed to see King and the draped figure of Cook resting in the cabinet at the same time, and he was permitted to take photographs. (Only a few survive, and most show Katie only. When the two are seen together, one of their faces is always obscured.)

In the spring of 1874, the séances moved back to Cook's home. There, Cook would materialize King in the privacy of her bedroom. Sitters were allowed to enter the dimly lit room to see and touch both figures. That was enough for Crookes to certify Cook as a genuine medium.

It's often been speculated that Sir William Crookes became Florence Cook's lover at some point during his investigations, which might have compromised his neutrality. Or, perhaps Crookes had been totally duped by her or he was merely naive. Then again, perhaps Florence Cook was the real thing.

Though Crookes obviously was sympathetic to spiritualists, he never really joined their ranks until three years before his death. He made the announcement of his conversion to spiritualism in the December 9, 1916, issue of *Light,* a spiritualist magazine. Apparently, medium Anna Eva Fay and photographs of spirits by a Mr. Hope had convinced him—despite the fact that both of them had been exposed of fraud.

A New Control Takes Control

In May 1874, in a sad farewell held behind a curtain, Katie King said goodbye to "dear Florrie." The next month, Cook's secret marriage to Edward Elgie Corner was revealed. Within months, Crookes and Blackburn, her patron, lost all interest in Cook.

Meanwhile, Florence Cook replaced Katie King with a new spirit control, Marie. In 1880, Cook sat for Sir George Sitwell, who grabbed Marie during the séance. He inspected the cabinet and found that Cook was no longer in her chair. Her supporters claimed that Cook walked in her sleep and had never intended to deceive her public.

Florence Cook was often caught in trickery. Fellow medium D.D. Home (perhaps out of professional jealousy, to further his own career, or to divert attention from his own suspicious actions) called Cook a "skillful trickster" and an "outright cheat." Nevertheless, she maintained a loyal following.

After two such shattering incidents, however, Cook took the unusual step of requiring that a sitter be bound in the cabinet beside her. Before long, Cook retired from the séance biz. She conducted one last séance as a test for the Sphinx Society in Berlin in 1899, where she materialized Marie as part of the examination. Cook died penniless in London on April 22, 1904.

Say "Cheese": Spirit Photography

Photography, invented in 1839, was less than a decade old when the Fox sisters first heard rappings in Hydesville, New York. It was only a matter of time before mediums began to use this new sensation as a tool to prove the existence of ghosts and spirits.

Technically, a *spirit photograph* is any ghost, phantom, or spirit of the dead captured on film. There's never been an authenticated spirit photograph, most are obvious fakes or simply oddities created when the photo was taken or flaws in its development. Still, about 10 percent of the photos that have been examined by photographic and paranormal experts cannot automatically be dismissed as fraudulent or caused by natural means.

Phantom Phrases

A **spirit photograph** shows a spirit or ghost on film. Spirit photography was originally used in posed sittings to capture the image of a loved one or other deceased person next to the subject of the photograph. In modern times, spirit photography is used in ghost hunting to try to catch a spectral image on film.

Mumler's the Word!

Spirit photography is generally credited to William Mumler, a jewelry engraver and amateur photographer in 19th-century Boston. Mumler took a self-portrait in 1861, and when he developed the plate, he noticed what seemed to be a ghostly face near to his own. Upon careful examination, he discovered that it was, of course, a double exposure. But, with interest in spiritualism at its zenith, Mumler immediately realized his discovery's financial potential.

Working as a (fraudulent) medium, Mumler photographed his subject. Then, when he developed the film, he added in the shadowy likeness of a loved one or a deceased celebrity. Needless to say, sitters paid high prices for such visible proof that the spirits of their dearly departed still surrounded them.

Spirit photographs helped spread belief in spiritualism worldwide, and Mumler had many imitators. Mumler's trickery was soon found out, however, because he made the mistake of inserting identifiable *living* Bostonians as ghosts. He left town in a hurry and set up shop in New York, but he was arrested there and tried for fraud in 1869. He was found not guilty, in part because of the flattering testimony of Judge John Edmonds from the U.S. Court of Appeals (who also just happened to be a spiritualist).

Abraham Lincoln is seen to hover over a woman believed to be his widow, Mary Todd Lincoln, in this famous spirit photograph probably taken by Mumler.

Wyllie on the West Coast

Ed Wyllie, a run-of-the-mill photographer in Los Angeles around 1900, began to have odd shapes and blurs, then extra faces, appear in his photographs. The Reverend Charles Cook, a noted skeptic of the paranormal, investigated him and his work in 1901. Cook allowed himself to be a spirit photography subject for Wyllie, and he oversaw all aspects of the sitting, from the loading of the camera to the development of the plate, to make sure there was no trickery. Nevertheless, his portrait showed an extra face floating next to him. And, more importantly, he could identify the spirit!

She was Flora Louden, who had been a college classmate of Cook's in 1866. She had died in Ohio in 1873. Cook could also make out hazy shapes of a star, cross, and heart, which were secret symbols used by Louden and Cook. Louden's image looked artificial, with the telltale cut-and-paste look of most spirit photographs. Yet, believing that there was no way Wyllie could have known about Louden, found her photo, or introduced it onto the negative plate, Cook declared the spirit photograph to be genuine.

Maybe it *was* real. But then, Cook may not have been the best judge. He was fooled on at least one other occasion by the fraudulent spirit photographer Alex Martin.

Wyllie was never caught in deception throughout his career as a spirit photographer.

The Crewe Crew

William Hope, another spirit photographer, claimed to have captured more than 2,500 "extras" (as he called the spirit faces). He headed an early 1920s group of spirit photographers in Crewe, England, that called themselves the "Crewe Circle." They actively invited inspection of their cameras, film, and equipment. They even allowed sitters to bring their own. They would start a sitting with prayers and hymns, followed by the taking of photographs.

Ghostly Pursuits

Sometimes William Hope didn't even bother to use a camera to take the spirit photograph. He would simply hold the sealed plate up to his forehead. The images of extras that appear on unexposed film are called "scotographs." Spirit writing has also allegedly appeared on photographs; British medium Reverend William Stainton Moses coined the term "psychography" to describe this phenomenon. In the 1960s, Ted Serios of Kansas City, Missouri, created a stir when he allegedly used "thoughtography" to create images on Polaroid film simply by staring into the camera.

In his 1924 book, *A Magician Among the Spirits,* Harry Houdini debunked the Crewe Circle. He pointed out that if the sitter wanted to supply the photographic plates, the Circle demanded that they receive them several days in advance in order to "magnetize" them. In that time, the plates could easily be doctored or switched.

On at least one occasion, a sitter secretly marked the plates he gave to the Crewe Circle. The plates that were returned had no markings. Another sitter reported that when he brought plates to the sitting unannounced, he caught members of the Crewe Circle trying to switch them while passing out the hymnals.

Despite frequent exposure, spirit photography remained popular well into the 20th century.

Ghostly Pursuits

Now I'm not saying that all spirit photographs are phony. Remember: At least 10 percent go unexplained. But you might want to try to make some spirit photos for yourself to see how the more obvious fakes may have been done:

Do you want to make your own spirit photographs to fool your friends? Here are some of the best methods:

➤ **Double exposures.** If you have a camera that allows you to manually forward the film between exposures, simply shoot a portrait of one person, then shoot another image (preferably slightly out of focus and off-center) without forwarding the film in between.

➤ **Long exposures.** Set your camera on a tripod and set it for a long exposure in low light. Have a person walk in front of the camera, stop briefly, or perhaps sit in a chair, then move out of frame. When the film is developed, the stationary objects will be crisp, but the moving figure will look like a ghost floating through the picture.

➤ **The camera strap ploy.** Let your camera strap (or any other similar object) dangle in front of the lens. As you shoot your photo, make sure the lens is focused on the distant objects or person, not the strap. (This will happen automatically with point-and-shoot cameras.) On the photo, the out-of-focus camera strap will come out looking like a hovering white streak.

Don't Touch That Dial!

In the 1970s, a new type of mediumship called *channeling* became popular, especially in the United States. Channeling is communication with a spirit through automatic speech and automatic writing. The channeler does this by allowing the spirit to take complete possession of his or her body.

Channelers do not limit themselves to spirits of the dead, however. (In fact, they rarely provide contact with the deceased.) They also claim to be in touch with angels, guardian spirits, demons, nature spirits, a Higher Self, or the Universal Mind. Channeling usually provides sitters with advice on spiritual healing and growth.

Probably the first famous channeler was Jane Roberts, whose channeled writings by the entity Seth became best-sellers. Among the many so-called Seth books (some of which have Seth attributed as the primary author) currently available are the following editions:

➤ *Dreams, "Evolution" and Value Fulfillment* (Amber-Allen, 1997)

➤ *How to Develop Your ESP Power: The First Published Encounter with Seth* (Lifetime Books, 1997)

➤ *The Individual and the Nature of Mass* (Amber-Allen, 1997)

➤ *The Magical Approach* (New World Library, 1995)

➤ *The Nature of Personal Reality* (New World Library, 1994)

➤ *The Nature of the Psyche* (Amber-Allen, 1996)

The belief in channeling is far from over, however. Even Hillary Rodham Clinton is said to have met in the White House with a channeler (who allowed the First Lady to chat with the spirit of Eleanor Roosevelt).

Phantom Phrases

Channeling is a form of spirit communication, especially popular in the United States during the 1970s and 1980s. During a channeling session, the unseen entity (seldom the spirit of a deceased human) takes possession of the medium (called a channeler) to impart spiritual guidance or wisdom.

Phantom Phrases

Cold reading is a technique used by pseudo-psychics, fraudulent mediums, fake mind-readers, and magicians to obtain information about a person, without any advance knowledge of the individual. This is usually accomplished through a series of statements and questions by the medium, responding to the verbal and non-verbal responses by the person being "read."

Hello, Heaven?

There will always be people claiming to be able to communicate with the dead as long as there are people willing to be believe that it's possible.

One of the newest media darlings in paranormal circles is medium and best-selling author James Van Praagh, who claims to be able to contact the Other World and chat with its residents. He says that after death, our souls move into a "different dimension" where our thoughts and emotions move on a "higher frequency." Van Praagh says he is able to tap into and understand the non-verbal "vibration" and "pure thought" as he makes his "spirit readings." In his book, *Talking to Heaven* (E.P. Dutton, 1997), he claims that anyone can do it! Van Praagh has made numerous talk-show appearances in which he demonstrates his ability to talk to the deceased loved ones of members of the audience, and some of these readings have been amazingly accurate.

Ghostly Pursuits

Paranormal skeptics point out that many mediums obtain their information through a technique known as "cold reading," in which the pseudo-psychic fishes for (and obtains) clues by offering "impressions" or making vague statements. For example, the medium makes an innocent remark such as "I sense a long trip," and immediately follows it with a generalized question, such as "Does that make sense?" The reading continues with a series of questions, answers, and declarations, as the medium makes a calculated reading according to what the sitter says or (in the case of body language) does. The technique is called "cold reading" because the medium meets the subject "cold," without any advance knowledge about the individual.

Perhaps there is a World Beyond, and perhaps there are mediums, channelers, and psychics who can peer through that veil. And maybe, one day, those of us on the mortal side of eternity will receive clear, indisputable proof. Until that time, there will be skeptics, scoffers, and paranormal investigators.

The Least You Need to Know

➤ D.D. Home, who was able to produce amazing physical phenomena during his séances, was one of spiritualism's most popular mediums.

➤ Florence Cook, attended by the spirit control Katie King, was perhaps the best-known female medium in the second half of the 19th century.

➤ Spirit photography purports to capture the images of ghosts on regular camera film, often in the same photo as a living person.

➤ James Van Praagh is one of the more visible contemporary mediums who claims to be able to communicate with the dead.

Part 3
Who Ya Gonna Call?

As the movie Ghostbusters cried, if you have a problem with ghosts, "Who ya gonna call?" Why not hire a ghost hunter? Quicker than you can say, "Boo!" spirit and paranormal researchers began to examine the claims of mediums. Before long, haunted houses were being staked out. Ghost sightings were studied. Some ghost hunters (and a ghostbuster or two) founded highly respected societies for psychical investigation.

And what about you? Could you be a ghost hunter? Once you learn the methods of the professional ghost hunters, you'll be ready to start out on your own—if you dare!

Finally, when the day is done (or, more likely, when the night is over and day breaks), how do you interpret what you've seen and heard? How can you tell if that noise you heard was a ghost or just a creaky floorboard? If the apparition or phenomenon you experienced wasn't a ghost, and you can't explain it away by some natural cause, what might it all have been?

Let's find out.

Chapter 10

Ghost Hunters and Ghostbusters

In This Chapter

➤ The Society for Psychical Research

➤ Early psychic and paranormal investigation

➤ Paranormal associations

➤ Ghost hunters Harry Price and Hans Holzer

For all practical purposes, the serious study of ghosts, apparitions, and paranormal phenomena began in earnest in the first half of the 19th century. Up until that time, ghosts were variously considered to be the spirits of the dead, demons, angels, or a combination of all three, depending upon the culture or civilization in which you lived.

I Will Survive

The goal of paranormal investigators has always been to come up with one workable theory that can accommodate all types of apparitional and spectral phenomena, including poltergeists, ghost or haunting apparitions, spirit communications through mediums and other means, and so on. Any practical theory that could accommodate *all* of these phenomena seems to be based on the acceptance of the principle of some form of life after death.

The Beginnings of the Society for Psychical Research

The Society for Psychical Research, or SPR, was founded in London in 1882. It was the first major association dedicated to the scientific research of paranormal activity. It was certainly a result of the spiritualism craze that swept England in the 1870s, but its purpose was to examine paranormal activity in the light of scientific knowledge and religious beliefs. In addition to ghost and poltergeist phenomena, the SPR also involved itself in the study of hypnosis, ESP, and other paranormal topics.

The key members of the original organization were Henry Sidgwick, Frederic W.H. Myers, and Edmund Gurney, all of whom were Fellows of Trinity College at Cambridge. Myers was fascinated by an appearance of the control John King at an 1873 séance, and he asked Sidgwick and Gurney to help him investigate. Myers then formed an informal association of friends and intellectuals for the purpose of research. Other original members of this Sidgwick Group, as it became known, were Arthur Balfour and his sister Eleanor (who married Sidgwick in 1876).

In 1882, Sir William Barrett, several spiritualists, and others joined the Sidgwick Group to form the Society for Psychical Research, with Sidgwick as its first president. Among the SPR's other early leading members was G.N.M. Tyrrell, who became known for his theoretical work on apparitions. Chemist/physicist Sir William Crookes (see Chapter 9, "Striking a Happy Medium") and author Sir Arthur Conan Doyle, both confirmed spiritualists, also joined. Years later, psychoanalyst Sigmund Freud and psychiatrist Carl G. Jung also became members.

How Do You Characterize a Ghost?
An Early SPR Survey

Well, where do you start? First, how do you define a ghost or apparition? Here's a simplified way of thinking about it: Imagine a material "being" without a physical occupant; in other words, a person from which all physical components (flesh and bones) has been removed, yet all other characteristics by which we perceive that person (including their personality, or soul) has survived. What remains would be the ghost or apparition.

One of the first studies undertaken by SPR was an investigation of apparitions, a Census of Hallucinations. Their initial survey split apparitions into three broad categories:

1. Apparitions of people who were still alive
2. Apparitions of the dying (including those that appeared to others at the moment of death)
3. Apparitions of the dead

The first question of the survey was: "Have you ever, when believing yourself to be completely awake, had a vivid impression of seeing or being touched by a living being or inanimate object, or of hearing a voice; which impression, as far as you could discover, was not due to any external physical cause?" Approximately 9.9 percent of 17,000 people sampled replied yes; interestingly, the clear majority were women.

As a result of their research, the society came up with some general, though sometimes conflicting, characteristics of ghosts. They:

➤ Often perceive and react to objects around them. They behave as if they were totally aware of their surroundings, coming in through doors, not walls. They move around furniture, not pass through it. If the ghost moves through a house, it uses staircases and hallways, established pathways or routes taken by the living.

➤ Can disappear or pass into walls, through closed doors, or through solid objects.

➤ Can be perceived by multiple viewers (a so-called "collective" case), although the ghost sometimes appears to some but not all of the people in the group.

➤ Are visible and audible only to certain people.

➤ Are sometimes, though rarely, tangible (that is, they feel solid to the touch).

➤ Are sometimes, though rarely, reflected in mirrors.

➤ Sometimes behave with regard to the lighting of the situation. In other words, they cast shadows or block the light if they pass in front of a lamp.

➤ Can be penetrated. You can walk or pass your hands through them without meeting any physical resistance.

➤ Appear and disappear in unexplainable ways, even in locked rooms.

➤ Disappear while you're watching them.

➤ Sometimes become transparent and fade away.

➤ Leave behind no physical evidence or traces, such as footprints.

➤ Are often perceived by animals, especially family or domesticated pets, even before (or instead of) by humans.

➤ Almost always occupy the center of your field of vision.

➤ Appear three-dimensional. You can walk all around the apparition, and it appears material, not like a flat projection.

➤ Are often accompanied by a feeling of cold. Either the room temperature drops, there is an icy breeze or wind, or, if the ghost touches you, the apparition feels cold.

➤ Sometimes first appear as a "presence": You wake up with a start or you "feel" something in the room. Often, you sense something staring at you from behind.

➤ Can create the physical sensation of a pressure weighing against your body.

In addition, master ghost philosopher Tyrrell noted seven major distinctions between human beings and apparitions:

1. When we approach an apparition, we might feel cold.

2. If we try to hold an apparition, our hands would go through it without resistance. (Then, not wanted to be captured or held, the ghost might choose to suddenly disappear.)

3. Only the human would leave footprints.

4. If a photograph were taken, only the human would appear in the developed print.

5. If a sound recording were made, only the human voice would be heard upon playback.

6. After a time, the apparition would disappear, either suddenly or gradually fade away.

7. The apparition might possess non-human characteristics: It might glow or transmute its appearance.

It's All in How You Perceive It

The survey perhaps raised more questions than it answered. Many of the characteristics appeared to conflict with one another. How could they all be true?

The answer lay in the percipient, the person who sees the ghost. Our senses deliver information to our brain, which then sorts and analyzes the data to make a perception. For example, we see something red with a long green tube attached; we touch it along the stem and feel a prick; we smell an attractive scent. Our brain decides that it's a rose.

Thus, each person who comes in contact with a ghost perceives it through the five—and some would add the sixth—senses. Some people see it; others might hear it; others experience some combination of these or other senses. Our brains analyze these sense responses to identify that we're seeing a ghost.

Ghosts *are* hallucinations, but not in the usual medical sense. In psychology, a hallucination is an auditory, visual, or tactile perception that has no real external cause or stimulus. Seeing a ghost, as we commonly use the word, *does* have an external cause: a material apparition.

The "material" essence of a ghost—the fact that something is really there—was proved by an interesting discovery. In all reported cases, if the percipients closed their eyes, they no longer saw the ghost. Perceiving the ghost depended on their being able to *see* it. If the ghost had merely been a psychological hallucination, it might have still been there even after they closed their eyes.

Ever See a Naked Ghost?

One of the earliest quandaries to puzzle investigators was, "Why do ghosts wear clothing?" A ghost is thought to be the spirit of a human being, but the clothing was never alive. It has no soul.

Then what is the clothing? Is the apparition wearing ghost pants?

This query, of course, immediately brings up the larger question, "Can any inanimate object become a ghost?" After all, in addition to wearing clothes, ghosts are sometimes accompanied by horses, carriages, or other non-human accoutrements, such as a walking stick. Where do these objects come from?

Paranormals decided that apparitions are perceived as a complete entity. The only way the mind can identify the spirit is in a recognizably human form, which would include all of its usual trappings.

Tyrrell suggested that the ghost is seen as part of a hallucinatory drama or theme, in which the person who sees the ghost fills in all parts of the dream as if it were real. Thus, one might see a ghost approach a door, open it, and pass through it, even though the actual physical door never moves. The percipient "sees" what is dramatically appropriate, whether or not is actually happens.

Baby, It's Cold Inside

Another question that still baffles investigators today is why haunted rooms have cold spots, icy breezes, or temperature shifts.

Even master ghost philosopher Tyrrell was stumped. He did theorize, however, that the percipient might be subjective physical reaction connected to seeing or sensing the apparition. In other words, perceiving an apparition might cause a person to biological react in such a way that the body temperature is reduced, thus producing a chill.

Other Research Organizations

The SPR was not the only group investigating paranormal activity. Other contemporary organizations, such as the London Dialectical Society (formed in the late 1860s) were conducting similar inquiries.

The Ghost Club, a private organization investigating ghost phenomenon, is based in London and actually predates the SPR. In fact, it's the oldest existing organization to research paranormal matters, having been around in one form or another since 1862. (It was predated by the Cambridge Ghost Club, which is no longer around.) The Ghost Club was established primarily to investigate the Davenport brothers (see Chapters 8, "Things That Go Bump in the Night," and 24, "The Magic Connection"). Over the years, the Ghost Club has shared many members with the SPR, but membership is now by invitation only.

In late 1884 or early 1885, the SPR helped found American Society for Psychical Research, or ASPR, in Boston. Except for some of its early years, the ASPR has operated independently of the SPR, although they share almost identical goals. The majority of ASPR's members were spiritualists, not scientists. In 1925, arguments over the investigation of the fraudulent medium Margery (Mina Stinson Crandon) led several members to break away and form a splinter group, the Society for Psychical Research. The group rejoined the ASPR in 1941.

In the 1950s, the ASPR became more involved with the investigation of extrasensory perception (ESP) and other psychic phenomena rather than ghost investigation. Many of their studies focused on the laboratory trials being performed by J.B. Rhine at Duke University.

As part of his experiments at Duke University, Rhine developed a deck of 25 playing cards whose faces consisted of five cards each of five designs: a circle, a cross, three wavy lines, a square, and a star. In the simplest of the ESP experiments, two participants would sit facing other with a shield between them. One person would mix the cards, turn them face up one at a time, and try to send the mental image of each design to the other person.

Ghostbusting

The Ghost Research Society has found that 70 to 85 percent of ghostly phenomena has explainable natural causes. (But what about the rest?)

The Ghost Research Society (GRS), originally called the Ghost Tracker's Club, was founded in the late 1970s in greater Chicago by Martin V. Riccardo. Dale Kaczmarek, the society's current president, became research director in 1982. Most of the group's investigations are carried out in the Midwestern United States, but it has done fieldwork farther afield. They mostly investigate ghost phenomena in private homes. The GRS also collects information about spirit photography, ghost lights, and electronic voice phenomena (EVP).

Here's a partial list of just a few more associations that have been formed in the last century to study ghosts and spirit phenomena:

➤ British College of Psychic Science (BCPS).

➤ Academy of Religion and Psychical Research.

➤ Spiritual Frontier Fellowship.

➤ Institut Metapsychique International (IMI), founded in France in 1918, whose first director was psychic researcher Gustave Geley (1868–1924). Under Geley, the IMI investigated noted French medium Marthe Beraud (who worked as Eva C.), among many others.

➤ Institut für Grenzgebiete der Psychologie and Psychohygiene (Institute for Border Areas of Psychology and Mental Health), founded in Germany in 1950 by Hans Bender (b. 1907).

➤ National Laboratory for Psychical Research.

➤ Parapsychology Foundation (PF).

➤ Winnipeg Society for Psychical Research.

➤ Committee for the Scientific Investigation of Claims of the Paranormal (CSICOP).

Harry Price (1881–1948) was, perhaps, the most famous ghost hunter of the first half of the 20th century. In his 1942 autobiography, *Search for Truth: My Life for Psychical Research,* he claimed to have had his first paranormal experience in a haunted house at the age of 15. He became interested in magic at an early age, and it was partly because of this that the SPR, which he had joined in 1920, sent him to investigate the spirit photographer William Hope (see Chapter 9). Price's results were inconclusive; some accused Price, not Hope, of trickery. Price also investigated Dorothy Stella Cranshaw, who operated as the medium Stella C. Price was actually quite impressed with her work, which caused consternation among both his magician friends and SPR associates.

Price founded his National Laboratory of Psychical Research, which is now part of London University, and he wrote voluminously about his investigations. Throughout his career, his methods, conclusions, and even his honesty, frequently came under fire.

Price is best known, however, for his high-profile investigation of "the most haunted house in England," the Borley Rectory, from 1929 until 1947. (We'll take a look at the Borley Rectory in detail in Chapter 15, "There'll Always Be an England.")

Price died suddenly of a heart attack on March 29, 1948. After his death, there were reports for a time that his spirit had returned. He supposedly appeared in Sweden by the bedside of a young man whom the case histories call Erson. Erson spoke no English, but he was able to figure out that the solid-looking phantom was named Price. The spectre began to appear regularly to Erson, his wife, and daughter. Erson attempted to take photographs of the ghost, but no image appeared. The phantom Price advised Erson to go to a particular hospital for a health problem. While he was there, Erson talked to a doctor who was interested in the paranormal. From Erson's description of the elderly phantom, the doctor was able to identify him as the British ghost investigator Harry Price. Now, why the ghost of Price would want to travel to a different country, materialize before someone who didn't speak English and had no interest in the paranormal … well, no one knows. It's just one of those mysteries.

The Ghost Hunter Himself: Hans Holzer

No list of ghostbusters and ghost hunters would be complete without a mention of Hans Holzer. Few paranormal investigators consider him a serious researcher, perhaps because of his reliance on the use of mediums at haunted sites.

Holzer's first book, *Ghost Hunter,* led to numerous television and radio appearances, for which he took his book's title as his sobriquet. A ubiquitous personality in paranormal investigation, Holzer has also produced and narrated several documentaries.

Today, the terms "psychical research," "parapsychology," and "paranormal activity" conjure up images of statistic research into ESP rather than the investigation of ghost activity. Certainly such research took a decided turn in that direction after the experiments of Dr. Rhine at Duke University.

Die-hard parapsychics, however, mourn the fact that the possibility of the existence of extrasensory perception is currently receiving more attention and credence than the possibility that ghosts exist. Parapsychic writer Spencer Brown bemoaned that the statistics revealed in ESP testing actually demonstrate peculiarities or quirks of randomness rather than proving genuine paranormal activity.

The fields of ghost and ESP research are inextricably linked, however, due to the early investigators' theories that some apparitions and other paranormal activity might be caused by one person planting the suggestion in another person's mind by telepathy. Some have even theorized something called super-ESP, a powerful form of extrasensory perception able to travel long distances that could explain collective apparitions. (You'll learn all about super-ESP in Chapter 12, "If Not a Ghost, Then What?")

The future of paranormal investigation may be *you!* Continue on to the next chapter to learn the guidelines set down by other researchers, and get ready to put together your own ghost-hunting gear!

The Least You Need to Know

➤ Although predated by other paranormal associations, the Society for Psychical Research was the first institution dedicated to the scientific investigation of ghost and spirit phenomena.

➤ Part of the early research process was defining an apparition and delineating its characteristics from those of living human beings.

➤ G.N.M. Tyrrell became renowned for his theoretical work on the nature of apparitions.

➤ Harry Price never shied away from publicity: He was one of the best-known paranormal investigators of the first half of the 20th century.

➤ Author/investigator Hans Holzer, the *Ghost Hunter,* has published more than 40 books on ghosts, paranormal phenomena, and related activities.

Chapter 11

A Method to the Madness: Conducting a Ghost Hunt

In This Chapter

➤ What's the difference between a ghost investigation and a ghost hunt?

➤ Tips and advice on conducting a ghost hunt from the pros

➤ The importance of doing your research

➤ What to take along in your ghost hunter's field kit

➤ Sorting through the data

Ready to go on a ghost hunt? Let's take a look at some of the pioneers in paranormal investigation, then apply their methods and discoveries to modern-day ghost detection.

You'll find tips to help you during all three parts of a ghost hunt:

➤ What you have to know and what preparations to make before you go

➤ What to look for and what to do while you're out there in the dark

➤ Perhaps most important, what to do with all the data you collect while you're out trying to track down a ghost

Hopefully, by the time you finish this chapter you'll be able to join a ghost investigation or set out on a ghost hunt of your own.

Ghost Investigations vs. Ghosts Hunts

Although the terms are sometimes used interchangeably, ghost investigations and ghost hunts are very different creatures, even though they have the same goal: to sight and record spectral activity. A *ghost investigation* is a carefully controlled, scientific research project of a location known, reported, or presumed (though usually with probable cause) to be haunted. Most investigations are instigated at the request of the owner or resident of the property, although researchers sometimes ask the owners/residents for permission to investigate properties that are reputed to be haunted.

There are a few reasons to carry out a ghost investigation:

➤ To prove or disprove a haunting

➤ To assist the owners of the property in their own investigation

➤ To help the ghosts leave the location and move on to their rightful place in the spirit world

To carry out their investigations, researchers use various tools, including audio and video recordings as well as still photography, which I'll discuss a little later in this chapter.

A *ghost hunt* is attempt to sight or catch a ghost (on audio, still photos, or video), often in a location where there has been no reported paranormal activity. Ghost hunters usually choose a location because there are rumors that the place is haunted or similar sights have known to be haunted (such as cemeteries, churches, or decrepit buildings).

Ghosts hunts are generally less controlled and scientific than a contracted or detailed investigation. Because the goal of a ghost hunt is to just go out to find a ghost, they're usually more loose-knit and fun than a formal investigation.

Ghost hunts are carried out by paranormal professionals as well as by hobbyists/ghost enthusiasts.

Phantom Phrases

A **ghost investigation** is a carefully controlled scientific research project, instigated to sight and record paranormal activity, usually at a location known or presumed to be haunted. A **ghost hunt** is an informal attempt to simply sight or record a ghost in a location similar to those known to be haunted.

Call in the Troops

You know how, when you get a leaky pipe, you crawl down under the sink with your wrench and pliers and you sorta get it fixed, then suddenly the whole pipe bursts open and you get soaking wet? So you wind up calling a professional plumber, which is what you should have done in the first place.

It's kind of like that with ghost hunting. You can set up your own cameras, tape recorders, and booby traps. But if you're really serious about tracking down a ghost, you'll probably need the services of a professional.

The Society for Psychical Research set the standard for paranormal investigations way back at the end of the 19th century. They, and other societies like them, have set up field studies of hundreds, if not thousands of sites over the past hundred years. Many of the organizations you might consider contacting were profiled in the last chapter. You can find their names and addresses, along with those of many independent ghost hunters, in Appendix B, "Continuing the Ghost Hunt."

Ghost Hunting Advice from a Pro

Just for the fun of it, let's say you want to stake out someplace on your own and conduct a ghost hunt. How do you begin?

Let's look to the experts for advice. One of the first "how to" guides on investigating haunted houses was written by ghost hunter Harry Price (whom you read about in Chapter 10, "Ghost Hunters and Ghostbusters") and published in pamphlet form. It was issued in conjunction with his examination of the Borley Rectory in 1937 and 1938. Among his many suggestions are the following:

➤ Establish a base in one room and keep all of your equipment there when it's not in use. This will prevent having to search for an item when it's needed.

➤ Keep a working flashlight in your pocket at all times.

➤ Be careful with flammable objects, such as matches, candles, and cigarettes.

➤ Always observe the area in question for the half-hour before and after dusk. These are especially active times for spirit phenomena.

➤ If you're part of a team and you experience a very strong phenomenon, or if a succession of phenomena occur, immediately contact the rest of your team (or a partner with whom you made previously arrangements) to record the activities in detail. Others may be able to assist you or corroborate your sightings.

➤ Be courteous to strangers and personal friends if they meet you on site, but don't allow untrained assistants to assist or join you. They may do more harm than good.

➤ Check measurement instruments regularly to be sure they're in working condition. Record all readings and the times at which they're taken. Note anything that appears unusual when you first notice it.

➤ Spend at least part of the day and night prior to an investigation in a totally dark room. This will get you accustomed to periods in the dark and will make your eyes sensitive to even the dimmest light.

The very much alive Harry Price (seated) is visited by a spectral women being. Though Price believed in spirit photography, he rejected this example as a double exposure. (Author's collection)

In the same guide, Price pointed out some types of possible phenomena ghost hunters might experience, along with his recommendations on what to do if they occur:

Ghostbusting

Outline moveable objects so that, later, you'll have proof that it actually did move. Put outlines around anything you suspect the ghost might want to move. Two good bets: anything that was owned a deceased person, or anything that's been reported as moving in the past.

➤ **Noises.** Try to judge where they came from. Record in a notebook at what time and for what duration they were heard. If the sound seems to move, try to determine its origin, the direction in which it travels, and its duration. If you can determine the type of sound, make descriptive observations (for example, in the case of footsteps, whether they were soft, heavy, shuffling, etc.).

➤ **Moving objects.** Outline any objects in chalk that you suspect might be able to or want to move. If an object is heard to move, determine in which room it occurred, what object moved, and in which direction it moved. Draw a rough map of the room, noting the path of the motion. Estimate how much force must have been needed to move it. Did the object float? Did it crash? If the object is seen in motion, record its speed, direction, force, and trajectory. In any case, examine the object after the motion for any changes, and return it to its original position within its outline.

➤ **Forms or apparitions.** If you see a ghost, don't move. Remain absolutely silent, try to control the rate and loudness of your breathing, and, most important, don't approach the spectre. Note at what time and for what duration it appeared. Record everything it does, including any mannerisms and gestures, that might help you identify the spirit later. Determine its path and the rate at which it travels. Observe its characteristics, such as height, shape, size, color, density, wardrobe or costume, accoutrements such as a cane, attendant animals or vehicles, speech, or sounds. If you have a camera, take as many photos as possible, being careful to minimize noise (such as that of the lens shutter).

Do Your Homework Before You Start

All of this advice by Harry Price of what to do once you're on the ghost hunt is excellent. It's as true today as it was when he wrote it in 1938. But, I can't stress enough the importance of prior, and proper, research before you begin your physical investigation. Your first tool as an psychic investigator is always research. Unless you first research the site that you're about to study, you won't know what you're looking for, and may not recognize phantom phenomena when you find (or see) it.

Although most of the tidbits you find during your pre-hunt research will lead nowhere, you might find that one piece of information that helps everything else fall into place. In addition, with a stack of documents under your arm, you'll boost your credibility and make your own findings harder to dispute or contradict later on.

For example, it's a good idea to find out who's already researched the site. Have other investigators been there before you, and if so, what did they find? Were their methods reliable? Do you agree with their findings?

Find out everything you can about the property and its history:

➤ The address

➤ Former residents

➤ Former owners

➤ Current resident

➤ Current owner, including liens on the property

Establish the owner of the property. Don't automatically assume the current resident is also the owner.

Look for the deed or title to the property. This will be filed with the County Recorder.

Where can you find all of this information?

➤ The County Registrar-Recorder office (look under the government pages in the local phone book) keeps records of deeds, real estate transactions, voting rolls, and birth, death, marriage, and divorce certificates for that county

➤ Public Utilities and Motor Vehicle Registration offices (privacy laws are being enacted in some areas to prevent the release of this information)

➤ The public library

➤ Historical societies (city, county, and state)

➤ Church and cemetery records

And, if you can get to these people, ask them directly:

➤ Current and former residents

➤ Current and former owners

➤ Current and former neighbors

That's right: Sometimes finding out all the information is as easy as knocking on the door of the house you want to investigate. If you want to do a ghost hunt on the property, you're going to have to talk to the residents at some point anyway. They can usually provide you with almost everything you need to know. And, if they can't, a nosy neighbors probably can.

You should establish all of the owners throughout the years, of both the land and the buildings or structures on it. Sometimes paranormal activity is attached to an event on the site before the structure was built.

Also find out *how* and *why* the property changed hands. This is especially useful if it's thought that the spirit is haunting the grounds to right a wrong or to complete some activity. In short, find out the personal histories of all the owners and residents, beginning with birth, marriage, and death certificates. Whenever possible, double-check and cross-check your information. Again, this will increase your credibility as a researcher among your peers, interested parties, and skeptics. It will also make the results of your investigation stronger and more valid.

Ghostbusting

While you're pumping the residents, neighbors, and owners for information on the history of the buildings and property, don't forget to ask them whether they've ever seen any ghosts of paranormal activity. You might be surprised by what you hear—and it may make your job a whole lot easier!

Look Before You Leap

Two words: permission and safety. And that's just to go on the property for starters. And as for safety, well, there's no sense getting killed. You're trying to see a ghost, not become one.

Some public areas, such as parks or cemeteries, may have restricted visiting hours. It may be unlawful to park on the shoulder of the haunted highway you want to stake out. Always check ahead of time.

Play it safe! The archetypal haunted house is old and has rickety stairs and rotted, easy-to-fall-through floors. If the house is in a state of decay, there will probably be lots of opportunities to step on rusty nails or get cut with shards of glass, so have your tetanus booster shot up to date. The building might be infested with all sorts of living creatures, like bats and raccoons, both of which have large rabies populations. Oh, then there are the spiders, and rats, and snakes, oh, my! Again, always be careful for your own physical well-being. No investigation is worth making *yourself* into a ghost!

Who Goes There?

If you do run into an apparition or spirit, it'll probably be a ghost. It was a living human at one time, and it's chosen to visit or remain in the material world at that specific location for some reason probably unknown to you.

Remember, ghosts usually aren't dangerous to mortals. They're attending to their own business. But, like humans, ghosts can be good or bad, so be as wary as you would of any stranger that you're meeting for the first time in a dark room.

In the Shadows: Tips from a Shadow Lord

Dave Juliano, who as Shadow Lord manages "The Shadowlands" Web site (see Appendix B), has had more than 30 years of experience investigating hauntings. He discourages untrained amateurs from conducting their own ghost hunts and directs them to several groups established for that purpose.

The following are among his many tips for those who insist on ghost-hunting on their own. You've already read some of these precautions, but it never hurts to reiterate this advice:

➤ Do your homework. Find out the history of the location. (Neighbors to the property and the local historical society can be especially helpful.)

Boo!

You don't want to be accused of trespassing on private property. Look for "No Trespassing" signs. And obey them! You want to protect yourself legally, especially should there be any damage or injuries during the ghost hunt. If it's posted, you could still ask the owner personally.

Boo!

There's also the very rare possibility that you'll run into a poltergeist or other non-human spirit on a ghost hunt. Since most of these spirits are malicious, if not downright malevolent, it's best to avoid them if at all possible. If you do suspect the apparition is a poltergeist or some demonic spirit, get outta there as soon as possible.

➤ Do a daytime reconnaissance so you will know the area in the dark.

➤ Historically, the most active times for ghost phenomena are between 9 P.M. and 6 A.M., although it's possible for spirit behavior to occur at any time. (Juliano notes that the best ghost photographs have also been taken in the dark.)

➤ *Never* go alone. Let me repeat that: *Never go alone!* If there are several people going on the hunt, break off into pairs or groups of three.

➤ Always take photo identification with you in case you're stopped and questioned by police, owners, or other authorities.

➤ Carry a log to record all activity. Record the date, the time, and the weather at the start of your ghost hunt, and enter any changes that occur.

Ghostbusting

Always work with brand-new audio, video, and film materials every time you do any ghost hunting. You want to avoid the possibility of acci-dental double-exposures or accusations of fraud for tampered evidence.

➤ To be sure you're working with clean, fresh materials (film, audiotape, plastic bags), wait until you're on site to open and load your film, videotape, and audiotape. Juliano suggests though that this will alert "aware" spirits of your intentions, which I suppose could be a good or a bad thing depending upon whether the ghosts want to cooperate.

➤ Make a quick walk of the area before setting up shop, noting conditions so that you can recognize any changes or activity when it does occur.

➤ Take videotape and still photos, and keep a tape recorder going continuously during the hunt. Be quiet. Don't even whisper. You don't want your voice picked up on tape and have it later be mistaken for electronic voice phenomena (EVP).

Boo!

Don't smoke while on a ghost hunt. First of all, fire, burning ash, and still-burning butts are safety hazards, especially if you're in an old, dry building or in a dry field. Plus, the dim glow of a cigarette may be mis-perceived by others as spirit phenom-ena. And no alcohol: You want to be in complete control of your senses!

Remember, we're talking ghosts here. Just because you don't sense, see, or hear anything, doesn't mean a ghost's not there and recordable. Quite often, ghost activity isn't discovered until much later, when the sound recording is listened to, the film is developed, or the videotape is watched.

Juliano adds two personal, optional tips. He recommends that you start any ghost hunt or investigation by asking for protection from whatever religious figure you worship. He also suggests that, as you finish up a ghost hunt, you ask any ghosts and spirits present to stay there and not follow you home!

Call me old-fashioned, but I'd also take a silver cross and some holy water.

Your Ghost-Hunting Bag of Tricks

You're going to be sitting out or walking for hours, probably at night, in your attempt to see a ghost. Few things could be worse than needing something and knowing that you left it at home.

You carry a first-aid kit on camping trips. What kind of kit should you be carrying with you on your ghost hunt?

Some of these are common-sense items. Others have been recommended by ghost-hunting experts. There are probably other things that you'll want to take along that are important just to you. When it's time to do the final packing for the ghost hunt, you'll have to decide for yourself what to take.

Nevertheless, here are *my* minimum daily requirements, the ones that I recommend you carry in your ghost hunter's field kit:

Ghostbusting

Some ghost hunters have had success taking photographs with infrared film, or simply placing a red gel over the flash unit. If you are using anything other than a point-and-shoot camera, learn how to set your camera to shoot in available light without the use of a flash.

➤ Appropriate clothing to keep warm and dry

➤ Food

➤ Water

With your basic physical needs out of the way, you'll also want to bring:

➤ A watch. (And a stop watch, if you're obsessive about timing the duration of phenomena.)

➤ At least one 35 mm camera with high-speed film (at *least* 400 ASA) for shooting in low light. You might consider a second camera loaded with high-speed black-and-white film.

➤ Video camera. Bring a tripod if you can't hold it steady or if it doesn't have gyroscopic correction for shakiness. Trust me, if you actually do see a ghost, chances are good you'll start shaking.

➤ Audio recorder with an external (not built-in) microphone, with a wind cover over the head of the microphone. Some experts recommend using high-grade metal tape; others say to never use chromium-oxide tape because it sometimes double-records voices. You may also want to carry a small, cheap, but reliable back-up tape recorder with a built-in microphone for when your hot-shot unit fails.

➤ More film and tape than you think you'll ever need. What if you finally see a ghost, and you're out of film?

➤ A flashlight (and an extra, for when you drop and break the first one), with extra batteries.

➤ Candles and matches. (For when you drop and break the second flashlight.) Or, if you prefer, a kerosene lantern.

➤ A basic first aid kit.

➤ A cellular phone in case of emergency or to contact other team members in a hurry. (It is the new millennium, after all!)

➤ A log or notebook, with sufficient pens and/or pencils. In addition to noting in the log all phenomena and the times that things occur, you'll want to record the *unseen*—what you feel and sense. Also, sketch floor plans of the haunted site and, if you can, draw a portrait of any apparitions you see.

➤ Clean, uncontaminated containers or plastic bags to hold evidence that you've assembled.

➤ Chalk, to mark paths and to outline objects.

➤ A compass. Some ghosts have been recorded as shifting magnetic fields; an unexplained change in the compass needle might indicate a spectral presence. A compass also comes in handy for navigation on back roads and to mark directions on maps you've sketched.

➤ A thermometer, to record temperature changes. Icy blasts and cold spots have been reported in almost all ghost literature; temperature shifts have been reported between six and 20 degrees. Use a standard mercury thermometer. It's thought that some electronic gadgets might be disrupted by spectres due to unaccountable magnetic fields that sometimes accompany them.

Good luck catching a ghost! Heck, good luck just trying to carry all that gear out to the car.

After the Hunt: Sorting Through Your Data

Let's say you spent all night staring into the inky darkness, and you didn't see or hear a thing. What do you do with all the data you've collected when you get home? Just throw it out?

No! That could be a big mistake!

When you have your 35 mm film developed, be sure to ask the lab to give you all of the negatives and make prints of all exposures. Some photography studios don't bother to print what look to be "bad" photos. But that white spot or streak that looks *to them* like light leakage or bad photography might be a ghost light, a globule, a vortex, or the spectral evidence you're looking for.

Watch those endless hours of video. You may have captured something without knowing it. Scan the entire screen: Not all ghosts automatically take center stage. If you see something odd or unusual, freeze frame the picture. If you're set up to do so, generate a computer printout. Have you captured the image of a ghost?

Likewise, listen to all your audiotapes, even if you didn't hear anything while you were recording. You'll be amazed to find out how much ambient noise you've picked up, on even the quietest of nights. First of all, identify what sounds you can. To assist you, check your log. You should have made a record of any identifiable sounds (such as a dog barking or a car horn) and the time at which you heard them. That'll probably leave only a few unidentifiable noises.

Remember, almost everything you see or hear, although unusual, will have a natural explanation. So if you have a recorded sound that you can't explain or pinpoint, don't jump to the conclusion that it's *electronic voice phenomenon*. EVP is very, very rare! If you have been lucky enough to capture a spirit voice, it'll probably have a rasping or grating sound, little more than a hoarse whisper. It may be only one or two words, probably less than a full sentence.

As you'll recall from Chapter 3, "Do the Dead Return?" Thomas Alva Edison was working on an electronic instrument to communicate with the dead. EVP has been seriously studied by a number of specialist organizations, including the Association for Voice Taping Research (VTR) and the Research Association for Voice Taping (AVT), both in Germany, as well as the American Association-Electronic Voice Phenomena.

EVP believers contend that the sounds are the voices of the dead; skeptics insist they are signals from radio, telephone, or television or imagined words formed from static or white sound. I usually chalk it up to the little voices talking to me from inside my head.

So, now you know how to get ready for a ghost hunt, how to collect your data, and how to analyze your results with logic, if not a healthy dose of skepticism. Part of that process is asking yourself, "If this spirit activity wasn't caused by a ghost, what did cause it?" So, for those who refuse to believe in spirits, let's take a look in our next chapter at what others have suggested might explain all this spooky, paranormal phenomena.

Phantom Phrases

The capture of spirit voices on magnetic tape as an audio recording is called **electronic voice phenomenon,** or **EVP.** Many times, no sound is heard while the tape is recording. It's only upon playback that the harsh, hushed voices can be heard.

The Least You Need to Know

➤ Ghost investigations are serious, scientific attempts to locate, identify, and deal with ghosts. Ghost hunts are much more informal, and often much more fun!

➤ Always thoroughly research the site at which you plan to set up a ghost investigation or hunt. Even a slight detail might help you track down a ghost.

➤ Always secure permission before walking onto private property.

➤ Safety should be a primary concern when out on a ghost hunt.

➤ Never discard your collected data until it's been thoroughly examined.

If Not a Ghost, Then What?

Reports of apparitions and ghost activities number in the thousands, if not tens or hundreds of thousands. Some are so solidly investigated and firmly established that the phenomena itself cannot be questioned. *Something* happened. All that remains is the explanation. *How* or *why* did it happen?

Now a lot of people, and probably most of the people reading this book, would like to believe that all of the weird things we see out there are ghosts, or at least caused by ghosts. But—and I don't know how to break this to you—but a lot of it ain't. So let's act mature about it and look at some of the other things paranormal researchers have suggested might cause some of the apparent ghost activity.

What Are Your Thoughts on That?

If apparitions aren't ghosts, what are they? What causes the spectral activity?

We have Edmund Gurney and Frederic W.H. Myers, founding members of the Society for Psychical Research (see Chapter 10, "Ghost Hunters and Ghostbusters"), to thank for much of the early modern theoretical work on this thorny issue. Unfortunately, they both decided that there were no such things as ghosts.

Let me rephrase that. Both Gurney and Myers believed that people saw what they thought were ghosts, but the apparitions were not actual physical entities. They believed that what people were experiencing were hallucinations caused by the dead. That's right: They thought the spirits of the dead somehow sent a *telepathic projection* of themselves into the minds of a living person. That person then formed a hallucination (the ghost) from the telepathically induced message. (As you'll see in Chapter 20, "Trains and Boats and Planes," Myers originally explained sightings of the ghost ship the *Flying Dutchman* as telepathic projection.)

Myers also believed that telepathic projection could be used to explain collective apparitions, where more than one person saw the same ghost (see Chapter 3, "Do the Dead Return?"). The spirit could be sending a telepathic projection to several people at the same time.

In their 1886 work *Phantasms of the Living,* Frank Podmore joined his fellow pioneering psychical researchers Myers and Gurney in suggesting that there was an underlying telepathic explanation for most, if not all, apparitions. They felt this was especially true for apparitions of the living, such as crisis apparitions that appear at a time of stress or the moment of death (see Chapter 3). How could it be a ghost, they reasoned, if the person wasn't even dead yet? In 1888, Myers theorized that *all* apparitions (those of the living and the dead) were telepathic in origin.

Phantom Phrases

The now-discredited theory of **telepathic projection,** first proposed by Frederic W.H. Myers, suggested that spirits of the dead sent mental messages to the living rather than physically returning as ghosts. The mortal's brain then interpreted the received information and used it to produce an external hallucination that resembled a ghost.

The Collective Dilemma: A Ghost for All People

Sometimes more than one person sees the same ghost. How can this be? Even if a spirit *were* able to send out simultaneous thought waves? Even if that's possible, why does the ghost look the same to everyone? Each individual would create a unique hallucination?

Edmund Gurney's main area of interest was this so-called "collective dilemma," in which several people, not necessarily all in the same place, see the same ghost at the same time. Gurney rejected Myers's theory. It was just too complicated to believe. The spirit would have to send out simultaneous, identical messages to several people, each of whom would then have to psychically transform the "broadcast" into his or her own personal apparition.

Instead, Gurney proposed a telepathic "infection" solution. The spirit would emit a telepathic message to only one specific person. He or she would receive the impulse and would, in turn, send it on to another person who would then, also, see the ghost.

Myers was quick to object to this theory. He pointed out that there was no research or evidence to suggest that any "normal or non-paranormal hallucinations spread in this fashion."

Doubters of "telepathic projection" and "infection" theories were quick to point out several problems with these explanations:

➤ If the ghost's image is being transmitted by one person, why doesn't it look exactly the same (including the same angle, distance, and perspective) to everyone else who sees it?

➤ If the ghost is only a hallucination, how can some of them move solid objects? Or do we also have to assume that hallucinations have telekinesis (the ability to move solid objects through the power of mind).

➤ Why do animals react when there are ghosts in the room? Do animals receive and react to telepathic messages as well? And, even if they do, animals often react to invisible presences in the room before humans do—in fact, many times, they react even though the people present sense nothing. Are the spirits of the dead sending telepathic projections to animals? And, if so, why?

➤ Finally, in order to believe in telepathic projection, you must first believe that telepathy itself exists. So far, there's been no definitive documented proof of ESP. So, pick your poison: Which is it easier for you to believe in? Telepathic communication or ghosts?

Eventually, all of the arguments against telepathic projection proved persuasive. By the time he wrote *Human Personality and the Survival of Bodily Death* (1903), Myers had abandoned his theory in favor of belief in actual apparitions. He suggested that the ghosts probably were made up of some sort of energy focusing into a kind of "phantasmogenic center."

Ghostbusting

The debate over whether animals can receive telepathic projections raises yet another interesting question: How do we know that when animals snarl, bark, or hiss at empty air that they're reacting to a ghost? Unless we see or otherwise sense the same ghostly activity at the same time, there's really no way for us to know for certain. The subject will no doubt continue to be discussed until animals learn to talk—but that's a whole different issue.

More Than Your Ordinary, Everyday ESP

In the late 1950s, American sociologist and psychical researcher Hornell Hart (1888–1967) coined the term *super-ESP* for a theoretical ability that's been debated since the earliest days of paranormal investigations. Essentially, super-ESP is an extraordinarily powerful form of telepathy that would allow mediums to mentally pick up information about the deceased from other living beings, even from great distances. Likewise, mediums possessing super-ESP could mentally project this information in the form of a hallucination, that could be perceived by themselves and others in the form of a ghost. This ability might be totally unconscious on the part of the medium.

If, indeed, super-ESP exists, then apparitions are not necessarily the returning spirits of the dead. Though super-ESP doesn't disprove or negate the possibility of survival after death, its existence could explain many, if not most, ghost sightings.

Phantom Phrases

Super-ESP is a theoretical powerful form of telepathy that allows a medium to unconsciously pick up information about a deceased person from other living people. Super-ESP might also account for ghosts: They could be the mental projections of a particularly strong medium.

What's the Objective?

So what's the bottom line? Are there actually ghosts out there? Or are we creating them all with our own minds? Unfortunately, there's no consensus; but just to be on the safe side, I suppose, some parapsychics delineate two types of apparitions:

➤ *Objective,* which are apparitions or phenomena that appear independent of our minds, and separate and distinct from our inner thoughts or feelings

➤ *Subjective,* which are apparitions or phenomena created by our own minds

Just to confuse the issue, some theorists suggest that some apparitions may be partially objective or partially subjective in nature.

Any questions?

Phantom Phrases

Objective apparitions are actual entities that appear independent of our mind, thoughts, or feelings. **Subjective apparitions** are created by our minds (i.e., hallucinations).

Any Other Bright Ideas?

If ghosts aren't real, and even the paranormal experts are backing away from their theories of telepathic contagion, what else could be causing all the apparitions and spectral phenomena?

Here are just a few more alternate explanations:

➤ **Mental illness.** You could be delusional or deranged—you know, just plain seeing things.

➤ **Legend.** A folktale, told often enough, sometimes comes to be believed or accepted as truth. A good example would be the Devil Baby of Hull House (see Chapter 14, "This Old House: Haunted America").

➤ **Deliberate distortion or general inaccuracy of the facts to make a better story.** And if the account is ever published, it's even more likely to be believed. Because, as everyone knows, if it's in print, it has to be true.

➤ **Indifference to the truth.** Many times, even after the ghostly phenomenon has been investigated and explained away, the ghost legend continues to be recycled because it's more interesting.

➤ **Hysterical mistakes.** The mind plays tricks. Under momentary mental or physical stress, you can mistake innocent objects and events of being ghosts and spectral phenomena.

➤ **Honest error due to illusion.** A shadow on the wall becomes a monster under the bed. A white curtain fluttering in the moonlight becomes a ghost. The settling of an old house becomes creaky footsteps of a phantom. A sudden, short breeze becomes the breath of the bogeyman. Need I go on?

➤ **Fraud.** Unfortunately, one of the more common possibilities.

> **Boo!**
>
> Are you beginning to get the *idea* that paranormal theorists are grasping at straws for some explanation—*any* explanation—for a spectral phenomenon, just so long as it isn't a ghost? Make sure any explanation *you* come up with for spirit activity isn't more outlandish than the possibility that you actually *have* seen a ghost.

In the next sections, we'll take a closer took at this last possibility, that of deliberate fraud.

A Real Cock-and-Bull Story: The Cock-Lane Ghost

In Chapter 5, "Poltergeists: They're Here!" we looked at one of the best-known modern examples of ghostly deception, the so-called Amityville Horror. But a similar hoax, perpetrated more than 200 years earlier, is the story of the Cock-Lane Ghost. In fact, some researchers date the modern age of ghost-hunting to 1762 when paranormal events started occurring in a house on Cock Lane in London.

According to legend, around 1760, a parish clerk named Mr. Parsons leased his house on Cock Lane to a stockbroker named Kent. After Kent's wife died, his sister-in law, Miss Fanny, came to serve as his housekeeper. Kent and Miss Fanny became close and named each other beneficiaries in their wills.

A 1762 engraving of the haunted Parsons house on Cock Lane in London.

Parsons borrowed money from Kent, which may have led to a disagreement. Regardless, for whatever reason, Kent moved out and soon sued Parsons for the money he was owed. Within two years, Miss Fanny died of smallpox, but Parsons spread the rumor that Kent may have poisoned her.

At the beginning of 1762, word spread that Miss Fanny had returned to the Cock Lane house to haunt the Parsons family. Elizabeth Parsons, the 12-year-old daughter, swore that she had seen the ghost, and the apparition said that Kent had poisoned her.

Although no one else actually saw the spectre, many people heard the knockings and scratching so often associated with ghosts. Soon, Elizabeth worked out a rapping code for the ghost to answer questions. Everyone wanted to hear the ghost, and Parsons was more than happy to admit them to his home—for a small fee.

A committee of local residents listened to Miss Fanny's ghost. It accused Kent of her murder and suggested that he be arrested and hanged for the crime. One of the members of the group was the Reverend Aldrich of Clerkenwell, who was pastor of Saint John's Church, where Miss Fanny's body was buried. The pastor refused to believe that the knocks he was hearing were actually being made by Fanny's ghost, so the ghost offered to travel to her crypt (in the company of Elizabeth, of course) and knock on her coffin lid to prove that it—the ghost—was real. (After all, if sounds came from inside the vault, didn't they have to be made by the person "living" there?)

Ghostly Pursuits

Elizabeth Parsons worked out the knocking code—one rap for "yes" and two for "no"—86 years before the Fox sisters in Hydesville, New York, used a similar system to communicate with their spirit. The Cock Lane incident was declared a fraud by most, whereas the events of the Fox sisters marked the birth of spiritualism and sparked a worldwide craze for holding séances.

Elizabeth stayed at the pastor's house the night before the ghostly visit was scheduled to occur. No one openly accused Elizabeth of making all of the noises and the ghost communications, but she had once been discovered knocking on a piece of wood she had hidden under her dress. So, just to prevent any trickery, the pastor had Elizabeth's bedclothes searched. There's no report whether anything out of the ordinary was found, but no rappings were heard in the clergyman's household that night, and, needless to say, the ghost also didn't appear in the vault the next morning, nor were there any knockings on the coffin.

But that wasn't enough evidence of fraud for some people. Kent was dragged in front of the coffin so that Fanny's ghost could accuse him directly. Still, no knocking was heard. But, rumors die hard. Someone suggested that the reason the ghost wasn't making any noise was because the coffin was empty. Someone must have stolen the body! So, the coffin was opened and what was left of poor Fanny was still there for all to see.

Ghostly Pursuits

According to local legend, some years after the Cock Lane incident, a man named J.W. Archer visited Saint John's Church, entered the crypt, and opened the coffin said to be that of Miss Fanny. By the light of a lantern, the corpse still seemed perfectly preserved. Archer noted that there were no smallpox scars on the flesh. Could some ingredients in a poison have helped preserve the body? Perhaps we'll never know the whole story unless Miss Fanny comes back a-knocking.

Kent reacted by suing Parsons, his wife, daughter, and several others for defamation. The trial was held on July 10, 1762, and the judge Lord Chief Justice Mansfield found in favor of Kent on all counts. In addition to monetary restitution, Parsons was sentenced to stand in the public pillory, then be imprisoned for two years.

Why had the people of Cock Lane been so slow to suspect Elizabeth? Even though she'd been caught in the act, as they say, most people didn't think that isolated incident could explain all of the rappings and scratching sounds they had heard. Or, perhaps they just wanted to believe in ghosts.

Frontispiece of a 1762 book detailing the "transactions and authentic testimonials respecting the supposed Cock-Lane Ghost."

T H E

MYSTERY REVEALED;

Containing a S E R I E S of

T R A N S A C T I O N S

A N D

AUTHENTIC TESTIMONIALS,

Refpecting the fuppofed

C o c k - L a n e G H O S T ;

Which have hitherto been concealed from the
P U B L I C.

—— Since none the Living dare implead,
Arraign him in the Perfon of the Dead.
DRYDEN.

L O N D O N:
Printed for W. BRISTOW, in St. Paul's Church-yard ;
and C. ETHRINGTON, York.
MDCCXLII.

Seeing Is Not Always Believing: The Cottingley Fairies

A naive and believing public can easily be fooled, even by their own eyes. In 1917 England, two little girls, Elsie Wright and her cousin Frances Griffiths, claimed that they had seen fairies in Cottingley Glen—and that they had taken the photographs to prove it! The fairies in the obviously faked photos were cut out of a popular children's book of the time, *Princess Mary's Gift Book,* and propped up for the camera.

Nevertheless, hundreds, possibly thousands, of people believed that the photographs were real. Among those duped was author Sir Arthur Conan Doyle, a devoted spiritualist and the creator of the oh-so-logical detective Sherlock Holmes. In later years, Elsie Wright said she never understood how so many people could have been fooled by their "little joke."

The story of the Cottingley Fairies was the subject of *Fairy Tale,* a 1997 film starring Peter O'Toole as Arthur Conan Doyle and Harvey Keitel as his friendly nemesis Harry Houdini.

One of the photographs taken by the girls of the Cottingley Fairies.

Why Resort to Fraud?

The reasons for fraud may be as varied (or individual) as those who perpetrate the deception. But here are some of the most common reasons:

- ➤ Attention
- ➤ Excitement
- ➤ Publicity
- ➤ Games, just for fun, especially children fooling their parents and friends
- ➤ To frighten people away from the area
- ➤ To destroy property values
- ➤ Money (the people who claim to be haunted may be planning to write a book about their experiences or sell their story)

Paranormal investigations will continue as long as people keep seeing ghosts. Fortunately, ghost hunters and ghostbusters are able to discover the natural causes for just about every sighting.

But, then, there are the others.

It's time for more than 100 pages of ghost stories—ghosts haunting houses and castles, battlefields and forts, theaters, schools, and libraries—well, you get the idea. Are you ready? That's the spirit!

The Least You Need to Know

➤ Frederic W.H. Myers and others suggested that ghosts are caused by telepathic projection by the deceased from the spirit world.

➤ Edmund Gurney suggested that collective apparitions were caused by the telepathic sharing of information from one medium to all of the other percipients (viewer).

➤ In theory, super-ESP is a powerful form of telepathy that allows mediums to create apparitions and obtain information about the deceased from the living.

➤ Fraud has been detected as the explanation for a great deal of spirit phenomena.

Part 4
Make Yourself at Home: The Hauntings

Here's what you've been waiting for: dozens of ghost stories to knock your socks off. You may not want to read these alone. And keep those lights turned up bright. I got goosebumply hearing and writing about these ghosts myself.

If you're a ghost-story addict, you've come to the right place. I've collected some of the most famous ghost tales in history, and I've thrown in lots more that are obscure but equally fascinating. After all, ghosts don't haunt only the big cities or famous places, like the Tower of London or the battlefields at Gettysburg. They might haunt a roadway that goes right by your door!

I've separated this enormous section into the types of places that ghosts haunt: houses, castles, churches and cemeteries, battlegrounds, theaters, roadways, schools, and many more. And, just for the fun of it, there's a whole chapter on Haunted Hollywood. Now, are you ready for your close-up?

Urban Legends

There was this young couple parked on lover's lane. The boy went out to check a strange noise and told his girlfriend not to leave the car. After a while, she started hearing a cracking on the roof of the car, but, terrified, she stayed put. Eventually, exhausted, she fell asleep. Police rescued her the next morning. As they ushered her into their squad car, she looked over her shoulder, and hanging from the tree over top of her car, his fingernails scraping the roof of the car, was …

Oh, you've heard this one before.

The paranormal world, too, is filled with such urban legends and folklore. These stories are passed down from one generation to the next. Like the many variations on the story of the hook-handed escapee from the mental institution or the dead boyfriend hanging from the tree—darn, did I spoil the surprise?—many ghost stories fall into genres.

Did you ever hear the one about …?

Going My Way? Phantom Travelers

Phantom travelers are ghosts of humans or even animals that haunt roads, way stations, or vehicles. They haunt a specific location, route, or type of transportation due to some tragedy or other strong emotional connection. Sometimes they're doomed to travel the route forever for committing some sin or transgression. (The story of the *Flying Dutchman,* which we'll look at in Chapter 20, "Trains and Boats and Planes," is a perfect example.)

Phantom Phrases

Phantom travelers are ghosts that haunt roadways or modes of transportation or are, for some reason, cursed to never-ending travel.

The earliest known recorded stories about phantom travelers date to around 1600 in Europe and Russia. The legends were certainly well-known in the United States by the time Washington Irving wrote his tale about a headless horseman in 1819 and 1820. (See Chapter 25, "Apparitions and the Arts.") Phantom travelers almost always seem solid and substantial—that is to say, real. They often appear from nowhere and can just as suddenly disappear.

Peter Rugg, Bound for Boston

A famous story of a phantom traveler forced to travel the earth is that of stubborn Peter Rugg of Boston. The tale was first told by a man named William Austin. In 1826, Austin was riding up front with the driver of a horse-drawn coach when they encountered a man, accompanied by a young girl, driving an open coach. As the coach sped by, Austin noticed that it seemed to be surrounded by storm clouds. As the coach passed, so did the clouds.

Austin's driver told him that he had seen the same coach many times before, driven by the same man, with the same girl as passenger, pursued by rain clouds. Rumor had it that the man occasionally stopped and asked for directions to Boston, but he never heeded the advice.

It was three years before Austin ran into Rugg again. Austin was standing on the front steps of a Connecticut hotel when Rugg, his coach, the girl, and the clouds approached. Austin flagged Rugg down and spoke with the man, who said that he was looking for Boston. Rugg refused to believe he was more than 100 miles away, and he took off in the opposite direction from what Austin told him.

The next time he was in Boston, Austin did a bit of detective work. He discovered that Peter Rugg's story was well known there. The bullheaded man had left his home on Middle Street in 1730 to take a trip with his daughter. On the way back, he visited a friend who warned him not to travel because of an impending storm. Rugg ignored the advice and headed homeward. He, his daughter, and his coach were never seen again.

The Mysterious Train Passenger

Phantom travelers were able to take longer trips on railways. Lord Halifax collected tales of British ghosts. In his 1936 work, *Lord Halifax's Ghost Book* (Geoffrey Bles, Ltd.), he tells the story of a Colonel Ewart who awoke in his train compartment to find a woman sitting opposite him. She was veiled and dressed all in black. She sat, as if holding a baby, rocking and humming a lullaby to her empty arms.

The train came to a screeching halt, and Ewart was knocked unconscious by a falling suitcase. After he awoke, he left his compartment to check on the condition of the train. Then he remembered the mysterious woman. She was gone. When he told a conductor his story, the railman said that she was a well-known ghost passenger who haunted the line.

Legend had it that just after she was married, the woman and her new husband were departing by train on their honeymoon. The husband leaned too far out the window and was decapitated by a wire. The head fell into the woman's lap. When the train arrived in London, she was discovered in the compartment, insane, cradling her husband's head in her arms as if it were a baby. She died shortly thereafter and had been haunting that particular railway line ever since.

Phantom Travelers of Heathrow Airport

There's a well-known phantom traveler who has haunted Runway 2-8 at London's Heathrow airport since 1948. He died when the plane he was on (a small Sabena Belgian Airways craft) crashed, killing all 22 aboard. He made his first visit almost immediately, appearing in his now-trademark dark suit and bowler hat. He walked through the fog and asked one of the rescue workers whether they had found his briefcase. A different ghost, dressed in a light gray suit, haunts the VIP lounges at Heathrow. The circumstances of his death and his reason for haunting the airport are unknown.

Stick Out Your Thumb: Phantom Hitchhikers

The phantom hitchhiker is the best-known type of phantom traveler and probably the single most popular type of ghost legend. Such stories probably originated in Europe, and they were well-established in the United States before the end of the 19th century.

In most variations of the story, the phantom hitchhiker is a girl or young woman—a damsel in distress—who is seen by a male driver, late at night along a remote stretch of highway. She suddenly appears in the headlights, usually dressed in white. Often she is soaking wet, even if it's not raining or there is no body of water nearby.

The driver stops and asks if he can help or can offer her a ride. She tells him where she's going: It's always to the town or destination that he's heading. He offers to take her directly to the address she gives. Sometimes she gives her name. She quietly gets into the back seat. He may give her his coat to wear to warm her. He constantly checks his rearview mirror, noticing how beautiful she is.

Ghostly Pursuits

A classic phantom traveler story involving an automobile is that of a person (who is actually an apparition) suddenly appearing in the middle of a roadway. A speeding driver sees the person too late, swerves to avoid an accident, and winds up crashing the car instead. When the driver checks the road, there is no one there. Or, the driver actually hits the person standing in the road. The driver usually hears and feels the impact. But when the driver stops to check under the vehicle, there's no one there, nor are there any marks on the vehicle.

When they reach her destination, he stops the car and turns to discover that the back seat is empty. The girl is gone. The seat is still damp, or there may be a puddle of water on the floor. Sometimes she leaves behind some object, such as a scarf or a book.

The driver goes to the door of the house where he's stopped and is greeted by a woman, or sometimes a man and wife. They tell him that this has often happened before—in fact, every year. It's the anniversary of their daughter's death. She was either murdered or died in an accident at the location where the driver first saw her. Every year, on that date, the girl tries to make it home, but she never succeeds. The disbelieving driver is shown a photograph of their daughter. It is, indeed, the woman he helped, wearing the same clothing. And here's the kicker: The man later visits her grave, and, if she disappeared wearing his jacket, it's draped over the tombstone.

Ooooo! Spooky!

Can You Give Me a Lift to the Cemetery?

The most famous phantom hitchhiker known by name is Resurrection Mary, who haunts the town of Justice, a suburb of Chicago. She takes her name from the district's Resurrection Cemetery, where she is thought to be buried. (There is no definite record of anyone having been buried there that matches her name and description. The closest in age is a young Polish woman named Mary, but there are no further details in the cemetery register.) Mary is most often described as a beautiful blonde with blue eyes and dressed in white.

According to legend, Mary was killed in 1934 in a car accident after an evening of dancing at the O. Henry Ballroom (later the Willowbrook Ballroom). Her ghost began appearing around 1939, appearing in front of an oncoming car in the middle of the road or jumping onto its side running board. The ghost would ask to be taken to the

O. Henry, where she would dance all night. Then, at closing time, she would catch a ride with a stranger traveling down Archer Road, back toward Resurrection Cemetery.

Usually Mary would disappear from the car as it neared or passed the cemetery. Sometimes the driver would stop, she would get out of the car, and then vanish as she melted through the closed gates of the cemetery.

Resurrection Mary has also been seen standing inside the cemetery. There were an especially large number of sightings while the cemetery was being renovated in the 1970s. Since that time, she has been sighted all over the Chicago area, but she always returns to Resurrection Cemetery.

In the past two decades, there have been varied reports of phantom hitchhikers attached to other cemeteries. For example, in the 1980s the ghost of a young brunette girl, tangible enough to be mistaken as being corporeal, was frequently seen hitchhiking rides in the area of the Evergreen Cemetery in west Chicago, where she is believed to be buried. One time, she even boarded a CTA bus headed for downtown. When the driver approached her for payment, she disappeared right before his eyes.

Boo!

Remember how your parents always warned you not to pick up strangers in your car? They might be axe murderers? I don't know which would be worse—being chopped to death or scared to death! If you see a female hitchhiker near a cemetery outside Chicago, you might want to think twice before you offer her a ride. It might be Resurrection Mary.

You're Giving Me Gray Hair!

Gray ladies are ghosts of women who have died for their love. Either they have pined away while waiting for their beloved to appear (or, more usually, to return), or they've died violently, often as a result of their love. They're called gray ladies because they usually appear dressed in gray; however, some gray ladies are seen wearing black, brown, or even white. The gray also refers to their emotional state.

Here are just three famous hauntings of gray ladies in Great Britain:

➤ Speke Hall near Liverpool is haunted by the ghost of Mary Norris, who died in the late 1600s. Distraught in her loveless marriage to Lord Sidney Beauclerk, she drowned herself and her baby son Topham in the moat. Her spectre is seen rocking the baby's cradle in the castle's tapestry room.

➤ Rufford Old Hall, a 15th-century house just a few miles from Speke Hall, is haunted by a

Phantom Phrases

A **gray lady** is the ghost of a woman who has died at the hands of her lover or while waiting for her love to appear or come back from afar. They are so-named because they usually appear dressed in gray and have mournful expressions.

gray lady and her husband. Though newly married, he departed for war and never returned. She died of despair shortly thereafter. On her deathbed, she swore to remain in the house until her soldier husband comes back to her.

➤ Heskin Hall, near Blackburn, acted as a hideout for Catholic priests during the English Civil War (1642–1649). A priest, discovered there by Oliver Cromwell's Roundheads, saved his own life by proving his devotion to the Puritans (rather than his own faith): He hanged the Catholic daughter of the owners (in front of them). The girl's phantom and its attendant rappings haunt the manse's Scarlet Room.

The reason that a gray lady returns to haunt the world of the living is simple: She's still hoping to be united with the person she loves. The apparition is often attended by poltergeist-like activity, such as objects moving by themselves, knocking, and rapping. Gray ladies have been reported all over the world, but the majority of sightings have been in England.

Ghostbusting

Even in modern-day Mexico, some parents use the legend to scare their children into behaving. For example, if the children are rowdy at bedtime, the mother might tell them to settle down or La Llorona will come for them!

Ghosts from Around the World

Many ghosts are specific to a particular country or culture. Jack-in-Irons, for example, is a British folkloric figure, a variation on phantom traveler legends. He only haunts deserted roads around Yorkshire, England. The ghost is tall, evil-looking, and, as his name suggests, wrapped in chains. He leaps out into the path of oncoming travelers simply to scare them; otherwise, he does them no harm.

Ghostly Pursuits

Jack-in-Irons is unusual in that few ghosts are actually seen bound in chains, despite the popular depiction in arts and literature. Perhaps the earliest recorded example of a ghost accompanied by the sounds of chains is the one that haunted Athenodorus (see Chapter 2, "In the Beginning: The First Famous Phantoms"). Probably the most famous example of a chains-encumbered phantom is Marley's ghost in Charles Dickens's *A Christmas Carol*.

Jimmy Squarefoot can also be found in English folklore, and he's said to haunt the Isle of Man. He's a ghost with a man's body and a pig's head. However, he also has tusks, like a wild boar. He grew the porcine features after his wife left him for throwing stones at her. He seems to have kept them now that he's a ghost.

The legend of Jimmy Squarefoot probably derives from an older story about an enormous pig, also named Squarefoot, which was carried about by a giant who threw stones. (Interestingly, in spirit lore, stone-throwing is one of the most common activities of poltergeists. See Chapter 5, "Poltergeists: They're Here!")

La Llorona is a ghost figure of Mexican and Mexican-American cultures. She's always seen as a weeping woman. According to folklore, while alive La Llorona was a woman who had several children, but she fell in love with a man who didn't want a family. In order to stand by her man, she drowned her own children. But then, overcome with grief and guilt, she killed herself. She's seen at night, usually along a river, a forest, or a deserted road, crying and looking for her lost children.

There are many variations to the La Llorona story. In some, she simply murdered her children and is doomed to be a ghost in eternity for her sins. In other versions of the tale, La Llorona behaves like a phantom hitchhiker. A man sees a weeping woman on a deserted road. He gives her a ride, then she vanishes from the car.

La Llorona is usually dressed all in black, but she is sometimes seen in white. She usually has long black hair and long fingernails. Most men would consider her sexy or at least seductive. But she has a dark side: To some, she appears without a face, or with the face of a bat or a horse.

Easter Island, famous for its giant basalt sculptures of rough heads and torsos (called *moai*, meaning "statue"), lies 2,200 miles off the coast of Chile. According to tradition, the ancient King Tuu-ko-ihu, who ruled sometime after A.D. 450, saw two *aku aku* (or "sleeping ghosts") in Puna Pau, one of the island's stone quarries. The ghosts had beards, long hooked noses, and earlobes that reached down to their necks. Their ribs stuck out so much that they looked emaciated. Tuu-ko-ihu knew that disturbing ghosts might make them angry, so he

Boo!

See what comes of throwing stones—especially at your wife? If you want to go through life with a pig's head and the tusks of a boar, well, let it be on your head (if you'll pardon the expression). Regardless, you shouldn't throw stones: Someone's just liable to throw them back!

Boo!

To some, La Llorona is a death omen: Anyone who sees her will die within a year. In less extreme versions of the tale, the percipient will merely have bad luck for a year. So, if you meet a mysterious sobbing woman dressed all in black down some back road in the middle of nowhere, be careful. That unearthly encounter could be your last.

crept away and hurried home. To remember what the ghosts looked like, the king immediately carved wooden sculptures of them. Ever since, islanders have carved *moai kavakava* (or "statue of ribs"), as small wooden replicas are called. Because of their unique look, kavakava are popular craft souvenirs among tourists.

A moai kavakava, or "statue of ribs," portraying the aku aku, *or "sleeping ghosts," of Easter Island. (Photo by author)*

Ghostly Pursuits

Czech composer Anton Dvořák's eighth opera is titled *Rusalka*. It premiered at the National Theater in Prague on March 31, 1901. (Its U.S. debut wasn't until March 10, 1935, in Chicago.) Although *Rusalka* is about a water nymph, its libretto more closely follows the legend of "The Little Mermaid," in which a naiad trades her soul to a witch in order to be able to join her mortal beloved on dry land.

In Russian folklore, Rusalka is the ghost of a virginal lass who drowns, either by accident or by violence, and is fated to haunt the spot of her death for eternity.

In most versions of stories about Rusalki (as the plural is known), the spectres are benevolent water nymphs. But, like a siren, Rusalka is so beautiful and bewitching that she may inadvertently (or sometimes deliberately) entice a young man to join her, entering the waters to his doom.

Mirror, Mirror, on the Wall ...

One of the most unusual types of apparitional manifestation is the appearance of a phantom's face or figure in a mirror. The concept of a haunted mirror is legendary. Perhaps the best-known example of a spirit-infested mirror is the one belonging to the Evil Queen in the story of Snow White and the Seven Dwarfs.

Apparitions have also been seen on other types of shiny or reflective surfaces, such as tabletops, and on wooden wardrobes and cabinets. Interestingly, there don't seem to be many reports of ghost reflections appearing on windowpanes, although seeing an apparition through the window (that is, from the other side) is common.

The concept of ghosts appearing in mirrors is closely associated with the practice of *scrying*, foretelling the future by consulting a shiny surface. A modern form of scrying would be peering into a crystal ball. In ancient times, wizards and seers peered into the shimmering surface of water.

Phantom Phrases

Scrying is a form of fortune-telling in which the seer sees visions of the future while gazing into a mirror, into a crystal (or crystal ball), onto a bowl of water, or at some other shiny surface.

A good example of a haunted mirror can be found in the St. Mathias Mission House in Huntington Park, California. The home was once occupied by an old couple who eventually died there. Several people have reported seeing an elderly person reflected in the mirror that hangs in what used to be their living room. Footsteps, moans, falling objects, and lights that turn themselves on and off have also been reported in the old mission.

While in Buenos Aires recently, I met a well-educated, non-superstitious woman who was attached to the U.S. Embassy, and, somehow, the subject came around to ghosts. She became quite agitated and confided that she owned a haunted mirror. It had belonged to her grandmother, and when she inherited it, she proudly hung the large mirror in her home.

At first, the woman would sometimes glimpse the figure of an elderly woman reflected in the mirror as she passed by. But sometimes she would see the unmistakable face of her grandmother peering out at her. The ghost didn't try to communicate with her in any way and expressed no emotion—neither happiness, sorrow, nor pain.

Well, the granddaughter freaked! Her first thought was to smash the mirror, but what if her grandmother's spirit was trapped in there and smashing the glass would some-how extinguish it? Or what if the mirror were some sort of portal between the worlds of the living and the dearly departed? And she couldn't sell the mirror: Sell her grandmother to a stranger? But she couldn't take having the mirror hanging in her house. It was just too creepy! So, she carefully and lovingly wrapped up the haunted mirror and placed it in storage, where it remains today.

Images of the Virgin Mary

Just before Christmas 1996, a strange, multi-colored image suddenly appeared on the mirrored windows of an office building in Clearwater, Florida. This highly publicized *Marian apparition*, which I've actually seen, spreads across several panes of glass, encompassing an area about 50 feet high by 35 feet wide. The image does indeed resemble a hooded figure whose head is surrounded by a halo or glow.

The Marian apparition in Clearwater, Florida. (Photo by Norman Deery)

Scientific consultants haven't been able to give a definitive answer as to the cause of the image. Because the stain wasn't noticed until palm trees covering the glass were trimmed, some experts thought the moving fronds shaped the curved image. Others suggested that the iridescent colors and swirls are a result of imperfections in the glass.

Still others say that the streaks were made by some bizarre combination of mineral deposits from rainwater, water sprinklers, and glass cleaners—despite the fact that no amount of washing has been able to remove the image.

Ghostly Pursuits

If you're in the area seeing the Marian apparition, you might want to visit two more weird (non-ghost) sites on the west Florida coast. In the 1940s and 1950s, an unidentifiable creature emerged from the sea onto Indian Rocks Beach in Clearwater, as well as nearby Dan's Island, Honeymoon Island, and Tarpon Springs. Those who saw it described the beast as walking on its hind legs, having a eight-foot stride, and a crocodilian head with sharp teeth. It left behind three-toed footprints. During excavation for Leverock's Restaurant in New Port Richey, a prehistoric altar covered with carved faces was discovered. The stone, probably used by Timucuan priests about A.D. 1 to make offerings to the gods, is on display at the restaurant.

It's estimated that since the appearance of the image of the Blessed Virgin Mary (or perhaps Jesus, as some claim), more than two million people have visited the site, causing the building's then owner (Mike Krizman-ich) and the Clearwater city council to convert the building's parking lot into a makeshift shrine. An unknown vandal damaged the Marian image in 1997, perhaps with the use of a chemical spray, but the Marian apparition is still plainly visible.

Apparitions of the Virgin Mary have been appearing for centuries, but only a few have been authenticated by the Catholic Church. Usually she appears in ghost-like form and identifies herself to the percipient(s). Usually, she brings a simple message of love and asks humankind to pray, be more faithful, and/or built a church or shrine dedicated to her on the site. The vision is often accompanied by other paranormal phenomena, such as heavenly music and angelic singing. After the sightings, miraculous healings often occur on the sites.

Boo!

If you want to see the Marian apparition in Florida for yourself, it's located on Highway 19, about half-way between Clearwater and New Port Richey (they're 19 miles apart) on the east side of the road. To study it, pull off the road or, better still, into the office building's parking-lot-cum-shrine. You don't want to be rear-ended while you're slowing down to gawking at the mysterious image.

View of Marian apparition in Clearwater, Florida. Part of the parking lot set aside for visitors as a shrine and viewing area can be seen. (Photo by Norman Deery)

According to Church doctrine, apparitions of ecclesiastical figures, such as Mary or the saints, are not ghosts; rather, they are special religious phenomena allowed by God. The best-known Marian apparitions are:

➤ Five appearances to Juan Diego in Guadalupe, Mexico, in 1531.

➤ Eighteen appearances to Bernadette Soubirous in a grotto along the Gave du Pau river outside Lourdes, from February 11 to July 16, 1858.

➤ Following three appearances of an entity identifying itself as the Angel of Portugal, Mary herself appeared to three young children. She visited them at the same hour and day for six more consecutive months. More than 50,000 people attended the final sighting on October 13, 1917. All but one of the visits occurred at a field called Cova da Iria in the parish of Fatima, north of Lisbon, Portugal.

Those Glowing Spectral Lights

In Chapter 4, "Something Wicked This Way Comes," we looked at ignis fatuus, spectral lights that folklorists believe are actually souls of the dead. There are other forms of ghost lights seen all over the world, however, that are generally not thought to be spirits.

These spectral lights are usually seen as ball-shaped or irregular, glowing patches. They are most often white or yellow, but some are red, orange, or blue. Although circumstances of their appearances differ from place to place, ghost lights almost always occur in remote areas. They can only be seen from certain angles or distances, and, if pursued, they can't be reached.

Paranormal skeptics suggest that the lights may be car headlights, swamp gas, phosphorescent gas, or other reflected or refracted light. Perhaps because there has been no definitive natural explanation, for them, the unusual luminous phenomena have caught the attention of ghost hunters.

The most famous examples of ghost lights include:

➤ Marfa lights, named for their appearance outside Marfa, Texas. They were first reported in 1883 by Robert Ellison. Spectral lights are also regularly seen in Anson and Abilene, Texas.

➤ Joplin lights, near Joplin, Missouri. They're visible almost every night from dusk until dawn.

➤ Brown Mountain lights, in the Brown Mountains (especially in Linville Gorge) near Morgan, North Carolina. They've been reported since 1913. Legends associated with the Brown Mountain lights say that they are the spirit of a Native American maiden seeking her brave or a slave searching for his master.

Ghost lights are not ghosts, per se, but they often appear in connection with ghost legends. Also, balls of light have been reported at places that are haunted by ghosts.

Luminescence is not limited to spirit lights. Although infrequent, there have been reports of apparitions appearing to glow. Phantoms sometimes appear within a disk or circle of light.

Ghostly Pursuits

Circles of light have been reported escaping the body at the moment of death. In 1907, Dr. Hippolyte Baraduc produced supposed photographic evidence of astral lights leaving the body of his recently deceased son. Six months later, the doctor's wife died, and he photographed globular mists and streaks of light departing her body almost immediately after her death. Even though the photographs themselves are suspect, his descriptions of the phenomenon match numerous accounts by people who've reported seeing mists and luminescence being emitted from a dying person's body.

Of course, luminous patches and shapes were also common manifestations in séances. Spirit faces often appeared bathed in low light. For the skeptic, however, the light was a necessary part of some spirit manifestations, since almost all séances were conducted in dim lights or darkness.

Screaming Skulls

Here's a weird one. Ghosts living in—or acting through—skulls, haunt a number of places, most of them in England. The skull, once placed in the house, seems to become comfy with its surroundings. Any attempt to remove the skull from the house, even to bury it in its rightful grave, results in loud screaming from the skull. Many times, poltergeist-like activity, such as bangs and thumping noises, accompany the screaming.

Some of the skulls belong to people who were, in some way, attached to the house during their lifetimes. Most of the people died by murder or some other violent means.

The two most famous screaming skulls are located at Wardley Hall, outside Manchester, England, and at Bettiscombe Manor, outside Dorset, England. According to legend, the Wardley Hall skull supposedly comes from the skeleton of Roger Downes, whose family owned the manor in the mid-17th century. Downes was decapitated during a sword fight on London Bridge, and his head was sent back home. All attempts to remove the skull from the home for burial resulted in screams as well as destructive paranormal activity.

The Bettiscombe skull is said to be that of a slave at the manor who, depending on the version of the story you hear, was either murdered or a murderer. In either case, after the slave's death, his corpse began screaming from its grave. The slave's body was disinterred so that it could be sent back to his native West Indies, but, again, the corpse screamed in protest. Eventually, all bones were lost but the skull, which currently sits near a staircase in Bettiscombe Manor.

Other lesser-known British screaming skulls are kept at Burton Agnes in North Yorkshire and at Tunstead Farm near Chapel-en-le-Frith.

Burton Agnes, built in 1598, was home to the Griffith family. Anne, one of the daughters living there, was struck by robbers nearby, and she died five days later. Her death wish was that her head be entombed in Burton Agnes. Instead, she was buried, her body intact, in the parish graveyard. Soon, odd sounds started coming from the grave. Her coffin was unearthed and opened: Her now-severed skull seemed to be smiling! The skull was moved to Burton Agnes, and all the noises stopped. Years later, the house was inherited by the Boynton family, who removed the skull. Again, the skull started screaming, so the owners reluctantly allowed it back into the house. The screeching stopped. A later owner of Burton Agnes walled up the skull somewhere within the house, where it presumably remains today.

A damaged skull, nicknamed "Dickie," is kept at Tunstead Farm. According to legend, noises emit from the skull when strangers come to the house, when a farm animal falls sick, or when a family member is about to die. Like its fellow screaming skulls, Dickie screeches if anyone tries to remove it from the house. Tunstead Farm also has its share of ghost stories: It's said that, far in the past, a girl was murdered in the room where Dickie is now kept. Another tale says that it was Ned Dixon, an ancestor of one of the farm's owners, who was murdered there. Also, in the 1800s, a female ghost supposedly appeared in the house as a death omen: Soon after the apparition was sighted, the tenant's daughter died.

Hi, How Are You; I'm Dead

Since the beginning of the electronic age, messages from the dead have been received from every form of communications device. Voices have come through telegraph and wireless, phonograph records, and loudspeakers. So many spirit voices have been heard coming over the radio that the paranormal activity's been given a name: *radio voice phenomena,* or *RVP.* The term *electronic voice phenomena (EVP)* is usually reserved for ghost voices picked up on magnetic (audio) tape.

Phone calls from the dead must be among the most shocking type of ghost phenomena possible. Imagine hearing the phone ring, picking up the receiver, and hearing the voice of someone you love whom you know to be dead!

Phantom Phrases

Radio voice phenomenon (RVP) is the reception of the voice of someone who's deceased through the speakers of an ordinary radio. Technically, it's a form of **electronic voice phenomenon (EVP)**, but this latter time is usually reserved for non-audible ghost voices recorded on tape.

Such calls been reported time and again. The calls generally have several similarities:

➤ The recipient of the call is tranquil or relaxed when the call arrives, and after the initial shock, the call is soothing rather than disturbing and stressful.

➤ The voice of the deceased sounds exactly the same as when the person was alive, although it may sound distant, progressively fading, or mixed with other voices in the background (as if wires were crossed).

➤ The call is usually brief—a few seconds to a few minutes—although some have been reported as lasting up to a half-hour. At the end of the call, the spirit may hang up, or the line may simply go dead.

➤ Most phone messages from the dead have a purpose: to impart information, to make a warning, or to say goodbye.

➤ Many occur on emotionally laden days, such as birthdays, Mother's Day, or the anniversary of the death.

➤ Most occur within 24 hours of the death of the person. Short calls usually come from people who have been dead less than a week; people who have been dead longer generally make lengthier calls. (I guess they have more to catch up on.) The longest recorded interval between a death and the receipt of a phone call from the deceased has been two years.

Phone calls have also been made from the living to the dead. People have reported calling and talking to someone whom they later discover was already dead by the time they chatted. A very few phone calls from the dead actually arrive person-to-person. Upon later investigation, it's discovered that the telephone company has no record of any of their operators having placed the call. Occasionally, spirit phones calls come from a stranger on behalf of a third party.

The current most popular explanations for phone calls from the dead are:

➤ They really *do* come from the dead.

➤ They're a prank or bad joke, although some think it may be a playful spirit and not a human being pulling the gag.

➤ The whole experience, including the telephone ringing and the recognition of the voice, is hallucinatory or produced by the subconscious.

There you have it: all sorts of ghosts and spirits whose appearances are so common that their stories have entered the realm of urban legends. It's impossible today to tell when the stories began, but it's certain that more, similar tales—and sightings—will be told in the future.

Let's do a ghost-hunter's Rorschach test. What's the first thing you think of when I say "ghost"? How many of you said "haunted houses"? Well, that's what's coming up next: tale after tale of haunted houses found throughout America. Flashlights ready? Let's step inside.

The Least You Need to Know

➤ Every culture has its unique ghost legends.

➤ Some ghost legends, such as the phantom traveler, magic mirrors, and spirit lights, transcend countries and civilizations.

➤ Apparitions of the Virgin Mary are a unique form of spirit phenomena.

➤ Ghost communications have been received through every form of electronic device. The most recent are phone calls from (and to) the dead.

Chapter 14

This Old House: Haunted America

In This Chapter

➤ America's haunted houses, region by region

➤ America's most haunted cities: Chicago, New Orleans, and Charleston

➤ Ghosts "living" in the nation's capital

➤ Abraham Lincoln, the White House's busiest phantom

Most people picture ghosts as "living" in haunted houses. They see a haunted house as being an old, boarded-up mansion. Sometimes a mysterious or unusual style of architecture is enough to have a house branded as being haunted: Perhaps it's one of those old New Englanders with a widow's walk and towering gables, or maybe a dusty Victorian manor with huge staircases and ancient oil portraits lining the halls.

The majority of houses that are reported as haunted, however, do not fit any of these stereotypes. True, most are old; many have what might be called a "history." But many have been renovated and are occupied—by the spectres alongside their human hosts. For most, it's an acceptable, if unusual, arrangement in cohabitation!

America the Haunted

The United States has more than its share of haunted houses. They can be found in every state in the Union, and they're located in the largest cities as well as the smallest villages.

In many towns, ghost tours have been set up to allow guests to visit haunted hideaways (see Appendix B, "Continuing the Ghost Hunt"). Some cities, such as Chicago, New Orleans, Charleston, and Washington, D.C., seem to be especially haunted. And there is so much legend and lore surrounding the glamorous and celebrity ghosts of Hollywood that I devote a separate chapter to it (see Chapter 22, "Haunted Hollywood").

There are numerous books available on haunted houses and other ghostly sites: One online book store lists more than 250 titles! Most books concentrate on specific regions or cities. There's even a national directory that lists more than 2,000 places, detailed state-by-state, where (according to the author) "events occur beyond our ability to explain them" (see Appendix D, "Haunted Places in the U.S. and Great Britain").

Later chapters in this book will deal with hauntings in different types of venues. In the meantime, here's a sampling of some of my favorite haunted houses found in the old U.S. of A.

Boo!

Remember, many of the sites mentioned throughout this book, even some haunted houses, are private residences. Never trespass on private property without the express permission of the owners or residents. Even when viewing a site from the road, be aware of possible loitering, trespassing, or invasion of privacy violations.

Haunted Houses of the East

The eastern seaboard, especially the Northeast, is the site of frequent apparitional activity. Perhaps the phantoms haunt the area out of a sense of history. People were living—and dying—in this part of the country long before the settlements out West. Here are some of the former residents who have never been able to pull themselves away from the East Coast!

Edgar Allan Poe House

The Baltimore, Maryland, home of the mystery and horror author Edgar Allan Poe is reportedly haunted, but not by Poe himself. Poe lived there from 1832 to 1835 with his grandmother Elizabeth Poe, his aunt Maria Clemm, and his cousin (and later his wife) Virginia Clemm. Elizabeth died there in 1835. The house changed hands many times during the next hundred years. It remained empty from 1922 to 1949. Since then it has been a museum, open to the public.

Phantom Phrases

In metaphysical jargon, a **sensitive** is someone who is aware of (that is, sensitive to) or can feel paranormal presences that cannot be picked up by the normal five senses. A sensitive may or may not be a mediums as well.

In the 1960s, visitors began reporting strange goings-on, especially in what were Virginia's bedroom and Poe's room in the attic. Spectral activity includes guests being tapped on their shoulders by invisible hands, voices, sounds, lights going on when no one is inside, and windows that open and close by themselves. Some *sensitives* have reported seeing the ghost of an elderly, overweight, gray-haired lady, dressed in gray 19th-century clothing, but no identification of the phantom has ever been made.

The Mount

The country home of author Edith Wharton (1862–1937), in Lenox, Massachusetts, is said to be haunted by several ghosts. Wharton built the neo-Georgian mansion between 1900 and 1902, moved out in 1908, and sold the property in 1912. Later it became Foxhollow School for Girls. The Mount is currently owned by an acting troupe, Shakespeare and Company and Co., which performed plays and opens the house to tourists in the summer months.

Visitors in the house have heard unexplained thumps, footsteps, and girlish laughter. Apparitions have been seen both day and night. A female ghost was seen alone, and at another time with a male ghost; they were later identified as Edith Wharton and author Henry James (a frequent guest in the house). The spectre of a pony-tailed man (James?) has been glimpsed in the Henry James Room, and a phantom thought to be Wharton has been seen walking the terrace. An unidentified man, in a cloak and hood, has appeared at bedsides, pressing down on the person in bed. The ghost of Edith's husband, Edward, among other phantoms, has also been reported.

Chase Home

Built in Portsmouth, New Hampshire, in the late 19th century, the Chase Home became an orphanage. For the past few decades, it has been a court-appointed children's home. Its spectral phenomena and apparitions include the following:

➤ Locked doors unlock themselves.

➤ Screams of a young girl are sometimes heard in the dormitory at night.

➤ Footsteps are heard walking and running on the vacant third floor (which at one time housed counselors).

➤ The ghost of a young girl who hanged herself in her dormitory is sometimes seen in the hallway of the dorm at night. When approached, she runs down the hall, then disappears.

Boo!

Sometimes it's better not to kid around with curses! It's said that anyone who sits in Amelia's chair at Baleroy will die within a year. So far, four deaths have been attributed to the curse coming true!

Ghostly Pursuits

Pennsylvania played a pivotal role in colonial and Civil War–era America. It only makes sense that ghosts haunt this Keystone state. There are at least three haunted mansions in Philadelphia, Pennsylvania:

➤ **Baleroy.** This splendidly restored and furnished mansion, owned by descendants of Civil War general George Meade (whose possessions, along with some of Napoleon's, decorate the house), is haunted. The ghost of Thomas Jefferson has appeared standing by a large clock in the dining room. A monk dressed in a brown habit has been seen in the master bedroom on the second floor, and a cranky, old woman with a cane has been spotted in the second floor hallway. A 200-year old wing chair located in the Blue Room is cursed: Only the ghost of a women named Amelia is allowed to sit in it on pain of death! There's even an unexplainable cold spot in the corridor between the Reception Room and the Blue Room. Still more ghosts have materialized at séances held at Baleroy over the years.

➤ **Bolton Mansion.** The beautiful building is a private residence at 84 Holly Drive in Levittown, a Philadelphia suburb. Visitors to the property have reported seeing the ghost of a woman outside the building, seemingly searching for something (or someone). The spectre of a little girl has been reported inside the mansion, darting from window to window, and looking outside. The two phantoms haven't been identified, but it's thought (although there is no factual evidence) that they may be related and, possibly, looking for each other.

➤ **Penn Rynn Manor.** Formerly the Biddle estate, Penn Rynn Manor is located on the Delaware River. The two ghosts reported haunting the grounds have been of a woman riding a white horse and a young man accompanying her from the house down to the river bank. According to legend, the son of the original owners fell in love with a maid. When the parents objected, the young couple committed suicide by drowning themselves in the river.

Farnsworth House Inn

Many ghosts reportedly haunt this inn located in Gettysburg, Pennsylvania, including:

➤ Mary, a Civil War-era phantom, who walks the halls at night

➤ Three Confederate sharpshooters at their post in the attic

➤ Another soldier, singing to still his wounded comrade, as he carries him to the basement to die

➤ A man carrying a child wrapped in a quilt (you can also hear him crying in a room upstairs)

➤ A midwife huddled over a woman in labor

Other spectral phenomena include cold spots throughout the inn. White balls of energy or "auras" have also been photographed. The Farnsworth House Inn has been investigated by psychic Carol Kirkpatrick and Ghost Hunters International, among others. The house has also been featured on TV's *Sightings* (Sci-Fi Channel) and *Unsolved Mysteries*.

Haunted Houses of the West

From the Southwest to the Pacific Northwest, ghosts are doing big business. Here are just a few representative manifestions to be found in the West.

McLoughlin House

John D. McLoughlin (1784–1857), "the Father of Oregon," was born in Quebec and had a early successful career as a physician for the Hudson's Bay Company. He acted as a company manager for their land interests in what is today Vancouver, Canada. In 1829, he moved his band of settlers south and founded Oregon City, Oregon.

His home, luxurious in comparison to his contemporaries, became a center for the town's business and social life. In a bitter legal battle with the U.S. government, McLoughlin lost the title to his property because he was Canadian. Ironically, the settlers he led were allowed to keep their claims.

After the death of McLoughlin, the home housed Chinese laborers and was, for a time, a bordello. In 1909 it was moved to a prestigious site on a hill overlooking the city, and it was refurbished as a public museum in the 1930s. The graves of McLoughlin and his wife were moved onto the new property in 1970.

Ghostly activity didn't start in the house until the mid-1970s, when Nancy Wilson became curator for the home and museum. The first phenomenon she experienced was a tap on the shoulder from an invisible hand. Soon, she and other employees were seeing the apparition of a large shadow

> **Ghostbusting**
>
> Ghostly manifestations and/or poltergeist activity starting after the arrival of a particular individual is not unusual. In Nancy Wilson's case, she discovered that among her ancestors is a Wells family that arrived in Oregon City in 1842. After Mr. Wells died, McLoughlin gave financial aid to Wells's widow and children. Wilson feels that perhaps McLoughlin is returning to collect the debt, or maybe to thank the community for restoring both his home and his good reputation.

(approximately the size of McLoughlin) moving along the upstairs hall and into the master bedroom. Other paranormal activity included:

➤ Footsteps

➤ The scent of pipe tobacco and coffee

➤ Hanging objects swaying without wind

➤ A child's bed being mysteriously disheveled overnight

➤ A rocking chair that rocked by itself

Physical manifestations stopped in the mid-1980s, but staff and visitors still report feeling the unseen but benign presence of McLoughlin in the house.

Barclay House

The Barclay House, situated next to the McLoughlin House, was the residence of Dr. Forbes Barclay. It, too, is now a museum. Visitors to the house have seen the apparition of a small red-headed boy so real that one guide thought he was an intruder and summoned the police. A spectral black-and-white dog occasionally leaves behind paw prints. A third resident ghost is said to be "Uncle Sandy," a brother of Forbes. He usually appeared in his old bedroom, standing next to the bed, especially when an overnight guest was staying there. So far, Forbes himself has yet to make an appearance.

Old Mill and the McCune Mansion

The McCune Mansion, located in Salt Lake City, isn't haunted by apparitions, but cold spots and seemingly locked doors (although they have no locks) have been reported. The owner often sees the lights going on in the empty house as he drives away. The building is also used for receptions, but if the hall is prepared the night before, the setup is often found disturbed and disheveled in the morning.

The Left Coast

People can hardly resist the sun and sizzle of California when they're alive. No wonder so many of them want to stay here after they're dead! Here are just a few of California's famous phantoms.

Haskell House and the Pardee Home

The cold breezes of the City by the Bay must appeal to ghostly presences. Among the many haunted houses in San Francisco is the Haskell House. There, the ghost of Senator Broderick can be heard pacing back and forth. Across the bay in Oakland's Preservation Park Historic District is the Pardee Home, residence of George Pardee, who was California's governor from 1903 to 1907. There have been no apparitional sightings there, but spirit photographs in the house have captured lighted orbs. Similar spirit orbs have been photographed throughout the park.

Winchester House

Located in San Jose, the Winchester House is a 160-room Victorian-style mansion, built by Sarah Winchester beginning in 1884, to appease the spirits of those killed by the Winchester rifle. She was still building onto the house when she died almost 40 years later.

The Winchester House in San Jose, California. (Photo courtesy of Winchester Mystery House)

The Honorable Fisher Winchester, nicknamed the "Rifle King," manufactured the popular rifle which bore his name. Because it was so widely used during the taming of the West, a staggering number of deaths can be attributed to the gun.

In 1862, Sarah married William Wirt Winchester, the son of Fisher Winchester. She was interested in the paranormal but became even more so after the death of her only child, Annie Pardee, when the baby was a month old. Her husband died from tuberculosis just 15 months later, leaving her with a fortune of $20 million.

Sarah consulted a medium in Boston who told her the spirits of those who had been killed by the Winchester rifle wanted her to sell her home in New Haven, Connecticut, and move out West. There, she was to build a home large enough to house the spirits of the avenging dead. If not, the spirits said they would kill her.

In 1884, she purchased a large mansion under construction in California. She hired a huge staff of servants and gardeners and employed up to 20 carpenters at a time. Her plan was simple: She would continue to add on to the house to placate the spirits, yet build the rooms in confusing designs to make it impossible for them to find her. (She would change bedrooms every night, for example, to evade their grasp while she slept.)

As a result, rooms were built at odd angles, doors opened onto solid walls, and some rooms were sealed so that no one could enter. Often, she would change designs, or have a completed room rebuilt, to further confound the spirits. Likewise, her massive gardens included trails leading to nowhere and trees planted closely together that she could hide behind to spy on approaching phantoms.

Ghostbusting

Sarah seemingly became obsessed with the occult number 13: There were 13 bathrooms, 13 windows and doors in the sewing room, and a staircase of 13 steps that led to nowhere. Even her will was divided into 13 sections, and she signed it 13 times.

No expense was spared in furnishing the house. She purchased Tiffany lamps and Belgium crystal, and laid parquet floors of imported wood. Silver and gold were used in the chandeliers; doors were ornamented in German silver and bronze. The house also boasted numerous innovations, including push-button gas lamps, state-of-the-art heating and sewage systems, and elevators.

Sarah Winchester was especially proud of her grand ballroom, in which she played the piano or an organ each night (despite severe arthritis in her hands) so that the invisible ghosts could dance. She also entertained at dinner each night, setting (and serving) 12 empty places besides her own at the table. She personally descended to the wine cellar to choose each night's vintage, but, after seeing a black handprint on the door to the cellar one evening, she had it walled up forever.

Except for her eccentric behavior regarding her house and her belief in vengeful spirits, Sarah was as sane as you and I. (Hmmm …) She was kind and thoughtful, even generous, to her construction staff and servants, but she was a recluse, living alone, and usually stayed indoors. When she did leave her property, she stayed in her carriage or, later, her lavender-and-gold Pierce Arrow car. Always, she veiled her face in public. She died of natural causes in 1922.

Over the years, the Winchester House has acquired a reputation for being haunted. Witnesses have heard unexplainable footsteps and doors slamming. The house is filled with cold spots, and floating lights have been reported. Sometimes, lights turn on or doors become unlocked by themselves. Piano or organ music is sometimes heard, even though the piano is no longer playable. The kitchen also seems to be haunted: There is often a strong odor of chicken soup, and at least one tour group saw what turned out to be the apparition of a lady seated at a kitchen table.

Today, the Winchester House is open to the public and is a popular California tourist attraction.

Santa Clara House and the Olivas Adobe

Located in Ventura, about an hour north along the Pacific coast from Los Angeles, is the Santa Clara House. Today the Victorian-style house is a restaurant, but it was once home to a young married couple. The wife had an adulterous affair with a salesman and became pregnant by him. She confessed to her husband, who left her. When the salesman never returned, the woman hanged herself in the attic. Her ghost has been seen peering out the window, looking for her salesman lover.

The Olivas Adobe, also in Ventura, is said to haunted by the ghost of another woman, who is seen at night standing in an upstairs window.

Hart Mansion

The home of the silent film star William S. Hart is located in Santa Clarita in southern California. The actor lived there with his sister. Both haunt the house, as does their nurse and Hart's dogs. Today, the house is a museum. Mr. Hart seems to recognize certain people and appears primarily to those he likes (mostly the docents). For some unknown reason, the spectral scent of coffee often wafts through the museum.

Early silent movie actor William S. Hart.

Whaley House

The Whaley House, built in San Diego by Thomas Whaley for his wife Anna Eloise deLaunay, was completed in 1857. The home was constructed on the site of an 1852 botched hanging: The gallows was too low, and instead of dying immediately of a broken neck, "Yankee Jim" Robinson slowly strangled to death.

Family members believed the house to be haunted by Robinson's ghost from the start. The Whaley children frequently heard footsteps.

Lillian Whaley, the last of the daughters, lived in the house until her death in 1953, after which the house rapidly deteriorated. It was saved as an historic monument and has since been refurbished with period furnishings and opened to the public. Visitors have identified the ghost of Anna Eloise Whaley, carrying a candle as she strolls from room to room. Non-apparitional activity—footsteps, windows opening and closing by themselves, a cradle rocking without assistance, cold breezes, and tripped burglar alarms—has also been reported.

The Windy (and Ghostly) City

Chicago has more than its share of fascinating ghosts and spirits blowing through. Perhaps it's the nip in the night air that draws them to the shores of Lake Michigan.

Allerton Mansion

There have been reports of a spectral "lady in white" at this Allerton Park abode. She has been identified through photographs as a frequent overnight guest of the original owner, Robert Allerton. Her ghost has been seen in the upstairs room she originally occupied, and her footsteps have been heard walking in the hall in front of the room as well as coming down the stairs. Her spectre has also been sighted walking by the fish pond in back of the mansion.

Beverly Unitarian Church

This structure was built as a private residence by Robert Givens in 1886 and became a church in 1942. Nicknamed the Irish Castle, the house was modeled after an actual castle Givens saw on the Emerald Isle. The church is haunted by the apparition of a young woman who appears in the living room or descending a staircase. Sometimes she appears as merely a flickering light, moving from room to room.

Hull House

Hull House is an excellent example of how superstition and gossip lead to a house's getting a reputation as being haunted. Charles J. Hull built the mansion as his home in 1856. In the 1880s, it began the first official welfare center in the United States, started by Jane Addams and Ellen Starr.

A rumor started in 1913 that a child was born in Chicago with a tail, cloven hooves, ascles, and pointed ears as a result of a curse. There were many variations of the story as to why the baby was born resembling Satan: It was a curse for marrying out of faith, for lying about a previous illegitimate baby, for promiscuity, for watching a performance of *Faust*, or for the father tearing a picture of the Virgin May off the wall. Regardless of the tale, the parents supposedly gave the baby to Jane Addams to care for.

Although there was no basis for truth in the story, it spread like wildfire. For six weeks, Hull House had hundreds of telephone calls and visitors wanting to see the "Devil Baby." Eventually the frenzy died down, but to this day some passersby claim to spot the Devil Baby in an upstairs left-attic window. Others claimed to have seen luminous ectoplasm ascend the staircase to the attic. The glowing mist has been caught on film, as have four monk-like apparitions ascending the staircase to the second floor.

Hull House is now a museum and is still on the itinerary of "Haunted Chicago" tours.

Schweppe Mansion

After his wife Laura died in 1937, Mr. Schweppe was inconsolable and committed suicide in 1941 by shooting himself in the head with a pistol. Their Lake Forest,

Illinois, home lay empty for 50 years. The bedrooms of the mansion are said to be haunted by the ghosts of the owners; the ghost of a servant haunts the many hallways. Interestingly, the windows of the master bedroom never seem to collect dust or need to be cleaned.

The South Shall Rise Again

Can't you just imagine the ghosts Scarlett O'Hara and Rhett Butler—well, if they were real people—haunting the antebellum homes of the Deep South? Let's take a look at some real ghosts of the region.

Bell House

In 1817, hauntings began on the farm of John Bell and his family near Adams, Tennessee. (This John Bell was no relation to the former resident of the Fox sisters' home mentioned in Chapter 7, "Spirit Move Me: The Birth of Spiritualism.") There are many variations of the Bell Witch story. In the most commonly heard version, the hauntings began with poltergeist-like activity, such as rappings and people being pinched and slapped by invisible hands. Betsy Bell, the 12-year-old daughter, was attacked most often. (Remember, someone of this age is often found in homes haunted by poltergeists.) The case received wide notice, including that of General Andrew Jackson, who was a neighbor.

Spectral animals appeared. One creature looked like a large dog. Another resembled a turkey. Finally, a ghost materialized. Over the next several months, the phantom variously claimed to be:

➤ "A Spirit from everywhere, Heaven, Hell, the Earth"

➤ The spectre of an unidentified immigrant who had buried a treasure nearby (though no hidden cache was every found, despite a great deal of searching).

➤ "Nothing more nor less than old Kate Batts' witch."

It was this last identity that stuck: The witch was, for then on, known as "Kate." Kate Batts was a local woman; she was obese, invalid, but still very much alive. Interestingly, townspeople didn't attack Batts herself as a witch: Times had changed since the witchcraft trials of Salem, Massachusetts, in 1692.

Kate swore to "haunt and torment old Jack Bell as long as he lives." Before long, Bell fell ill and took to his bed. On December 19, 1820, Bell was discovered in a near coma with a strange bottle of medicine by his bed. The liquid was tested on a cat, which died after drinking it. Bell, too, died the next day.

The Bell Witch soon left, but she promised to return in seven years. She did, announcing herself by dropping a large round rock down the chimney. She departed again after two weeks, promising to return in 107 years to curse all of Tennessee and the rest of the country. Fortunately, there's no record of her return.

The two other most popular versions of the Bell Witch place the legend in North Carolina. One identifies the spirit as the ghost of an overseer whom John Bell killed in anger; the other says she is the ghost of the widow Kate Batts who was engaged to John Bell. Bell asked to break off the engagement, she refused, so he locked her in a cellar, where she died.

Mysterious Charleston, South Carolina, lays claim to being the most haunted city in the Southeast. And why not? Take a look at these four representative haunted houses:

➤ **Heyward House.** The young James Heyward accidentally shot himself to death through the jugular vein in a hunting accident in 1805. His ghost, dressed in hunting clothes, has been spotted in the library of his house by later owners and residents.

➤ **Ladd House.** This white stucco home was built in 1732. It's haunted by Dr. Joseph Brown Ladd, who lived there in the 1780s and died in a 1786 duel. His ghost is usually preceded by a cold draft, footsteps, and occasionally the sound of his whistling an English ballad (his favorite) in the halls. The presence of a second ghost, a little girl from the Savage family who lived in the house in the 1830s, is sometimes felt in a room on the second floor and on an outside walkway.

➤ **Medway.** Jan Van Arrsens built Medway, the oldest building still standing in South Carolina, in 1686. His ghost smokes an invisible pipe in the upstairs south bedroom. The ghost of a later resident, a young bride, is sometimes seen standing at a downstairs window. She is waiting for her husband, unaware that he has died in a hunting accident.

Ghostbusting

Visitors to Charleston can enjoy Ghost Tours—popular walking tours through the city's most haunted areas. (See Appendix B for more information.)

➤ **Yeoman's Hall.** This development of luxury homes was built on the site of the old Goose Creek Plantation. In its latter years, the plantation was haunted by one of its early residents, an old Irish woman named Mary Hyrne. She often appeared whenever someone living there swore, missed church, or worked on a Sunday. She has since materialized in Yeoman's Hall, the modern clubhouse, appearing as a frowning old woman, wearing a white hat and period black dress.

The Cajun and Bayou country, dotted with its above-ground tombs and sepulchers, with the night air stirred by the rhythm of jazz and the chants of voodoo priestesses, makes New Orleans uniquely qualified to claim its stake as perhaps the most haunted city in the United States. All of Louisiana seems to be under a spectral spell of hauntings. Here are the stories of just some of the haunted houses in New Orleans.

Beauregard House

Also known as LeCarpentier House, this mansion was built in 1812. General Pierre Gustave Toutant de Beauregard, the commander of the Confederate soldiers at the calamitous Battle of Shiloh, lived there until 1860. Sometimes, around 2:00 A.M., the ghosts of Beauregard and his soldiers appear in full spit-and-polish military uniform outside the ballroom. Then, their uniforms change into torn and bloody rags.

Gardette-LePetrie House

In the 1790s, enemies of a Turkish sultan murdered the entire household of his brother (including the wives and servants) who were living in this mansion located at the corner of Dauphine and Orlean streets. The brother's corpse was buried under a date tree (nicknamed the Death Tree) in the courtyard. For years, until the house was broken up into apartments, apparitions were seen near the tree and Turkish music was heard.

Hermann-Grima House

The ghosts haunting this house spread the scents of lavender and rose in the parlor, and on cold mornings they have been known to light the fire in the fireplace.

Lalaurie House

This mansion was built at 1140 Royal Street in 1832 by the wealthy socialite Delphine LaLaurie. She secretly kept her slaves chained; those she imprisoned in the attic were tortured and maimed. In 1833, one slave girl escaped. LaLaurie chased the girl with a whip across the roof, and the girl jumped to her death. The ensuing scandal led to authorities forcing LaLaurie to sell her slaves, but friends bought them and returned them to LaLaurie.

On April 24, 1834, a cook accidentally set the kitchen on fire. Firemen found the body of the slave cook chained to the floor; the bodies of seven other slaves were found on torture devices in the attic. LaLaurie and her husband were driven out of town, and she was later fatally gored by a wild boar near her new home in southern France. Around 1900, the house was turned into apartments. Residents report seeing the ghost of LeLaurie, a tall black man on the staircase, and various other hooded figures. Spectral sounds include the classic rattling chain being dragged down the stairs, screams in the attic, and the cries of a young girl in the courtyard.

Laveau House

Born an illegitimate mulatto in 1794, Marie Laveau was the undisputed Voodoo Queen of New Orleans. She sold charms and medicines, led voodoo dances in Congo Square, and held pagan rites at St. John's Bayou at Lake Ponchartrain. She seemed to stay eternally young. Many speculated that there were really *two* Marie Laveaus, a mother and daughter. (There are actually two tombs said to be hers in the old French Quarter cemetery.)

By 1895, she (or they) had disappeared, but her ghost still practiced voodoo along with her phantom followers in her home on St. Ann Street. Her apparition has also been spotted strolling down St. Ann Street in a long white dress with her trademark, seven-knotted handkerchief around her neck. On at least one occasion, she was seen to slap a man and then float to the ceiling in a French Quarter pharmacy. Laveau's voice can also be heard singing at St. John's Bayou on St. John's Eve.

D.C. Denizens of the Dark

Finally, our nation's capital houses contain some of the most famous haunts in the nation. The ghosts include military heroes and even presidents, located everywhere from Georgetown to the White House.

Decatur House

Stephen Decatur was one of the country's great early naval captains. He received his first ship in 1803, and in 1807 he sat on the commission which court-martialed Commodore James Barron, commander of the *Chesapeake,* for boarding the British ship *Leopold* without authorization. Barron never forgave Decatur, who went on to distinguish himself in the War of 1812 as the new commander of the *Chesapeake.*

After the war, Decatur and his wife Susan moved into a house in fashionable Lafayette Square in central Washington, D.C. Barron's insistent insults led to duel with Decatur on March 14, 1820. The war hero, mortally wounded, was returned to his home, where he died.

A year later, Decatur's ghost began to appear, staring out his bedroom window, where it is said Decatur stood in contemplation the night before the duel. Although the window was walled over, the ghost continued to return. The ghost has since been seen leaving the back door of the house, carrying a box of dueling pistols, and the echoes of a woman's crying, said to be that of Susan's ghost, have also been heard throughout the house.

Today, the house is maintained as a public museum.

Halcyon House

Benjamin Stoddert, the first Secretary of the U.S. Navy, built Halcyon House overlooking the Potomac River in historic Georgetown, just outside Washington, D.C. During the Civil War, the owners allowed their home to be a way-station of the Underground Railway for runaway slaves. A tunnel (closed off in the 20th century) was dug from the river to the basement. Moans and crying have been heard throughout the house ever since, reportedly from the ghosts of slaves who, weakened and ill from their journeys, died there.

In the 1930s, Albert Adsit Clemons bought the house. He developed a belief that he would never die as long as he continued to build onto the house. (Sarah Winchester, who we talked about earlier, had a similar obsession with her home, the Winchester House!) Needless to say, his incessant building didn't prevent his death in 1938. (As part of his will, he insisted that his doctor pierce his heart to be sure that he was actually dead before burial.)

After Clemons's death, hauntings increased in Halcyon House—belying the home's name. The ghosts of a man resembling Stoddert and a female phantom have appeared. Two separate house guests reported that they awoke to find themselves floating above their beds. Others woke up to find themselves reversed in bed. In addition to continued cries and sighs, shut windows are found open, unusual sounds emanate from the attic, and artwork has fallen from the wall.

Today, the privately owned house is an historic landmark.

Ghostly Pursuits

By 1938 when Clemons died, it was common practice to embalm corpses before burial. Besides preservation of the remains, it also ensured (as a side benefit, I suppose) that the person being buried was really dead. Before the Civil War, when embalming first became a science, this was not necessarily the case. Those in a coma or a narcoleptic sleep could easily be mistaken for dead. They could be buried, then wake up later to find themselves emtombed or six feet underground. The fear of this happening was so great that devices were patented in the United States to allow victims of premature burial to alert those passing by cemeteries. Edgar Allan Poe (1809–1849) made this morbid preoccupation a theme in at least two of his stories: "The Fall of the House of Usher" (1839) and "The Premature Burial" (1850).

The Octagon

This three-story house was built on an oddly shaped plot of land near the White House in the early 1800s for Colonel John Tayloe, a planter from Virginia and friend of George Washington. Tayloe nicknamed his new home The Octagon, although it had only six sides. (Perhaps he thought it more mellifluous than The Hexagonal.) Among its most famous features is a spectacular, oval central staircase.

The Octagon is said to be the most haunted private home in Washington, D.C., and there were reports of ghostly goings-on well into the latter part of the 20th century. The first apparition to haunt the property was one of Tayloe's daughters, who fell to her death over a railing and down a stairwell shortly after Tayloe argued with her over an unsuitable suitor. (Some say she committed suicide rather than stumbling.) Sometimes, only a shadow of a candle floating up the steps is seen, followed by a scream and a thud at the bottom of the stairs.

Tayloe and his family moved out during the War of 1812, and miraculously the house was not burned by the British. The White House was, however, and Tayloe loaned the house to President James and Dolly Madison during the renovation of the White House, and they stayed there from 1814 to 1817.

After the Tayloes returned, the father had an argument with a second daughter at the top of the stairs over her elopement. Tayloe brushed his daughter aside to pass her, and she, like her sister, fell to her death. Her ghost is also said to haunt the house.

A gambler, accused of cheating, was killed in one of the house's upstairs rooms during the Civil War. As he slumped to his death, he clutched the bell cord that was used to summon the servants. Ever since, the gambler's ghost has been seen performing this action.

The house's most famous phantom is that of Dolly Madison herself, whose ghost first appeared in the late 19th century, dressed in period wardrobe and perfumed with lilac.

Boo!

It should go without saying, but never get into a rough-and-tumble argument with someone at the top of a staircase. Chances are better than not that at least one of you is going to wind up being a ghost!

Other spectres and phenomena include carriages and footmen, various unrecognizable human shadows moving up the staircase and out the back door to the gardens, footprints left behind in dust, the clashing of swords, the aroma of food, and groans and cries. Rumor has it that loud thumping, heard throughout the house for more than a century, is caused by the ghosts of runaway slaves (from when the house purportedly acted as a station of the Underground Railroad), from Union soldiers who died there (from when the house acted as a rooming house/hospital), and/or from a slave girl who was murdered by her lover, a British soldier, who walled up her corpse within the house.

The Octagon is open to the public as a museum.

Woodrow Wilson House

After serving two terms as President, Woodrow Wilson moved in 1921 to a house on Embassy Row near the Executive Mansion. Wilson died just three years later, and his spirit has been seen in the house, now a museum, sitting in his favorite rocking chair. Staff members have also heard the shuffle of a man with a cane climbing the stairs as well as the quiet sobs of a man's voice.

The Capitol Building

The home of the federal government's legislative branch is haunted by numerous ghosts. The ghost of a stonemason who was sealed alive in a wall during the construction of the Capitol is seen in the Senate chambers. Legend has it that he was struck with a brick during an argument with a carpenter, who then sealed up the mason while he was still alive. A ghost of another worker, carrying a tray, is sometimes seen floating in the Rotunda, where he was killed.

The spirits of Congressional rivals Joseph G. Cannon and Champ Clark, both former Speakers of the House of Representatives, have been spotted late at night debating in the House chambers. Their materialization is often accompanied by the rap of the Speaker's gavel.

Dark stains on the steps outside the House gallery mark the spot where Kentucky congressman William Taulbee was shot and killed in the winter of 1890 by newspaperman Charles Kincaid. All attempts over the years to remove the stains have been futile. Staff workers say they have seen and heard the murdered congressman near the steps whenever a reporter slips on the slick stairs.

Other ghosts haunting the Capitol include Presidents John Quincy Adams and James Garfield, the World War I's Unknown Soldier, and a large cat. Some say the marble figures in Statuary Hall come to life on New Year's Eve.

The White House

Several rooms of the Executive Mansion (or White House), built to serve as the residence for the President of the United States while in office, are haunted. Several of the ghosts are those of U.S. presidents. The ghost of William Henry Harrison is frequently heard in the attic. Andrew Jackson revisits his bed in what is now called the Queen's Bedroom, and his guttural laughter has been heard there for more than a century. Thomas Jefferson is heard practicing his violin in the Yellow Oval Room.

The ghost of Abraham Lincoln also reportedly haunts the White House. Phantom footsteps on the second floor have long been attributed to Lincoln. Supposedly, the first person to report seeing his spirit was Grace Coolidge, the wife of President Calvin Coolidge. She saw Lincoln's silhouette standing at one of the windows in the Oval Office, dolefully looking out over the Potomac. Many have since reported seeing (or, in the case of poet Carl Sandburg, sensing) Lincoln in that same pose.

Lincoln is also said to haunt his old bedroom, now called the Lincoln Room. Overnight guests in the room have heard spectral footsteps in the hall; one has seen Lincoln sit on the bed to put on his boots. Queen Wilhelmina of the Netherlands, on a state visit to President Franklin D. Roosevelt, stayed in the Lincoln Room. One evening she heard footsteps and a knock at the door. She opened it to find Abraham Lincoln, in a frock coat and top hat, standing before her! Like any respectable lady of her generation who found herself in such a situation, she fainted.

Eleanor Roosevelt claimed that she often sensed Lincoln's presence late at night, and the family dog, Fala, would often bark for no reason, seemingly at an invisible presence. President Harry Truman also heard footsteps that he attributed to Lincoln. During Ronald Reagan's tenancy, his daughter Maureen saw Lincoln's ghost in the Lincoln Room.

As the saying goes, you can't keep a good man down. Lincoln's ghost has not been restricted to the White House. He's been seen at a number of sites around the country. His ghost haunts the Loudon Cottage (now Eamonn's restaurant) in Loundonville,

New York. The house was once owned by one of the women sitting next to the President when he was assassinated in Ford's Theatre.

Lincoln's phantom footsteps have been heard at his gravesite in Springfield, Illinois, where popular lore says his tomb is empty. His image appeared in a portrait taken of his widow Mary Todd Lincoln, when she sat under an assumed name for spirit photographer William Mumler. And the phantom Lincoln funeral train is seen every year on the anniversary of his cortege (see Chapter 20, "Trains and Boats and Planes").

Yes, ghosts haunt houses in every corner of the United States. But many owners and residents of these homes have denied rumors of haunting. Only recently have they opened the ghost-closet door to admit their spectral secret to one and all. England, on the other hand, accepts its distinction as, perhaps, the most haunted country in the world. Great Britain touts its ghosts with pride, so next we'll cross the pond to peek into the haunted houses of the British Isles.

The Least You Need to Know

➤ Every state in America has houses that are reputed to be haunted.

➤ Chicago, New Orleans, and Charleston are three of the nation's most haunted cities.

➤ Today, many historic haunted houses are museums that are open to the public.

➤ Old politicians never die; they just haunt the halls of the District of Columbia forever.

Chapter 15

There'll Always Be an England

> ## In This Chapter
>
> ➤ Great Britain, the world's most haunted country
>
> ➤ Borley Rectory, England's most haunted house
>
> ➤ Ghostly tales of the great manors of England
>
> ➤ Haunted houses in the Commonwealth countries

Perhaps no country on Earth is as haunted as Great Britain. For as far back as anyone can remember, any castle or venerable manor worth its salt had at least one resident ghost. Remember, this is a country where children *and* adults commonly believed in the existence of fairies, leprechauns, and other elfin spirits.

When spiritualism first reached British shores from America in the 1850s, it started a craze of mediums, séances, and ghost sightings unmatched anywhere else in the world. It's no accident that one of the first serious groups to investigate the paranormal and ghostly phenomena, the Society for Psychic Research, was founded in London.

Here are just a few of the more famous examples of haunted houses found in England, Scotland, and Ireland. We'll start off with the subject of one of the most intense paranormal investigations ever of a haunted house: the Borley Rectory.

The Most Haunted House in England

Located about 60 miles northeast of London in Essex County, the Borley Rectory was called "the most haunted house in England." Although spectral activity was considerable and supposedly occurred for more than 50 years, ghostly goings-on at the Borley Rectory were really rather ordinary: the usual rappings, footsteps, levitations, and so on. What made the case sensational was the incredibly thorough investigation by paranormal expert Harry Price between 1929 and 1938 as well as the massive amount of publicity his research generated.

The rectory, a somber if commonplace red-brick structure, was built in 1863 by the Reverend Henry Bull, and his family lived there for about 70 years. When Henry died, his son Harry was made rector.

It was during the Bull family's residency that the house obtained its reputation for being haunted. A phantom nun often floated over the property, especially down one path the Bulls nicknamed "the Nun's Walk." Once, she was spotted at the same time by four daughters of Henry Bull. The ghost nun was usually seen at dusk (an especially active time of day for paranormal activity), but she was also seen at night as well as in broad daylight. For some unexplained reason, her ghost always appeared on July 28. The house was also haunted by a phantom horse-drawn coach. Harry Bull claimed to have once seen it driven by two headless horsemen!

Ghostly Pursuits

Legend has it that these hauntings were related to a monastery that occupied the site in medieval times, although historical records dating back to the 12th century show that no monastery has ever existed on the site. According to the folkloric tale, a nun from a nearby convent eloped with a monk from the monastery, and they escaped by carriage with the aid of a brother monk. All were caught. As punishment the nun was buried alive in a monastery wall; her lover and his aide were hanged. There are multiple variations on the tragic tale.

After Harry Bull's death, Borley Rectory sat vacant for a number of years. Because of the house's reputation, a dozen clergymen declined the position at Borley before it was accepted by the Reverend G.E. Smith. Neither he nor his wife believed in the paranormal.

Enter Harry Price

Harry Price, the well-known ghost hunter, entered the picture in 1929 after reading several articles about the rectory in the *Daily Mail*. He and his secretary, Lucie Kaye, visited the property on June 12, 1929. According to Price, the Smiths confided that they'd been experiencing ghostly phenomena ever since they arrived, including:

➤ Footsteps

➤ Whispers and murmurs

➤ Harry Bull's ghost

➤ Black, irregularly shaped figures

➤ The phantom nun (also seen by two maids)

➤ Lights seen in the windows of unused rooms

➤ A woman moaning, followed by her cry, "Don't, Carlos, don't!" (No word on who Carlos was—or the woman, for that matter.)

Price talked with the staff to put together a list of all the paranormal activity that had occurred over the previous half century. In addition to the events experienced by the Smiths, others reported banging doors, bells ringing, sudden temperature changes, spontaneous combustion, unexplained scents, frightened animals, moving objects, broken pottery, writing on the walls, spectral music and choirs singing, and the sounds of invisible horses and coaches. In all, Price claimed to have interviewed more than a hundred eyewitnesses to ghostly activity.

During subsequent visits, Price himself experienced poltergeist-type phenomena, especially bells ringing and thrown objects.

On July 15, 1929, the Smiths left the rectory. They claimed not to have changed their disbelief in the paranormal; rather, they left because they found the rectory uncomfortable. Three months later, on October 16, 1930, the Reverend Lionel Algernon Foyster (who was related to the Bulls) and his wife Marianne moved into the rectory.

Within a year, Price received word that the poltergeist activity had picked up and had become increasingly violent. According to Price, the most important manifestation were notes addressed to Marianne, written in strange, tiny lettering on the rectory walls. Price called these the "Marianne messages." He later concluded that Marianne somehow subconsciously evoked the poltergeist activity that wrote these messages, because none appeared after the Foysters moved out in 1935.

Price Moves In

In 1937, Price rented the Borley Rectory so that he could conduct a detailed, controlled investigation.

Ghostbusting

If you even suspect that you may have experienced paranormal activity, make a record of the activity. Write down as much as you can remember, in as much detail as possible. Include *what* you saw or felt, *where* it happened, and *when*. You never know when someone like Harry Price will come along years later asking what you may have experienced.

Ghostbusting

Harry Price advertised for ghost hunters; he trained those he selected on the spot. Interested in becoming part of a team yourself? Consider offering your services to an established, bona fide ghost hunter who's already out in the field. You'll find the names and contact information for several in Appendix B, "Continuing the Ghost Hunt."

He advertised in the newspaper for research assistants. Of the 200 respondents, Price selected 40 men to help. He drew up a master plan to document all spectral phenomena, using technical equipment such as movie and still cameras as well as paranormal paraphernalia such as Ouija boards and planchettes. He circled all moveable objects with chalk outlines to measure any changes in their positions.

There were three mediums on Price's team: S.H. Glanville, his son Roger, and his daughter Helen. They were allowed to conduct séances in the rectory in an attempt to contact any spirits present. During one sitting, Harry Bull allegedly appeared to disclose that a nun and a monk, named either Fadenoch or Father Enoch, were buried in the garden.

On another occasion, the spirit of a nun named Marie Lairre explained through a planchette that she had been convinced to break her vows and marry. Her fiancé murdered her on May 17, 1667, and he buried her in the cellar. (Price had already discovered the skeleton of a female buried in the basement.) The nun said that she would haunt the rectory until she received mass and a Christian burial.

On March 27, 1938, medium Helen Glanville received a spirit message with her planchette that "Sunex Amures and one of his men" would start a fire over the hall and burn down the rectory that night at 9:00 P.M. The deadline came and went but no fire materialized.

Price finished his investigation and left the rectory on May 19, 1938. While activity had been recorded, most of it was minor or mundane, and none of it was conclusive. Price claimed that the phantom nun was seen in February 1938, and there were reports of apports; however, none of the evidence was indisputable.

Nevertheless, in his book *The Most Haunted House in England* (1940), Price called Borley Rectory "the best authenticated case in the annals of psychical research." Although most of the activity seemed to suggest a poltergeist, there were also many sightings of ghosts. Price concluded that the phenomena he experienced was caused by lingering mental impressions of former occupants. He conceded that readers could label these remnants "spirits," if they wished.

Within a year of the planchette warning to Helen Glanville, the rectory did burn down, at midnight on February 27, 1939, but the cause was not supernatural in origin. Captain W.H. Gregson had begun living in the rectory (or Borley Priory, as he called it) in December 1938. He dropped a paraffin lamp, which started a blaze over the hallway and eventually engulfed the house. It has never been rebuilt.

Finding Fault with the Master

Price's methods—and the authenticity and conclusions of his research—have been debated by parapsychics ever since his book about his investigation was published. For example, all of his researchers were untrained non-professionals. There was no common log book to record activity and compare data. And the results from mediums, while interesting, were certainly neither scientific nor reliable.

Criticism picked up in earnest after Price's death in 1948. Psychical researchers Eric Dingwall and Kathleen M. Goldney, along with paranormal skeptic Trevor H. Hall, revisited Price's observations and conclusions.

They discovered Charles Sutton, a *Daily Mail* reporter, who claimed to have caught Price, his pockets full of pebbles, faking a stone-throwing activity that hit him on the head. It was noted by Lucie Kaye, another witness to the incident, that stone-throwing poltergeist activity never seemed to occur when Price wasn't around.

In 1949, Mrs. Smith came forward, saying that she believed Price had caused all the paranormal activity during her tenure at the rectory. She claimed nothing out of the ordinary had ever happened to them before Price's arrival, and that she and her husband were overwhelmed by all that occurred when Price was there. The Smiths had only asked the *Daily Mail* for the name of a reliable psychic research society so that she and her husband could put the rumors to rest about the rectory being haunted. Instead, the articles in the *Mail* flamed interest in the ghost stories.

In their book *Haunting of Borley Rectory* (1956), Dingwall, Goldney, and Hall concluded that all of Price's data, even if true, was too unreliable. None of his observances was corroborated, and all of them were subject to interpretation. As an example, they noted a time that the Reverend G.E. Smith mistook a column of smoke for an apparition. Price reported only the paranormal interpretation, not the possible (and probable) natural cause.

Speculation about the Borley Rectory has refused to die. In 1953 and 1954, newspapers reported ghosts on the grounds. It's said that a phantom nun still haunts the nearby church. Also, a newspaper reported that playful boys removed some bricks from the ruined rectory and buried them in the playground of their school in Willingborough; soon after, one of the boys reported seeing a ghost at the school.

Even if all of the poltergeist activity during Price's visits had been faked, that leaves decades of previous sightings unaccounted for. The truth about the Borley Rectory may never be known.

Boo!

Be careful what you wish for: It may come true with a vengeance. If you do request the services of a ghost hunter, be prepared for your life and your property to be turned upside down. Ghost researchers, if thorough, will investigate every nook and cranny of your house. They won't hesitate to ask questions, no matter how personal, to get the information they need to help them catch the ghost.

Boo!

Did a brick moved from the Borley Rectory really set off a haunting at a Willingborough school? If it occurred, it would be unique in the annals of paranormal investigation. There have been very few tales of a ghost moving its haunting from one location to another. And there's never been a case history where a ghost has tagged along with something as inconsequential as a single brick.

Cheery-OH!: Ghosts of the British Isles

Ghosts flourish throughout the British Isles. The phenomena they produce are strikingly similar, from white apparitions to knockings and mournful cries in the dark. Just imagine yourself walking down a cobblestone street in a heavy London fog, or perhaps you're wandering alone across a Scottish moor as clouds drift past the face of a blood-red moon. It's not so hard to imagine a ghost or two in jolly old England now, is it? Here are some of the most popular stories.

Ash Manor House

In his book *The Haunted Mind* (1959), psychical researcher Nandor Fodor described his investigation of the ghost at Ash Manor in Sussex, England. The original Ash Manor House was built in the 13th century during the reign of Edward the Confessor, but most of it had been rebuilt by the time Mr. and Mrs. Keel (names assigned the owners by Fodor) bought the house and moved in on June 24, 1934, unaware that the house was said to be haunted.

Almost from the first night, the Keels were awakened by thumping in the attic; by November they were hearing banging at their bedroom doors. Finally, on November 25, around 3:00 A.M., first Mr. Keel then his wife encountered the ghost of an old man, dressed in a green smock and a hat, with a red handkerchief around his neck, and wearing muddy breeches and hose. They tried to grab the phantom, but their hands passed right through him.

Hauntings continued, despite numerous attempts by both priests and lay exorcists to rid the house of its unwelcome guest. Fodor began his investigation in July 1936, and he invited the medium Eileen J. Garrett to assist him. Once entranced, Garrett's control Uvani revealed that the ghost was drawn to the negative energy and tension between the Keels. The ghost took possession of Garrett and revealed himself to be Charles Edward, a former landowner who had his property stolen by the Earl of Huntingdon. Edward was betrayed by his friend Buckingham and thrown into prison, where he died.

During a second séance in the house, Uvani accused the Keels of psychically holding onto the ghost as an excuse to embarrass each other and avoid working out problems in their marriage. As soon as Keel confessed that Uvani was correct about the marital difficulties, the ghost never returned. Why not? I guess only the shadow knows.

Ballechin House

Ballechin House was built in Perthshire, Scotland, in 1806 on the ancestral home of the Steuart family, who were descendants of King Robert II of Scotland. Major Robert Steuart, who had inherited the property in 1834, died in 1876 and left the property to John Steuart, one of his nephews.

Shortly after obtaining the house, John Steuart ordered all of the dogs on the estate to be shot. While serving in India, the major had become a believer in reincarnation. In fact, he often expressed the hope that his soul would be able to return to possess the body his favorite black spaniel.

The Major was still freshly in his grave when haunting began at Ballechin House. Phenomena included loud thumpings, the scent and touch of invisible dogs, limping footsteps (the Major's one leg had been lame), and apparitions (including a hunchback man, spectral dogs and dog paws, and a misty human figure). Sessions with a Ouija board and automatic writing directed an investigator to a nearby glen, where she encountered a ghost dressed like a nun.

The hauntings continued for about 20 years. The accounts were made public in 1899, much to the chagrin of the remaining Steuart clan.

Bow Head

In late 1669 or 1770, Thomas Weir, one of the most respected citizens of Edinburgh, Scotland, unexpectedly, and without explanation, announced that he was a witch, performed black magic and necromancy, practiced bestiality, and had been involved in an incestuous relationship with his sister Jean for almost 40 years before turning to young girls. Jean also later confessed to incest and witchcraft. Both were tried, convicted, and executed (Thomas by strangling at the stake, then burning—along with his staff—Jean by hanging) on April 11 and 12, 1670, respectively.

Almost immediately, reports circulated that Weir's ghost was seen throughout Edinburgh at night. He returned to haunt his house, Bow Head, and phantom carriages (reportedly arriving to take Weir and his sister away to hell) were seen at Bow Head's front door.

The haunted house remained vacant for more than a century. (An elderly couple moved in for one night, but were scared away by a spectral demon cow staring at them through a window.) These were odd lights and sounds coming from inside the house, perpetuating its notorious reputation. Weir's ghost sometimes appeared from the alley behind the house, mounted a horse, and rode off in a trail of fire. The last sighting of ghost activity at Bow Head was reported in 1825, and the house was leveled five years later. Today, it's unknown exactly where Bow Head stood.

Chingle Hall

Located at Goosnargh, Lancashire, England, six miles north of Preston, Chingle Hall was built in the 13th century. In the 1600s, the Wall family owned Chingle Hall. St. John Wall, who was hanged as a religious martyr in 1679, was born there. Legend has it that his head was removed, returned to the Hall, and buried in the basement. His ghost has been seen and heard (e.g., rappings, scratching sounds, footsteps) in the house and over the property. Several Benedictine monks who were reportedly murdered there during the 16th and 17th centuries have taken up residence at Chingle Hall. Some spirits have shown up in photographs.

In addition to the apparitions, visitors have reported seeing table objects and pictures on the wall move on their own. They have also been touched and pushed by invisible spirit hands. Visitors sometimes experience sudden chills and "flashbacks" from the manor's past. (You'll learn more about this type of residual haunting in the next chapter.) Chingle Hall is open to guests from April to October (see Appendix D, "Haunted Places in the U.S. and Great Britain"); you can even arrange to spend the night!

Coolmoney House

Here's a more recent ghost story: Built in 1837, Coolmoney House is located in the Wicklow Hills area of what is today the Glen of Imaal army camp in County Wicklow, Ireland. According to local legend, the house is haunted by the ghost of Nelly, a local 19th-century servant who was made pregnant by a member of the upper class. The scoundrel murdered Nelly and threw her body from an upstairs window. Her ghost has haunted the manse ever since.

Boo!

Don't jump to conclusions when you're doing your ghost investigations. Just because a spot looks like dried blood, it could be a stain from all sorts of things. Before making extraordinary claims, back your research up with evidence, tests, double-checks, and careful analysis.

In addition to the ghost, there is a large mark on the floor in an upstairs room which is allegedly a blood stain. No one's been able to remove the stain, and even when the floor boards have been replaced, the mark has returned. (Apparently, no tests have been done to analyze the spot, so natural causes have not been ruled out.)

Rumors of the ghost resurfaced when, in February 1998, the *Irish Times* reported that Ms. Yvonne Croke, the 22-year-old daughter of the camp commandant, had seen the ghost of a slim, pretty girl on several occasions. She described the apparition as a "see-through person," about 15 or 16 years old and 5'6" tall, with black disheveled hair and wearing a simple white dress with a black belt. Supposedly, Ms. Croke did not know the Nelly legend before her first sighting.

Fifty Berkeley Square

Although no paranormal activity has been reported in modern times, the home at Fifty Berkeley Square in London was known, in Victorian times at least, as "the most haunted house in England." The mansion was owned by George Canning, a Prime Minister of England. After his death in 1827, a Miss Curzon then lived there until she died in 1859. The next owner, a Mr. Myers, apparently went mad. While living in the house as a virtual hermit, Myers allowed the house to fall into ruins: Its deteriorated and abandoned appearance led to its reputation as being haunted.

Strange sounds emanated from the house and standard poltergeist activity—including stones, books, and furniture flying through the air—was reported throughout the 1870s and 1880s. According to some tales, overnight visitors have been frightened to death, unexplainably, in an upstairs bedroom. Some say the house is haunted by a woman who threw herself out of a window to get away from an incestuous uncle; the ghost reportedly still holds onto the window ledge, screaming.

Ghostly Pursuits

Each generation seems to have its "most haunted" site. In Victorian England, it was Fifty Berkeley Square. In the 1930s, it was the Borley Rectory—at least according to Harry Price. The Octagon has been pronounced the most haunted house in Washington, D.C. Depending who you talk to, Chicago, New Orleans, or any of dozen other cities is the most haunted in America. Is there a definitive "most haunted" anywhere in the world? Unfortunately, no. The title pretty much depends on who's doing the ranking, who's publishing the list, and, all too often, whether it helps sell a book, film, or sightseeing tour.

In another story, two sailors stayed in the vacant house overnight on Christmas Eve 1887. While investigating unusual noises, they encountered an apparition (variously described as "dark and shapeless" and that of an ashen-faced man). One sailor ran off; the other was found the next morning impaled on the outside railings to the basement.

The Morton Case (Also Known as the Cheltenham Haunting)

A house in Cheltenham, England, built for Henry Swinhoe in 1860, was the site of a haunting by a female apparition on and off for more than 90 years. The majority of the sightings occurred between 1882 and 1889, but the phantom was viewed independently by at least 17 persons.

Swinhoe's first wife died in 1866. He remarried in 1869, but his new wife, Imogen Hutchins Swinhoe, left him shortly before his death in 1876, in part because instead of giving her his first wife's jewelry, he hid it in a safe under the living room floor. Imogen, who died two years after her husband, never returned to the house while she was still alive; however, she is thought to be the one who returned to haunt the house.

After Mr. Swinhoe's death, the house's next lessee, a Mr. L., died six months after moving in. The Cheltenham house sat empty for the next four years, until Captain Despard and his family took the house in March 1882. Although paranormal phenomena had apparently occurred earlier, hauntings now began in earnest, with 19-year-old Rosina Despard (later Rosina Morton) being the one who most often saw the spectre: a tall woman, dressed in black, holding a handkerchief over part of her face (which made positive identification impossible). The ghost often passed down the stairs; she almost always paused in the living room before moving down the hall to the door to the garden, where she disappeared. On at least one occasion, one of the Despard daughters saw her in the garden. The phantom appeared to be solid and aware of her surroundings (moving *around* furniture, for example), but she never acknowledged anyone's attempt to communicate with her.

Eventually, almost everyone in the household saw the figure, including, apparently, the family dogs, who often howled or shrank in fear even when no apparition was visible. In addition to the human apparition, the house experienced the traditional knocks and bumps in the night.

In 1885, the Despard home was investigated by Frederic W.H. Myers of the Society for Psychical Research. (Rosina had published her own experiences in the society's journal the previous year.) At Myers's suggestion, Rosina attempted to take photographs of the spirit, but none produced a recognizable image.

Sightings slowed after 1887 and stopped completely two years later. The Despards moved in 1893. After a boys' school leased the property in 1898, the ghost returned, sometimes appearing in daylight to walk from the garden and down a path. The school closed shortly thereafter, and until the house was renovated and converted into apartments in 1973, no tenant stayed at the property for more than a few years (although ghost sightings were never given as a reason for departure).

Interestingly, ghosts have been seen elsewhere in Cheltenham, and at least two were similar to the Despard apparition. All of these phantoms appeared in structures dating back to the time that the Despards lived in Cheltenham.

Ghostbusting

For whatever reason, animals (especially dogs and cats) seem to be very sensitive to a ghostly presence in the room, even when there's nothing to be seen. So if your family pet suddenly starts acting up for no good reason, look sharp: A ghost may be in attendance, and you don't know it. Yet.

Raynham Hall and Houghton Hall

Located near Fakenham, Norfolk, in England, Raynham Hall has been haunted by the apparition of a "Brown Lady" for more than 250 years. The mansion is the family seat of the Marquises of Townshend, and the ghost is thought to be that of Lady Dorothy Townshend, wife of the second Marquis of Townshend.

Dorothy married Lord Charles Townshend, her childhood sweetheart, about a year after the death of his first wife in 1711. Some say Lord Townshend learned that prior to his marriage to Dorothy, she had been a mistress to Lord Wharton; in a fit of rage and jealousy, Townshend locked Dorothy in her own section of the Raynham Hall. There, it's said, she died of either a broken heart, smallpox, or a fall down a stairwell.

The apparition has been identified as Lady Dorothy because of its resemblance to her official portrait, in which she was dressed in brown. The ghost has been seen by numerous reputable people, including:

➤ In the early 19th century, then-regent George IV.

➤ Around Christmas 1835, a Colonel Loftus. The ghost visited him on two successive evenings.

➤ Shortly thereafter, novelist Captain Frederick Marryat.

Marryat saw the ghost while accompanied by two of Lord Charles's nephews. He fired his gun at the phantom, but it immediately disappeared. His bullet was found in the wall the next morning.

The apparition wasn't seen again for almost a hundred years, reappearing next in 1926 to the Marquis Townshend, then to a boy, and to one of his friends. Ten years later, Lady Townshend hired Indra Shira and his assistant, Mr. Provand, to photograph the rooms of Raynham Hall. As they photographed the staircase, Shira saw a white form appear on the steps. At his instruction, Provand shot up the apparently empty staircase. When the film was developed, an image of the Brown Lady, dressed in white and wearing a veil, appeared. The spirit photograph, published in the December 1, 1936 edition of *Country Life* magazine, has never been proven to be a fake.

Ghostbusting

Consider the source. A ghost sighting is more believable if the person who claims to have seen a ghost (or had some other paranormal experience) has an excellent reputation for telling the truth and, indeed, no reason to lie. The story is even more credible if the observer has nothing to gain (and in some cases, much to lose) by telling the story.

The ghost of Raynham Hall. This spirit photograph, taken in 1936 for Country Life *magazine, is of the Brown Lady of Raynham Hall. Many experts think it's authentic, and it's possibly the most famous ghost photo ever taken.*
(Photo by Captain Provand, courtesy of Country Life Librarys)

The Brown Lady has also been reported at Houghton Hall, which was the estate built on the ancestral family grounds by Sir Robert Walpole, who was Lady Townsend's brother and the first prime minister of England. Lady Townsend was also the daughter of Robert Walpole, a member of Parliament for Houghton, and she spent much of her happy childhood in the district. Perhaps it's only natural that her spirit would want to return there.

Sawston Hall

This 16th-century manse in Cambridgeshire, England, is said to be haunted by the ghosts of Queen Mary Tudor (Mary I) and an unidentified lady in gray. Ready for a quick lesson in 16th-century English history? Mary Tudor (1516–1558) was the daughter of Henry VIII and Catherine of Aragon. When her parents divorced, Mary was forced to leave the court.

Edward VI, Henry's son and successor, died at a very young age, but not before he was persuaded to name Lady Jane Grey, rather than his sister Mary, as his heir. (Grey was a distant relative, the daughter of a niece of Henry VIII.)

Upon Edward's death in July 1553, Lady Jane's father-in-law, the Duke of Northumberland, presented the 15-year-old girl to the Privy Council to have her proclaimed queen. Nine days later, the rest of the country embraced Mary as their rightful monarch. Mary took the throne and jailed Lady Grey in the Tower of London, where she was beheaded seven months later.

Okay, back to our little book about ghosts. What does all this have to do with Sawston Hall? Well, the Duke of Northumberland wanted to imprison Mary to quiet her supporters and ensure Lady Jane's ascension to the throne. So Mary went into hiding at Sawston Hall, which was owned by the Huddleston family. When the Duke discovered Mary's whereabouts, he had the Hall burned to the ground; but Mary escaped in disguise. After she became queen, Mary had Sawston Hall rebuilt to thank the Huddlestons for their loyalty and kindness.

Today, the ghost of "Bloody Mary" (who got her nickname for her persecution of the Protestants) is sometimes seen floating slowly through Sawston Hall or rapidly through the gardens. A lady in gray (not Lady *Jane* Grey) sometimes knocks three times at the door of the Tapestry Room, then glides across the floor. In addition to the apparitions, spirit sounds have been reported in Sawston Hall, including knockings at doors and rattling of the latches, girlish laughter, and music from a spinet piano.

Willington Mill

For most of the 19th century, a house adjacent to a flour mill in Willington Mill, England, was the site of unexplained hauntings. The Unthank family knew that the house had a reputation as being haunted when they moved there in 1806, but they lived there for 25 years without experiencing any paranormal phenomena. Their cousins, John Proctor and family, were the next residents, and it was for them that ghostly activities began in 1834.

At first, thumping and the heavy pacing of footsteps were heard by the maid, followed by members of the Proctor family. The sounds were heard both day and night. The white phantom of a woman was seen in an upstairs window; later a glowing priestlike figure appeared there. Beds shook, floors vibrated, and spectral sounds included a clock winding, whistling, sticks snapping, a bullet smacking into wood, and beating on a drum. Human cries, moans, and voices (saying such things as "Never mind" and "Come and get it") were heard. Occupants of the house sometimes experienced icy blasts and strong pressure on their bodies from unseen forces.

The phenomena slowed around 1840, then increased in May the next year. A young son, Edmund, saw and felt a ghost monkey. Other family members saw some small figure disappear under the bed. Another son saw the phantom of a man come into his bedroom, open the window, shut it, then leave the room. A ghostly face glared down the stairs leading to the attic. None of the ghosts was ever identified.

Finally, enough was enough, and in 1847, the Proctors moved out. The house was subdivided into two apartments. The new residents occasionally heard unusual sounds and saw at least one ghost, but nothing like what the Proctors had endured. New residents in 1867 were disturbed as well.

While the property went up for sale, Edmund Proctor held a séance in the house, conducted by a medium from Newcastle-on-Tyne, but they were unsuccessful in receiving any conclusive proof of spirit habitation. Around 1890 the house was further divided into tenements, and no further ghost activity was ever recorded.

Throughout his family's stay at Willington Mill, John Proctor kept a diary of the strange events. It was published, with additional remarks by his son Edmund, in the *Journal of the Society for Psychical Research* in 1892.

The White Witch of Rose Hall Great House

There are haunted houses found in every nation that is or once was part of the British Commonwealth, from Australia to the Caribbean. One of the more fascinating case histories is that of Rose Hall Great House.

Jamaica has a colorful occult past, filled with tales of magic, witchcraft, and voodoo. Rose Hall Great House, built in the late 1700s and located on a 6,600-acre plantation about nine miles east of Montego Bay, is said to be haunted by the ghost of Annie Palmer (d. 1831), the house's second mistress. Known as the White Witch, Palmer was infamous for beating her slaves and is reputed to have killed three husbands and numerous lovers, including the plantation keeper. For years after her murder under mysterious circumstances, the stories of her ghostly return frightened off prospective buyers. Restored to its original splendor in the mid-1900s, Rose Hall Great House is today a popular Jamaica tourist attraction.

Rose Hall Great House in Jamaica, haunted by the ghost of Annie Palmer, the White Witch.
(Photo by author)

What a whirlwind visit to the great haunted manors of Great Britain! With plenty of ghosts to boot, from kitchen maids to queens! No wonder many people think that England's the most haunted country on Earth. In fact, in the next chapter, we'll take a peek inside some of the most famous haunted castles in Great Britain—and even one across the Channel in France.

The Least You Need to Know

➤ Spirits and ghosts are considered commonplace in England, perhaps the most haunted country in the world.

➤ Borley Rectory, once called "the most haunted house in England," was the site of one of the most thorough, if imperfect and inconclusive, paranormal investigations.

➤ The spirit photograph of the Brown Lady of Raynham Hall has never been discredited. Many experts think it's the real thing.

➤ No part of the British Empire was immune to haunting.

Castles in the Air

I don't know about you, but when I think "castle," I automatically think "ghost." It's easy to imagine spirits haunting those dark, torch-lit, drafty corridors—not to mention the dank, subterranean dungeons and torture chambers.

Europe is dotted with hundreds of ancient castles, many in total or partial ruin or decay. Still others have been restored, refurbished, or modernized. But no amount of renovation can keep out a ghost if it wants to live there!

It would be impossible to tell the tales of all the haunted castles, towers, and palaces in Europe and Great Britain, so I've concentrated on just a few of the most familiar.

Apparitional England

From the time of the Norman Conquest up to today, castles and palaces have housed royalty and noblemen throughout England. Odd thing about the British: They pride themselves on their resident ghosts. And why not? One of these tantalizing stories may make you want you to have a resident ghost of your own!

Hampton Court Palace

Several ghosts are said to haunt this famous castle, which lies about 15 miles southwest of London. It was built as a private residence by Cardinal Thomas Wolsey, who later made it a gift to King Henry VIII to secure the monarch's favor. (It was Henry VIII, king of England from 1509 to 1547, who replaced the Catholic Church throughout the realm with the Church of England.)

The ghost of Wolsey was seen under an archway in 1966. Often, unidentified footsteps are heard and other paranormal phenomena are experienced in the adjoining Old Court House on the anniversary of the death of the famous architect Sir Christopher Wren (1632–1723). Wren lived there while overseeing renovation of the palace, and he died there on February 26, 1723.

King Henry VIII lived at Hampton Court with five of his six wives. Two of them still haunt the palace grounds. Jane Seymour, who was the sovereign's third wife, died there a week after giving birth to the boy who would become King Edward VI. Seymour's spectre is frequently seen carrying a lit torch on the anniversary of the baby's birth.

Catherine Howard was the fifth wife of Henry VIII, but she was beheaded for adultery in 1542. Her ghost is frequently seen in the so-called Haunted Gallery, the walkway in which she ran in vain to escape capture and where she pleaded for forgiveness from the king. Her spirit often materializes on the anniversary of her arrest. An apparition of Howard's ringed hand has also been seen hovering in front of her official portrait in the gallery.

Catherine Howard, the fifth wife of Henry VIII. (Taken from Guiley's Encyclopedia of Ghosts and Spirits*)*

The ghost of Sibell Penn, who nursed Edward after the death of Seymour, has also been seen at Hampton Court. There are two popular explanations for her return. She died of smallpox in 1568, and she was buried close by at St. Mary's Church. After being damaged by lightning in 1829, the church was rebuilt. When Penn's tomb was relocated, however, some of her remains were disturbed and dispersed. It's thought that she haunts the palace to which she was attached until she receives a proper and complete burial.

According to another legend, odd whirring sounds and unintelligible murmuring was heard coming from behind a palace wall shortly after Penn's death. When the wall was broken down, a secret room holding a spinning wheel was discovered. Had it belonged to Penn?

In addition, two sentries as well as Princess Frederica of Hanover spotted the apparition of an old woman wearing a hooded gray robe in the same area. The ghost, thought by some to be Penn, was promptly nicknamed the Lady in Gray (no relation to any of the other gray ladies we've discussed).

Among the other numerous ghosts that haunt Hampton Court are:

➤ A mysterious White Lady.

➤ The headless Archbishop Laud.

➤ A spectral party of two men and seven women (reported by a police officer during World War II).

➤ Two officers from King Charles I's army. Until their remains were given a proper burial, the ghosts haunted the Fountain Court with loud noises throughout the night.

Boo!

The Lady in Gray was a common name for any of the dozens of gray ladies who've been spotted over the centuries. Some ghosts do get around. They've been known to haunt more than one location. So you have to be careful when you identify a ghost who's called a Lady in Gray. It may or may not be the same spirit you've already met at some other haunting.

Windsor Castle

Windsor Castle lies 20 miles outside London and has been the summer residence of England's royal family for 900 years. A wooden castle, of which nothing remains, was built on the site by William the Conqueror around 1078. The first stone castle was begun by Henry I around 1110.

Windsor Castle is haunted by the ghosts of four of the English rulers who are buried there:

➤ King Henry VIII

➤ Queen Elizabeth I

➤ King Charles I

➤ King George III

Other spirits of non-royals—thought to be courtiers, soldiers, and servants—have been sighted there as well. Among the most recent of these apparitions is the ghost of a royal guard who committed suicide in 1927.

Henry VIII is sometimes seen walking along the castle ramparts, but he is more often spotted in the cloisters. Percipients often report that they can hear his moans as he drags his ulcerated leg behind him. Queen Elizabeth I, who was Henry's daughter and the last of the Tudor monarchs, has haunted the library since her death in 1603. Her phantom has been seen there by no less than Her Royal Highness Princess Margaret and the Empress Frederick of Germany, among others.

Two other royal spirits also haunt the Windsor Castle library: King Charles I, who was beheaded in 1649 at the end of the English Civil War; and King George the III, who ruled England from 1760 to 1820 and spent the final years of his life within the castle walls. The most famous non-royal ghost haunting the castle is that of Herne the Hunter, who has been seen regularly since the woodsman hanged himself from an oak tree on the grounds centuries ago. He appears in the nearby forest of Windsor Great Park on a *Wild Hunt,* riding on a phantom black horse, accompanied by spectral baying hounds. The phantom can't be mistaken: He wears chains and has stag's antlers growing from his head.

Phantom Phrases

A **Wild Hunt** is a group of ghost huntsmen, horses, and hounds in procession, always seen at night. The legend of the Wild Hunt dates back to Norse and Teutonic mythology. In Norse tales, the god Odin led mounted huntsmen across the sky; among the northern Germans, the pack was led by Holda, the goddess of motherhood. The ghost of Sir Francis Drake has also been seen leading a Wild Hunt (see Chapter 18, "That These Honored Dead").

According to popular lore, Herne was a royal huntsman of Richard II, who reigned from 1377 to 1399, or possibly Henry VII or Henry VIII. Herne saved the life of his king by throwing himself in front of a wounded stag that was charging the monarch. A wizard suddenly appeared and told the king that he could save Herne by cutting off the stag's antlers and tying them to the hunter's head. Miraculously, Herne recovered. Feeling indebted, the king showered Herne with attention and rewards. His fellow huntsmen became jealous and eventually convinced the king to oust Herne from the court. Cast out and in despair, the loyal hunter hanged himself.

Henry VIII was among the many people who've reported seeing the apparition of Herne the Hunter. When the oak tree from which Herne purportedly hanged himself blew down in 1863, Queen Victoria ordered the wood to be burned in order to release his spirit. The ghost of Herne the Hunter is still said to appear whenever England is in crisis, as he did before the 1931 Depression and again before the outbreak of World War II. In 1962, he appeared on horseback in Windsor Great Park before an entire group of boys. Other sightings have been in connection with alleged witchcraft covens in the forest and Herne's leadership of a Wild Hunt.

The Tower of London

The Tower of London, which once served as a prison and an execution site, is one of the most haunted places in England. Most of its ghosts are unidentifiable, and many are headless. They're thought to be the spirits of the many people—of both sexes and all ages—who lost their lives there. Ghosts have been known to walk the grounds, pass through doors and windows, or dolefully stare out of tower windows.

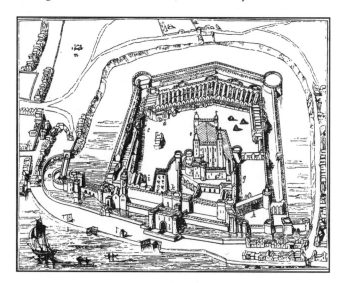

The Tower of London, the prison and execution site known for its multitude of famous ghosts, as it appeared in 1597.

There are many notable ghosts that haunt the Tower as well. Perhaps the first famous ghost to be recognized at the Tower was that of Thomas à Becket, archbishop of Canterbury, who was first seen in 1241, 71 years after he was murdered in Canterbury Cathedral. It's thought that, although Becket didn't die on the Tower grounds, his ghost has returned there because he was once constable there.

Also among the Tower's ghosts is the headless Anne Boleyn, the second wife of Henry VIII. She was beheaded at the Tower in 1536. Her spirit has been spotted walking in front of the Tower chapel, in the hall below the room in which she was imprisoned the night before her execution, and strolling toward the Thames River (which runs beside the Tower).

Another one of Henry VIII's unlucky wives was Catherine Howard. Some say her screaming ghost

Ghostbusting

It's not all that unusual that Catherine Howard haunts both Hampton Court and the Tower of London. Many ghosts, especially celebrity ghosts, it seems, have been known to haunt a number of places. Ghosts can return to haunt any location, though they usually haunt places with which they had some association (happy or unpleasant) during life.

is seen, still running the length of the corridor outside her prison apartment. (Yes, she *also* haunts the hallways of Hampton Court. You can't keep a good ghost down.) The ghost of King Henry VIII himself has also been reported by sentries.

As we learned during our mini-lesson in British history in our last chapter, Lady Jane Grey was executed in the Tower of London after reigning for only nine days as queen of England. Her ghost has often appeared in the Tower, primarily throughout the 1950s (a full 400 years after her death), and usually around the anniversary of her beheading on February 12, 1554.

Margaret, the Countess of Salisbury, had a grisly end at the Tower in 1541. The executioner missed his mark on the first three tries. He finally connected on the fourth swing, but his ax only succeeded in cutting her head halfway off. The fifth chop was the *coup de grâce*. The horrific screams of the Countess are sometimes still heard on the nights of the anniversary of her death.

Other famous phantoms at the Tower of London include:

➤ Sir Walter Raleigh, who was executed in 1618 by the order of King James I

➤ King Edward V and Prince Richard, the brothers who were executed while still children by their usurping uncle, King Richard III

➤ The Duke of Northumberland, who appeared so often that sentries dubbed the usual path he took between Martin Tower and Constable Tower as "Northumberland's Walk"

In addition to the ghosts of the nobility, a phantom veiled lady has been spotted roaming the Tower. She remains unidentified, because where there should be a face, there is only darkness. Phantom funeral carriages have also been reported on the Tower grounds.

Boo!

Don't believe every ghost legend you hear. Glamis Castle is probably best-known as the traditional site of Macbeth's assassination of King Duncan. A non-removable bloodstain is also said to mark the stop where King Malcolm II was murdered. But almost all of the events and locations in his tragedy are mere literary invention.

Spooks in Your Sporrans: Glamis Castle

Along the dark moors and the Highland heath, the Scottish landscape is dotted with scores of castles, some still standing, many in ruins. Most served as the ancestral homes of the various northern tartan-clad clans. Perhaps the most famous castle in Scotland is the notorious Glamis Castle, the setting of Shakespeare's *Macbeth*. Is it any wonder that Glamis has been haunted for as long as anyone can remember?

Glamis Castle is the oldest inhabited castle in Scotland— and easily one of the most impressive. The historic home of the Earls of Strathmore and Kinghorne, Glamis Castle has been a royal home since 1372 and is the family home of Her Majesty Queen Elizabeth and the Queen Mother.

Among the many apparitions said to haunt Glamis Castle are:

➤ A small, unidentified Gray Lady (yes, yet *another* gray lady), who has most often been seen in the chapel

➤ Shadowy figures near the Blue Room

➤ A woman without a tongue, madly pointing toward her mouth as she darts across the grounds

➤ "Jack the Runner," a thin man running up the driveway

➤ A young black boy thought to have been a mistreated servant, who appears near the Queen Mother's bedroom

➤ A wild man seen on dark and stormy nights bounding across a portion of the roof known as "Mad Earl's Walk"

➤ A female figure bathed in a red glow, floating above the clock tower (She's thought to be a Lady Glamis, who was burned at the stake for witchcraft and attempting to poison King James V.)

➤ A tall, unidentified figure, dressed in a long cloak

➤ An unidentified woman, with a pale face and sad eyes, looking out an upper window

Glamis Castle, which legend and literature (though not historical fact) identifies as the site of Macbeth's murder of King Duncan.
(Photo courtesy of the Strathmore Estates)

Glamis Castle has its share of other paranormal phenomena. Invisible hands have removed the bedclothes of some overnight visitors. A door opens by itself every night, even when bolted. The sound of hammering and knocking is sometimes heard coming from a room in the oldest part of the castle.

A local legend says that during the reign of James II of Scotland, Lord Glamis argued with Alexander, the fourth Earl of Crawford (known as "Earl Beardie"), over a game of dice. When they cursed God for their bad luck, the devil appeared and sentenced their souls to play dice in that room for eternity. To this day, the spectral sound of dice being rolled can be heard coming from an overhead tower. The ghost of Earl Beardie has also been seen in the castle, most often in the Blue Room.

Ghostly Pursuits

Glamis Castle is also known in horror circles for the legend of the Monster of Glamis. Supposedly, around 1800 a monster-child was born the rightful heir of Glamis. Because of his unspeakable appearance (egg-shaped, with no neck, and stubs for arms and legs), he was denied his title and locked up in a secret room. Only his successors were told of his existence. The monster is said to have lived to a remarkably old age: Some accounts say he didn't die until 1921. There are, of course, no written records of a Monster of Glamis or any hidden chambers, but in 1985 the then-current Lord Strathmore was quoted as believing that there was a corpse or a coffin walled up somewhere within the castle.

The Shamrock Shores of the Emerald Isle

When it comes to sprites and spirits, Ireland is best known for its leprechauns, the wee elves with pots of gold found at the ends of rainbows. But Irish legend and literature is filled with ghostly tales of terror as well. Feast on this double dose of creepy Celtic castles.

Antrim Castle

Built in 1662, the first Antrim Castle was destroyed by fire. It was restored in 1816, but was again burnt in 1922. Hundreds of visitors to the ruins have reported loud breathing or hissing sounds in what was once the right wing of the castle. The noises remain unexplained, but some investigators have attributed them to owls and other birds that nest in the walls, the castle's porous stones and masonry, or underground caverns.

Leap Castle

Overlooking the Slieve Bloom Mountains, the ancestral home of the O'Carrolls was built around a large, central square tower known as the Chapel. A door opened at one end of the room into a secret chamber that was used as a dungeon. Wings were later added onto the tower; one of the hallways ended in the so-called Priest's House. The castle was almost completely destroyed by fire in 1923.

Several guests have described seeing what's been called an "It"—a phantom standing about four feet tall, with black holes for eyes, bony hands, and smelling of rotting flesh.

One overnight visitor awoke to feel a cold pressure against his heart. He turned to see a tall, spectral woman, dressed in red and illuminated from within, with an upraised right hand. As he lit a match to see her better, the ghost disappeared.

Other ghosts seen at Leap Castle have included:

➤ A shaven monk, wearing a cowl, who floats out of a window in the Priest's House

➤ A small elderly man, dressed in a green cutaway coat, brown breeches, and buckle shoes. He is sometimes accompanied by an aged lady, also wearing period clothes. (Their attire suggests that they were servants or, perhaps, guests at the castle.)

➤ An invisible "bedmate," which lies down beside guests. The mortal visitors can feel the phantom's weight pressing into the mattress and against their night-clothes.

Local legend has it that one of the inhabitants, about to be jailed for rebellion, hid his treasure somewhere in the castle. He was eventually released, but he had gone mad in prison. As a result, he could never find the gold and jewels. The treasure has never been located. One psychic attempting to find the cache indicated a spot along one of the hallways. When the wall was torn open, two skeletons were found.

Fit for a King: The Palace of Versailles

Of course, Great Britain has no monopoly on haunted castles. In medieval France, as in all of Europe during the Middle Ages, every fiefdom was dominated by the lord's castle. And then there were the palaces built by the kings. Versailles, the most spectacular of these palaces, was surrounded by gardens and outer buildings, some of which have been reported as haunted for almost a hundred years.

The Petit Trianon, made up of several outer building and gardens on the grounds of the palace of Versailles, outside Paris, was allegedly the site of one of the most fascinating ghost materializations of the 20th century. The buildings were originally commissioned by King Louis XV for his mistress, the Marquise de Pompadour, and construction started in 1762. The structures were enlarged over the years to accommodate the king's subsequent mistress, Madame Dubarry, and later, King Louis XVI's wife, Marie Antoinette.

Now to the spooky stuff. In 1901, two English scholars, Annie Moberly and Eleanor Jourdain, visited Versailles. As they approached the Petit Trianon, they felt the air become totally still, then oppressively thick. For about a half hour, they observed several men in late 18th-century garb working and strolling throughout the gardens. Moberly also saw a woman in period costume sitting on the grass outside the main house.

The women didn't discuss their strange experience or compare notes for a week. Once they did, they decided that they had experienced a haunting. After a bit of research, they decided that the phantom woman on the lawn that Moberly had seen was Marie Antoinette; one of the male ghosts was her friend the Comte de Vaudreuil.

To test their theory, the ladies decided to return to the Petit Trianon. In January 1902, Jourdain encountered phenomena similar to what they had experienced on their first visit. Moberly accompanied Jourdain in July 1904. This time, nothing paranormal occurred. In fact, nothing looked or felt the same: "The commonplace, unhistorical atmosphere was totally inconsistent with the air of silent mystery by which we had been so much oppressed," they later observed.

Moberly and Jourdain wrote a book about their walk on the wild side titled *An Adventure,* which they published in 1911. They concluded that they had somehow traveled back in time, back to the time of Marie Antoinette. In fact, they even determined the exact date they thought they had visited: August 5, 1789.

If the events did occur as they suggested, it would be a documented report of *retrocognition.* Also sometimes called *postcognition* or a *residual haunting,* this very rare phenomenon is a sudden displacement in time during which you see into or experiences the past. Often times, you'll find yourself standing in a three-dimensional world, but there's no interaction between you and the spirit.

Retrocognition is not the same a déjà vu—when you think you've seen, heard, or done something before. Rather, it feels as if somehow you have suddenly stepped into the past. An example might be a person walking into a room and seeing it furnished and populated exactly as it had been in an earlier century.

Nor is retrocognition a case of regression of memory. Subjects experience events that have no connection to their personal lives or family history.

Think of it as an audio and video playback of an event from the past. Most paparanormal experts think that residual hauntings are not earthbound or returning ghosts. Rather, they feel, the people and events are made up of psychic energy that's somehow imprinted itself on some atmospheric ether—just like audio and videotape are electronic impulses laid down onto oxidized tape.

Phantom Phrases

Retrocognition, also sometimes called **postcognition,** or **residual haunting** is a sudden shift or displacement in time in which you find yourself in the past, seeing or experiencing events of which you have no prior knowledge.

Needless to say, as much as paranormal investigators may have wanted to believe Moberly and Jourdain, they just couldn't accept their story as being an authentic case of retrocognition. First of all, their sighting was totally uncorroborated. Also, the tale was considered unreliable because they had waited so long to write down what supposedly happened. Memory plays tricks, skeptics pointed out, and they dismissed the claims one by one by offering possible natural causes for each event. Even the Society for Psychical Research felt that there was insufficient proof that Moberly and Jourdain had experienced a true paranormal event.

Over the years, there have been other reports of spectral sightings near the Petit Trianon:

➤ In 1908, John Crooke, his wife, and son heard phantom band music and watched at length as a phantom lady sketched on a piece of paper.

➤ In 1928, Clare M. Burrow and Ann Lambert felt the dense air and depression described by Moberly and Jourdain. They, too, then encountered phantom men and women in period wardrobe. At least one of the ghosts vanished suddenly.

➤ On October 10, 1949, Jack and Clara Wilkinson and their four-year-old son saw a woman in 18th-century costume who, although not appearing to be a ghost, disappeared in the blink of an eye.

➤ On May 21, 1955, a London lawyer and his wife saw two men and a woman in period wardrobe walking near the Petit Trianon. Within seconds, the three phantoms vanished.

These and subsequent claims were all investigated by ghost hunters. Some suggested that the percipients had seen living persons dressed in 18th-century costumes, perhaps in rehearsal or as part of an historical pageant. Also, it was pointed out, it was once common for visitors to Versailles to dress in period wardrobe just for the fun of it.

Despite the healthy doses of skepticism, the many spectral sightings at Versailles have never been completely dismissed, and they continue into modern day.

And now it's time to escape from those dusty dungeons and castle corridors. Do you hear that carillon out in the distance? For whom do those bells toll? Well, they toll for thee! Let's get you to the church on time to meet the many ghosts who haunt cathedrals, monasteries, nunneries, and graveyards.

The Least You Need to Know

➤ Hampton Court, Windsor Castle, and the Tower of London are just three of England's best-known haunted castles. All are visited by the phantoms of legendary kings and queens.

➤ Glamis Castle, the traditional (if not historical) setting for Shakespeare's *Macbeth*, is haunted by numerous apparitions.

➤ Ireland, known for its shamrocks and leprechauns, also has a folk tradition that includes ghosts and other spirit phenomena.

➤ Haunted visions at Versailles may be attributed to retrocognition, a sense of seeing or being transported into the past.

Get Me to the Church on Time

In ancient Greece, it was believed that evil and dangerous ghosts rose from their graves and would attack passersby. It was best not to get too close to their tombs, especially at night. Throughout its history, the Catholic Church has accepted spectral visitations by the spirits of martyrs and the Virgin Mary. Survival after death is a major belief of most of the world's more prominent religions.

Is it any wonder, then, that churches, cathedrals, and cemeteries—especially those in ruins—have become prime targets for ghost hunters in their attempts to catch a glimpse of a spook? Let's take a look at some of the more infamous places.

Oh, Brother! There'll Be Nun of That!

Dozens of cases of hauntings by phantom monks have been reported throughout Great Britain and the United States. In almost all instances, the religious spectres haunt their former monasteries, abbeys, cathedrals, or, occasionally, the family homes where they were born. The phantoms have been seen haunting ruins as well as modern structures built on ancient sites. Often, groups of phantom monks are seen walking in procession, as if going to meals or vespers. Sometimes percipients hear chanting or singing. Phantom monks have also been known to talk to those who see them. It's believed that some phantom ghosts return to the locations at which they were martyred for their beliefs; others return to a spot that they loved during their lives. Phantom nuns have also been reported at similar sites.

Ghostly Monks and Nuns of the British Isles

For some unknown reason, there seem to be more ghostly monks running around than nuns, and both are much more common in the older ruins of the United Kingdom than here in the United States. Phantom monks and nuns aren't exclusive to England, of course. Wherever there are Catholics, there's the chance that you can find phantom monks. There have also been reports of phantom nuns, though not nearly so many sightings as there have been of monks. You'll recall that Henry Bull reported seeing a phantom nun on the so-called Nun's Walk at Borley Rectory in the 1860s (see Chapter 15, "There'll Always Be an England"). Here are a few of their favorite haunts.

Iona

The whole Isle of Iona seems to be haunted. Iona's one of the Inner Hebrides off the coast of Scotland, and it's dotted with ancient ruins and graveyards, plus the tombs of 60 Irish, Norwegian, and Scottish kings.

A monastery founded in 563 by St. Columba was the home for the monks now thought to roam the island as ghosts, both singly and in procession. Reports of phantom monk sightings didn't begin until the Reformation, when many of their graves were defiled and the crosses used to mark their graves were thrown into the sea. The monks have been seen indoors as well as out, but they're always Columban monks, wearing brown robes and hemp rope belts. They never speak. In fact, they make *no* sound at all, but they are sometimes accompanied by twinkling blue lights. So many phantom monks have been seen on Angels' Hill that many local residents fear going there after dark.

The Isle of Iona is also haunted by spectral music, invisible "presences," and phantom Viking longboats (especially on White Sands beach, where invading Danes landed on the island on Christmas Eve 986).

Boo!

The legendary "Call of the Island" beckons unwary listeners, creating an overwhelming urge to travel to Iona. Many have heard it and traveled from halfway around the world. For some, it's their last holiday: Either they choose to stay in Iona, or the spirits don't let them go—at least not alive. Many visitors have died under mysterious circumstances. If you hear the siren call from Iona, plug your ears. The trip could be your last!

Beaulieu Abbey

In 1928, a woman visited this abbey in Hampshire, England and encountered a phantom monk, who asked her to dig at a particular spot in the ground. She found a small box containing two small stones and a few bones. To assuage the monk, she re-interred the remains with a Christian burial. Ever since, visitors have heard occasional chanting from phantom monks.

Bolton Priory

Found eight miles east of Skipton, North Yorkshire, England, the ruins of Bolton Priory are haunted by the Black Canon, so-named because the ghost always appears dressed in a black robe, cape, and hat. The unidentified phantom seems to be in his 60s, and he's appeared during the day as well as at night.

Bury St. Edmunds

A church was built on this site in Suffolk, where St. Edmunds, King of the East Angles, was killed by the Danes in A.D. 870. While writing a book about the martyr, a local rector was allegedly visited by a phantom monk. The ghost revealed that the saint's body had been secretly moved from its original tomb and was buried in a hidden tomb elsewhere within the church. This might explain why the saint's remains have never been found.

Holy Trinity Church

Found in Micklegate, York, Holy Trinity Church is supposedly haunted by the ghost of an abbess. Soldiers who came to destroy the building during the Reformation killed the abbess, who was head of the Benedictine convent located there. As she lay dying, she swore to haunt the site. Indeed, her phantom did return to the ruins, and she moved in to haunt the Holy Trinity Church when it was built on the location.

The church is also said to be haunted by the ghosts of an unidentified woman and her child. The woman's husband died and was buried near the organ within the church. Their child died of the plague and was buried outside the city walls. Soon, the woman also died, but she was buried next to her husband. It's said that the spirits of the mother and child cannot rest because they're buried apart, and that the phantom abbess leads the ghost child from its grave into the church to visit the mother.

Whalley Abbey

Monks first lived on the abbey grounds of Whalley Abbey, located near Clitheroe, Lancashire beginning in the 13th century. The Crown seized the property in 1537 after the head abbot, John Paslew, was tried, convicted, and executed for treason. Today, the ruins of the abbey are haunted by a procession of monks, who walk with heads bowed and hands clasped in prayer. The monks have also been heard singing a *Te Deum*. Paslew's ghost also haunts the ruins. Poltergeist activity often signals his impending appearance.

Battle Abbey

William I (William the Conqueror) built this now-haunted church and monastery on the site where he defeated King Harold at the Battle of Hastings in 1066. William placed the High Altar at the spot where Harold fell; now, a ghostly fountain of blood supposedly appears there on occasion.

Ghostbusting

Things aren't always what they seem. Before you call a ghost a ghost, make sure of what you're seeing. The victorious Normans, for example, called the site of the Battle of Hastings "Senlac," which means "Lake of Blood." The name probably comes from a natural phenomenon: After a rainstorm, puddles of water appear red because of iron content in the ground. To the ancients, this liquid might have appeared to be blood.

In the 19th century, the ghost of an unidentified woman was frequently seen on the grounds. A phantom monk has also been spotted along Monk's Walk at the abbey. Some people think that the apparition is that of a monk who cursed Sir Anthony Browne after the nobleman accepted the abbey as a gift from Henry VIII in 1538. Others believe it's the ghost of the Duchess of Cleveland, who once rented the property.

Glastonbury Abbey

According to tradition, Glastonbury Abbey, the earliest Christian Church in England, was established in A.D. 166. Some experts claim it was founded as early as A.D. 47, and that it stands on the site of the island of Avalon, the final resting place of King Arthur. According to most versions of the Arthurian legend, the king was mortally wounded in battle with Modred, his illegitimate son and usurper of his throne. Arthur was whisked away on a boat by three fairies, but he will triumphantly return from his enchanted, healing sleep when Britain is in its greatest hour of need.

King Arthur.
(Daniel Beard illustration from the first edition of Mark Twain's A Connecticut Yankee in King Arthur's Court, *1889)*

In 1907, an amateur group, the Somerset Archaeological and Natural History Society, began excavations at Glastonbury. Frederick Bligh Bond, a professional architect who had been fascinated with the Middle Ages and Glastonbury for years, joined the team.

For reasons he never explained, Bond consulted a medium, retired navy captain John Allen Bartlett, to help him with his excavations. According to Bond, they contacted "the Watchers," a group of spirits of monks who had lived at the Glastonbury monastery, who gave them details of the abbey's layout and structural design, including the location of the lost Edgar Chapel. Over the next several years, working as directed by his spirit guides, Bond was able to uncover four other chapels, the perimeter wall, and the northern section of the abbey, along with many outer buildings.

Bond didn't mention his paranormal connections to his peers until 1915. It was three more years before he told the entire story in a book *The Gate of Remembrance* (1918). Bond didn't believe that the Watchers were actual ghosts of monks, by the way. He believed in a form of *collective unconsciousness,* an eternal pool of human experiences and memories; Bond thought he had somehow connected into that grand reserve.

Despite his great success in excavations, Bond was eased out of direct archaeological work (though apparently for reasons other than his paranormal leanings). He was finally dismissed in 1922.

Bond's interest in Glastonbury never diminished, however. Throughout the rest of his life, he was involved with several paranormal societies, including the British College of Psychic Science, the ASPR, and Survival Foundation, Inc. (dedicated to returning spirituality to America). Bond died in Wales, leaving behind an unpublished book chronicling his spirit communications with his great-uncle, Captain William Bligh of the *Bounty.*

Phantom Phrases

According to the concept of the **collective unconscious,** your unconscious mind contains symbols from all of humanity's collective past and not just from your own past. The collective unconscious is central to analytical psychology, developed by the Swiss psychiatrist Carl Gustav Jung (1875–1961), a friend and follower of Sigmund Freud, the founder of psychoanalysis.

Monastery at Leicestershire

Along the deserted road between Shepshed and Whitwhick, in Leicestershire, England, there's a large fenced-off field within which are the ruins of an old ivory-covered monastery. Popular legend has it that two ghosts, purportedly a monk and possibly a servant, haunt the grounds. The phantoms seem so real that the local bus has sometimes stopped for them on occasion because they seemed to be standing at the bus stop across from the ruins.

Ghostly Monks and Nuns of the United States

Belcourt Castle

Belcourt Castle, in Newport, Rhode Island, used to house a statue of a monk near the staircase. Oddly, a phantom monk was sometimes seen nearby. Once the statue was moved into the chapel, however, the ghost never returned.

Monresa Castle

This castle in Port Townsend, Washington, was once inhabited by monks. It's said that one of the brothers committed suicide by hanging himself, and that, on some nights, you can hear his phantom body swaying on an invisible rope.

Collingwood Arts Center

This building on Collingwood Avenue in Toledo, Ohio, used to serve as a dormitory for nuns, and several have apparently decided to stay on after death. One phantom nun is sometimes seen walking from the balcony down to a particular seat in the downstairs auditorium. Once she is settled, she vanishes. It's said that this spectre gives off negative and angry vibes and is, therefore, very disturbing to encounter. A kinder, gentler phantom nun has been seen sewing in the attic. The Arts Center is haunted by at least three other lay ghosts: There is a male ghost in the basement and another in one of the apartments, and the ghost of a bride who committed suicide after being left at the altar haunts the building's west hallway.

Bonanza Inn

The Bonanza Inn in Virginia City, Montana, used to be a frontier hospital. The ghost of a nun who used to serve there has occasionally been seen throughout the building.

Once again, we have our own share of church-going ghosts on this side of the pond. Many churches throughout the United States have a reputation for being haunted, by everything from the ghost of a Confederate soldier to a businessman dressed for work in his coat and tie. Let's take an alphabetical romp through eight states:

➤ **Alabama.** The chapel of the University of Alabama is haunted by the ghost of a Confederate soldier, in uniform.

➤ **Connecticut.** The Church of Eternal Light, constructed around the end of the 19th century, was one of three churches built in Bristol by the Sessions family. Balls of ghost light have been filmed in the chapel, and an apparition has been seen in the bell tower.

➤ **Illinois.** There are at least three haunted churches in Chicago: Beverly Unitarian Church (see its earlier listing as a haunted house in Chapter 14, "This Old House: Haunted America"); Holy Family Church (parishioners and clergy have seen an unidentified white apparition); and St. Turbius Church (an unexplained spectre has been seen near the altar).

Also, the sanctuary of the First Methodist Church of Evanston is haunted by the ghost of an unidentified man wearing a black business suit. He is usually seen walking down the side aisle between the pillars and the wall. He often pauses behind the pillars, as if hiding, but if you check to look, he's never there.

➤ **Louisiana.** Sometimes on early rainy mornings, the ghost of Pere Dagobert can be heard singing a funeral mass in the St. Louis Cathedral in New Orleans. Legend has it that the phantom voice still continues from a service he conducted in 1769 for several townspeople executed for attempting to overthrow the Spanish occupation.

➤ **Maryland.** Featured on television's *Sightings: The Ghost Report,* Baltimore's Westminster Church dates back to the 18th century. Among those buried here is horror author Edgar Allen Poe. (Remember the Edgar Allen Poe house from Chapter 14?) Although no apparitions have been reported in the church or its graveyard, many people have heard voices or felt mysterious presences. Several ghost hunters have checked out the location. Despite the use of an EMF (electronic magnetic field detector) and audio recording apparatus for EVP (electronic voice phenomena), there has been no conclusive ghost evidence collected.

➤ **Nevada.** The spirit of an unidentified woman can be seen in an upstairs window at St. Paul's Episcopal Church in Virginia City.

➤ **Virginia.** The ghost of a woman who was killed in the Aquia Church in Fredericksburg has been seen haunting its belfry.

➤ **Wyoming.** Likewise, the belfry of St. Mark's Episcopal Church in Cheyenne is haunted by the ghost of man who was killed while building the tower.

Ghostbusting

According to legend, a phantom "Pink Lady" appears on the night of June 15 every other year in the Yorba Family Cemetery in Yorba Linda, California. Ghost hunters from all over flock to the cemetery each year on that date, hoping to catch a glimpse of her. If you're in the area, why not drop by? You might get lucky!

It's a Grave Situation

There's an old wives' tale that you should whistle to keep away the ghosts if you have to walk through a graveyard in the dark. I personally have always thought it would take more to scare away a creature from the Beyond. But, hey, whatever works!

Given the great numbers of haunted churches, castles, and homes in Great Britain, it's odd that there aren't more cemeteries there with the same reputation. Perhaps the United States has more than made up for that. Here are just a few of the dozens of (allegedly) ghostly graveyards right here in America.

Bachelor Grove Cemetery

Located on a one-acre plot near the Rubio Woods Forest Preserve in Midlothian, Bachelor Grove Cemetery is one of greater Chicago's most active cemeteries. It gets its name from the number of unmarried men who once lived in the area.

There have been more than a hundred sightings between its opening in 1864 and 1965, when reports of apparitions and paranormal activity tapered off. Perhaps because of its ghostly reputation, the cemetery has experienced a great deal of vandalism, including gravestones being defaced or smashed and coffins being disinterred and opened.

Among the many ghosts and phenomena seen in the cemetery have been:

➤ A hooded monk

➤ A so-called "White Lady" or "Madonna of Bachelor's Grove," the latter seen carrying a phantom baby, and only during the full moon

➤ A farmer along with his horse and plow

➤ Various vehicles

➤ Men walking out of the lagoon, which was a common dumping place for bodies during the gang wars of the Prohibition era

➤ A ghostly farmhouse, located at various places on the property, with reports dating only to the 1950s

➤ Ghost lights

Graceland Cemetery

Not to be confused with Elvis's estate, this Chicago cemetery, opened in 1860, is the home of numerous ghosts and haunted statues. Among them is Inez Clarke, who died in 1880. Her ghost roams the grounds, and the glass-enclosed statue on her grave frequently disappears at night, especially during rainstorms, only to reappear the next morning. The area around the colossal tomb of Ludwig Wolff is haunted by a green-eyed monster that howls when there's a full moon. The statue of a seven-year-old girl seems to cry and has been seen walking through the cemetery.

Jewish Waldheim Cemetery

The ghost of an unidentified 1920s-era flapper has been seen near this cemetery in North Riverside (greater Chicago), Illinois. Her ghost was especially active in 1933, then again in 1973. (Perhaps you'll want to check this place out in 2013!)

St. Louis Cemetery

This old cemetery in the French Quarter of New Orleans hosts the ghost of Marie Laveau, the infamous 19th-century voodoo queen (see Chapter 14). There are two unmarked tombs speculated to be that of Marie (or that of Marie and her daughter), one in each of the two sections of the graveyard. Although she doesn't haunt the cemetery in a recognizable humanform, some say she flies over her tombs in the guise of a giant black crow. Others think she takes the shape of a large phantom black dog that's frequently seen on the grounds.

Well, that's enough to keep me out of a cemetery at night. And, if I do have to pass one, I'm gonna whistle a happy tune as I walk on by.

All right, it's time now to put on your uniform and check out your battle gear. We're going to take a look at the ghosts of famous war heroes and haunted battlefields.

The Least You Need to Know

➤ Phantom monks and nuns have been reported haunting monasteries and convents throughout the world.

➤ England is perhaps the most haunted country on Earth; this is particularly true of its ancient cathedrals and abbeys, many of which are in ruins.

➤ More modern churches throughout the United States also have their share of ghosts. In fact, they can be found in every state of the Union.

➤ For those fearful of ghosts, cemeteries have always been off-limits at night. There have been reports of hauntings in graveyards since the time of the ancient Greeks.

Chapter 18

That These Honored Dead

In This Chapter

➤ Phantoms of military greats

➤ Phantom armies on the move

➤ Revolutionary and Civil War spirits

➤ Ghosts from the taming of the West

Some of the greatest tales of courage come out of war. And so do some of the spookiest ghost stories. Ghosts have returned to their old battlefields and forts. Some are famous phantoms; most are among the anonymous millions who have served their countries in the hours of need. It seems that the bloodier the battle, the more likely that ghosts will return to haunt the fields of glory. Let's walk across that Thin Red Line to see them for ourselves.

Hero Worship

Military heroes are often larger-than-life characters, if not during their careers, then certainly in legend. Sir Francis Drake and "Mad Anthony" Wayne are certainly no exception. So when their ghosts come back, you know they mean business!

Sir Francis Drake: Spirit from the Sea

Sir Francis Drake (1540–1596) was an English navigator, and, perhaps because of his prowess in battle, many of his contemporaries thought that he was a wizard. He was the first Englishman to circumnavigate the globe (between 1570 and 1580). Along the way, he found Spanish ships and sacked their settlements in the New World. In 1580, he was knighted by Queen Elizabeth I. Drake's fame lies mainly in his defeat of the Spanish Armada in 1588.

Despite his seeming invincibility, Drake was eventually beaten by a Spanish force in the West Indies in 1595. The next year, he fell ill and died aboard his ship off Puerto Bello, Panama.

Ghostbusting

The sound of phantom drums beating is a recurrent theme in battleground ghost stories. And don't forget the poltergeists: Along with stone-throwing and fire-starting, it was one of the most popular activities among pre-20th-century poltergeists. Remember the Drummer of Tedworth from Chapter 5? If, some spooky night, you hear a rattle-tat-tat coming from that toy drum in the kids' play chest, you might just be haunted.

Before his death, he ordered that his battle drum be taken back to his home, Buckland Abbey, in Devon, England. He swore that, should England face peril again, he would return from the dead, striking the drum, to lead his troops and his country. (As you learned in Chapter 17, "Get Me to the Church on Time," a similar legend surrounds King Arthur; he is to awaken from his eternal sleep on the island of Avalon when England is in its greatest danger.)

Indeed, Drake's drum was supposedly heard beating throughout Western England in 1914 as the country entered World War I. A single loud drum beat was supposedly heard onboard the British ships surrounding the defeated German fleet at their surrender in 1919. Some claimed they also heard the beating drum at the beginning of World War II.

Two final ghostly notes about Sir Drake: According to legend, Drake sometimes appears as the leader of a Wild Hunt (see Chapter 16, "Castles in the Air"). Also, some occultists believe that, over the centuries, Drake's spirit has returned several times, reincarnated into various British admirals, including Viscount Horatio Nelson (1758–1805).

He's Mad, I Tell You: Major General Anthony Wayne

The American Major General Anthony Wayne (1745–1796) was nicknamed "Mad Anthony" because of his single-minded determination in pursuing and beating his enemies during the American Revolution. Apparently, he *is* tenacious, because his spirit has apparently refused to depart this earth.

His ghost is said to haunt Fort Ticonderoga, where he was commandant in 1771. The phantom most often appears in the dining room of his former quarters or sitting in a chair in front of the fireplace. He's usually seen smoking a long-stemmed pipe or drinking from a pewter mug.

While Wayne was stationed at Ticonderoga, he and Nancy Coates, a local woman, became lovers. Convinced that Wayne had turned his attentions to another lady, Penelope Haynes, Coates drowned herself in the lake. Nancy Coates's ghost is seen in and around the fort and floating in the lake. People often hear her crying as well.

Wayne's ghost also appears at Lake Memphremagog in Vermont, which he first visited in 1776 while hunting for bald eagles to train. After Wayne's death, his spirit appeared at the log fort (by then a fur trader's post) next to the lake. The ghost was also seen on nearby paths with one eagle perched on each wrist and walking across the waters of the lake.

Ghostly Pursuits

The battlefield outside Fort Ticonderoga was the site of another famous haunting. Several years earlier in Scotland, Major Duncan Campbell had given refuge to a man in his castle, unaware that the vagabond had killed Duncan's cousin, Donald Campbell. Donald's ghost began to haunt Duncan, but the Scotsman had given his word and never turned the murderer over to the police. Finally, the killer fled. That very night, Donald's apparition awoke his cousin in a burst of light, crying, "Farewell, Duncan Campbell. Farewell 'til we meet at Ticonderga."

Even when he was later stationed at Fort Ticonderoga as part of the British forces guarding against French invasion, Campbell paid no heed to the mysterious prophecy. As Campbell was hurt during a skirmish, the ghost appeared one last time to declare, "Farewell, Duncan Campbell." The major died two weeks later from his battle wounds.

To this day, some have claimed to see the ghosts of both Campbells on the old battle-grounds. The folktale served as the inspiration for Robert Louis Stevenson's 1889 novel *The Master of Ballantrae: A Winter's Tale.*

In 1779, at the command of George Washington, Wayne was ordered to warn the American troops of an upcoming attack on the British troops at Storm King Pass near Stony Point, New York. He made a daring ride during a stormy night on his horse, Nab, to alert the troops. The spectral ride re-occurs to this day when storms approach the area. Wayne, with his cape rippling behind him, is seen hunkered over Nab, the horse's hooves and flanks sparking fire as the duo gallop through the mountain passes.

Finally, Wayne's wraith is said to visit the ruins of a Georgian-style brick home owned in 1779 by Philip Nolan. Construction on the house, located near Rogue's Road in Loudon County, Virginia, was never completed. Wayne last stopped at the Nolan house as he traveled to Virginia to surrender Fort Ticonderoga to General Burgoyne. The reason for Wayne's haunting the house is uncertain. The residence is also suppos-edly haunted by the ghosts of two Hessian soldiers who fled their nearby camp during the Revolutionary War. They hid in the house, but were found and shot. Their spectres haunt the basement as they bang and scratch on the walls.

Ghostly Pursuits

Two other haunted spots connected to military figures are also notable:

➤ Fort Warren in Boston, Massachusetts, has been haunted since the Civil War by the ghost of a lady dressed in black. She's thought to be the wife of a Lieutenant Andrew Lanier, who was imprisoned there. During an attempt to help her husband escape, Lanier's wife mortally wounded her own husband when her gun misfired. She was captured and hanged for her effort.

➤ The Waverly estate was built by Colonel George Hampton in 1852 in Columbus, Mississippi. Hampton's ghost sometimes appears in mirrors hanging in the mansion (see "Mirror, Mirror, on the Wall ..." in Chapter 13). The property is also haunted by the ghost of Major John Pytchlyn riding his phantom horse. The house is also visited by dozens of other ghosts, including the phantom of a young girl, who is seen and heard weeping.

Tramp, Tramp, Tramp, the Boys Are Marching

In the heat of battle, more than one soldier has experienced visitations from spirits. Sometimes they're of loved ones; sometimes they're spectral angels.

Others have reported seeing entire phantom armies on the move. Sometimes the ghosts pass by silently. Other times, the percipients experience all of the noise and brouhaha associated with battle.

The Dieppe Raid Case

In late July and early August 1951, two Englishwomen, called Dorothy Norton and her sister-in-law Agenes Norton in later paranormal investigations, were on holiday with Dorothy's two children and a nurse at Puys, near Dieppe, France. On the morning of August 4 at about 4:20, the women were suddenly awakened by the sounds of war coming from the direction of the beach. The noises included gunfire, men shouting, screams, and, later, planes. The sounds continued in various degrees of intensity for about two-and-a-half hours before disappearing completely. Throughout the disturbance, they saw no apparitions of men or machines.

The women knew that a battle had taken place on that stretch of beach during World War II, but they knew none of the details. They also knew about the retrocognition experienced at the Petit Trianon in 1901 by two other British women (see Chapter 16), so they knew the importance of independent verification of what they had heard.

First, they surveyed the household to see if anyone else had heard the commotion. No one had, so the two ladies wrote down separate accounts of what they heard and the times at which they occurred. The accounts were almost identical, but what was truly amazing was that, upon further research, they discovered that the times and sounds nearly matched the events of the actual battle that taken place on August 19, 1942. (In her testimony, Dorothy Norton claimed that she had also heard the phenomena on August 3, but she had not wanted to alarm her sister-in-law, who had not awakened.)

Psychical researchers G.W. Lambert and Kathleen Gray investigated their claims. They were impressed by the ladies' seeming honesty and conviction, but, of course, their statements couldn't be tested. Skeptics were quick to point out that there were several other possibilities to explain what the Nortons might have heard.

The Legend of the Legionnaires

An uninvestigated haunting appears in the records of Rene Dupre, who was stationed in Algeria with the French Foreign Legion. In May 1912, his company and two others were crossing the sands outside their fort when they were attacked by the warriors of an Arab tribe. They eventually repelled their assailants, but not before five Legionnaires, including two soldiers named Leduc and Schmidt, were killed. The Legionnaires buried their comrades and returned to the blockhouse.

Two weeks later, Dupre was standing guard just after midnight. He saw a man in Legionnaire uniform staggering outside the fort across the sand. He seemed to be searching for something or someone. As the phantom drew closer to the fort, Dupre realized that he could see right through the figure. It was a ghost! Dupre called for others, who also saw the phantom. One man recognized it as Leduc. The ghost vanished, but it reappeared four nights later.

Three nights after that, Dupre was again on guard when he and others saw a different lone figure on the sands: the ghost of Schmidt. Like Leduc's ghost, he seemed to be moving along purposefully, as if looking for something. The ghost disappeared but, again, came back two nights later. One Legionnaire suggested that perhaps Schmidt was looking for Leduc, who was a friend as well as comrade in life.

Finally, on the 15th night after Dupre first spotted the ghost of Leduc, two phantom figures were seen walking together far out at a distance. The Legionnaires speculated that the ghosts were Leduc and Schmidt, and that they had finally found one another in the Other World. As the ghosts walked over the horizon, one raised a hand, as if in salute and farewell to their fellow Legionnaires back at the fort.

Touched by an Angel: The Angels of Mons

A famous battlefield sighting, the spectral armies or angels of Mons, was precipitated by a hoax. Between August 26 and 28, 1914, British and French troops were overwhelmed by German forces in a fierce World War I battle at Mons, France. Despite their eventual retreat, the British and French suffered more than 15,000 causalities.

On September 14, 1914, the *London Evening News* published "The Bowmen," a short story by British journalist, Arthur Machen. According to the tale, the British and French troops had seen spectral bowmen and other medieval soldiers holding back the German troops during their retreat. The ghostly soldiers were thought to be from the 15th-century battle of Agincourt, which is located near Mons.

The story prompted sensational confessions from soldiers. Indeed, many had seen angels rather than soldiers. Some of the British had seen St. George. Many of the French identified the heavenly hosts as the archangel Michael or St. Joan of Arc. Soon, there were similar stories from other battlefields.

Then, in a devastating confession, Machen admitted that he had made the story up, that no soldier had ever told him about seeing visions. Nevertheless, many soldiers continued to swear by their stories.

Ghostly Pursuits

In 1930, Friedrich Hezenwirth, the director of German espionage, put a new twist on the Angels of Mons. He claimed that during the battle, German aviators had projected movies of angels onto the clouds. The intent was to convince the Germans that God was on their side. It was thought that the soldiers, convinced of their moral right, would fight even harder.

Who was telling the truth? Indeed, Machen had made the story up. But that did not necessarily mean that the troops had not seen something. Perhaps it took the Machen story for them to confess their visions. Perhaps it was a collective apparition. Paranormals have suggested that soldiers were seeing the mass departure of the souls of the dying. It might have been hysteria, or hallucination, or wanting to believe in the protection of a Higher Power. Or perhaps what Friedrich Hezenwirth claimed was there. People believe what they want to believe, and, especially in cases like this, that's all that matters.

Haunted Wartime Habitats

There are haunted spots throughout the United States—especially in the Northeast and Atlantic states—that date back to the years between the Revolutionary War and the War Between the States. Many of the spirits who haunt them are of soldiers; in other instances, the buildings themselves are connected to the military.

The Spy House

The Spy House Museum in Port Monmouth, New Jersey, was an inn during the Revolutionary War era. It got its nickname because the owner welcomed British troops into the tavern, overheard their plans, then passed the information on to General Washington's troops. Prior to that, pirates had used the house to store their treasure, and they supposedly buried some of their murdered victims in the basement. There have been modern reports of the ghosts of pirates, soldiers, and a child thought to have died there.

Fort McHenry

The 18th-century star-shaped Fort McHenry stands guard over Baltimore harbor. Its bombardment by the British on September 13 to 14, 1814, during the War of 1812, inspired 35-year-old poet and lawyer, Francis Scott Key to write the poem "The Star-Spangled Banner." The fort was never attacked again, but it remained an active military facility, on and off, for another century. During the Civil War, Union forces used it as a prison camp for Confederate soldiers and southern sympathizers. During World War I, it served as an army hospital, and the Coast Guard trained there as recently as World War II. Fort McHenry became part of the National Park Service in 1933.

Over the years, many ghosts and spectral activity have been sighted at the fort, including:

➤ A silhouetted figure moving on the parapets

➤ A malevolent spirit in the corridor leading to the public bathrooms

➤ Furniture that levitates or moves on its own

➤ Spectral lights

➤ Disembodied voices heard by the staff after closing time

In addition to the regular guided tours, there have been walking Ghost Tours conducted at the fort. (See Appendix D, "Haunted Places in the U.S. and Great Britain.")

Todd's Farm

Todd's Farm, also known as Todd's Inheritance, in Fort Howard, New Jersey, dates back to before the War of 1812. Among the many ghosts that have been seen there is a young woman standing at the attic window, holding a candle. She is said to be waiting for her husband or boyfriend, a soldier, to come home from war. She is still waiting. In addition, a much more gruesome sight is sometimes seen: the apparition of slaves hanging from trees on the property. The house is no longer occupied and has no electrical service, but, according to legend, if a prowler or vagrant enters the house, the rooms light up.

How the West Was Won

One of the sorriest episodes of America's past is the treatment of Native Americans during the colonization of the West. As settlers pushed westward and were resisted by Indian forces, the colonizers demanded government protection. Army troops were sent in to contain the native uprisings. Many times, this erupted into full-scale battle.

Fort Laramie

Fort Laramie in Wyoming was one of the great legendary Western frontier forts. From March 1834 to March 1890, it served to protect and assist settlers moving into the Pacific Northwest.

Apparently, many of its residents from those pioneer days have chosen to stay. In Quarters A (also known as the Captain's Quarters) bolted doors have unlocked and opened themselves. People have heard tromping on overhead wooden walkways and floorboards, and a security guard reported feeling himself grabbed and slapped on the back by invisible hands. The apparition of a man in a cavalry uniform has also been reported. Also, a ghostly woman dressed in green riding on a spectral black horse is said to appear on the grounds outside the fort every seven years.

Fort Dodge

Old Fort Dodge, built in Dodge City, Kansas, during the taming of the West, still stands and is a retirement home for soldiers. Several of the structures are more than 150 years old, and many have seen paranormal activity. Ghostly Indians and soldiers have been seen at Fort Abercrombie in Abercrombie, North Dakota, and at Commanche Look-out Hill in San Antonio, Texas.

Fort Sill

Fort Sill, an army base in Lawton, Oklahoma, was built on former Indian land. In fact, the grave of Geronimo, the great Apache chief, is located there. Lawton was the site of a bloody fight between Indians and settlers in the early 1800s. Strange noises are often heard there at Fort Sill, and there have been apparitional sightings of Native American spirits.

Custer's Last Stand

Perhaps the most famous personality of the Indian wars was General George Armstrong Custer (1839–1876). On June 24, 1876, he and his troops were killed by Sioux forces commanded by chiefs Crazy Horse and Sitting Bull at the battle of the Little Bighorn (also called "Custer's Last Stand"). Some call Custer an American hero; others deride him as flamboyant, impetuous, and a glory seeker.

Say what you will about him, but Custer commanded attention. He still commands attention at the house he and his wife occupied prior to his traveling to Little Bighorn.

The Custer House was recently rebuilt in Ft. Lincoln National Park, in Mandan, North Dakota, and it's supposedly already occupied by the general's ghost and, possibly, that of his wife.

There have also been many sightings of apparitions of unidentified soldiers in residential apartments located near Reno's Crossing, a bend in the Little Bighorn River where brutal fighting occurred, and in a stone house, formerly the park guard headquarters, located near the battlefield cemetery.

Remember the Alamo

Around this same period, the territory of Texas sought to declare its independence from Mexico. The Alamo, one of the most mythic structures in the United States, was built as a Catholic mission in the 18th century. The property was first used as a military post in 1803. During the Texas War of Independence, 189 defenders of the Alamo lost their lives. Among them were David "Davy" Crockett and Jim Bowie. At least 1,200 Mexican soldiers also lost their lives in the battle; few received proper burial. Needless to say, many of the spirits of the dead are thought to haunt the Alamo and its environs. Although no apparitions have been seen in the Alamo itself, unexplained cold spots and a sometimes-overwhelming feeling of sadness pervade the mission.

Can't You Be Civil?

Abraham Lincoln, America's 16th president, is synonymous with the Civil War. You can't think of one without thinking of the other. A heroic and tragic man, Lincoln believed in the spirit world. During his tenure at the White House, Lincoln and his wife sat with several mediums, including J.B. Conklin, Nettie Colburn, Mrs. Miller, Mrs. Cranston Laurie, and Cora Maynard.

Lincoln had several premonitions of his own death. The first occurred just before his first election in 1860. He saw two separate, simultaneous reflections of himself in a mirror: one face hardy, the other pale. Ten days before his assassination, he foresaw his own death in a dream. He reported that, in his dream, he had an out-of-body experience, seeing his own corpse laid out in the East Room of the White House. The day of his murder, Lincoln told his bodyguard, W.H. Crook, that he had dreamed about being killed for three straight nights.

As you'll see in Chapter 20, "Trains and Boats and Planes," the ghost of Lincoln's funeral train can still be seen traveling the route from Washington, D.C., to Springfield, Illinois, on April evenings. And Lincoln's ghost has been witnessed many times throughout the residence area of the White House, most frequently in the so-called Lincoln Bedroom and the Oval Office (see Chapter 14, "This Old House: Haunted America").

Skirmishes during the Civil War were particularly acrimonious, pitting metaphorically—and sometimes literally—brother against brother. The battles were horrific. The pain and misery associated with the war have caused many spirits to remain behind, hoping to ease their psychic wounds.

Abraham Lincoln had several premonitions of his own death.

The Battle of Antietam in Maryland was particularly bloody. Today, it's one of the most haunted battlefields in America. The ghosts of Civil War soldiers are also sometimes seen walking around Fort Jackson in Buras, Louisiana.

The town of Harpers Ferry, West Virginia, is home to many ghosts. The best known is John Brown himself: His ghost is so lifelike some modern tourists, thinking that he was a costumed actor, have asked him to have his picture taken with them. Most of the other Harpers Ferry ghosts are also from the Civil War era, although some have been identified as more recent residents.

Civil War soldiers haunt the environs of Mark's Mill in Warren, Arkansas. One ghost is that of a Rebel who was blinded (and later died from his wounds) from artillery fire while trying to keep a trainload of Confederate gold away from the Yankees. Other phantoms belong to soldiers whose comrades hurriedly dumped their corpses down a well rather than burying them. Sometimes you can hear their cries coming from the well, begging to be given a decent burial.

Almost every night, a strange fog rolls across the Chickamauga Battlefield in Chickamauga, Georgia. Oddly, the fog seldom extends beyond the environs of the park. The apparition who is most frequently seen is "Green Eyes," a Confederate soldier who was killed by

Ghostbusting

After her husband's death, Mary Todd Lincoln became even more involved in spiritualism. She went to spirit photograph William Mumler under a pseudonym to have her portrait taken. The result was a now-famous photograph in which the faint shadow of the President can be seen over her shoulder (see Chapter 9, "Striking a Happy Medium").

his twin brother, who was a Yankee. The soldier's eyes are often observed glowing in the dark over Snodgrass Hill. Legend also has it that the ghost of a woman in a wedding gown haunts the battlefield in September and October. She is said to be visiting the grave of her fiancé, who was killed in battle.

Ghostly Pursuits

As the 20th Maine division approached Gettysburg to join the battle, they weren't sure which way to go. Suddenly, a glowing phantom on horseback—an officer wearing a tri-cornered hat—appeared in front of them. The men soon recognized him: It was George Washington! The general spurred the soldiers to the capture of Little Round Top, which they then successfully defended against Confederate advance.

The story of Washington's ghost became so widespread that Edwin Stanton, Secretary of War, held an official investigation. Hundreds of soldiers, including General Oliver Hunt and several of his fellow officers, claimed to have seen and been able to identify the phantom as being Washington. Colonel Joshua Chamberlain, who led the Maine division, declared, "We know not what mystic power may be possessed by those who are now bivouacking with the dead. I only know the effect, but I dare not explain or deny the cause. Who shall say that Washington was not among the number of those who aided the country that he founded?"

The most famous battlefield of the Civil War is located in Gettysburg, Pennsylvania. The apparitions of dozens of individual soldiers have been observed there over the past century, including Captain William Miller (who stopped haunting Gettysburg after his tombstone was inscribed to record his Medal of Honor) and a headless horseman on Little Round Top. The phantom cavalry officer (who is *not* George Washington) is still seen today. Some people have claimed to see (and sometimes hear) entire phantom battles! One of the most poignant visions is that of a dog, thought to have belonged to General William Barksdale. The dog was killed while trying to deliver a message from its owner, across the battlefield, to another general.

Miscellaneous Military

Just to round off this chapter on the Armed Services, here are three more martial mysteries:

➤ A World War II bunker placed at the point of Cape May, New Jersey, once housed cannons to protect the coast from German submarines. Ghostly soldiers have been seen on the beach beneath the bunker as well as inside the bunker itself.

➤ Fort Sheridan in Highland Park, Illinois, a military base that's open to the public, has been the site of many reported hauntings, even by local police. People have heard spectral voices and laughing. The water tower is haunted by a young woman who drowned there. Also, according to legend, some of the rooms in which people died were so haunted that they were exorcised, then closed up with bricks.

➤ People have reported seeing the upper torso of a man floating around the larger of two barracks in Fort Howard, Maryland. And at Nellis Air Force Base in Las Vegas, Nevada, an unidentified gray figure is sometimes seen, and unexplained footsteps are often heard.

War is hell. Maybe that's why the ghosts prefer to roam the earth. In any case, things are getting too serious. It's time to play, or at least, it's time to go *see* a play. Let's go indoors to visit some of the most haunted theaters in the English-speaking world.

The Least You Need to Know

➤ All over the world, ghosts haunt the sites of the great battlefields in which they lost their lives.

➤ Although most battlefield spectres are strictly anonymous, some, like generals "Mad Anthony" Wayne and George Custer, are famous phantoms.

➤ Paranormal sightings are not limited to individual ghosts: Entire phantom battles and armies have been reported.

➤ Ghosts have been reported from every American conflict, including phantom fighters from the Revolutionary War, the War of 1812, the Indian uprisings, the Texas War of Independence, the Civil War, and the World Wars.

Alas, poor Yorick,
I knew him well...

You still do!

Chapter 19

All the World's a Stage

In This Chapter

➤ Great ghosts of the British theater

➤ A tour of some of England's most haunted theaters

➤ Haunted theaters of the United States

➤ A quick survey of theater ghosts across America

I've heard of a dead audience, but this is ridiculous!

The life of an actor is unpredictable at best. They never know what their next role will be—or when it will come along. So, who knows? Maybe a few of the theater ghosts decided that, once they got the gig in the theater, they'd just stay there, even if it meant hanging around after the fall of life's curtain.

By and large, stage actors are a superstitious lot. They believe all sorts of things could bring disaster to a production: wishing a fellow actor "Good luck" instead of "Break a leg," whistling in the dressing room, or mentioning the "Scottish play" by its actual name inside the theater (but lots more about Shakespeare's *Macbeth* in Chapter 25, "Apparitions and the Arts"). So is it any wonder that the theater world is, shall we say, "receptive" to the belief that ghosts haunt their playhouses?

Raising the Curtain on England's Haunted Theaters

England, home of the Bard, has some of the world's most haunted theaters. Some activity, such as lights flickering, occur in almost all of the West End theaters, but these are often attributed to their age rather than any paranormal activity. But some of the theaters are paid regular visits by their resident ghosts, and the phantoms are seen by cast, crew, and, occasionally, patrons.

Adelphi Theatre

The ghost of actor William Terriss haunts the famed Adelphi Theatre located on London's Strand. In December 1877, Terriss was stabbed to death as he exited the stage door. Among the phantom phenomena attributed to him have been:

➤ Unidentified footsteps

➤ Lights that turn on and off by themselves

➤ Stage elevators that run by themselves

➤ Furniture that moves by itself (including a famous 1928 incident in which many spectators saw the couch from his dressing room move on its own while a young lady was sitting on it)

From 1955 to at least 1972, Terris's ghost, decked out in a gray suit and white gloves, has also been sighted on many occasions at the Covent Garden underground station by several ticket takers, engineers, signalmen, and the like. In addition, a ghostly nun, whose appearance seems to foretell a lucky life for whoever sees her, sometimes haunts Covent Garden itself.

Coliseum

At London's Coliseum, the ghost of a soldier in World War I-era uniform sometimes appears to take a seat in the Dress Circle just as the show is about to begin. Legend has it that the young man, in love with a leading lady, went directly from the theater to the front lines of the war, where he was killed. He is believed to appear on the anniversary of his death.

Ghostbusting

To avoid any confusion for non-British readers, any theater that received the royal patent was able to call itself Theatre Royal. (Think of it as a seal of approval from the monarchy.) Several theaters held and used the title concurrently because, once the honor was bestowed, it was theirs to keep and advertise unless or until the throne withdrew it.

Drury Lane

The Drury Lane, Theatre Royal in London is one of the world's most haunted theaters and has had dozens of authenticated sightings. Today's theater is actually the fourth to stand on that site.

Drury Lane's most famous ghost is the so-called "Man in Gray," who usually appears—*when* he appears—between the hours of 9 A.M. and 6 P.M. He's been spotted by not only the actors but matinee audiences as well. He also appeared from time to time during World War II when the Entertainers National Services Association (ENSA) occupied the building.

The ghost is thought to be that of a nobleman from the 1770s. He appears with powdered hair, wearing a tri-corner hat, dress jacket, ruffled sleeves, riding boots, a cape or cloak, and a sword.

According to legend, the nobleman frequented the theater because he was in love with one of the leading ladies. A jealous rival stabbed the nobleman to death and walled his corpse into a seldom-used service passage on the left side of the stage. The skeletal remains remained there until they were discovered during renovation of the theater in 1848.

No one seems to be able to get closer than about 40 feet to the Man in Gray. He's silent and undemonstrative. When he appears, he enters the auditorium on the orchestra level by walking through a wall, then passes through several doors (without opening them) and walks up the stairs to the Dress Circle. He crosses the front of the Dress Circle, descends the staircase at the other side, and leaves the theater by passing through the wall opposite where he entered.

The spirit of actor Charles Macklin, who lost his temper and killed fellow actor Thomas Hallam, usually appears backstage. He was never convicted for his crime, and he lived to be an emaciated, unattractive man, 107 years old. It's said he's doomed to wander the corridor where the murder took place for eternity.

Ghostbusting

The Man in Gray usually manifests in Drury Lane Theatre just before the theater is about to open a long-running hit. (Needless to say, he's a rather welcome spirit!) He appeared, for instance, during rehearsals—once to more than 70 cast members—for the original London productions of *Oklahoma!, Carousel, South Pacific,* and *The King and I.* Of course, maybe he just likes Rodgers and Hammerstein tunes.

Other, more pleasant, ghosts inhabit Drury Lane Theatre. During the 1947 run of *Oklahoma!* the spirit of King Charles II was spotted. One of the cast members, American Betty Joe Jones, reported feeling herself guided about the stage by an invisible presence to help her improve her blocking. When she got it right, the ghost congratulated her with a pat on the back. Seven years later, cast member Doreen Duke reported receiving a similar spirit guide and "well done" pat during the opening night of *The King and I.* Some say that the ghost who helped the young ladies was none other than that of Joe Grimaldi, the celebrated clown and actor, who often played Drury Lane and was beloved for his willingness to help new talent.

Duke of York's Theatre

Strange sounds and knocks are heard at the Duke of York's Theatre in London (currently housing the Royal Court theater company). Staff members attribute the noise to the ghost of Violet Melnotte, a flamboyant, strong-willed owner/manager of the theater who died in 1935.

The Haymarket

The Haymarket, Theatre Royal is the second-oldest London theater still in use. Located between Piccadilly Circus and Buckingham Palace, the original theater was built in

1720 and replaced with the current structure a hundred and one years later. The theater is haunted by the ghost of John Buckstone, who spent 30 years with the theater, first as an actor and later as manager (from 1853 to 1878). The first sighting of Buckstone's ghost in the theater occurred within a year of his death.

Buckstone appears in one of the theater boxes, dressed in a frock coat. The door of his old dressing room has also been seen to open and close by itself. Another ghost, an old man who walks the hallways, is thought to be that of Henry Field, and actor-manager of the theater in the early 1700s.

Ghostly Pursuits

Among the notable actors who have seen the ghost of John Buckstone at the Haymarket, Theatre Royal was actress Margaret Rutherford. One night in 1963, it was hard to get home after a performance of *School for Scandal* because of an extremely heavy fog. She and her husband decided to stay the night in her dressing room. The next day, she claimed that in the middle of the night she looked across the room and saw the hairy leg of a man, then looked up and noticed his period clothes and his face. It was Buckstone! She later gave a similar report to the magazine *Psychic News*. Rutherford is still fondly remembered for her zany portrayal of the medium in a play about ghosts, Noel Coward's *Blithe Spirit*.

Although Buckstone's apparition is rarely seen today, there are plenty of unusual occurrences in the theater of the type often associated with ghosts and poltergeists: lights going on and off by themselves, doorknobs jiggling, and props disappearing from one place and reappearing at another.

Her Majesty's Theatre

Also located between Piccadilly Circus and Buckingham Palace, Her Majesty's Theatre was built for actor-manager Sir Beerbohm Tree in 1897. After his death in 1917, Tree's ghost returned to the theater. His apparition was seldom seen but often felt, and presumed to be his. The presence was always accompanied by a drop in temperature. It usually appeared backstage on Fridays, or paydays. When the spirit was in the house, it usually occupied a top box on stage right, which was Tree's favorite seat in the theater. Audience members sitting there during a performance have complained of the box opening by itself, then air becoming icy cold. On one celebrated occasion in the 1970s, Tree's ghost was seen by many people at one time (a collective apparition). During the run of Terence Rattingan's *Cause Célèbre,* the entire cast on the stage—including the show's star Glynis Johns—saw Tree's ghost crossing at the back of the stalls (orchestra seating).

Today, Her Majesty's Theatre has a new phantom, who is probably set to "haunt" the theater for many years to come: It's current, long-running tenant is Andrew Lloyd Webber's *The Phantom of the Opera*.

Sadler's Wells Theatre

The upper gallery of Sadler's Wells Theatre in London is thought to be haunted by the ghost of Lilian Baylis, who built the playhouse in the early 1900s. Another apparition, dressed as a clown and thought to be Grimaldi, sometimes appears in one of the theater boxes at midnight.

Theatre Royal, Bath

The Theatre Royal in Bath is haunted by a Gray Lady. According to legend, she's thought to be the ghost of an actress who performed there. She became, shall we say, "romantically" involved with a gentleman who booked a box seat every night to watch her on stage. Unfortunately, the actress was married, and when her husband found out about the affair, he challenged his wife's lover to a duel. They fought with swords; the lover lost, pierced through the heart. The actress, grief-stricken, played one last performance wearing her costume of a gray gown and a headdress of gray feathers. After the show, she went to her room next door at the Garrick's Head Hotel and hanged herself. She was discovered in the morning, still wearing the gray dress: She returns in it as a phantom. Her ghost usually appears in the box where her lover sat admiring her.

The same Gray Lady is said to haunt Garrick's Head Hotel as well. Her ghost is often accompanied by the strong scent of jasmine perfume. She is also said to play tricks: knocking on doors, moving candles across the bar, and stealing small objects such as coins or cuff links and returning them to vacant, locked rooms. The ghost has also materialized in Popjoy's Restaurant, located to the side of the theater.

Theatre Royal, York

The Theatre Royal in York is haunted by the ghost of yet another Gray Lady, a gray-and-white apparition of a female. The spectre, which has been seen by both playgoers and actors, usually appears in a small room just off the Dress Circle and is thought by some to be a phantom nun. The theater was built on the site of a hospital that was operated by nuns from the 12th to the 18th century. According to one legend, the phantom nun was bricked up alive in her convent cell as punishment for breaking her religious vows.

Nottingham Theater

Just after World War II, a Methodist church in the Nottingham city center was turned into an amateur theater. Many people have reported seeing the ghost of a man, dressed in a suit, or have heard his footsteps or breathing, usually in the right-hand side of the building.

The phantom has been seen coming through the auditorium up to the area in front of the stage, then passing through a wall and into the box office. In another sighting, the ghost was followed through the upstairs rehearsal rooms until it passed through a wall and into the wardrobe area. He's also been spotted in the passage running outside along the length of the theater. On one of these occasions, a member of the troupe was opening the gates at one end of the alleyway and saw the man walking toward them down the passage. As the spectre reached the gate, he disappeared.

Boo!

Although the FBI certified that the corpse of the man shot outside the Biograph Theater was Dillinger, some identified the body as that of another career criminal, Jimmy Lawrence. The FBI claimed that Dillinger's appearance had been altered by plastic surgery. The moral to the story: Always be certain about your corpses. You don't want to wind up being haunted by the wrong ghost!

Ghosts of the American Theater

They may hold *royal* patents, but British theaters have no patents on ghosts. More than a few theaters in the States also are haunted. In fact, our phantoms aren't snobs: Some even haunt—shudder—movie theaters. For example, the Biograph Theater, a movie house on Clark Street in North Chicago, is haunted by the ghost of a man running down the alley next to theater. It's thought to be the ghost of John Dillinger, who was ambushed by police and died in a hail of bullets in 1934.

Why, Oh, Why Ohio?

Ohio can hold its own when it comes to claims on ghost-infested theaters. During renovations in the 1980s, it was discovered that the Music Hall in Cincinnati was apparently built over a pauper's cemetery. This might explain the strange paranormal activity seen by the crew. Angry whispering and female voices have been overheard. A security guard investigated laughing coming from one of the ballrooms and discovered the ghosts of men and women dressed in 1880s period dress. This occurrence was especially unusual because the haunting was repeated the next day, when it was witnessed by several women.

Another Ohio theater, the Akron Civic Theatre, is protected by the ghost of Fred, its former long-time custodian. He returns during special events, such as high school proms, and frightens away would-be vandals. The phantom of a young, weeping woman is also seen near the canal that runs under the theater and much of the city. Although the style of her clothing offered no real clues, she's thought to be have lived during the heyday of canal boat travel.

California Dreaming

The Pasadena Playhouse, named the official State Theater of California in 1937, is haunted by its founder Gilmor Brown.

Gilmor Brown.
(Photo courtesy of the
Pasadena Playhouse)

Born in North Dakota in 1886, Gilmor had a diverse career in acting and theater company management, touring throughout the country and Canada before settling his troupe, "The Gilmor Brown Players," in Pasadena in 1916. His newly dubbed Community Players performed in several facilities there, including the Savoy, a renovated burlesque house. Finally, in 1924, the cornerstone was laid on a new theater, the Pasadena Community Playhouse, and the company moved in the following year.

During its Golden Years from 1925 to 1937, the Playhouse produced more than 500 new plays, including 23 American and 277 world premieres. Being close to Hollywood, the Pasadena Playhouse often drew film stars to its casts. Over the years, many of today's stars—such as Dustin Hoffmann, Gene Hackman, Rue McClanahan, Jamie Farr, and Sally Struthers—received some of their early training at the Playhouse's theater school. Following Gilmor's death in 1960, the Playhouse fell into decline, finally closing its doors in 1969. Restoration of the theater began in 1979, and in 1986 the Pasadena Playhouse once again started a full subscription season of plays and musicals.

There have been reports for decades of Gilmor Brown's ghost playing pranks throughout the theater. Although his apparition has never been seen, a presence thought to be Gilmore's is often

Ghostbusting

Staff members at the Pasadena Playhouse know that if the house ghost starts acting up, all they have to do is quietly chide him with a "Now, Gilmor, that's enough," or "Not now, Gilmor, I'm busy." And he'll go away! Imagine that—a ghost with manners!

felt. Most often, he performs harmless practical jokes. The activity is so frequent that, these days, almost anything unusual that occurs at the Playhouse is blamed on Gilmor.

The interior of the haunted Pasadena Playhouse. (Photo courtesy of the Pasadena Playhouse)

One of the house mangers, Betty Jean Morris, has kept a journal of some of the more recent ghost activity at the Playhouse:

➤ Some personal objects, such as Morris's own binoculars, have disappeared from the otherwise empty theater.

➤ Staff members have reported leaving some small item (such as a file of documents) in one location, only to find it only minutes later in another part of the theater.

➤ One time, the front door could not be unlocked; later, the same lock unlocked on its own.

➤ During the Sunday matinees of one particular production, and at exactly the same time each week for about a month, the house lights in the theater would come up on their own. The electrician could find no natural cause or explanation.

➤ For a time, the controls and earphones in the overhead booth would be rearranged when the sound and light crew left for their break during intermissions, even though the booth was locked. They finally posted an usher as guard during intermissions. No one entered the booth, yet the controls still somehow were reset.

➤ The elevator frequently stops at the third floor, even if it's not the passenger's destination. For many years, Gilmor Brown kept his office on the third floor.

The Montgomery in Chinatown

Another California theater was the old Montgomery Playhouse in San Francisco located on Broadway near the Chinatown district, it was filled with phantoms. Cindy Freeling, an actress who also helped the tech staff after hours, tells how she was puzzled, but not frightened, when costumes or props were invisibly pushed or yanked out of her arms. She mentioned the phenomena to some of the crew, who said, "Oh, don't you know? The theater's haunted. The building used to be a Chinese mortuary. If you go down into the basement you can still see the slabs."

The ghosts were never malicious, but they liked to let the actors and crew know they were there. Freeling remembers the time that the actors were all backstage in line, ready for a curtain call. Every one of them, from the back to the front of the line, felt an invisible body elbow its way to the front in order to take its bow.

Ghostly Pursuits

The Montgomery Playhouse saw the last stage performance of actor Sal Mineo. He finished up a run in James Kirkwood's play *P.S. Your Cat Is Dead,* and transferred with the production to Los Angeles. It was just before opening night in L.A. in February 1976 that the 37-year-old actor was murdered by a stab wound to the chest as he was getting out his car behind the West Hollywood building where he lived. Mineo had starred in the 1955 film *Rebel Without a Cause* with James Dean, Natalie Wood, and Nick Adams. All three of these co-stars also died violent or mysterious deaths.

After the theater lost its lease, the neighborhood was renovated. Yet, for the longest time, none of the local developers wanted to touch the old Chinese mortuary. They were afraid there were just too many ghosts, and they didn't want to disturb them. Since the building's eventual make-over, however, there have been no more reports of hauntings.

From See to Shining See

Here are about a dozen thumbnail sketches of some other theaters from one coast to the other in which the spectres are the stars:

➤ **Maine.** A room on the second floor of the Boothbay Opera House in Boothbay Harbor is haunted by an unidentified spectre, and Revolutionary-era soldiers are sometimes seen at the Ogunquit Playhouse in Ogunquit.

➤ **New York.** At least two ghosts haunt the Cohoes Music Hall in Cohoes. The one most frequently seen is that of a woman, dressed in 1930s or 1940s apparel. She always appears to be angry. The other phantom is male and is thought to be a former stage manager who was crushed to death by a falling sandbag. His apparition has been seen and heard in the wings and on the stage. (You'd think he'd know better! You're supposed to be quiet offstage when the play's in progress.)

➤ **Pennsylvania.** Many people have reported seeing the shade of an elderly woman walking across the balcony of the Majestic Theater in Reading. Unidentified ghosts also haunt the Pittsburgh Playhouse.

➤ **Maryland.** The old Opera House building in Westminster (today the home of the Opera House Printing Company) is supposedly haunted by an actor who was murdered just outside the stage door after a performance. (Talk about critics! Could you get a worse review?)

➤ **Wisconsin.** Say cheese! A foglike apparition has been spotted in the balcony of the Majestic Theater in Milwaukee, and the ghost of a former theater manager has appeared in the Grand Theatre in Wausau.

➤ **Illinois.** The ghost of "One-armed Red" is seen and heard in the Lincoln Theatre in Decatur.

Ghostly Pursuits

Richard Miller, an 18-year-old usher at the Guthrie in 1967, was a shy and sometimes bumbling loner. On Saturday, February 5, 1967, he committed suicide by shooting himself with a newly purchased gun and ammunition while sitting in his car in a Sears parking lot on Lake Street. His body, still dressed in his usher's uniform, was not discovered until two days later, on Monday.

Soon, patrons seated in Row 18 (which had been part of Miller's assigned area) at the Guthrie began complaining of a rude usher pacing the adjacent aisle and staring at them during performances. The young man never spoke or made any other sound. Their descriptions of the boy, which included a distinct mole on his cheek, matched Miller. Dozens of staff members have seen the apparition in the house, on the stage's catwalks, or in a seating area known as the Queen's Box. Sightings have tapered since an exorcism was conducted in 1994.

➤ **Tennessee.** The Orpheum Theatre in Memphis is home to the ghost of a little girl named Mary. People have felt her as they sit in one particular seat in the theater: Obviously, it's her favorite. According to legend, she died in the fire that burned the original Orpheum Theatre. Some think she was actually killed on nearby Beale Street rather than in the theater itself.

➤ **Minnesota.** The famed Guthrie Theater in Minneapolis is allegedly haunted by the ghost of a teenage usher who committed suicide. He's seen standing in the aisles during performances after the house lights have gone down.

➤ **Iowa.** Ever since a 1986 renovation, theater staff of the Grand Opera House in Dubuque have heard ghost voices and footsteps. Beginning in 1991, apparitions started appearing at the back of the auditorium.

➤ **Kansas.** The Purple Masque Theater on the campus of Kansas State University is haunted by several ghosts, including that of Nick, a football player who died in an accident while enrolled at KSU. He's a noisy one, banging objects and rear-ranging chairs. The ghost of a Confederate soldier also sometimes appears on the stage, seated in a phantom chair.

➤ **Wyoming.** At least two unknown ghosts haunt the Atlas Theatre in Cheyenne.

Ford's Theatre: A National Tragedy

Ford's Theatre in Washington, D.C., is perhaps the most famous, or infamous, theater in the United States. On April 14, 1865, during a performance of the play *Our American Cousin,* John Wilkes Booth entered Box 7 and assassinated President Abraham Lincoln. After firing the fatal shot to Lincoln's head, Booth jumped from the president's box to the stage, breaking his leg in the fall. Booth managed to escape from the theater.

Twelve days later, Booth was hiding in a barn on Richard Garret's farm near Bowling Green, Virginia, when he was surrounded by soldiers. They set the barn on fire, and Booth died either in the blaze or the accompanying gunfire.

Shortly after Lincoln's assassination and Booth's death, noted photographer Matthew Brady shot several photos of the interior of Ford's Theatre. In one of his photographs, a hazy figure resembling Booth could be seen standing in the presidential box.

John Thomson Ford, who built the theater, was jailed, tried, and acquitted of conspiracy in the assassination. Congress forced him to sell the theater, then closed it to the public. In 1893, part of the building collapsed, killing 28 people. Ford's

Ghostbusting

Interestingly, because of damage to the corpse from the fire, Booth's body was never positively identified. Conspiracy theorists believe that Booth may have actually somehow escaped the carnage. Of course, if that's the case, how do you explain the sightings of his ghost almost immediately thereafter?

Theatre was finally renovated by the National Park Service and reopened to the public in 1968 as a museum and playhouse. Ever since, actors, audiences, and staff in the theater and museum have reported seeing Booth's ghost. In addition, actors often feel an icy presence, become ill at ease, nauseous, shudder, or forget lines when standing near the spot at left-center stage where Booth landed.

Lincoln's ghost hasn't appeared in the theater, but it has been seen across the street at Petersen House, where he was carried, mortally wounded, and subsequently died. Lincoln's ghost also haunts the White House and Loudon Cottage as well as his tomb in Illinois (see Chapter 14, "This Old House: Haunted America"). Every April, the phantom of his funeral train appears along the route between Washington, D.C., and Springfield, Illinois (see Chapter 20, "Trains and Boats and Planes").

So there you have it. Next time you're sitting all alone in a theater, and the lights go down, look carefully to your left, then to your right. Shakespeare wrote about the Seven Ages of Man. Maybe, if you're lucky, you'll be seated next to someone who's in the Eighth.

Now let's ease on down the road to look at some of the world's most famous haunted roadways and modes of transportation.

The Least You Need to Know

➤ Old theaters are always suspected of being haunted. Some really are!

➤ England has more than its fair share of theater ghosts. Most are long-time owners, managers, or actors associated with their respective theaters.

➤ Both movie and legitimate theaters are haunted in the United States, and some of these hauntings are well-documented.

Chapter 20

Trains and Boats and Planes

In This Chapter

➤ Lincoln's ghost train

➤ The *Flying Dutchman* and Cruises to Eternity

➤ James Dean's death car

➤ Phantom pilots from flights of doom

With each new technological advance, every mode of transportation has entered the Ghost Age. Yes, first it was only phantoms on foot, then on horseback and in coaches and carriages. If we follow the natural—or perhaps supernatural—progression, we'll find that there have been ghost boats, railways, cars, and planes.

Of course, this has caused quite a controversy in paranormal circles. The sightings can't be denied. But how are they possible? According to most paranormal theorists, humans can return as ghosts because they have some spirit, essence, or soul that survives death.

But do horses? And planes, boats, and trains? So far, ghost hunters haven't come up with a good answer to explain them. But they *have* come up with some good ghost stories about travel vehicles. So fasten your seat belts: It's gonna be a bumpy night!

The Little Engine That Could: Railway Phantoms

Ghosts and phantoms have been reported on trains and along railroad tracks for as long as there has been an Iron Horse. During the Golden Age of Railroads, steam- (and then early diesel) driven trains were fast, they were modern, but they could also be deadly. Collisions and derailments were a regular part of train travel.

At one time, British railways maintained a small makeshift morgue at many stations to house those who died on railway property until the corpses could be claimed. People have claimed to see the ghosts of those whose bodies lay nearby in the station's "dead house," as such structures were known.

Here in the United States, the Cody Road Railroad Bridge in Independence, Kentucky, is supposedly haunted by a woman who was killed by a train at the overpass. A ghost at the Old Depot House in New London, Minnesota, has been identified as passenger Ey Wtizke. There are endless examples of such hauntings by individuals.

Got a Light?

There's a whole genre of ghost lights that haunt railways. One of the best-known railroad legends concerning a spirit lantern is the so-called Summerville Light of Summerville, South Carolina. According to local lore, every night at midnight, a local woman would meet her husband, a conductor on the rail line. She would always arrive carrying a lantern and a meal for him. One dreadful night, the train never arrived. The train had derailed, or crashed, and (according to most versions of the story) her husband was beheaded. The woman became deranged and never accepted the loss of her husband. She still showed up at the station every night at midnight, swinging the lantern as she paced along the tracks.

Of course, eventually she, too, died. But that didn't stop the Summerville Light, the ghost light of her lantern. They say that if you go to the old train stop at night, at exactly midnight all sounds of the evening (crickets, frogs, whatever) suddenly stop! (Perhaps they sense the presence of the woman's ghost.) Then, a light can be seen far off in the distance; it slowly comes toward you, and if you run, it chases you. Finally, it passes on and moves off into the night. You've seen the light of the sad, mad widow, waiting for her husband who will never arrive.

There are other ghost lamp stories from all across the United States. For example, television's *Unsolved Mysteries* retold the tale of a phantom man and his ghost lantern haunting the tracks outside Gurdon, Arizona. Ghosts have also been seen holding swinging lanterns by the train depot at Arcola, Illinois. Legend has it that the shadow of a man appears, swinging a ghost lantern, every time a train stops at the Maco Station near Wilmington, North Carolina. It's thought to be the ghost of Joe Baldwin, a conductor who was run over by a train at the station one night in 1867.

Ghostbusting

I've said it before, but it bears repeating: There's plenty of evidence that animals perceive spirits. Just like dogs can hear high-pitched sounds inaudible to human ears, perhaps animals operate some paranormal wavelength that humans don't yet understand. All I know is, if your critters suddenly quiet down—or go crazy—be on the lookout. There might be a ghost right around the corner.

Lincoln's Haunted Funeral Train

No doubt the most celebrated haunted train—or at least the one that carries the most famous passenger—is the annual spectral visit of Abraham Lincoln's funeral train.

After his assassination in 1865, President Lincoln's body was transported back for burial from Washington, D.C., to his home in Springfield, Illinois. The unique cortege by black-draped funeral train passed slowly on the tracks. All along the route, people lined the tracks to pay their last respects to their already-fabled leader.

Ever since, on the anniversary of Lincoln's assassination, many people living along the rail line claim to see the funeral train pass by. The train is always described as being black, and some imaginative percipients see a crew of skeletons.

Abraham Lincoln's funeral train, at the Pennsylvania Railroad station in Harrisburg, Pennsylvania, 1865.

Ghostly Pursuits

It's not just kooks and crazies who see ghosts. Sometimes, they're reported by legitimate news organizations. Here's just one account of the Lincoln ghost train, as described by the *Albany Times*:

It passes noiselessly. If it is moonlight, clouds cover over the moon as the phantom train goes by. After the pilot engine passes, the funeral train itself with flags and streamers rushes past. The track seems covered with black carpet and the coffin is seen in the center of the car, while all about it in the air and on the train behind are vast numbers of blue coated men, some with coffins on their backs, others leaning onto them.

My Body Lies over the Ocean

There have probably been legends of phantom boats and ships as long as people have set sail on the waters. Here are just a few of the best-known nautical nightshades.

Come Fly with Me: The Flying Dutchman

Probably the most famous ghost ship is the legendary *Flying Dutchman*. Spotting the ancient sailing vessel is supposed to be an omen of disaster. Depending upon which version of the story you hear, the ship is supposedly cursed to sail for eternity without reaching port either because of a challenge of (or oath against) God or as punishment for some sin. The ship is said to appear during storms off the Cape of Good Hope in South Africa. (Of course, the cape is infamous for its sudden, strong storms that can easily overpower and sink sailing vessels.)

There are many variations of the *Flying Dutchman* story. According to the Dutch version, Captain van Straaten swore that he could round the Cape of Storms (now the Cape of Good Hope) in a tempest. Needless to say, the ship sank and all aboard perished. The captain and his crew are now doomed to haunt the Cape forever.

In 1821, a British magazine published what has become one of most popular versions of the legend. During a storm off the Cape, the crew begged their captain to head for a safe harbor. He refused and swore that even God couldn't sink the ship. A silent, unidentifiable apparition appeared on the ship. Was it there to answer the captain's challenge? Or to offer help? Before the crew could find out, the captain cried, "Who wants a peaceful passage? I don't, I'm asking nothing from you."

The captain ordered the spectre to leave. When it didn't, he drew his pistol and fired, but the pistol blew up in his hand. The spirit then cursed the vessel, saying, "And since it is your delight to torment sailors you shall torment them, for you shall be the evil spirit of the sea. Your ship shall bring misfortune to all who sight it." The phantom then let the *Flying Dutchman* sink, killing all aboard.

Heinrich Heine (1797–1856), the 19th-century German Romantic poet, wrote his own version of the saga, in *Memoirs of Herr von Schnabelewopski* in which the captain

Boo!

Legend isn't always reality. Take the story of the *Flying Dutchman*. The Cape of Good Hope is infamous for its sudden, strong storms. A ship seen through a thick veil of rain, illuminated by cracks of lightning and towering overhead on the crest of a wave would seem ghostly indeed. No wonder that folklore about ghost vessels sprang up in the region!

Ghostbusting

It's the Heine version of the *Flying Dutchman* story that German composer Richard Wagner (1813–1883) used as the basis for his opera *Der Fliegende Hollander* (1843). In Wagner's libretto, the captain's name was van Derdeeken, and the lady whose love he sought was named Senta.

is allowed to bring the ship to port once every seven years. If he can win the true love of a virginal maiden, he can break the curse, and the ship and its crew can finally come to rest.

One of four sailors who spotted what they thought was the *Flying Dutchman* off the Cape of Good Hope in 1923 reported it to Sir Ernest Bennett, a member of London's Society for Psychical Research. One of the other seamen corroborated the account. Bennett wrote up the encounter in his 1934 book *Apparitions and Haunted Houses: A Survey of the Evidence*. Bennett agreed with fellow SPR member Frederic W.H. Myers, that the phantom ship sighting was probably an image caused by a telepathic projection by the vessel's dead crew. (Most paranormal researchers have since discounted the telepathic projection theory as an explanation for ghosts.)

Skeptics and scientists do not deny the sightings. They just deny that they're apparitions. The most probable cause, they say, is refraction, which casts the image of an actual ship, not visible but just over the horizon, up into the air and against the clouds.

Please Be My Palantine

Yet another Dutch ship, *The Palantine,* is the basis for another nautical ghost legend. The lights of the blazing phantom ship are supposedly seen near Block Island off Rhode Island. According to one version of the legend, *The Palantine* left Holland in 1752 bound for Philadelphia, but it was badly damaged by a storm off New England. The crew mutinied, killed the captain, robbed the passengers, and then deserted the ship. *The Palantine* ran aground on Block Island. Local pirates known as the Block Island Wreckers plundered the ship, but not before giving the passengers safe passage to shore. One woman, who had gone mad during the storm and mutiny, refused to leave the ship, even though the pirates were going to set it on fire. As the ship was washed back out to sea, engulfed in flames, the woman's screams echoed to the shore. The light of *The Palantine* on fire can still be seen on stormy nights.

In another version of the tale, the ship was German, and the captain and crew deliberately wrecked and plundered their own ship. In yet a third variation, the ship ran ashore because of pirates setting up decoy warning lights. In both of these versions, the passengers weren't rescued before the ship was set ablaze and sent back out to sea.

The *Palantine* light, as the apparition is known, has been seen on and off by residents of Block Island, usually just before stormy weather, from the late

Ghostbusting

Belief in ghost legends often depends more on faith that on fact. *The Palantine* was plundered more than 200 years ago, so the last pirate of the vessel is long since dead. By most versions of *The Palantine* tale, the ghost lights should never return. Yet return they do. Perhaps the ghosts of the pirates have come back, too. If so, *The Palantine* light might go on forever.

18th century through the 19th century and, on rarer occasions, in the 20th century. Many people believed that the light was God's punishment of the pirates who had killed *The Palantine*'s passengers and crew, and that when the last pirate died, the *Palantine* light would never return.

Watertown *Wraiths*

In December 1924, there was a fatal accident onboard the SS *Watertown,* a large oil tanker owned by Cities Service Company and bound for the Panama Canal from the Pacific Ocean. Two crew members, James Courtney and Michael Meehan, were cleaning one of the cargo tanks when they were overcome by toxic gas fumes and died. They were both accorded the traditional burial at sea.

The next day, the first mate saw two phantom faces in the trail of unsettled water behind the ship. He immediately pointed out the watery images to Captain Keith Tracy. Soon, the whole crew was intrigued. Everyone agreed that the ghostly images were those of Courtney and Meehan. The faces trailed the ship for days, and virtually all of the crew saw them. When the ship reached port at New Orleans, the captain made a report of the strange occurrence. One company manager, S.J. Patton, gave Tracy a roll of film and told him to take some photos should the faces ever show up again.

Of course, such things never happen when you have a camera, do they? But this time, it did! The faces appeared, the captain quickly got his camera and he took six photographs. When the ship returned to New Orleans, the captain gave Patton the film. To prevent any trickery, Patton took it to a commercial photographer to have it developed. Five of the shots showed nothing by waves. But on the sixth, there were outlines (possibly caused by light and shadow) that many swear are the faces of the dead seamen.

Boo!

The SS *Watertown* incident demonstrates the importance of timely investigation. By the time paranormal investigators got to the case, eyewitnesses and evidence had long since dispersed or disappeared. Analyze any data from a ghost hunt as soon as possible after you collect it, when it's still fresh in your mind. The less time that elapses, the less chance there is for errors to creep in.

Although the story apparently was widely told within Cities Service circles, it didn't become public until the tale was published in the company magazine *Service* in 1934. The noted psychical researcher Hereward Carrington tried to investigate the sighting, but in the 10 years that had elapsed since the apparitions were seen, both the first mate and Patton had died. The rest of the crew of the SS *Watertown* had dispersed, making firsthand documentation nearly impossible. The company could not even locate an original photo for Carrington, even though copies have since been widely published. To this day, the faces following the SS *Watertown* remain an unsolved mystery.

The **Queen Mary** *Mirages*

Perhaps the best-known and best-documented haunted ship is the *Queen Mary*. When she was christened at her Scottish shipyard in 1934 by Britain's King George V and Queen Mary, the *Queen Mary* was the largest ship in the world and the jewel of the Cunard Line. From 1936 to 1939, it sailed transatlantic voyages mostly between England and New York.

From 1940 to 1946, the ship was used for military service, acting primarily as a troop transport ship. Painted battleship gray to help camouflage her at sea, the *Queen Mary* was nicknamed "the Gray Ghost." Although she escaped harm from enemy vessels, on October 2, 1942, the *Queen Mary* had a tragic collision with one of her escort cruisers, the HMS *Curacoa*. The smaller ship was literally sliced in half, killing 338 of the sailors aboard.

From July 31, 1947, to December 9, 1967, the *Queen Mary* resumed service as a transoceanic cruise ship. Today, the ship is permanently moored in Long Beach, California, as a hotel and tourist attraction.

The Queen Mary, *now moored in Long Beach, California, is the world's best-documented haunted ship.*
(Photo by author)

There have been literally hundreds of sightings of various ghosts throughout the ship, and they continue to the present day. Many of the ship's staff, tour guides, and visitors to the ship, as well as overnight guests at the hotel, have reported seeing them.

Boo!

So far there have been no ghosts reported from the recent discovery, examination, and excavation of the wreckage of the RMS *Titanic*. You never know what spirits may awaken from their unearthly sleep. Some of them may not take too kindly to being disturbed.

One ghost who is regularly seen is that of 18-year-old John Pedder, who was trapped and crushed on July 10, 1966, when a watertight door in the engine room, next to the propeller shaft, closed on him. Because of the area he haunts, he has earned the nickname "the Shaft Alley Spectre."

The ghost of Senior Second Officer W.E. Stark has been spotted in his former sleeping quarters as well as on deck. He, too, died in an accident. On September 18, 1949, he drank a mixture of carbon tetrachloride and lime juice: The deadly cleaning fluid had been stored without proper warning in an old gin bottle. He treated the mistake lightly, but the next day he fell into a coma and died three days later.

The phantom of a man in a mechanic's white boiler suit has also been seen and heard near the engine room. Likewise, a man in blue-gray overalls, with black hair and a long beard, has been spotted below deck.

Ghostly Pursuits

Ghosts don't return just to haunt tragic sites; sometimes they come back to recall the good old days! Several different phantoms have been seen by the *Queen Mary*'s indoor first-class swimming pool, including an elderly woman wearing an old-fashioned, one-piece swimsuit and a bathing cap, as well as a young woman in a miniskirt. Their identities are unknown, but neither was a result of a reported drowning in the pool. They must be back just for the fun of it.

The ghost of another unidentified woman, the so-called Lady in White, seems to be attached to a specific piano. When it was in the Main Lounge, she was sometimes seen there, wearing a white evening gown and waltzing by herself. Sometimes she would stroll over to the piano. When the piano was moved to another lounge, now called Sir Winston's Piano Bar, the ghost moved with it.

In addition to the many ghosts sighted on the *Queen Mary*, there have been traditional haunting phenomena, such as unexplained voices and moving objects. Several séances have been held on the ship, at which mediums claim to have contacted resident spirits. The spirit most often mentioned is that of Lieutenant Carlo Giovetti, an Italian fighter pilot who was shot down by the British over North Africa. Giovetti died onboard the *Queen Mary* while being transported as a prisoner of war. He died primarily due to complications from injuries he suffered during the plane crash, and, like many others who died onboard during the War years, was most probably buried at sea. So far, his appearances have been confined to séances, but you never know …

Deadman's Curve: James Dean's Haunted Car

James Dean (1931–1955), the legendary Hollywood movie star, died in a fatal car crash in September 1955. For most of the summer preceding his death, he was on the set of the movie *Giant* just outside Marfa, Texas (home of the Marfa ghost lights; see Chapter 13, "Urban Legends"). After returning to Los Angeles, Dean bought a silver-gray 1955 Porsche Spyder.

Dean loved the car and nicknamed it "Little Bastard," but many of his friends were leery of it. For some reason, it made them feel uneasy. Driving the car on the way to the races at Salinas, California, Dean collided head-on with another car, which had paused while making a left-hand turn. The other driver was only slightly hurt; Dean's passenger, his mechanic Rolf Wuetherich, was thrown from the vehicle and badly injured. Dean was killed instantly.

Soon, a legend grew that the mangled remains of Dean's car were cursed. George Barris, a car designer and a friend of Dean's, bought the wreckage for salvage. While the car was being unloaded back at his garage, the car slipped and fell on Barris, breaking one of his legs. Barris sold two of the wreck's tires to a man, who reported that both tires blew out simultaneously just a few days later. Fans of the late actor were injured trying to steal souvenir parts from the wreckage.

Troy McHenry, a physician, bought the engine for his race car, and William F. Eschrid, another doctor, bought the drive shaft. Both raced with cars using the parts from Dean's car for the first time at Pomona, California, on October 1, 1956. McHenry spun out of control, hit a tree, and was killed. Eschrid flipped his car on a curve and was seriously hurt.

Over the next four years, Barris allowed the wreckage to be used for exhibition. Almost without exception, death or injury followed the car. In 1960, following an exhibition in Miami, Little Bastard was crated up and shipped back to Barris in Los Angeles. It never arrived.

Some people believe that certain objects can become cursed if they're involved in tragedy or violence. Was the wreckage of Little Bastard, an inanimate object, haunting others with just such a curse? Until it's found, we'll never know.

Many of James Dean's close friends and associates also met with some sort of tragedy or death:

➤ In 1968, his mechanic Rolf Wuetherich was convicted of murdering his wife. He pled insanity but was sentenced to life in prison.

251

➤ Also that year, Nick Adams, a friend who had dubbed some of Dean's voice during post-production of *Giant,* died of a drug overdose.

➤ Sal Mineo, Dean's co-star in *Rebel Without a Cause,* was stabbed to death in 1976.

➤ Lance Reventlow, an heir to the Woolworth fortune, had met Dean on his way to Salinas; he died in a plane crash.

Perhaps it wasn't Little Bastard that was cursed. Perhaps it was Dean himself!

Ghostly Pursuits

Other ghostly car legends concern death cars whose interiors carry the scent of death—whatever that may be—because a previous owner had died in the car, and the corpse wasn't discovered until it had begun to decompose. Although the details of the death and the make and year of the car may vary, the story always starts with a car that's inexpensive—a deal too good to pass up. It's only after the new owner buys the car that the ghastly smell of the former owner is noticed. No attempts to remove the smell are successful. Eventually the new owner sells the car at a loss or returns it to the dealership. The death car legend started in the United States around the 1930s, and it spread to England within 20 years.

Flying the Frightening Skies

Flying is scary enough for some people. How can something as heavy as a plane stay up there? Well, sometimes it doesn't. And two crashes in particular have led to well-documented ghost stories.

Before you read this section, you better check to see where the two nearest exits are located. And don't forget, they—or *something*—may be located right behind you.

The Crash of British Dirigible R-101

The British dirigible R-101 crashed on her maiden voyage in 1930. It lifted off in England on October 4, and fell to the ground the next day in France. And Irish medium, Eileen J. Garrett (1893–1970), knew it was going to happen!

Garrett received her first vision of the flying airship, even though it had not yet been built, while walking her dog in Hyde Park in London in 1926. Two years later, she saw it again, but this time in distress and sending off smoke, while strolling near London's Holland Park. Shortly thereafter, the construction of two new dirigibles was mentioned in the press, and Garrett received a psychic impression that one of them, the R-101, would crash. She sent a warning to Sir Sefton Brancker, the director of civil aviation. He pooh-poohed the warning; he would later die in the crash.

Ghostly Pursuits

Eileen J. Garrett was one of the few mediums who actually encouraged scientific investigation and testing of paranormal phenomenon. She entered mediumship reluctantly, mostly at the urging of psychic researchers such as Hereward Carrington and Nandor Fodor, and was a subject of many investigations. Garrett became a U.S. citizen in 1947; four years later she founded the Parapsychological Foundation (PF) to encourage paranormal research through grants and conferences. Although she contacted the spirit world through Uvani and other occasional controls, she remained open-minded as to whether she was actually contacting spirits of the dead or tapping into an inner or collective unconscious.

Later in 1928, Garrett claimed to have received a message during a séance from the spirit of the deceased Captain Raymond Hinchcliffe. He came from the Beyond to warn his friend Ernest Johnston, who was to be the navigator on the R-101 maiden voyage, not to go because the ship would crash. Johnson, too, ignored the plea and lived—or rather, died—to regret it. Then, in 1929, Garrett had a third and final vision of the airship in flames while flying over London. When the ship did plunge to the ground the following year, Garrett said she felt it before the press had learned of the disaster.

Ghostbusting

If you start getting messages from the spirit world—maybe not just one, but two, three, or four?—hey, pay attention! They're trying to tell you something! If they're coming all the way from the Other Side just to talk to you, it's probably important. And even if it's not, it'll sure be worth listening to.

Now comes the real ghost stuff: Three days after the crash, Garrett held a séance to try to contact the spirit of Sir Arthur Conan Doyle, who had died the previous July. Instead, Garrett's control Uvani started receiving messages from Flight Lieutenant H. Carmichael Irwin, who had been the captain of R-101. He gave very precise and detailed technical information about his craft. Ghost researcher Harry Price was at the séance; he was so convinced that the information was not only real but possibly top secret that he sent a transcript of the sitting to Sir John Simon, head of the Court of Inquiry that was investigating the airship disaster.

News of the séance also appeared in the newspapers, and a friend of Brancker's, Major Oliver Villiers, became interested in Garrett's work.

In a subsequent séance, several spirits of those who had died aboard R-101 contacted Garrett. Joining Irwin were Brancker and Johnson, among others. The ghosts explained that there had been a gas leak that was ignited from a backfire from the engine. They also claimed that officials knew the dirigible was unsafe—it was too heavy to reach a safe altitude, and it had bad air and fuel pumps—but the maiden voyage was commanded to proceed as scheduled.

Villiers, believing he had actually heard from the ghosts of the dead crew, gave Simon transcripts from the seven séances in which Garrett contacted the dirigible victims. Though fascinated, Simon said that ghost testimony was inadmissible in a court of law.

The Ghost of Flight 401

Throughout the 1970s, several crews and passengers have variously reported seeing, hearing, and receiving messages and warnings from, the ghosts of Captain Bob Loft and second officer and flight engineer Dan Repo of Eastern Airline Flight 401, which crashed in Florida's Everglades on the night of December 19, 1972. In every case, the apparitions, as well as other paranormal activity (such as cold spots, objects suddenly appearing, and sensing invisible presences), occurred on jets that were using salvaged parts from the downed L-1011.

Ghostly Pursuits

Two 1978 made-for-television movies dealt with incidents surrounding an L-1011 that crashed in the Everglades. Neither film mentioned people involved in the doomed Eastern Airlines flight by name.

As its title suggests, *Ghost of Flight 401,* written by Robert Howard Young and Robert Malcolm Young, focused on the spirit aftermath of the crash. The cast, directed by Steven Hilliard Stern, included Ernest Borgnine, Gary Lockwood, Kim Basinger, Tom Clancy, Howard Hesseman, and Russell Johnson.

Crash of Flight 401, directed by Barry Shear, also told the story of the doomed flight, but not its ghostly outcome. The cast included William Shatner, Eddie Albert, Adrienne Barbeau, and George Maharis.

A hundred passengers and crew, including Loft and Repo, died in or as a result of the crash. Loft and Repo both survived the impact, but Loft died about an hour later, before rescue crews could reach the plane. Repo died in the hospital about 30 hours after the crash. The investigation concluded that it was a combination of possible mechanical failure and human error. Printouts said the landing gear wasn't operating properly; as the two pilots were checking the data, they didn't notice that they were letting the plane lose altitude. By the time they noticed, it was too late.

Eastern salvaged the wreck and allowed parts to be used for repair and maintenance on other L-1011s in the fleet. Before long, Loft's and Repo's ghosts began appearing on those planes, including several leased to other airlines and especially on Eastern's plane number 318. Management refused to believe the sightings. Besides, if they did acknowledge anything unusual, they knew the media would have a field day reporting about Eastern's haunted planes. The reports became so plentiful and persistent that eventually Eastern quietly removed all of the recycled Flight 401 parts.

Repo was seen more often than Loft, but both were frequently seen, recognized, and identified by crew members who had worked with them. Here are just a few of the major reported sightings of Repo and Loft:

Boo!

Do spirits feel guilt in the after-world? Ghost experts say that they do, and that the spectres sometimes return to the mortal world to right wrongs and atone for their sins. That might explain why Repo, who carried the burden of the loss of a hundred lives under his care, returned to check the safety of other planes. He was not able to let such a crash happen again—not on *his* watch!

➤ Repo liked to visit the galley, where his face would appear reflected in the oven door. Even when he wasn't seen, flight attendants sometimes sensed his or some other presence, and the galley would feel cold and damp.

➤ A flight attendant watched as an engineer fixed an overloaded circuit on an oven before take-off. Only after later seeing Repo's photograph did the flight attendant realize she had seen his ghost fixing the circuit!

➤ Repo's ghost was particularly concerned about safety. He would appear in the cockpit, sitting at the engineer's instrument panel or simply reflected in the instruments. He even told one engineer he had already run the pre-flight inspection.

➤ Before one flight, Repo warned about an electrical failure. He alerted the crew to a problem with hydraulic fluid on another flight, and a fire onboard a third. He was always found to be correct in such warnings, and due to his alerting the crew in advance, disaster was prevented.

➤ Loft often appeared sitting, in uniform, in an unoccupied first-class seat. On at least one occasion, he was instantly recognized by the captain, then the ghost simply disappeared.

➤ Loft also appeared from time to time in the small crew compartment. He even spoke over the public address system on flight safety, informing passengers on the proper use of the lap belt, etc.

As strange and sad as some of these tales of vehicular hauntings may be, could anything possibly be more tragic than the loss of a school-age child to the Great Unknown? Many student spirits have chosen to return to haunt the hallways of their youth. And, while we're talking books and learning, let's stop by the library. Maybe the ghosts haunting *them* are simply returning their overdue books.

The Least You Need to Know

➤ There are reports of hauntings on all forms of vehicles and modes of transportation.

➤ Most ghost legends of the railroads are connected to deaths caused by collisions, disrailing, or other tragedies: A famous example is the appearance of the ghost of Lincoln's funeral train.

➤ As long as humankind has explored the oceans, there have been legends of ghost ships, including those of the *Flying Dutchman* and the *Palantine* light; and the appearance of ghost crews and passengers, such as on the SS *Watertown* and the *Queen Mary.*

➤ Spirit visits from the crew of the downed British dirigible R–101 were discounted because the contact came through séances; the frequently seen apparitions from Eastern Airlines Flight 401 couldn't be dismissed so easily.

Chapter 21

School Daze: America's Most Haunted Schools

In This Chapter

➤ Student ghosts stay after school

➤ Sshh! Spirits in the library stacks

➤ Teachers who ignored the "final bell"

➤ Haunted halls of higher education

It was the best of times. It was the worst of times.

No, I'm not quoting Dickens. I'm talking about being a kid. A *school* kid. It's possibly the most exhilarating and liberating time of life. Anything and everything in the world is possible. If only there's time to do it all.

But sometimes, there's not.

It's a fact of life: People die every day. And, unfortunately, some of them are children and young adults. When they do return as ghosts, it's common for kids to haunt the happy (and, sometimes, not so happy) halls of their schools and dorms.

Let's take a class trip across the United States to look at a cross-section of some of America's haunted educational institutions, region by region. And, while we're at it, we'll hit some of the country's libraries, and maybe check out a few books on ghosts and hauntings (that's 133.1 in the good old Dewey Decimal system).

Hurry up, or you'll be late for homeroom.

Northern Nightshades

Colonial America started in the Northeast, and the region is home to the nation's oldest schools, which means the area's also home to the country's oldest spooks—not that you could tell by looking at them. Most of them look as young as they did the day they first entered these schoolyards.

If you've got a hall pass to the Spirit World, let's take a look around.

Maine

Haunted Oak Grove Academy lies in the woods of Vassalboro. Legend has it that several students were murdered here and hanged from meathooks, and the killer was never found. Spectral voices whisper the children's names, their ghosts are seen on the main school building's roof, and lights flicker throughout the academy.

Over in Brunswick, the old high school is haunted by a schoolgirl, but no one knows who she is or why she's returned. The custodians have named her Mimi. She moves objects and slams doors, and her apparition is occasionally seen walking the halls of Brunswick High.

Vermont

Also in the upper United States, the University of Vermont is located in Burlington. Henry, a former medical student who committed suicide there in the 1920s, haunts Converse Hall. The ghost of Margaret "Daisy" Smith haunts Bittersweet House. She lived in the building from the 1930s to the 1950s; today, it houses the school's environmental department. She usually appears wearing a period ankle-length skirt and a blouse with a high collar.

In the 1960s, five students from Winooski High School in Winooski were killed in a car crash while returning from a trip to Canada. A memorial service was held for them in the school gym, ever since, custodians have reported apparitional activity in the gymnasium.

Ghostbusting

The entire fourth floor of Shelton Hall is usually reserved for writing majors. Perhaps that's why Eugene O'Neill haunts the floor: Maybe the playwright feels comfortable with fellow writers. Of course, his tragic life influenced much of his own work. By haunting the dorm, is he giving his successors something to write about?

Massachusetts

Sessions House at Smith College in Northampton was once a farmhouse and served as a station on the Underground Railroad. It's been haunted since before being incorporated into the college. The ghosts are thought to be those of slaves who died when one of the secret tunnels into the basement collapsed and accidentally killed them. The first floor of Martha Wilson House, also on campus, is haunted by an unknown presence. Its footsteps can be heard pacing the floor, windows are discovered to have been opened by themselves, and occasionally, all the doors on the floor slam shut simultaneously without human assistance.

The famous playwright Eugene O'Neill is said to have died in what is now Room 401 in Shelton Hall of Boston University in Boston. Since his death in 1953, he has haunted the entire floor of the residence facility.

New York

Drop down to Schenectady, the home of Union College. There's a beautiful garden behind the central campus that belies its horrific history. Each year, on the first full moon following the summer solstice, the ghost of "Alice" strolls along the creek running through the garden. According to legend, she was burned at the stake for witchcraft on the site hundreds of years ago.

Ghostly Pursuits

The legend of Alice being burned at the stake for witchcraft in Schenectady, New York, is improbable. Few people were burned for witchcraft in the United States; most were hanged. Now and then, one was pressed to death by having large stones placed on the their chest to force a confession. The last notable hangings and pressings occurred as part of the witchcraft hysteria and trials at Salem Village in the Massachusetts Bay Colony in 1692. Of course, that's not to say there couldn't have been a local burning here and there.

Pennsylvania

Pennsylvania is one of the most haunted of the original 13 American colonies. With the writing of the Declaration of Independence there, you could say that Philadelphia is the site of the birth of a nation. Ghosts can be found all over the greater city area, not just from the Revolutionary War days, but from all eras of its historic past:

➤ **Civil War Library and Museum.** Phantom soldiers have been seen playing cards on the second floor of the Philadelphia museum. In fact the site has been featured on TV's *Unsolved Mysteries*.

➤ **Grundy Memorial Library.** The ghost of man said to have been a king of Spain has been spotted in a phantom rowboat on the Delaware River behind the library in Bristol. He holds a lantern and calls out the name of a lost little girl. Reports date back to before the library was built when there was a private residence on the site.

➤ **Bucks County Community College.** Tyler Hall at this Doylestown college is haunted by a female ghost who's thought to be Stella Tyler, a former school administrator.

➤ **Tate House.** In the 1770s, a Hessian solider was buried in the cellar of the house in Newtown. The former residence, now part of The George School, is haunted by the Revolutionary mercenary.

The ghost of a female student haunts Butz Hall at Cedar Crest College in Allentown. Like the Converse Hall student at the University of Vermont, the Butz Hall resident is said to have committed suicide in her dorm. Just down the road in Bethlehem, an unidentified elderly man haunts the library of Lehigh University. A few miles in the opposite direction, Central Catholic High School in Reading is haunted by a man who hanged himself in the attic there, back when the building was a private residence. Students report seeing combination locks on lockers spinning by themselves and the distinct sound of chains rattling sometimes echoes down the halls.

Ghostly Pursuits

As I signed out several books on ghosts from the library, the librarian noticed the titles and raised an eyebrow. "I had a ghost," she offered dryly. I've learned in such a situation to simply say, "Tell me about it." When the woman first moved to Hollywood, she moved into a small apartment. Almost immediately, ghostlike phenomena—especially floating objects— started happening. She'd be sitting at a table, and her cigarette would float up from the ashtray, across in front of her eyes, then drop: a definite fire hazard! Her cats were always the first to know when spirit activity was coming. They'd arch their backs, bear their teeth, hiss, and spit. Soon, she found out that a man had died in her apartment some time before. Perhaps his ghost thought he was still a tenant!

She was never afraid of the ghost or the phenomena, but after six months, it became too frustrating and unnerving. She moved.

Out at the other end of the state, Carnegie Library in Pittsburgh was supposedly built over an ancient cemetery, and people think that ghosts of the graveyard visit the building at night after closing hours. It's said that Room 201 of Bruce Hall, a dorm on the campus of the University of Pittsburgh in Pittsburgh, is haunted. On the Johnstown campus of the University of Pittsburgh, Laurel Hall as well as the Living and Learning Center are haunted by several nighttime spirits, including a woman, a boy, and an elderly man who hollers and wakes students from their sleep.

All of Gettysburg seems to be haunted, what with the catastrophic events that took place there during the Civil War (see Chapter 18, "That These Honored Dead," for more on Gettysburg's haunted battlefields). But the haunting of Stevens Hall at Gettysburg College only dates back about a hundred years. "The Blue Boy," as the spectre is called, ran away from an abusive home and sought shelter among the young college women in the dorms. One frigid, snowy night, the boy hid on a window ledge when the headmistress did her room checks. The woman seemed to take an eternity. When she left, the girls ran to the window to let the boy back in, but he had disappeared. Terrified that he had fallen and injured himself (or worse), they rushed outside. The boy wasn't there. He was never found. But residents of the dorm now report seeing a young boy, blue as if frozen to death, in and around the dorm.

The main campus of the Pennsylvania State University is located at University Park in the exact geographic center of the state. Schwab Auditorium, the site of many of the university's special events, is supposedly haunted by a handful of ghosts. One is thought to be George W. Atherton, the seventh president of the university, who is buried beside the hall. Another may be Charles Schwab, for whom the building is dedicated. Perhaps he hangs around his namesake auditorium hoping to be recognized.

The ghost of Old Coaly, a mule that was used during construction of the university in the 1850s, often has been seen and heard haunting Watts Hall. Also, a third-floor room of the dormitory Runkle Hall was the site of unexplained poltergeist activity in 1994.

Ghostbusting

Could Old Coaly really have returned from the dead? Most people believe that a ghost is a soul in spirit or apparitional form. Does that mean that animals—and many, many have been sighted as ghosts— have souls? Paranormal experts, religious theorists, and many pet owners still debate the issue.

The Lower Depths: Dixie and Southwest

There's an old song about how nice it is to live and die in Dixie. Well, apparently a lot of southern belles and beaus (and their counterparts in the Southwest) have decided there's a third verse to that song—something about coming back to haunt those of us still here.

But they're good kids: They've decided to stay in school! They weren't going to let a little thing like dying get in the way of a better education.

Virginia

Even the youngest children return to their happy haunts. At least two elementary schools are haunted in Virginia. At the first, William Bass Elementary School in Lynchburg, spectral voices are heard, and doors open and shut on their own at some of school's special events. The spirits of two African-American boys who were killed in the 1960s by an unknown segregationist still attend Matthew Whaley Elementary School at 301 Scotland Street in Williamsburg.

Several ghosts haunt the College of William and Mary, which is also located in Williamsburg. In 1980, a female student committed suicide in a classroom in Tucker Hall. Ever since, students have reported seeing her ghost in the hallways there. Two phantom Native American boys who were forced to attend the school in the 17th century are still "sensed" in Brafferton Building; one is sometimes seen on the campus grounds. Also, ghosts of a French soldier and the college's first president, the Reverend James Blair, have been spotted in President's House.

Finally, a spectre identified as Lucinda, a former student, haunts the stage, a room below, and the balcony of the theater in Phi Beta Kappa Hall. (Lucinda was to have performed in an upcoming college production of Thornton Wilder's *Our Town* when she was killed in an automobile accident.) The spectre of Revolutionary War soldier who died of gunshot wounds on the third floor of the building also returns to haunt Phi Beta Kappa Hall.

North Carolina

Here's a grisly one: Corpses are regularly sold or donated to medical schools for use in the classroom. But, apparently one girl wasn't too happy about hers being sold to Founders College in Charlotte, North Carolina. In the 1930s, her green-eyed, slender ghost regularly haunted Chambers Hall on the small campus that used to be located in the center of the city.

South Caldwell High School in Lenoir has not one but two ghosts, although neither appears as an apparition. The first is a female student who died while rehearsing a school play. She's now a theater ghost (see Chapter 19, "All the World's a Stage") and plays tricks just before opening night of any play, such as moving props backstage and creating havoc with the lights and sets. The other ghost is that of a man who fell down the shaft while working on the elevator one night. The elevator now seems to have a mind of its own. It often goes up and down on its own, sometimes four or five times, around the hour of his deadly accident.

Florida

Flagler College is located in northern Florida, in St. Augustine. Although there are several ghost legends of sightings on campus, most of the activity occurs in Ponce de Leon Hall, which is the girls' dorm. Supposedly, the fourth floor is haunted by the ghost of the mistress of Henry Flagler, who hanged herself in the fourth-floor room back when the building was a hotel.

The old women's dormitory of the Ringling School of Art and Design in Sarasota in southern Florida also used to be a hotel. The building is haunted by the ghost Mary, who committed suicide back in the 1920s on the stairwell between the second and third floors. (That section of stairs is now used only as a fire escape.) Mary's apparition has been seen in the halls, but usually just out of the corner of one's eye. Students who live in what was once Mary's room sometimes come in to find their paintbrushes slowly spinning in their cups of rinse water!

To the west, Cawthon Hall on the campus of Florida State University in Tallahassee is revisited by a female student who was killed while sunbathing on the roof. She was struck by lightning during a freak, sudden storm. According to a 1971 story in the university newspaper, *The Florida Flambeau,* students have reported poltergeist-like activity in the dorm for years. Residents who occupy what was once the girl's room are especially haunted: Objects such as books or photos move by themselves, there are unusual sounds in the room at night, and often the ghost's "presence" can be felt.

Alabama

The stars fall over Alabama, but do ghosts fall out of the sky as well? It's said that a student who died in McCandless Hall at Athens State College in Hunstville is still seen from time to time in the halls of his old dorm. Two ghosts haunt Hunting-don College in Montgomery: A Red Lady (named for the color of clothing she wore in life, and still wears in death) visits the older dorms of the college. A lonely student who was unable to make any friends at the college, she hanged herself in despair. Apparently, she's returned, still hoping to make the friends she never acquired while alive. You can't see the other spectre. He's called the Ghost on the Green because he shot himself on the campus green and now walks there at night. Percipients have felt him grab at their clothing, muss their hair, or blow in their eyes.

Also in Alabama, students have seen unexplained ghosts and heard spectral footsteps at Decatur High School in Decatur.

Boo!

There's an old saying, "Life is not a dress rehearsal." Apparently, a lot of ghosts don't agree. They come back to do things they never got around to when they were alive. Trouble is, most of them don't succeed when they're dead either. They just spend eternity trying. There's a lesson to be learned: Do it now! This is probably your only real chance to make it happen.

Louisiana

We've already looked at several of the haunted homes and cemeteries of Louisiana, and you've read about phantom monks and priests. Put them all together, and you have Saint Charles Borromeo College in Grand Coteau. The college's main building has been Ursuline Convent and a training center for the Society of Jesus religious order. It's haunted by an elderly priest who can be seen walking the halls.

Texas

Texas is known for its size. Everything is huge! So is it any wonder that its high schools, colleges, and universities have more than their share of spirits?

Texas's institutes of higher education are especially active:

➤ The University of Texas Medical Branch at Galveston (UTMB). Over the years, people have imagined seeing phantom faces on everything from window glass to cinnamon buns. But there's a long-standing legend of an unidentified face appearing on the side of a building on the UTMB campus.

➤ The University of Texas at Brownsville used to be Fort Brown. Phantom soldiers have been seen at night, marching their drills.

➤ At Institute of Texas Culture in San Antonio, budgeted under University of Texas at San Antonio (UTSA), unexplained pipe smoke is smelled in exhibition rooms, books rearrange themselves in the library, and phantom footsteps can be heard coming from the audio/visual room.

➤ The Agriculture building at Texas A&M University in College Station has a haunted elevator. Local legend attributes it to the victim of a murder that was supposedly committed in the elevator.

➤ The Housing Office and adjacent buildings of Angelo State University in San Angelo are haunted by a murder victim, a young female student who was killed in the 1970s by an ROTC cadet. Apparently, the suitor went murderously insane when she rejected him.

Two more Texas terrors: The old library building in downtown Houston is haunted by a ghost who plays the violin late at night. According to some legends, the spirit was a maintenance man in the 1920s and 1930s. Sealy High School in Sealy has an elevator that operates by itself. Doors on the second floor also open and close all by their lonesome, although the activity might be connected to the unexplained footsteps coming from up there.

Arkansas

A little further west, Old Charlie Fowler Christian School in Mountain View has unexplained footsteps heard descending the staircase at night. Water drips from the ceiling, even during droughts, and spectral voices chatter away in the cafeteria. Rumor has it that the school was built on an ancient Native American burial ground. Paranormal theorists say this might explain some of the activity.

The ghost of a female student haunts Henderson State University in Arkadelphia. She goes from dorm to dorm, looking for the boyfriend who deserted her. According to most versions of the tale, she died of a broken heart.

Nevada

Over in Nevada, the ghost of Miss Suzette, a former teacher, still strolls across the school grounds at Fourth Ward School in Virginia City. That's some recess supervisor! In Reno, there's a ghostly legend at Wooster High School involving the suicide of a football player. Back in the early 1970s, the Wooster Colts lost a big game to their rivals, the McQueen Lancers. Later that night, one of the defeated players went onto the field and shot himself. Now, whenever the two teams meet, players say they sometimes fumble over an invisible something—or someone—out on the field.

Also in Nevada, four different houses are reputedly haunted, each by its own resident ghost, at The College of Saint Rose in Albany. They are believed to be:

➤ A gardener

➤ A priest

➤ A musician who committed suicide in Chicago (no one knows how his ghost wound up in Nevada)

➤ A seven-year-old girl who was killed in a fire

It's unknown why these ghosts have chosen to haunt these particular buildings.

The Nation's Breadbasket

A nation moves westward ... and so does its belief in ghosts. Perhaps the telling of ghost stories is just another one of those good old, traditional family values for which the country's Midwest is justly proud. With almost 4,000 miles between its coasts, the United States has plenty of space to be haunted, and hundreds of ghosts attend classrooms and take up residence in dormitories every day.

Illinois

Here's a gruesome one. There's a clearing outside Gurnee that's referred to locally as The Gate. A small schoolhouse used to stand on the property, but it's long since been torn down, and the road to the site is closed. All that still stands is a large black cast-iron gate.

According to legend, a lunatic burst into the school and killed all the students. He decapitated several of the children and stuck their heads onto the pointed

Boo!

The road to The Gate and its site were obviously closed for a reason. Never go on private property unless you have permission from the owner and/or current resident.

Boo!

Suicide is never the answer. It doesn't really solve problems: Often, it just carries them over in the next world. Look at how many suicides have returned as ghosts, and they still can't seem to put an end their troubles. Work on meeting your challenges now, in this life, so you can rest in peace in the next.

spikes on the top of the gate. It's said that, even if you don't know the story, looking at gate produces an overwhelming sense of grief in the onlooker. Every so often, phantom heads appear on the gate's spikes, and the screams and cries of the phantom children can be heard in the wind.

It's said that the English building on the Champaign-Urbana campus of the University of Illinois used to be a girls' dormitory. One of the students who supposedly committed suicide there still haunts the structure.

Spectral activity takes place at the library in Williams Hall at the Illinois State University in Normal. Books fall from the shelf one by one without the help of human hands, and people have seen the flicker of a moving white object out of the corner of the eye. The apparition is thought to be that of the hall's first librarian, Angie Milner.

Indiana

Next door in the Hoosier State, a Gray Lady has been seen in the Willard Library in Evansville.

Several spots of the Indiana State University in Terre Haute are haunted. Spectral activity such as objects that move by themselves and spirit whispers and noises have been reported in Burford Hall. Also, the 12th floor of Cromwell Hall, which was a male dorm, is haunted by the spirit of a student who committed suicide by jumping out of the window of his room (Room 1221). His restless spirit now paces the hall. Residents have also heard other odd noises.

The University of Notre Dame in South Bend was built on lands once occupied by the Potawatomi Indians. Columbus Hall, one of the university's earliest buildings, is haunted by phantom Native Americans on horseback, galloping up and down the front steps. Notre Dame is world-famous for its football team, and according to some, one of the university's star players, George Gipp, haunts his old dormitory, Washington Hall. The building now houses the theater of the university's drama club, and Gipp supposedly returns to visit the stage and the backstage green room (where actors and their guests visit and relax before and after performances).

Iowa

In the late 1800s, a woman was descending the staircase from the third-floor College Hall at Simpson College in Indianola when she stumbled and fell. The fall broke her neck, killing her instantly. Ever since, according to school tradition, if you stand on the college seal on the grounds outside the hall at exactly midnight on any Friday the 13th, the woman's face will appear at (or on the glass of) a third-floor window.

Several buildings at the University of Northern Iowa in Cedar Falls are haunted. The spirit of a solider named Augie returns to a dormitory named Lawther Hall. He died there when the building was used as an infirmary. Student residents also have felt cold spots, heard unusual noises, and seen moving objects—all standard ghost and poltergeist activity. The Strayer-Wood Theatre, also on campus, is haunted by a ghost whom theater students have nicknamed Zelda.

Over in Ames, at Iowa State University, there's an unexplainable low moaning sound that can always be heard in Memorial Union. The building is dedicated to the memory of graduates of ISU who died at war, and the noise is said to be the haunting voice of the only female graduate of Iowa State to die in World War II.

Kansas

Well, now we *are* in Kansas, Toto. Kansas State University is located in Manhattan (Kansas, that is). The ghost of Duncan, a pledge who died from hazing by the Theta Xi fraternity, haunts its building, which now houses Phi Gamma Delta. (Two other fraternity houses, Delta Sigma Phi and Kappa Sigma, have also been reported as being haunted.)

Jesse Baird haunts the third floor of the Baird Music Hall at Morehead State University in Morehead. Some people claim to have seen his apparition; others have heard sounds and detected certain scents distinctive to Baird.

A depressed student committed suicide by jumping from the sixth floor of the Fine Arts building at Murray State University in Murray. Several faculty members have seen his apparition roaming up and down the aisles of Lovett Auditorium, which is located in the building. People have also reported soft piano music coming from the third-floor practice room when no one was there.

Ghostbusting

Zelda's case history is quite unusual in ghost lore, because she moved locations as her primary haunt. She originally haunted an older theater on the University of Northern Iowa campus, but she moved along with the theater department to their new building. Zelda has not been seen as a ghost; rather, she's responsible for producing spectral piano music, strange noises, and operating some of the theater's equipment.

A former head of maintenance who died at Paola High School in Paola seems to have liked his job—he's still there. A girl who died by falling down the stairs during a fire drill haunts Jackson Independent School in Jackson. And the girls' restroom of the third floor of Madison Middle School in Richmond is also haunted. A cheerleader was found there, beaten to death, in the 1950s, and it's believed her ghost is causing the weird sounds coming from the empty room in the morning and late at night when the school is closed.

Michigan

The Ladies' Library in Ypsilanti was once the residence of the Starkweather family. Maryanne Starkweather bequeathed the building to the city upon her death on the condition it be used as a library. About 15 years ago, however, the building was changed into office space. Ever since, people working after hours have heard footsteps on vacant floors overhead. Is it Maryanne, unhappy about the fact that the building's no longer a library?

Minnesota

Some students at the Minneapolis College of Art and Design in Minnesota claim to have been awakened in the middle of the night, unable to move and hearing the sound of screaming inside their skulls. They blame the phenomenon on the unsettled spirit of a female student who had allegedly been raped and killed in one of the basement apartments years earlier.

The third and fourth floor of Heffron Hall, a dormitory at St. Mary's University in Winona, are said to be haunted by a phantom priest, Father Laurence Michael Lesches. On August 25, 1915, Father Lesches shot and killed Bishop Patrick Heffron (after whom the dorm was later named). Father Lesches was committed to the State Hospital for the Dangerously Insane in St. Peter, Minnesota, where he died in 1943.

There's a spook alive in the darkroom at the College of Visual Arts in St. Paul. Objects move on their own in the dark, and the timer resets itself. Other ghost activity occurs throughout the building: Night custodians have reported the lights turning on and off by themselves, and they sometimes hear the disembodied sounds of children as well as other strange noises. Rumor has it that a former owner was cheating on his wife with the maid. They often used the darkroom for their assignations. When the man refused to leave his wife for the maid, the servant hanged herself in despair on the banister of the main stairwell. Some have claimed to see the man himself, dressed in flannel.

Missouri

Cottey College in Nevada, Missouri, has two resident ghosts. One, named Vera, is the spirit of a former student who accidentally caught her nightgown on fire while making candy in her room—killing her and burning down her dormitory, Rosemary Hall. Now she haunts the whole college, playing pranks on some girls and being kind to others. The second ghost at Cottey dates back to Civil War days. He's been reported as a man dressed in black or possibly an African-American man. It's thought that, for some unexplained reason, he is desperately seeking Vera.

At Stephens College in Columbia, Senior Hall is haunted by a young lady who hanged herself in the bell tower of the dorm. She killed herself after watching her boyfriend, a Confederate soldier she had hidden in her dorm, be discovered and shot.

Nebraska

Former music teachers haunt two colleges in Nebraska. The music professor who haunts Hastings College in Hastings often appears as a ghost light in that college's Music building. He's also been seen in human form, walking the halls. Lights that turn on and off by themselves have also been attributed to him.

Another ghost haunts the Music building at Nebraska Wesleyan University in Lincoln, where he taught the organ. His ghost is most often seen sitting near the instrument. Often, organ music can be heard wafting from the empty music hall. The professor's ghost has also been seen and heard in his former apartment.

Ghostly Pursuits

The current ghost at Nebraska Wesleyan University is the second music professor to haunt the institution—and in the university's second music building! In a famous sighting on October 3, 1963, Mrs. Coleen Buterbaugh, Dean Sam Dahl's secretary, entered a room in the C.C. White Memorial Building, the school's original music building, and noticed a musty scent. Then, she saw the ghost of a tall, thin woman standing in a corner, reaching for papers on a high shelf. Just as surprising, Mrs. Buterbaugh looked through the window and realized that it appeared to be a sunny, summer day, with flowers blooming. The apparition disappeared, and, just as suddenly, the outdoor scene returned to its usual autumn gray.

Buterbaugh described the vision to the dean, who discovered that Miss Clara Urania Mills, a former music teacher at the school from 1912 to 1936 who fit the description of the ghostly woman, had her office in that room. Moreover, Mills had died in the room across the hall on that date, October 3, in 1936.

The C.C. White Building was demolished in 1973.

A teacher who was killed at York High School in York has returned as a ghost. She's been reported walking into her regular room, turning on the lights, and sitting at her desk. Then, for some unexplained reason, she scatters all the papers sitting on the desk in front of her.

Ohio

The Hinckley Library in Hinckley was once a private residence owned by Vernon Stouffer, who founded Stouffer Foods. During its conversion into a library in 1973, workers reported seeing a young woman in a 19th-century-era blue dress and a man wearing a hat standing on the staircase. An indistinguishable ghost was also seen on the basement stairway. Staffers feel unusual, unexplainable presences on the upper floors of the former mansion, and small, self-levitating objects (such as paper clips) have been reported. Although no one's been able to positively identify the spirits, none of them resembles Stouffer. They're thought to be the ghosts of a Dr. Nelson Wilcox and his sister Rebecca, who lived in a cabin located on the grounds around the time of the Civil War.

Columbus State Community College in Columbus was apparently built on top of an old Catholic cemetery. The original residents must not be too happy: Several of them haunt the college.

A female ghost has been heard walking the third floor of the Lucas County Public Library in Toledo long after closing time. Percipients decided it was a woman because the noise sounded like high heels on linoleum.

Oakwood High School in a southern suburb of Dayton has had a haunted reputation for years. The fast-moving figure of a male spectre, as well as footsteps, are said to be those of the ghost of a student who hanged himself in one of the hallways in the 1960s or 1970s. The second apparition, of which little is known, is that of a pretty young girl who is almost always seen in the same hallway as the one haunted by the boy, although the two spirits never appear together. Several people have also reported seeing the girl sitting on one of the benches that lines the hall.

Tennessee

At a women's residence hall at East Tennessee State University Campus in Johnson City, students regularly hear noises overhead that sound like someone is dropping marbles, one at a time, onto the floor above. The noise is supposedly caused by the ghost of the so-called "Marble Boy," who died in the hall's elevator. If you yell at the boy, he loses his marbles. (Well, okay, he drops all his marbles at one time.)

Go West, Young Man

"Recent" is a relative term when you're talking about eternity. But the ghosts of the West are certainly newer that their East Coast counterparts. After all, colonial America had a head start.

North Dakota

At the University of North Dakota in Grand Forks, numerous sightings have been reported of the often-legless ghost of a girl in the tunnel connecting Wilkerson Dining Hall with the five campus dormitories. As recently as 1988, three students saw her in the West Hall tunnel. The spectre is always described as being about 5'5", with short dark hair, and wearing a nightgown. The ghost is thought to be that of a young female student who froze to death about 60 feet from West Hall around 2 A.M. in December 1962, before the tunnels were built. It's believed that she was trying to go to the dining room, but slipped on the ice, fell, and died of exposure.

South Dakota

Sparky, as the ghost has been named, haunts the stage area and auditorium's storage room in Stevens High School in Rapid City. He has supposedly made chairs burst into flames (hence his nickname) and caused nails to fall out of cement ceilings. The school is supposedly located on the site of a house fire in which an entire family died. Its cause: Sparky made chairs in the home burst into flames.

Wyoming

In Byron, Rocky Mountain High School (which actually houses elementary through senior classes) has been haunted since 1952. Students, teachers, and superintendents have all felt presences. Much of the activity occurs in or near the weightlifting and wrestling room, which was the former library. Phenomena includes:

➤ Electrical appliances working, though not plugged in

➤ Floating, moving mist or fog

➤ Foul odors

➤ Icy cold spots

➤ Lights turning on and off by themselves

➤ The sensation of an invisible body passing by

➤ The sound of doors opening and shutting on their own

➤ Spectral footsteps

So far, no one's been able to explain the phenomena or attribute it to any individual or event in the past.

Washington

On the West Coast, an old one-room schoolhouse in Coupeville is today being used as a rental property. The ghost of a small girl dressed in old-time clothing has been seen on the front porch and peeking out the window of the old school.

Oregon

One seat in the auditorium of South Eugene High School in Eugene is haunted by a student who died while sitting there. Meanwhile, since the 1940s there have been hundreds of reports by students and faculty of spirit activity in Knight Hall in Forest Grove. Two ghosts are also regularly sighted. The building used to be the music building for Pacific University.

California

The San Francisco Arts Institute is said to have been built over a cemetery after the great earthquake of 1906. Ever since, the building has been haunted by unhappy spectres that believe the grounds to have been desecrated.

Down the road in Sunnyvale, Homestead High School has a ghost—only seen at night—that walks the second-floor hallway. Other times, students and faculty have "felt" its presence. In one teacher's case, it was literal: The invisible phantom tapped the teacher on the shoulder. The spectre also locks and opens doors when no one's around.

According to Modesto High School legend, some years ago a male student fell to his death from the balcony of the auditorium onto the carpeted concrete ramp below. His ghost has been reported walking back and forth along the balcony railing. Also, there have been rapping noises heard in the main hall by the Home Economic rooms.

During some of the big basketball games, the gymnasium of Bakersfield High School in Bakersfield is haunted by a student couple, about 16 to 18 years old. They appear on the top row of a particular area on the "home side" of the bleachers. The girl—oddly for a basketball game—is wearing her prom dress, and her boyfriend is wearing his football jacket with BHS on the back. They sit watching the match or make out throughout the game. As is common with apparitional sightings, when they appear, that entire area of the bleachers drops in temperature. And even those who don't see the apparitions have the sensation that they're being watched.

Down in southern California, William Cook Anaheim High School Auditorium is the site of spectral activity, even though no apparitions have been reported, but disembodied voices are sometimes heard in the house, and irregular, wandering footsteps can be heard on the roof.

What do you want to be when you grow up—that is, if you're not trapped in high school as the prom ghost? Well, each year there are a lot of graduates who decide they want to move to California to become stars. Do you have what it takes?

In the next chapter we'll take a nighttime tour of Tinseltown. So get out your autograph book. Who knows how many filmdom phantoms we'll meet on our tour of Haunted Hollywood?

The Least You Need to Know

➤ Ghosts return to places where their mortal counterparts enjoyed life and/or met tragic ends. School students are no exception.

➤ Ghosts can be found in schools in every state of the Union.

➤ Be careful checking out books: There are haunted libraries in every region of the United States.

➤ The spirit world is an equal-opportunity employer: Ghosts of every rank (students, faculty, and other staff) and age (young and old) haunt schools and libraries.

Chapter 22

Haunted Hollywood

In This Chapter

➤ Famous phantoms of filmdom

➤ Tales from celebrities who say they've been haunted

➤ Haunted homes of the stars

➤ Spectral visions at movieland venues

Nothing lives forever. Even the stars in the heavens finally fade and die. But how about the stars from *movies and television?* Do you think some of them could live forever? I mean, other than on video and in syndication. Maybe—if they come back as a ghost!

A Star Is Born (Again)

Many stars of the silent and early sound eras of filmmaking were fascinated with spiritualism and the occult. Charlie Chaplin once quipped that ectoplasm seemed to hover over Hollywood "like smog." Rudolph Valentino, Jean Harlow, and Mae West, among other stars, frequently attended séances. In fact, West sometimes *conducted* séances, acting as the medium. On occasion, she even produced spirit voices (or DVP).

All the world watches Hollywood, so when one of its stars returns as a ghost, all the world notices. Let's take a look at some of the more well-known celebrity "comebacks."

Jean Harlow

In 1932, film siren and "blonde bombshell" (about whom the phrase was coined) Jean Harlow (1911–1937) was married to director Paul Bern in the living room of her home at 1353 Club View Drive in Los Angeles. They moved into Bern's Bavarian-chalet style mansion at 9820 Easton Drive in Benedict Canyon in Beverly Hills. Just two months later, Bern committed suicide there, in Harlow's bedroom.

Jean Harlow, the "blonde bombshell."

Devastated by her husband's suicide, Harlow tried unsuccessfully to kill herself the next day, in the master bedroom on the second floor of the house. Harlow moved to 512 North Palm Drive. Just five years later, while filming *Saratoga* (1937), the 26-year-old star died suddenly at her home of uremic poisoning. She is buried in the Great Mausoleum of Forest Lawn Cemetery in a private niche purchased by her fiancé, actor William Powell.

Ghostly Pursuits

Hairstylist Jay Sebring purchased Paul Bern's home in 1966. Sebring was dating Sharon Tate at the time, and he asked her to housesit for him one night when he was out of town. Tate awoke to see the ghost of Bern, running around the bedroom and crashing into furniture. Tate fled downstairs and was horrified to see an apparition of Sebring tied to the post of the staircase, bleeding with his throat slashed. Banging sounds continued from the bedroom upstairs. Eventually, the visions faded and the noise ended, and Tate, exhausted, finally fell asleep. The next morning Tate confided to Sebring what she had experienced, but the evening's events were soon forgotten. Within two years, Sebring, Tate, and three others were bound and murdered by Charles Manson and his followers in a house located just down the canyon from the Bern–Harlow home.

According to some of the later owners of the Benedict Canyon house, Harlow occasionally reports to haunt her upstairs bedroom. There have even been a few reports of her apparition at her old home on Club View Drive.

Ozzie Nelson

Ozzie Nelson (1907–1975), whose beginnings were in radio, went on to star with his wife Harriet and their two sons Rick and David in the long-running television show, *The Adventures of Ozzie and Harriet* (1952–1966). In 1973, Ozzie and Harriet—without their sons—returned to television for one season in *Ozzie's Girls*.

Ozzie Nelson, television star.

For 25 years, the real-life Nelson family lived at 1822 Camino Palermo in Hollywood. Harriet continued to live there after Ozzie's death for another five years.

The Nelson home in Hollywood.
(Photo by author)

Almost immediately upon moving in, the new owners reported paranormal activity throughout the house, such as lights and faucets that turned on and off by themselves and doors that opened and shut when no one was near. The owners believe that the ghost of Ozzie Nelson is pulling the pranks, even though his apparition hasn't been seen.

Ramon Novarro

Silent-screen star Ramon Novarro (1899–1968) was a Latin-lover type—a rival yet close friend of Rudolph Valentino. Novarro is best remembered for his title role in the 1926 film *Ben Hur;* he was also the male lead in Greta Garbo's *Mata Hari* (1932). A lifelong bachelor, Novarro was brutally murdered on Halloween 1968 during a struggle with two young men he had met on Hollywood Boulevard and brought back to his home at 3110 Laurel Canyon. Novarro's naked body was found, beaten to death, in the master bedroom. Visitors to the estate often claim to feel an uneasy presence; many believe the house is haunted by Ramon Novarro, who died so violently.

Ramon Novarro, silent-screen star and Latin lover.

George Reeves

George Reeves (1914–1959) is best known for his role as Superman in the popular television show *The Adventures of Superman* that ran from 1951 through 1957. He was found dead of a gunshot wound to the head on the floor of his bedroom at his home at 1579 Benedict Canyon. The gun lay between his legs. The police ruled the death a suicide, claiming that Reeves had been upset over his career downturn after the end of the series.

Reeves's mother, among many others, believed that he had actually been murdered. She shipped her son's body to the East Coast, supposedly until she could prove her claim. His remains were quietly returned eight months later, cremated, and interred in an unmarked urn at an undisclosed cemetery.

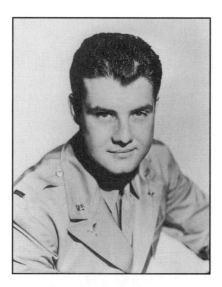

George "Superman" Reeves.

At least one set of subsequent owners of Reeves's home moved because of paranormal and ghostly activity inside the house. Others who also think Reeves was murdered sometimes hold séances on the property in an attempt to contact his spirit. Look! Up in the sky! Is it a bird? It is a plane? Or is it the ghost of Superman?

John Wayne

The Associated Press wire service reported in the 1980s that the Santa Monica, California, lawyer who had purchased the *Wild Goose,* a yacht once belonging to John Wayne (1907–1979), regularly heard—and sometimes saw—the Duke's ghost walking the deck on board late at night. He also heard invisible beer mugs clinking together in the ship's bar.

On one evening, the boat was on a chartered cruise when the engines were accidentally cut off, and the yacht started to drift. Oddly, the boat moved against the current and the wind, finally stopping right in front of John Wayne's old harborside home.

Clifton Webb

Clifton Webb (1891–1966) was one of Hollywood's most popular character actors, usually portraying pompous, upper-class types. He was nominated for three Academy Awards for his work in *Laura* (1944), *The Razor's Edge* (1946), and *Sitting Pretty* (1948). In his later films, he played a stuffed shirt (including his signature character, Mr. Belvedere) in a string of comedies.

Webb lived with his mother, Maybelle, at his 1005 North Rexford mansion in Beverly Hills, where he often threw gala parties. After his mother's death in the house in 1960, Webb kept her clothes and other belongings locked in her room.

Famous character actor Clifton Webb.

Webb reported seeing the ghost of his friend Grace Moore, a Metropolitan opera star and film actress who had once leased the house. According to some sources, Webb also saw the ghost of his mother.

Metropolitan opera and film star Grace Moore, who died tragically in an airplane accident. (Photo courtesy of Collector's Bookstore, Hollywood, California)

In 1967, a year after Webb's death, the house was bought by producer Douglas Cramer and his wife, columnist Joyce Haber. They have both reported seeing two shadowy phantoms in the house whom they believed to be Clifton Webb and Miss Moore.

Webb was buried in a crypt in the Sanctuary of Peace at Hollywood Memorial Cemetery (now under new management and renamed "Hollywood Forever"). His ghost is said to walk the halls of the mausoleum where he is interred.

The crypt of actor Clifton Webb.
(Photo by author)

One of the mausoleum hallways actor Clifton Webb is said to haunt. White lilies mark his crypt in this photo.
(Photo by author)

Ghostly Pursuits

Hollywood doesn't only bury its actors. Many of the stars buried their beloved animal companions. Los Angeles Pet Cemetery is one of the most popular among the Hollywood elite. Hopalong Cassidy's horse, Mary Pickford's dog, and Petey, the Little Rascal's dog all have their final resting places here. Rudolph Valentino may be buried in Hollywood Forever, not far from Clifton Webb, but Valentino's Great Dane, Kabar, is interred at Los Angeles Pet Cemetery. The dog died in 1929, but has apparently returned as a ghost. Several people who have passed the canine's grave have heard panting or been licked by a phantom tongue—presumably that of a dog.

Spirit Stalkers: Warning from Beyond

It's not always the celebrity who returns to do the haunting. Sometimes, it's the stars who become the haunted.

James Cagney

Well, I'll be a Yankee Doodle Dandy. James Cagney believed that he was saved from a fatal car crash when he received a warning: He heard the disembodied voice of his father, who had died years earlier.

Telly Savalas

Who loves ya, baby? Telly Savalas, star of TV's long-running *Kojak,* often told the story of how he was assisted by a ghost, a phantom driver and car. Savalas was driving across a remote stretch of Long Island around 3:00 A.M. when he noticed that his car was running low on gas. He stopped at an all-night diner to ask directions to the nearest gas station.

Savalas came out of the café and noticed a man standing by a black Cadillac. The guy asked him if he needed a lift, and Savalas allowed himself to be driven to get a can of gas. As he went to pay, however, Savalas realized he had lost his wallet. His driver loaned him the money, but Savalas made the man write down his name and address so he could repay him.

The man drove Savalas back to his car. Savalas filled his tank, and when he looked up, the man was gone. Savalas wanted to thank him properly, so the next morning he looked up the man's name and address in the phone book. He called, but a woman answered the phone. She told him that her husband had been dead for five years.

So that the woman didn't think he was simply playing a cruel joke, Savalas visited the widow and showed her the paper. It was her husband's handwriting. She asked what the man who claimed to be her husband was wearing. It was the suit he had been buried in.

Elke Sommer

Elke Sommer, the sexy blonde film star from Germany, truly believes that a ghost saved her life, and she frequently tells the story on radio and television talk shows. She had just married writer Joe Hyams in 1964, and they moved into their new home in Beverly Hills. The first night, they heard poltergeist-like banging and thumping downstairs in the dining room. At first, they suspected burglars, but none were found. The next night, and the next, they heard the same noises, and always from the dining room.

One fateful night there was a loud pounding on their bedroom door. Joe opened the door, but no one was there. Then he noticed thick, black smoke rising from down-stairs. Joe fought his way down to the dining room, found it on fire, and put out the flames.

Elke Sommer says that she consulted several mediums, and they all agreed that a mischievous poltergeist had set fire to the dining room, but when the fire got out of hand, the poltergeist woke them up to warn them of the danger.

Now that's some smoke detector!

Map to the Stars' Homes

As we've seen time and time again, it's usually *places,* not *people,* that are haunted. Hollywood is no exception. Some of the town's celebrated residences are haunted, though not always by the stars themselves. So let's pick up one of those maps to the stars' homes as we continue our ghost tour of haunted houses into the Hollywood Hills.

The Houdini Mansion

The property often referred to as the "Harry Houdini estate" is a four-acre tract of land in Laurel Canyon (at the corner of Laurel Canyon Boulevard and Willow Glen Road) in West Hollywood. In early 1999, DBL Realtors of Beverly Hills had it listed for $1,777,777.77. (The owner, a Georgia antiques dealer, considers seven to be a lucky number.)

R.J. Walker, a Los Angeles department store magnate, built a 40-room mansion on the tract between 1911 and 1924. The mansion and adjoining structures on the property burned in the 1950s.

The renovated stairway and hillside leading up to the ruins of Houdini's haunted estate. (Photo by author)

Houdini's name never appeared on a deed, so there's always been some question as to his actual connection with the property. The *Los Angeles Times* names the Laurel Canyon Land Company as the earliest owner of record. Walker owned stock in the company, but then, Houdini also invested in the company when he came west in 1919 to act in two films, *The Grim Game* and *Terror Island*. Most likely, Houdini stayed in the guesthouse, which burned with the mansion.

Houdini in the film Terror Island. *(Photo from the collection of Mark S. Willoughby)*

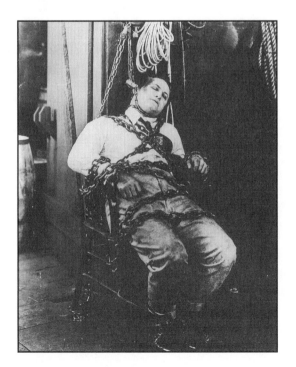

In 1998, while clearing brush, the Georgian owner discovered iron gates which he claimed bore the names "Houdini" and "Walker" and the date "1919," as well as other artifacts that possibly place Houdini on the site. The owner is also restoring walkways, stairs, and the stonework of a garage used as quarters for the chauffeur.

Before the estate's recent renovation, nearby residents have reported seeing and hearing unusual events such as ghost lights and unexplained sounds among the ruins on the uninhabited site. During the 1960s, it was reported a hang-out for occultists and paranormal types. Some think that the estate is haunted by Houdini himself.

Pickfair

In 1918, Douglas Fairbanks, Sr. (1883–1939) bought a tract of land in undeveloped Beverly Hills. When he married Mary Pickford (1893–1979) two years later, they remodeled a hunting lodge on the property as their new home. A reporter dubbed it "Pickfair," from the names Pickford and Fairbanks. The 42-room residence was glamorous for its day: Their swimming pool, for example, was the first one built in Beverly Hills.

The couple divorced in 1936, and Pickford received the property as part of the settlement. She married actor Buddy Rogers in 1937, and they lived at Pickfair until Pickford's death. Sports entrepreneur Jerry Buss purchased the home in 1980.

There were intermittent rumors of paranormal activity at Pickfair while Buss owned Pickfair. The ghost of a man, thought to be Fairbanks, was sometimes seen in the mural-lined entryway. The ghost of a maid occasionally appeared in the staff quarters, and there were at least two other unidentified ghosts seen in the hall.

In 1988, singer Pia Zadora bought Pickfair. Two years later, she razed the building to its foundation, and built a new house on the property. There have been no new reports of hauntings in the new residence, so whatever spirits may have been lingering must have been attached to the original Pickfair.

Haunted Hollywood Landmarks

Ever since Hollywood became the movie capital of the world, it's been famous for its glittering stars and fabulous nightclubs, as well as its notorious sex scandals, suicides, and murders. In such a festive atmosphere, why would any spirits want to leave? Wouldn't you want to stay to enjoy the party?

Ghosts and paranormal activity have been sighted at more than a few Hollywood landmarks. Let's take a drive down the streets of Tinseltown to see if we can turn up a macabre sight or two of our own.

Mann's Chinese Theatre

Probably the best-known Hollywood landmark, Mann's Chinese Theatre (originally Grauman's Chinese Theatre) was built by Sid Grauman in 1927 and opened with the

Boo!

There's a lesson to be learned from the deaths of Ramon Novarro and Victor Killian, both of whom were brutally murdered: Don't invite strangers back to your place. They may help you onto your way to becoming a ghost!

premiere of Cecil B. DeMille's silent film epic *The King of Kings*. The movie palace, located at 6925 Hollywood Boulevard, is famous for the hand prints and footprints of movie stars enshrined in cement in the forecourt.

It's been said that the ghost of actor Victor Killian has haunted the forecourt since 1982. Supposedly, he walks back and forth along the sidewalk looking for his murderer. According to police reports, Killian befriended a man at a nearby bar and invited him back to his apartment. The man allegedly beat Killian to death. Killian's body was found the next morning. His killer was never identified.

Mann's Chinese Theatre. (Photo by author)

The Comedy Store

The Comedy Store, a nightclub featuring established and up-and-coming comedians, is located in West Hollywood. W.R. Wilkerson opened the building as Ciro's in 1939. Herman Hover subsequently owned it from 1942 to 1957. In its heyday, Ciro's was one of the largest and glitziest nightclubs on the Sunset Strip.

After Ciro's closed its doors, the club operated as a rock 'n' roll venue through much of the 1960s. Then in the 1970s, Mitzi Shore reopened the club as The Comedy Store.

Comedians and night watchmen have regularly reported that the club is haunted. Chairs move without help, and sometimes the lights and sound seem to have a mind of their own. For some unknown reason, this happened especially whenever the late comic Sam Kinison was onstage. Although most spirit activity there occurs at night, more than one person has reported seeing apparitions during the day, including the ghost of a man in a brown leather jacket and other men dressed in the styles of the 1940s. The back room dressing room area and the basement storage area under the stage seem to be particularly haunted.

The Comedy Store.
(Photo by author)

On January 11, 1999, Mitzi Shore, the owner of The Comedy Store, had paranormal investigators visit her Hollywood Hills house in which several comedians—including Richard Pryor, Robin Williams, and Mitzi's son Pauly Shore—had roomed while performing at The Comedy Store. Several comedians reported paranormal activity, including seeing shadows moving through the house and doors opening and closing by themselves—"standard poltergeist activity in a haunting situation," according to investigators.

Dr. Larry Montz, a parapsychologist, led the investigation; Daena Smoller, a psychic medium, also attended. High-tech tools used to pinpoint ghosts included a *magnetometer* (which measures the presence and fluctuation of magnetic energy) and a temperature gauge. Often, in paranormal investigations, a two-, five-, or even 10-degree temperature change is recorded. (Indeed, a five-degree drop in temperature was registered at the Shore house.)

Ghostbusting

Dr. Barry E. Taff and members of a parapsychology team from UCLA investigated Shore's house in 1982, but their data was inconclusive. Taff, who holds a doctorate in psycho-physiology and frequently appears on radio and television as a paranormal expert, was a research associate with UCLA's former Parapsychology Laboratory from 1969 through 1978.

During the investigation of Shore's home, the ghost hunters sensed a man who had been shot dead and dragged down a set of stairs. They "saw" an "invisible" stain at the foot of the stairs. Eventually, they claimed that they felt three figures—two male, one female—all killed in the 1920s. The female, named Flo or Florence, supposedly died from a botched abortion.

Phantom Phrases

A **magnetometer** measures the presence of a magnetic field as well as its strength, direction, and fluctuation. Normally, a magnetometer is used in geophysical and astronomical surveys, but some paranormal investigators believe that spirits have a detectable, measurable magnetic or energy aura.

Researchers are now looking for historical pictures, evidence, or other information to corroborate what they felt.

Hollywood Roosevelt Hotel

The Hollywood Roosevelt Hotel, located diagonally opposite Mann's Chinese Theatre on Hollywood Boulevard, has long been a mecca for ghost hunters.

The luxury hotel in central Hollywood opened its doors in 1927. Over the years, most of Hollywood's elite have walked through its doors, either staying as guests or attending one of the swanky parties held under its roof. Remember, the hotel is right across the street from the Chinese Theatre, where so many movie premieres took place. In fact, the first Academy Awards banquet was held in the hotel's Blossom Room in 1929.

The Hollywood Roosevelt Hotel.
(Photo by author)

In 1984, the hotel underwent a multimillion-dollar renovation, restoring it to its former glory. Since that time, there have been dozens of reported sightings of apparitions. No doubt hundreds more have gone unreported.

In 1985, prior to the hotel's grand reopening, a cold spot credited to spirits was felt in the Blossom Room. The spot, 30 inches in diameter, measured about 10 degrees cooler than the rest of the room.

The same year, a staff member was looking into the mirror in the hotel manager's office, when she noticed the reflection of a blonde woman standing there. It was Marilyn Monroe! The employee turned to look, but there was no one behind her. Yet, when she faced the mirror again, Marilyn's reflection was still there.

The mirror once hung in Suite 1200, which was often occupied by Monroe. The mirror has since been moved and is said to be the one now hanging beside the elevators on the hotel's lower level. Many people have reported seeing the ghost of Marilyn Monroe reflected in its glass.

The haunted mirror, located in the lower level of the Hollywood Roosevelt Hotel. The ghost of Marilyn Monroe is said to appear reflected in its glass.
(Photo by author)

Ghostly Pursuits

That Marilyn gets around! Not only does she haunt a mirror in the Hollywood Roosevelt Hotel, but her ghost has also been seen hovering near her crypt at the Westwood Memorial Cemetery in Westwood, California.

Actor Richard Conte, known for his Italian cop and gangster roles in the 1940s and 1950s, is also buried at Westwood Memorial Cemetery. Oddly, the years "1910–1975–?" are marked on his grave marker. Why the question mark? Did he intend to come back? Perhaps reincarnated? Or as a ghost?

Ghostbusting

While researching the Roosevelt Hotel, I talked with some guests who had come to town to take part in a Walk of Fame ceremony. (That's when a celebrity gets his or her own star set into the sidewalk in Hollywood.) One visitor reported seeing a phantom woman at the foot of her bed, calmly brushing her hair. Another saw the ghost of a man reflected in the room's mirror.

Monroe isn't the only celebrity ghost spotted at the Roosevelt. Montgomery Clift lived in Room 928 for three months in 1952 while he was filming *From Here to Eternity*. Maids have reported feeling cold drafts in the hallway outside his room. Others have reported seeing strange shadows. And in 1992, a guest staying overnight in Room 928 reported feeling a spectral hand on her shoulder.

Several people have reported seeing the ghost of an unidentified man in a white suit. Other phantom phenomena at the hotel include guests being bolted out of their rooms from the inside and phone calls being made from locked, unoccupied rooms. Other times, phones are knocked off their receivers inside vacant suites. The spirits seemed to have a field day when a television crew came to shoot a report on the sightings in 1989. Equipment failed without explanation, hotel lights went out by themselves, and smoke detectors set themselves off.

Pacific Theater (Formerly Warner Theater)

In 1927, Warner Brothers was filming a revolutionary movie *The Jazz Singer*. It would be the first feature-length "talkie." For its West Coast premiere, the four Warner brothers—Harry, Albert, Sam, and Jack—began work on a new flagship movie theater on Hollywood Boulevard. Sam Warner personally supervised the installation of the sound equipment. Unfortunately, the theater was not completed in time and it's said that Sam cursed it. The day before the film's premiere in New York, on October 6, 1927, Sam Warner died in Los Angeles of a cerebral hemorrhage.

The Warner Theater finally opened six months later, and a plaque commemorating Sam Warner was placed in the lobby. Over the years, there have been sporadic sightings of Sam Warner in the theater's lobby, the auditorium of the theater, and in the offices upstairs. Two men on a cleaning crew saw Warner's ghost walk across the lobby and enter an elevator. Others have heard noises—scratching and chairs being moved—in vacant offices overhead.

For its last several years of operation, the theater was part of the Pacific Theater chain. It's currently closed awaiting renovation.

The Palace

The Palace opened in 1927 as the Hollywood Playhouse to house legitimate theater. Since that time, it has housed radio shows, a nightclub, television shows, and, most recently, a rock 'n' roll venue. With such a history, it would actually be unusual—by Hollywood standards, anyway—if it *weren't* haunted. But don't worry: It is!

Spectral phenomena have included:

➤ A piano, locked inside a room, playing jazz music on its own

➤ Cold drafts

➤ The scent of perfume

➤ Phantom taps on the shoulder

One security guard reported seeing the apparition of a tuxedoed man with no face. The ghost was standing but had no feet: It was seemingly standing on a the former surface slightly beneath the level of the current stage. The phantom was also sensed and chased by the guard's dog.

Phantom voices have often been reported coming from the theater's balcony. At least two apparitions (an elderly couple) have been sighted there.

Ghosts have also been blamed over the years for electronic troubles that have plagued bands playing at the theater. Also, printouts from the theater's adding machines and cash registers often contain odd, nonsensical combinations or groups of numbers. Are they coded messages from the Other Side?

Pantages Theatre

The Art Deco Pantages Theatre was built by Alexander Pantages as the West Coast jewel box of his namesake vaudeville chain. Howard Hughes acquired the theater as part of his purchase of RKO Pictures in 1949. He and his two sons had their offices on the second floor. In 1967, Pacific Theaters bought the Pantages and, in association with the Nederlander Corporation, restored the theater.

Since that time, there have been reports of a presence and cold drafts in Howard Hughes's old office. The scent of cigarettes and the clacking sounds of brass drawer knobs sometimes waft through the air. The large apparition of a man, thought to be Hughes, has been seen at least twice in the hallway outside his former office. Following a 1990 vandalism of the balcony area, there have been repeated spectral thumpings and bangings there. Did someone disturb a ghost?

Since 1932, the disembodied voice of a woman has been heard singing in the theater, sometimes during the day but usually at night when the theater is closed. Legend says it belongs to a woman who died in the mezzanine during a show. Once, her voice was even picked up by a microphone during a performance!

And so our tour of the stars' homes and the famous sites of filmdom's capital comes to a close. But there're plenty more places to visit. Before we finish off our section on hauntings, let's do a catch-all chapter of other venues and facilities that have attracted ghosts.

The Least You Need to Know

➤ The ghosts of several stars of film and television have been reported throughout the Hollywood area.

➤ Many stars have had paranormal experiences; some even say they owe their lives to warnings from ghosts.

➤ Stars return from Beyond to visit places they loved and frequented during life—be it their homes, theaters, nightclubs, or hotels.

➤ Many of Hollywood's top tourist attractions, including Mann's Chinese Theatre, the Hollywood Roosevelt Hotel, and several other theaters, are said to be haunted.

Chapter 23

Where (Else) on Earth?

In This Chapter

➤ Haunted hospitals

➤ Phantoms that play in the park; others imprisoned for eternity

➤ Ghostly auras from lonely lighthouses

➤ Ghosts who never grew up: haunted orphanages

➤ Musty old museum spirits bring history alive

➤ A final catch-all cornucopia of ghostly haunts

By now you'd think we've looked at just about every place a ghost could hide. But, no, there's still plenty more. To paraphrase the movie *Field of Dreams:* "If you build it, they will come … and haunt it!"

In this chapter we'll take a quick look at—get ready—hospitals, theme parks, outdoor recreational areas, jails, orphanages, museums, newspaper offices, government buildings, restaurants—even lighthouses. Can you think of any kind of place else that could be haunted? If so, jot it down. Next time, we'll add it to the list.

Phantoms in the Infirmary

There are haunted hospitals of all types scattered across America. While these places provide health care and cures, they're also sites of great sadness, pain, misery, and death. Paranormal theorists believe people's spirits can stay in or be drawn back to locations where they have experienced such strong, negative emotions.

Before proper inoculations and medications were discovered to prevent and treat tuberculosis, the disease was one of the world's most hideous killers. The symptoms as patients sickened and died were horrific, from uncontrollable bleeding coughs to insanity. Patients were often quarantined or treated in special wards or sanitariums to prevent contagion.

Boo!

The old Louisville TB ward has been declared off-limits by police due to numerous cases of vandalism and injuries on the site. If you do go hunting for haunted buildings, remember to always have permission, be respectful of the property, and be careful!

In Orlando, Florida, the Sunnyland Hospital has stood vacant for almost 20 years. The third floor remains locked, yet late at night, footsteps can be heard shuffling on the floor overhead. The sounds of whispering and objects dropped on the floor have also been reported. The ghosts of suffering patients, perhaps?

There's a former hospital in Louisville, Kentucky, off the Dixie Highway that housed many TB patients. Many ghost spotters have seen a small girl standing at a third-floor window in the vacant building.

Mental hospitals have been the sight of many grim encounters. It's easy to imagine the shrieking of the mad inmates, who sometimes have to be restrained to prevent doing violence to themselves or others, carrying over into their spirit lives.

An old mental hospital in Tallahassee, Florida, which has been closed for many years, is rumored to be haunted. Its staff had the reputation for being unkind to its patients. Indeed, it's thought that many patients died under their care. Several people driving by have claimed to see lights on inside the building and people staring out of the windows. When they stopped to look, the phantoms at the windows vanished.

Belleview Mental Hospital, located in the Pine Hills section of Orlando, Florida, is closed now. Still, there have been numerous reports of poltergeist activity, spirit voices, and screams coming from within.

Many haunted hospitals date back to one of the saddest parts of America's history: the Civil War. The melancholy and weariness attached to the old Civil War hospitals may be what's holding so many of its lost souls.

Carnton Mansion in Franklin, Tennessee, is one such example. A historic residence, the house served as a Confederate Hospital following the Battle of Franklin during the War Between the States. Local paranormal investigators have recorded unusual sounds there that they claim are gunshots, drum beats, battle cries, and the tramping of running soldiers. They have also produced photographs, but they, too, remain inconclusive.

Patients, visitors, and staff members at the Heather Hill Hospital in Chardon, Ohio, have all heard knocking on their walls at times when there was no one awake in the rooms next door, above, or below. The hospital also has a colorful resident ghost: "the knickers boy."

Ghostly Pursuits

"The knickers boy" is the ghost of a young boy dressed in old knickers (hence, the nick-name) and is regularly seen by nurses and nurses aides in Area C of the Heather Hill Hospital. No one's been able to identify him as any of the hospital's former patients. He's always alone and is spotted running in and out of rooms. If someone follows him into a room to catch him, he's not there.

On occasion, elderly patients see the boy when a staff member is in the room. The worker never sees him, and the patient, not realizing the boy is a phantom, sometimes starts talking to him. When the nurse or aide asks whom the patient is chatting with, the patient describes "the knickers boy."

Today, the Scallabrini Villa of North Kingstown, Rhode Island, is a resident nursing home for retired nuns and priests, under the direction of the Scallabrini Fathers. The villa is comprised of two buildings. The newer one was erected in 1995, but the older wing was once a children's hospital. Visitors have claimed that the former hospital is still haunted by the ghosts of children who died there. Their spectral laughing and crying, and the sound of children at play, have been heard. For some reason, Room 103 is said to be the home of many of the phantoms.

Here are just a few more of America's haunted hospitals:

➤ The Telfair Hospital of Savannah, Georgia, is a former ladies' hospital. It's said Mary Telfair herself haunts the building, roaming the hallways in a brown dress.

➤ Salem Hospital in Massachusetts is haunted by the ghost of a woman who died while giving childbirth. She's been seen in the halls on various occasions.

➤ The Old State Hospital of Kalamazoo, Michigan, has some of the most regular activity on record. Local residents say red lights, odd sounds, and mysterious handwriting on the walls appear almost every night between 11:00 and mid-night. The apparition of an unidentified person is also sometimes seen at one of the windows.

➤ Can you imagine being frightened by a ghost on your way to surgery? Aren't things bad enough? One ghost apparently walks the halls by the operating theater in the Community Hospital of Fulton, Missouri. (Lab workers have also reported the dank scent of sweat, even though there are no people around. Where's your roll-on when you really need it?)

Ghostly Pursuits

Whenever the subject of ghosts came up, my brother-in-law would bring up his own phantom encounter. His father died during his first wife's pregnancy, never getting to see the first grandchild he wanted so badly. After the baby was born and brought home from the hospital, the parents kept the child in a crib at the foot of their bed at night.

One morning around 3 A.M., the father awoke to see a spectral form standing over the crib, looking down at the baby. As his eyes focused, he recognized the ghost: It was his father! Realizing he had a bit to drink the night before, he nudged his wife to let her share in the joke. But, with a mixture of awe and fear in her voice, she replied, "I'm awake. And I see him, too!"

They're Not Amused: Ghost-Ridden Theme Parks

Amusement parks should be the happiest places on Earth. They are for most, unless tragedy strikes. The ghosts of those who have died on the attractions sometimes never get off the carousel. They haunt the park forever.

Of course, the juxtaposition of death opposite the joy and innocence of a day at the park has helped create all of these urban legends. Did the deaths ever occur at all? And if so, has anyone ever really seen these people's ghosts? Still, some of the stories are hard to shake.

Paramount's Great America

For example, it's said that the ghost of a 10-year old boy who was killed on a park ride at Paramount's Great America in Santa Clara, California, still wanders aimlessly around the open area where the attraction used to stand.

King's Island

Several ghosts supposedly roam the grounds of King's Island amusement park outside Cincinnati, Ohio. Seen most often is the spectre of a little girl with blonde hair and blue eyes and wearing a blue dress. She usually materializes after the park is closed, appearing to tram drivers near the Water Works. Staff members don't think she died at the park. Instead, it's believed that the girl is buried in a cemetery that's located between the parking lot and an adjoining campground.

A second spirit at King's Island belongs to a young man who, intoxicated, fell to his death while trying to climb the park's mock Eiffel Tower. "The Beast," as a third phantom is known, takes his name from the roller coaster that he haunts. He often appears in the cars, sitting in an empty seat next to a park-goer riding the coaster. Another patron, said to have died on "The Octopus" ride, stays on in spirit to haunt the attraction.

Disneyland

At least seven ghosts—not counting the mechanical ones in the Haunted Mansion attraction—are thought to haunt Disneyland in Anaheim, California. There is one ghost said to reside in the Haunted Mansion itself. But more about her in Chapter 24, "The Magic Connection."

Ghostly Pursuits

Kate Ward, a receptionist at the Magic Castle, tells of seeing a ghost at the exclusive Victorian Inn on the Park in San Francisco. More than a hundred years old, Victorian Inn on the Park was once a magnificent private home. During one stay at the bed-and-breakfast-style hotel, Kate stayed up late reading as her husband slept beside her. She heard a faint female voice whispering, as if the sound were coming from the next room. She paid it little attention until she, later, got up and entered the bathroom. Standing at the mirror, Kate could plainly see the reflection of a translucent female figure standing behind her. Kate turned, and, of course, the ghost was gone. It suddenly became obvious to Kate that the murmuring must have come from the bathroom. It had been the spectral voice of the ghost. The identity of the ghost remains unknown.

The old People Mover attraction is now gone from Tomorrowland, but for years it was supposedly haunted by the ghost of a young man who is said to have died on one of the annual Grad Nights held at the park. According to the legend, the boy apparently jumped out of his moving car, tripped, and was dragged underneath to his death. It's said that he grasped at his girlfriend's long blonde hair trying to pull himself to safety. From that night on, there were sporadic reports from girls riding on the attraction—especially those with long blonde hair—that they felt an invisible presence violently tugging their hair.

Two or more apparitions have been seen on Tom Sawyer's Island after it was closed for the night. Cast members searching the island invariably came up empty-handed. It's thought that the ghosts may belong to the (at least) three boys who are said to have drowned in the Rivers of America surrounding the island during Grad Nights. (The "river," by the way, was never more than five feet deep.)

The "It's a Small World" attraction, populated by singing dolls dressed to represent people from all the regions on Earth, debuted at the 1964 World's Fair in New York. It's still a crowd-pleaser a third of a century later. In fact, it's said that three cast members loved it so much, their spirits have returned to haunt the attraction. It's said that lights inside the attraction turn on and off by themselves, and, after hours, the dolls sometimes move when there's no electricity working them.

The most infamous ghost story about Disneyland—and probably the saddest—is that of Dolly's ghost, who haunts the Matterhorn ride. According to legend, Dolly was riding in the front of a toboggan-style car and turned to check her two children riding in the back of the car. For some reason, she felt she had to undo her seat belt and stand to do this. The car entered a sharp decline (now known as "Dolly's Dip"), she was thrown out of the car, up over the heads of her children, and onto the track behind them. She was then promptly run over by the next toboggan.

Boo!

Accidents happen, especially when you take unnecessary risks, when you're not paying attention, and after dark. Whether you're at an amusement park (where you think nothing could possibly go wrong) or you're out in the middle of nowhere during a ghost hunt, be careful at all times. The ghost you prevent could be your own!

Park It Right There, Buster

Any place where people have gone for fun and pleasure, where the day suddenly turns to tragedy, is ripe for haunting. Many times the people who have undergone the trauma return as phantoms to haunt those coming to frolic.

Take, for example, the so-called "White Lady" of Indian Wells State Park in Shelton, Connecticut. Some think she was killed there on her wedding day. Others believe it to be the phantom of a child who was killed in the 1930s while playing on the nearby railroad tracks.

The Wood River Camp in Baker Creek, Idaho, is haunted by an immigrant miner that many call "Russian John." Sightings date back to the 1920s. Down the road, the ghost of Manuel Sato is seen along the shores of Loon Creek in Boise, Idaho.

Two girls have returned as phantoms to Indian Head Park in Willow Springs, Illinois. It's said they were drugged, raped, murdered, and their bodies tossed into a bog on the property. Likewise, a Lady in White searches the beach of Durand Eastman Park in Rochester, New York, looking for her daughter who was supposedly raped and murdered there.

Jailhouse Rock

Jails hold some of the most vicious and brutal types that humanity has to offer. Prison walls have enclosed so much violence, pain, misery, and, of course, death, that it somehow seems only natural that residents of the spirit world are holed up here.

In some instances, the identity of the apparitions is known because it's the ghost of a former inmate. Pickens County Courthouse in Carrollton, Alabama, is haunted by the ghost of Henry Wells, a prisoner who was killed while confined there. Cell 5 on the third floor of Burlington County Prison in Burlington, New Jersey, is haunted by Joseph Clough, who, it's said, was chained in this cell during his last days on Earth (as a mortal).

Three prisons deserve special note: Yuma Territorial Prison, the Old State Penitentiary in Baton Rouge, and Alcatraz:

➤ The spirits haunt Yuma Territorial Prison, which is now a state historic park in Yuma, Arizona. One ghost likes to pinch people who visit the "hole," a cell with no light where unruly prisoners were thrown as special punishment. The ghost is especially attracted to children and people who dress in red. The other spectre likes to play with the money—especially dimes—in the museum's cash drawers.

Ghostbusting

Ironic, isn't it? You'd think that after spending your life in prison, that death would set you free. But for some of the unlucky ones, that's not the case. They're free, at least their bodies are, from earthly shackles. But they're not free to leave. Their spirits remain bound, for whatever reason, to the jailhouse site forever. Are these are true ties that bind?

➤ The Old State Penitentiary in Baton Rogue, Louisiana, today houses the Louisiana State Police Headquarters and barracks. The old morgue and execution chamber are now offices. Spectral activity includes the sound of footsteps and radios turning on and off by themselves. Dark spots in the old basement seem to be the home of some malevolent presence.

➤ The most famous haunted prison of all is Alcatraz, located in San Francisco Bay. Originally called La Isla de Los Altraces (the Island of the Pelicans), Alcatraz was an Army fort and prison until it was converted into a federal penitentiary in 1934. Society's most hardened criminals were sent there, and it was considered inescapable. Among its many residents were Robert "The Birdman" Stroud, "Machine Gun" Kelly, and Al Capone (who, after five years, went insane, at least in part due to advanced syphilis). It was closed as a prison in 1963 and is now a popular tourist attraction.

Alcatraz was the site of beatings, suicide, murders, and mutilations. Several inmates were killed trying to escape. Guards and tour guides have reported hearing the sounds of cells being opened and shut, footsteps, whistling, screams, and voices echoing down the halls. Banjo music has been heard coming from the shower room: Capone was allowed to keep and play a banjo. Many visitors have reported cold spots throughout the facility, especially around the solitary confinement "holes" in Cell Block D. Often guests report the feeling that they're being watched by invisible presences.

There really is no escape from Alcatraz—it's the site of many ghosts and paranormal phenomena.

Shine That Light over This Way

Everyone knows that ghosts like the dark. And what could be darker than the inky blackness surrounding the beam of a lighthouse? Lighthouses are also often isolated and lonely places, a big plus for phantoms. And if the lighthouse's beam should fail, the result could be disastrous should a ship stray too close to the rocky shores. No wonder there are dozens of legends about lighthouses being haunted.

Supposedly Ledge Lighthouse in New London, Connecticut, was haunted by Ernie, a lighthouse keeper who committed suicide by leaping to his death on the rocks below. His wife had run off with the captain of the local Block Island Ferry. There's no record of either event, but that doesn't stop folklore. Footsteps were heard on the stairs heading up to the lamp, chairs moved, and doors opened and shut by themselves. Also, Ernie's ghostly presence was sometimes felt. All phantom activity ended when the lighthouse became automated on May 1, 1987.

A former lighthouse keeper haunts St. Simon's Island Lighthouse in Georgia. His phantom footsteps can be heard climbing the stairs.

The Old Lighthouse on Hilton Head Island, South Carolina, is haunted by the ghost of a young girl who died there during the hurricane of 1898. Her name is Caroline, although she's more commonly referred to as the Blue Lady. People who drive by the lighthouse often report hearing her crying. She most often materializes right before a hurricane or during the fall hurricane season.

Ghostly Pursuits

Hilton Head Island is also home to the ghost of William Baynard. After Baynard's death from yellow fever in 1849, his body was placed in a family tomb (Baynard Mausoleum) in Zion Cemetery. During the Civil War, Union soldiers ransacked the mausoleum looking for treasure that was supposedly buried with the corpses. Baynard's body was removed from the crypt and has since disappeared.

Today, Baynard's ghost is sometimes seen leading a phantom funeral procession from his plantation to the cemetery. The carriage stops briefly at every former plantation along the route, long enough for Baynard to approach each gate. Ghost servants bring up the rear of the cortege.

Baynard's mistress, Eliza, haunts the so-called Eliza Tree, a large oak at the intersection of Matthews Drive and Marshlands Road. Eliza was hanged from the tree for poisoning Baynard's wife.

Fort Lincoln at Point Lookout State Park in Maryland was a Union hospital and prisoner-of-war camp named Camp Hoffman during the Civil War. The lighthouse there, now converted into a residence, is guarded by a male phantom dressed in a Civil War uniform. He is usually seen leaning against the doorway to the stairs leading to the top of the lighthouse. Some people claim to have caught him on film. Several other ghosts have been seen at the fort, as has the ghost dressed as soldiers and at least one sailor.

Three ghosts haunt the lighthouse on Anastasia Island near St. Augustine, Florida. All of them were reported while the lighthouse was undergoing renovation in the 1980s:

➤ A small girl who was hit and killed by a train nearby around 1900.

➤ A presence felt in the basement of the lightkeeper's house.

➤ An unidentified man who hanged himself there. Workers saw his ghost hanging above them.

Little Orphan (Apparitional) Annie

Few places are sadder than orphanages. The charges have been abandoned at birth and never knew their parents, they've lost their families, or they've been victims of abuse and placed there for their protection. Regardless, the trauma and melancholy are magnets for spirits to return.

The ghosts of young students who died in a fire at Highland Orphanage in Jackson, Kentucky, have returned to haunt the facility. When not seen, they're frequently heard. Ghost children also haunt the burnt ruins of Gore Orphanage in Medina, Ohio.

The spectres of several boys and one of the staff have returned to the now-vacant boys' home in Guthrie, Oklahoma. The worker hanged himself in the belfry, and people still hear his footsteps leading up to the tower. On quiet nights, he's heard gasping for air, and the bells ring by themselves in the middle of the night.

Dry and Dusty Museum Denizens of the Dark

Museums hold more than ancient artifacts. They also often contain the ghosts attached to their historical objects. Wouldn't it be great if they could also be put on display?

According to tradition, an Egyptian mummy (Exhibit 22542) in the British Museum in London, England, is cursed and, perhaps, in a sense, haunted. The mummy is said to have been responsible for 13 deaths before it was brought to the museum. One of the victims, for example, received a fatal cut while moving the mummy, even though it has no sharp edges or protrusions. Also according to legend, photographs taken of the mummy come out blank or fuzzy, and the photographers soon die under unusual circumstances.

Ghostbusting

Even to an amateur ghost-hunter, mummies and other ancient Egyptian artifacts must seem kinda spooky. No wonder they attract ghosts! Ghosts seem to hang out in creepy places and with creepy things. You might increase your own chances of spotting a spirit if you visit a place filled with mystic objects or that has ghost stories already associated with it.

Likewise, the mummy case is haunted at the Cincinnati Museum of Art in Ohio. Guards there have reported seeing a black "blur" rise from a mummy sarcophagus on exhibit. The ghost floats up and through the ceiling. They've described the phantom as being seven feet tall with no facial features. Other times guards would run up against a hovering, glowing face, which would block their path, then suddenly vanish.

The Pioneer's Museum in Colorado Springs, Colorado, is haunted by a manager who was shot and killed by an employee over a salary dispute. The man's ghost is most strongly felt in his former apartment. Several people have seen a phantom playing the piano at the Captain's Museum in Brownville, Nebraska. Many more have reported hearing piano music wafting from inside the museum at night after closing time. A Lady in Purple, among other ghosts, has been spotted in the Utah State Historical Society in Salt Lake City, Utah.

On and On: More Ghostly Venues

Ghosts can appear at any venue, anywhere, anytime. I don't know why, but of all places of business, newspaper offices seem to have more than their fair share of ghosts. (Do you think it has anything to do with the Obituary pages?)

The offices of the Bakersfield *Californian,* for example, are haunted by a former editor, a security guard, and a German shepherd. "George" haunts the *Sullivan County News* in Blountville, Tennessee. Up the road, at *The Record* in Sacramento, California, the ghost of an elderly woman in Victorian clothing appears.

How do you get a haunted hotel? Simple: The guests check in, but they don't check out. You couldn't even begin to finish a list of all the haunted hotels and their ghost lodgers. Room 17 at the St. James Hotel in Cimarron, New Mexico, for example, is haunted by the ghost of a man who was killed there after winning the hotel in a poker game. The scent of perfume pervades "Mary's Room" at the same hotel, and the ghost of "The Imp," a short man with a pockmarked complexion, has been seen there, too. (The St. James Hotel has been featured on television's *Unsolved Mysteries*.)

Out in Cheyenne, Wyoming, the Plains Hotel is haunted by several ghosts, including one of a man who was murdered by being pushed out of a window on the fourth floor. Across the state in Yellowstone National Park, Old Faithful Inn is haunted by the apparition of a man wearing a large black hat and a bride who was decapitated by her husband on their wedding night. One amusing haunting there concerned a couple who woke to find their room sweltering hot. Their bedclothes had somehow been removed and were folded neatly at the foot of their bed.

Even government buildings aren't exempt from phantoms. Queen Liluokalani haunts the State Capitol Building in Honolulu, Hawaii. The ghosts of former maintenance crew members haunt the capitol buildings of Lincoln, Nebraska, and Albany, New York. A Gray Lady, a phantom Indian, and a ghost soldier haunt Liberty Hall in Frankfort, Kentucky.

Be careful who sits down next to you when you're eating in a restaurant. Big Nose Kate's in Tombstone, Arizona, is haunted by several cowboy ghosts, some of whom have been photographed. A spectral woman in white appears at a dark, corner table in El Fandango Restaurant in San Diego, California. Full Circle Cafe in Georgetown, Colorado, was featured on television's *Sightings:* It has at least 15 to 20 ghosts. Some restaurants, which are converted from private homes, are haunted by their former owners. These include Alpha Paynter at the Homestead Restaurant in Jacksonville, Florida; Pirate Captain Flint at Pirate's House Restaurant in Savannah, Georgia; and Elizabeth Ford at the Country Tavern in Nashua, New Hampshire.

Still hungry? How about a quick snack before bed? Because that just about wraps up our Spirit Survey. Now turn out the light, say your prayers, and try to get a good night's sleep.

Then it'll be time to turn to our last section and see how ghosts and spirit phenomena have been reflected in our popular culture.

> ### The Least You Need to Know
>
> ➤ The sadness, trauma, and deaths that occur in hospitals have led to a large percentage of hauntings in their facilities.
>
> ➤ Sites connected with joy and innocence that suddenly turn deadly, such as deaths or murders at amusement parks and recreational areas, are ghost magnets.
>
> ➤ Ghosts can—and do—appear anytime, anywhere, in any type of venue.
>
> ➤ Spirits seem to be comfortable in dark, deserted, or desolate like fog-shrouded lighthouses and dusty, or musty, museums.
>
> ➤ Sites of long-term human tenure, like orphanages and prisons, sometimes keep hold of their residents after death.

Part 5
We Are Not Alone

Lots of people think that ghosts are real. Maybe some of them are. But for others, they're all just an illusion. Ask the famous magicians profiled in these pages who created ghosts (or, to be fair, the illusion of ghosts) for their audiences.

Ancient wizards and sorcerers were condemned for practicing necromancy to call up spirits of the dead. Modern stage magicians trade on this accusation of forbidden knowledge and deviltry in their advertising and their performances. Then there are the 20th-century conjurors, like Houdini and the Amazing Randi, who set out to debunk frauds claiming supernatural powers, often by exposing their secret methods.

Ghost stories make up a major part of our literature, be it in the form of books, plays, or films. Everyone has a favorite, so in this section I've profiled just a few of the most popular in each genre.

Ready to learn some secrets? But remember: You can never reveal how the tricks are done. The spirits will find you!

Chapter 24

The Magic Connection

In This Chapter

➤ Ancient magic and the spirits

➤ The Davenport brothers tour as mediums

➤ Magicians include ghostly phenomena and pseudo-séances in their acts

➤ Houdini exposes fraudulent mediums

➤ The popularity of the spook show and other stage shows

➤ Modern-day séances

Can you keep a secret? Magicians throughout history have used their special skills to create the illusion that they were able to summon up ghosts and spirits. Often, priests or tribal leaders used their "tricks" to demonstrate their power over the spirit world.

Way back in Chapter 2, "In the Beginning: The First Famous Phantoms," we looked at one of the earliest recorded examples of a magician-cum-necromancer using an illusion to create a ghost. Remember the story of the Witch of Endor from the Old Testament? What else could the spirit of Samuel have been except for a smoky phantom produced by magic—I mean, of course, unless the Witch of Endor really *was* a witch.

Well, let's see how magicians pulled off the illusion of creating ghosts and other spirit phenomena. Along the way, we'll discover how magic tricks were used by fraudulent spiritualists in the 19th century and how the experience of the séance lives on in modern recreations. Finally, we'll visit some spooky stage shows and venues where magic's being used to produce a hauntingly good time.

Remember, a good magician never tells how the tricks are done, so you'll keep all this under your top hat!

Open Sesame: Spirit Doors

One magical effect in classical Greek and Roman times that always produced awe was when gigantic and massive temple doors opened by themselves, as if by the invisible hands of powerful spirits. In an illustrated manuscript, Hero of Alexandria explained one secret technique to produce this phenomenon. The heat from a fire built on the altar warmed the air in a bladder bag hidden below. The bag inflated, pulling a rope over a pulley, which turned concealed columns that were connected to the doors.

Spirit doors. Lighting the altar fires produced the magical effect through pneumonics.
(From a manuscript by Hero of Alexandria)

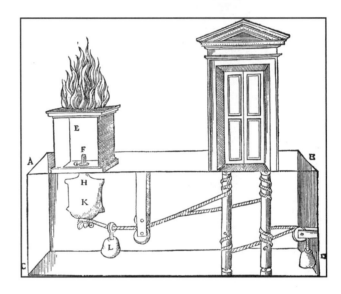

Imagine going to visit an oracle at a temple dedicated to the god Apollo. You need convincing that the priestess is able to get in touch with deities and spirits from the underworld. What more convincing would you need after the massive doors to the temples swung open by themselves? I'd be sold, wouldn't you?

Throughout the Dark and Middle Ages and even into the 16th and 17th centuries, wizards and sorcerers, steeped in the occult teachings of the *Kabbalah,* sought to contact angelic and demonic forces to do their bidding. As we've seen, these magicians would also use necromancy to try to invoke or manifest spirits of the dead.

It was during these dark days of the Inquisition, that—if they weren't careful—wizards and alchemists were branded heretics and imprisoned or burned for witchcraft.

By the late 18th or early 19th century, however, the performance of magic was accepted as a legitimate form of stage entertainment. No longer were magicians branded as devils—at least, not usually.

It was an age of scientific discovery, and magicians used many of the new principles to create their illusions. One of the most popular effects was the production of ghosts on the stage. In 1784, Belgian stage performer Robertson (Etienne-Gaspard Robert) debuted his "Fantasmagorie" in which images were projected onto smoke. Ten years later, he presented the ghost illusion during a six-year run in a Paris theater. Then, in 1803, magician Paul de Philipsthal created his own version of the trick, which he called "Phantasmagoria."

Standing within the safety of a magic circle in the middle of the stage, de Philipsthal would wave his wand to produce spectres of the "Dead or Absent." In a more superstitious time, viewers would have sworn that what they were seeing on the stage was a real materialization of a real, honest-to-goodness ghost. To ensure that he wouldn't be accused of actually performing witchcraft under the guise of magic, he advertised that the entertainment was performed "to expose the Practices of artful Imposters ... and to open the Eyes of those who still foster an absurd belief in Ghosts or Disembodied Spirits."

Other magicians followed Robinson's and de Philipsthal's lead. Henri Robin produced his "Living Phantasmagoria" in 1847.

Phantom Phrases

The **Kabbalah** is a not an individual book, but a collected way of thinking based primarily on ancient spiritual writings, primarily Jewish, and their mystic interpretation. The word Kabbalah (also seen as "Cabbala," "Cabala," "Kabbala" or in the Hebrew form *qabbalah*) is based on a root word *kbl* (in Hebrew *qibbel*), meaning "to receive." The Kabbalah is thought to be "received" wisdom revealed by the god(s) or other Higher Power.

PHANTASMAGORIA,
THIS and every EVENING,
AT THE
LYCEUM, STRAND.

With a wave of the wand, de Philipsthal conjured up a phantom "each and every evening" at the Lyceum Theatre on the Strand, in London, England.

... and Mirrors: The Pepper's Ghost

In the 1860s, Dr. John Henry Pepper created an elaborate stage trick using a mirror to create the illusion that the performers on stage were interacting with translucent ghosts, spirits, skeletons, and the like. The illusion and the principle itself are now known to magicians as Pepper's Ghost.

It worked like this: The actors were really standing behind a wall of glass, angled so that the audience was seeing not only the actors on stage, but also the reflection of other actors standing in a pit located in front of the stage but below the audience's line of vision. With the use of special and precise lighting, the translucent reflection of the actors in the pit, costumed as ghosts and other entities, would appear to be standing right next to the actors standing on the stage.

The creative French conjuror, Jean Eugene Robert-Houdin (1805–1871), often called the "Father of Modern Magic," used the Pepper's Ghost principle in a Paris stage production named *La Czarine* at the Ambigu Theatre, in Paris 1868.

With the assistance of a Mr. Walker, Pepper adapted his ghost illusion in the 1870s. Using gradual light changes, he could make the ghostly reflection fade away at the same time that whatever was behind the wall of glass slowly appeared, or vice versa. From the audience's point of view, one object would change into the other. For example, a living person could visibly turn into a ghost.

Phantom Phrases

Spirit theater is a general term used by modern-day magicians to describe shows, acts, or tricks in which ghosts or other spirit activity is apparently produced.

Pepper called the new illusion "Metempsychosis." Years later, it would be adapted by American stage illusionist Harry Kellar (1849–1922) under the title "the Blue Room" for use in a playlet as part of his full-evening touring show.

Today, many magicians use the term *spirit theater* to refer to individual tricks, routines, acts, shows, or events in which ghosts or other paranormal phenomena are apparently produced. Magician Eugene Burger and his work personify spirit theater. Burger is considered by fellow magicians to be the authority on the subject, and his 1986 book *Spirit Theater* is considered a modern classic magician's text on the subject.

Coming out of the Closet: The Davenport Brothers

As we've seen, the heyday of spiritualism was from the mid to late 1800s. Almost from the start, mediums were frequently accused of using the magicians' tricks to produce their controls, ectoplasm, and other spirit phenomena.

As it turns out, one of the first mediums to appear on stage actually *was* an act: That is to say, they were two professional entertainers—magicians—who performed as mediums. Though personally never claiming to be mediums, the Davenport brothers (whom you met briefly in Chapter 8, "Things That Go Bump in the Night") were hailed as spiritualists worldwide.

The Brothers Start to Rap

The Davenport brothers, Ira Erastus (1830–1911) and William Henry (1841–1877), from Buffalo, New York, performed one of the most celebrated séance acts of the 19th century. They staged their first public show in 1855, just seven years after the Fox sisters first produced ghostly phenomena in nearby Hydesville (see Chapter 7, "Spirit Move Me: The Birth of Spiritualism").

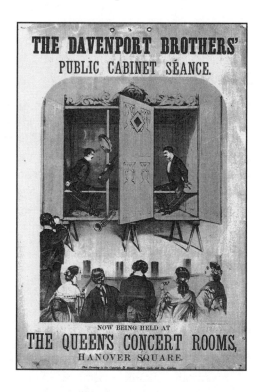

The Davenport brothers.

Having heard reports of spirit noises in Rochester (perhaps produced by the young Margaret Fox, who was living there with her sister Leah at the time), the boys' father decided to try a sitting around the family table. Rapping began almost immediately. At one gathering, Ira shot a pistol in the dark, and there was a materialization! The surprised spectators briefly saw a flash of a spirit. It was John King, the control who was to manifest himself for the brothers for the rest of their career.

The King Family Takes Control

King claimed to have been Henry Owen Morgan in life, the 17th-century English pirate who ransacked Jamaica before being knighted and made its governor by Charles II. King had a daughter, nicknamed Katie, who in life had been Annie Owen Morgan. She reportedly died young, at 23, after murdering her own two children. (Katie sometimes appeared as a spirit control at a few later Davenport séances.)

According to the Davenports, in 1855 John King ordered the boys, then aged 14 and 16, to "go public," so the family rented an auditorium to perform a séance before a paying audience. Their professional debut included spirit rappings and table tipping, musical instruments being played by invisible ghosts, and spectral hands touching the sitters at the table.

Ghostly Pursuits

Some controls were very popular, appearing for many different mediums. John King, first produced by the Davenport brothers, was especially in demand, appearing for many of the top 19th-century mediums, including Mrs. Guppy and Eusapia Palladino (see Chapter 8). This was not unusual: Other contemporary mediums often usurped well-known and colorful controls. For example, although first materialized by the Davenports, Katie King became the main control for famed medium Florence Cook (see Chapter 9, "Striking a Happy Medium"). As a result, depending on the medium, the same control often spoke in an accents or had a different appearance. Katie King, especially, was much more beautiful when manifested by Cook than by the Davenport brothers.

Out of Bounds

By the end of year, the Davenport brothers were appearing in New York City, where, for the first time, they had themselves bound in ropes as proof that they didn't perform the spirit shenanigans themselves. An audience member suggested that the brothers also be enclosed in a box to prevent any outside assistance. Realizing that anything could be accomplished out of the sight of the audience, the Davenport brothers immediately embraced this new condition.

The first spirit cabinet (or simply, cabinet), as such armoire-like enclosures came to be known, measured seven feet by six feet by two feet and sat on three sawhorses up off the floor. It had three doors on the front. The two brothers, tied up in ropes, sat facing each other from opposite ends of the cabinet. A low bench holding musical instruments sat between them. The center door had a diamond-shaped window to let in air and to allow the audience to see the spirit manifestations.

During a séance, the brothers would be tightly tied, and the doors would be shut. Instantly, music was heard from inside the cabinet. Phantom hands waved through the window. No matter how often the doors were opened, the Davenport brothers were always still securely bound. Sometimes, audience members were invited to sit in the center section of the cabinet, tied to the brothers. Still, the Davenports never seemed to escape from the ropes until they were finally released by the audience at the end of the séance.

The Davenports created a sensation—and controversy—wherever they traveled. The brothers billed their act as a séance, but they never called themselves (or claimed to be) mediums. Nevertheless, they were embraced by spiritualists as being authentic, but detractors denounced them as clever magicians.

During a tour of England in 1865, the Davenport brothers were bound so painfully at a Liverpool engagement that they refused to perform. A riot ensued. Similar violence met them in Hudersfield and Leeds, so the brothers quickly moved on to France. A four-year tour of Europe followed, during which they performed before many of the crowned heads of state.

Ghostbusting

The magic world is actually a small community. Most of the professional performers know, and have often worked with, each other. Early in his career, Harry Kellar, who later toured the Blue Room as part of his own illusion show, worked as an assistant and then an agent for the Davenport brothers. On his first magic tour (to South America and England), he worked with Fay, another Davenport assistant.

A Sudden End; a Final Farewell Visit

In 1876, the Davenport brothers traveled to Australia, where, the following year, William suddenly died in Sydney. Ira attempted to bury William beneath a gravestone engraved with a rendering of their spirit cabinet, ropes, and musical instruments, but Church officials refused to allow the memorial to spiritualism on sacred grounds. Devastated, Ira buried William outside the hallowed walls of the cemetery, and returned home to New York to retire.

In 1910, Harry Houdini met up with Ira Davenport in upstate New York. According to Houdini in his book, *A Magician Among the Spirits,* Ira confessed that the brothers, too, were escape artists, and he taught Houdini many of their secrets. (As it turns out, magician Harry Kellar used a similar wrist binding known among magicians today as the "Kellar Rope Tie.")

Magicians Supply the Phantom Paraphernalia

Let me be clear: Séances were *not* magic shows. They were supposedly legitimate attempts to contact the spirits of the deceased. Although almost all mediums were suspected of trickery from time to time, there were many, many who were never caught in the act.

Often, any "magic" that occurred took place in the sitters' minds. The setting, lighting, and atmosphere instilled a muted sense of dread, fear, and expectation. The slightest movement, special effect, or sound—and *especially* the silence—were magnified out of proportion by the sitters' imaginations.

Nevertheless, to remain popular, mediums had to produce results. As a result, many of them resorted to trickery. Magic supply shops were more than willing to provide the tools necessary for fraudulent mediums to fool their clients.

Ghostly Pursuits

For about 30 years, beginning in the late 1920s or early 1930s, Robert (Bob) Nelson was one of the top suppliers of "magical" effects for pseudo psychics and mendacious mind readers. The late T.A. Waters, himself a performer and a one-time employee, liked to tell the story of making a follow-up phone call regarding an order to one of the shop's customers who was a swami. The woman who answered explained that the Swami couldn't come to the phone because he had recently "ascended to a higher plane." (He had died.) But she asked Waters an odd question. She asked, "Is there any message for him?"

Magicians also purchase the supplies and paraphernalia to duplicate séance phenomena. Among the most popular pieces of apparatus are:

➤ Spirit slates, similar to those used by Henry Slade (see Chapter 8)

➤ A rapping hand (a mannequin hand which, when set on the table, rocks and taps by itself)

➤ Mechanical talking skulls

➤ Spirit cabinets

➤ Floating and tipping tables

In 1999, a New York illusion builder offered a new and improved "one-man floating table," which seems to rise, float, and tilt on its own (or at the magician's command) for only $795.

Magicians have always been well aware of the reputation that they've carried with them from the days of the Inquisition. No, modern stage performers aren't trafficking with the devil. But they don't necessarily shy away from the association.

Magicians still incorporate this "dark side" in their acts and in their advertising. Posters from the first half of the 20th century (and even a modern poster by performer Ricky Jay) show miniature devils whispering into the magicians' ears. Illusionist Howard Thurston (1869–1936), for instance, took advantage of the public's fascination with spiritualism by asking the question, "Do the Spirits Come Back?" on several of his posters. The spectral séance activity illustrated on his posters implicitly answered, "Yes."

Left: Abbott's Spirit Séance, a complete spirit act as offered in the catalog of Abbott's Magic Company of Colon, Michigan. Right: Abbott's Floating Table, a magical version of the spiritualists' tipping table.
(Used by permission of Abbott's Magic Company, Colon, Michigan)

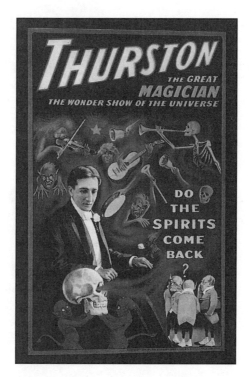

An advertising poster of illusionist Howard Thurston, asking, "Do the Spirits Come Back?"

Houdini Among the Spirits

The most famous magician of the 20th century was Harry Houdini (1874–1926). He was best known as an escape artist, but, in the last years of his career, a sizeable portion of his full-evening show was given over to recreating and exposing spirit séances.

How much of a believer in spiritualism was Harry Houdini? Was he a complete skeptic, or, as many suggest, was he actually seeking a real medium so that he could once again communicate with his beloved mother? The truth will probably never be known.

What is known is that Houdini was a master showman, and he knew that spiritualism was a craze. He realized that by debunking famous mediums as part of his act, he would draw huge audiences to his shows.

Houdini began a crusade, exposing the methods of mediums, challenging them to produce true phenomena under test conditions, and writing articles, pamphlets, and even a book (*A Magician Among the Spirits*) about his experiences.

Harry Houdini, escape artist.
(Photo from the Mark S. Willoughby collection)

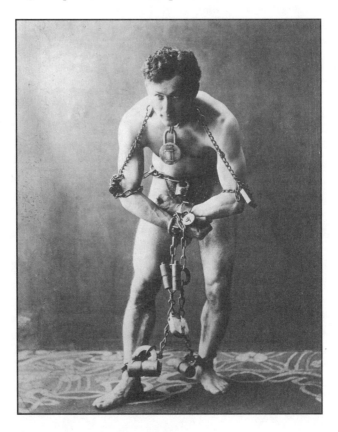

Houdini, Meet Sherlock Holmes

Houdini was a friend of Sir Arthur Conan Doyle, but Doyle's blind belief in spiritualism sometimes caused tension between them. Doyle, for example, believed that Houdini escaped from a locked trunk by changing into spirit form, passing through cracks in the box, and rematerializing on the other side. Nothing the magician said could convince him otherwise. In fact, Doyle frequently asked Houdini to admit his spirit-like abilities for the sake of the spiritualism movement.

At one séance they attended together (some say the medium was Doyle's wife), Houdini received a message supposedly written by his deceased mother. But the writing was in English, a language his Hungarian mother had never learned. Doyle's comment that Houdini's mother must have learned English on the Other Side infuriated the master magician.

Boo!

Sherlock Holmes explained how he solved his cases: "Eliminate the impossible, and all that's left is the possible." (It's hard to believe Sir Arthur Conan Doyle penned those words. As an avid spiritualist, he frequently chose to ignore rational explanations.) *You* should heed Sherlock's advice, however. Don't automatically assume that the spirit phenomena you've witnessed is proof that ghosts exist. Eliminate all other explanations first.

The Scientific Investigation of Margery

In 1924, the prestigious *Scientific American* magazine formed a committee to investigate mediums. It was really the inspiration of J. Malcolm Bird, the magazine's associate editor. Two prizes of $2,500 each were offered, one for a demonstration of true mediumship, the other for an actual psychic or spirit photograph. The five judges were American psychic researcher Walter Franklin Prince; Hereward Carrington, an English-born writer about the paranormal who had a fascination with magic; magician Harry Houdini; Daniel F. Comstock (who developed Technicolor for movies); and Bird.

The committee's major investigation was of Mina Stinson Crandon (1884–1941), a Boston medium who worked under the name of "Margery." Houdini left the committee after a year, claiming that the rest of the group ignored Margery's obvious trickery. The rest of the committee continued séances with Margery on-and-off for a half year. All but Carrington eventually agreed with Houdini. The contest was ended, and no award was ever given out.

Houdini demonstrates how a spirit cabinet is no impediment to a trained trickster in this booklet exposing the medium Margery.
(From author's collection)

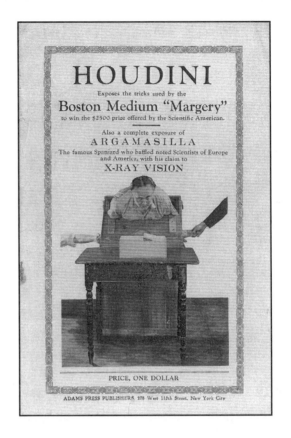

Houdini Performs an Encore

Houdini died of peritonitis on Halloween 1926. It was rumored that he and his wife Beatrice had worked out a coded message so that, should the survivor ever receive the words in a séance, there would be proof of contact with the afterlife.

Although a number of mediums claimed to have contacted Houdini, it was years before Beatrice agreed that one of them, the American medium Arthur Augustus Ford (1897–1971), had actually received the message from her dead husband. There's still controversy surrounding this stunning announcement.

Magical historians have come up with a number of different possible explanations:

➤ Ford had read, overheard, or otherwise learned the secret message.

➤ Beatrice was sick and unaware of what she was agreeing to.

➤ Beatrice simply agreed with Ford to stop the constant flood of mediums claiming to have contacted her late husband.

➤ She was still grieving over the loss of Houdini.

➤ She confused Ford's communication with the coded message.

➤ Beatrice conspired with Ford to promote a lecture tour.

Beatrice flatly denied that she was in cahoots with Ford. Further, she retracted her endorsement, saying that she had been too ill to be totally accurate. For many years, however, in an attempt to contact Harry, she held a séance on Halloween on the roof of the Knickerbocker Hotel, which had just opened its doors in Hollywood in 1925. After 25 years, she called an end to the ritual, saying that it was her opinion that if Houdini *had* survived death, he wasn't coming back.

The Knickerbocker Hotel in Hollywood, site of the annual Houdini séance for 25 years after his death. (Photo by author)

The New Skeptics

Although several magicians carried on Houdini's tradition of debunking paranormal claims, the gauntlet was really picked up by performer and author Milbourne Christopher (1914–1984). In his books *ESP Seers and Psychics* (1970), *Mediums Mystics and the Occult* (1975), and *Search for the Soul,* he examined the role that magic, outright fraud, and superstition play in fooling a gullible public that wants to believe in the paranormal.

In more recent years, the role of professional skeptic has been assumed by James Randi (b. 1928). A recipient of the MacArthur Foundation "genius" grant, Randi is perhaps best known for his attempts to debunk the Israeli psychic Uri Gellar.

Right Before Your Very Eyes

The *spook show,* also known as a ghost show or more colloquially as a spookeroo, was a magic show especially designed to target audiences with a fascination for horror and ghosts. The heyday of the Spook Show was the post-War 1940s and the 1950s, although they did continue into the 1960s.

The show usually began around midnight and featured horror-themed magical tricks, such as sawing a person in half or chopping through a neck with a guillotine (without hurting the volunteer, of course). Sometimes, they would re-create a spirit séance onstage. Often, there were short sketches: In the two most famous, the Frankenstein monster was brought to life, and Dracula visibly turned into a bat and flew out over the auditorium. Spook shows almost always included the showing of one or two horror movies.

Phantom Phrases

A **spook show,** also called a ghost show or spookeroo, was a magic show, most popular in the 1950s, that featured horror- or ghost-themed tricks. Often, one or two horror movies were shown as part of the evening's entertainment.

The climax of the spook show was always the dark segment, or blackout, in which ghosts, spirits, and other creatures of the night supposedly traveled out into the audience. Audiences were told what they would experience, such as the touch of the cold clammy hands of the mummy, or worms and maggots crawling up their legs. Then, in the dark, assistants dressed in black raced up and down the aisles, brushing people with their ice-cold fingertips as they passed. To create a real panic, the men in black would throw strands of cooked wet spaghetti or macaroni into the crowd. Likewise, glowing ghosts, luminous skeletons, and the like (all painted models on strings, of course) would fly over the heads of the audience.

People of all ages attended spook shows, but they were particularly popular with the dating crowd. During the scary dark segment of the show, young ladies would often leap with fright into the arms of their boyfriends—or vice versa!

Many magicians have performed spook shows as a segment of their full-evening shows. Some performers specialized in the genre. William Neff (1905–1967), presenting his *Madhouse of Mystery* show, George Marquis, and Jack Baker (working as Dr. Silkini) were among the best-known performers in the field.

Conjuring Under Canvas

In addition to magic shows that performed in theaters, there were several shows that toured under canvas throughout the early and middle parts of the 20th century. Perhaps the best known in the United States was the full-evening illusion show performed by Harry Willard (1896–1970), known as Willard the Wizard. He first performed magic in Ireland in the 1860s, then moved to the United States in the 1880s.

One of the features of his show was the recreation of a spirit séance, including, as one of his posters promised, Nellie Davenport producing "startling feats of Spirit and Power in full gas light." In the spirit séance segment, Davenport would have volunteers from the audience tie her wrists and neck with strips of cloth, then nail the ends to the bench on which she sat. She was then enclosed with a curtained-draped framework, which acted as her spirit cabinet.

Immediately, according to one advertising broadside, "knocks are heard … tables and chairs float in mid-air … [spirit] hands and faces are plain[ly] seen and musical instruments are played and passed to the audience. Flowers are materialized and etherealized spirit forms are seen on the stage." Spectators were promised "Spirit Concerts Upon a Dozen Instruments, All Playing at One Time without a Living Soul Touching Them."

Advertising piece for the Willard the Wizard show. The wizard promised to produce genuine spirit phenomena during his performance. (Courtesy of Frances Willard and Glenn Falkenstein)

The remarkable spirit cabinet act is still convincingly performed today by Willard's daughter, Frances, who began her career as an assistant to her father. Acting as the medium, she performs a modern yet traditional version of the spirit cabinet routine with her husband, mentalist Glenn Falkenstein. Frances Willard is generally recognized as the best performer of the spirit cabinet in the world.

Spirit activity surrounds the bound medium, Frances Willard, as Glenn Falkenstein opens the spirit cabinet.
(Photo by Cory Flynn; courtesy of Frances Willard and Glenn Falkenstein)

The Haunted Mansion

In our last chapter, we talked about all the real ghosts at Disneyland. But Disneyland also has its own haunted house. According to the legend created to go with the attraction, there are "999 Happy Haunts" residing in the park's Haunted Mansion.

The southern antebellum mansion was built in New Orleans Square in the Magic Kingdom in 1963, but the Haunted Mansion didn't open its doors to the public until August 16, 1969. According to a well-publicized quote, when asked in 1962 about the design of the haunted house, Walt Disney reportedly said, "We'll take care of the outside, and the ghosts will take care of the inside." Actually, many of the special ghost effects use magical methods dating back to the 1800s.

Let's Go for a Ride: A Guided Ghost Tour

It's amazing how many ghost legends are represented in the mansion's haunted halls. Here's a ghost tour, room by room:

➤ *Stretching Gallery.* Guests are ushered in small groups from a reception room into a tall, windowless art gallery. Soon, oil portraits on the wall stretch to twice their length, and the spectre of a man hanging from a noose appears overhead.

➤ *Hallway to Limbo.* You walk down a long corridor in which eyes in the portraits follow you, and the scenes on the paintings change right before your eyes.

➤ *The Conservatory.* You're helped into a small coffin-shaped car, called a "carriage," that takes you on your spectral journey through the house.

➤ *Corridor of Doors.* There are tons of novelty spook effects, including doorknockers that rap by themselves, bulging doors, and a candelabra that floats in the middle of an endless corridor.

➤ *Séance Room.* Here you'll get to see fluorescent, rattling tambourines and spirit horns levitating overhead (see Chapter 8). You circle a large round table that holds a giant crystal ball, inside of which is the disembodied, live and talking head of your medium, Mme. Leota.

➤ *Grand Ballroom.* You view this lower-level room as if you were looking down from a balcony. Ghosts appear out of a carriage hearse, fly through the air, and dance around and through the table. Two spectres fight a duel by emerging from their portraits, turning toward each other, and firing their pistols. A phantom musician bangs out notes from a huge pipe organ at one end of the room.

➤ *Attic.* Your ride through the attic is interrupted by screaming ghosts mischievously popping out of trunks to frighten you. You pass a ghost bride, who has no face, but you can't help but notice her glowing, red heart beating through her wedding dress.

➤ *Graveyard.* Seemingly hundreds of ghosts fly overhead and around you. Sculpted headstones come to life and sing to you. Just like you'd find in your ordinary, everyday cemetery (see Chapter 17, "Get Me to the Church on Time").

➤ *Exit Crypt.* Leaving the graveyard, you'll be confronted by three phantom hitchhikers (see Chapter 13, "Urban Legends"). Next, you'll find yourself looking into a giant magic mirror (also Chapter 13). A ghost suddenly appears in the car beside you (or, at least in your reflection). Then, as you pass down a hallway lined with many mirrors, your particular ghost (every car is different) moves along with you. As you leave the attraction, a tiny ghost of a woman perched to one side bids you farewell.

In another story, a female cast member working near the exit caught a glimpse of a man in a tuxedo. Because he was in wardrobe, she assumed that he was another cast member, but when she turned to talk to him, nobody was there. He later reappeared and walked right past her. She turned to look at him: The hallway was empty. Later that night, the mysterious man tried to talk to her, but no sound came from his lips. He walked behind her and put his hand on her shoulder. She turned to face him, but he had disappeared.

Also, the tale is told of a woman who wanted to spread the ashes of her recently deceased young son in the Haunted Mansion, because it was his favorite attraction. She asked permission, but, of course, Disneyland couldn't allow it. Nevertheless, the mother snuck in the ashes and scattered them anyway. From that time on, several guests and cast members have seen a phantom boy, sitting and crying, near the exit of the Haunted Mansion.

Finally, here's one that's not a legend or folklore. It's absolutely true! Gordon Williams, a sound designer of the Haunted Mansion at Disneyland, was putting finishing touches on his work in the attraction prior to its opening, when he heard the oddest noise: soft, non-stop music coming from behind one of the walls. There were no speakers on the other side of the wall, and the music wasn't bleeding over from another part of the attraction.

Williams thought that, perhaps, a radio had accidentally been walled over, or maybe a makeshift ham radio had been created by crossed wires or pipes touching—it's possible—so he waited hours, then days, for a radio announcer or a station's call letters to break in. The music never stopped. With no time to tear down the wall to find the source of the haunting refrains, he placed a large speaker right in front of the wall. The attraction's theme music completely covered over the quieter, ghostly sounds. For all anyone knows, the unexplained phantom music is still playing behind that wall to this day.

Magic Castle

The Magic Castle, located in Hollywood, California, was created by Milt Larsen and his brother William W. Larsen, Jr., as a private club for magicians and their friends. It's the official clubhouse for the Academy of Magical Arts, which fosters education and fraternity in the magic society. The Magic Castle, unique in the world, can be visited only by its members or by invitation by a member.

The Magic Castle opened in 1963, housed in a Victorian mansion built by the Rollin B. Lane family in 1908. In addition to dining and bar areas, there are three showrooms featuring magical entertainment each evening.

One of unique rooms is the Houdini Séance room, which must be specially reserved for use by a private party. Ten guests are served a special dinner at a large circular table, after which a medium joins the sitters to summon the ghost of Houdini. As part of the séance, the lights are darkened, a tambourine shakes and flies through the air, the table floats, and the chandelier sways and lowers.

The Magic Castle in Hollywood, California. (Photo by author, with permission by the Magic Castle)

The Houdini Séance room at the Magic Castle. (Photo by author, with permission by the Magic Castle)

Ghostly Pursuits

The Ballroom of the Haunted Mansion is the largest Pepper's Ghost ever built. It's also the most popular. With slight variations in design, the Haunted Mansion, complete with its ballroom and other special ghost effects, can be found at all four Disney theme parks: Disneyland, Walt Disney World, Tokyo Disneyland, and Disneyland Paris (where the attraction's called the Phantom Manor).

While designing the Ballroom sequence and its secret workings for Disneyland, the late Yale Gracey created a small-scale prototype, in which tiny ghosts appear inside a doll-size room. Gracey donated this original model to the Magic Castle, a magician's clubhouse you'll read about shortly. The still-working miniature is on display as part of the Magic Castle's museum collection.

The True Ghosts of the Haunted Mansion

Is it possible that the Haunted Mansion is really haunted? Well, there are several legends that say it is. According to one, two cast members swear they watched a woman in their security monitors as she entered one of the cars. She rode through the attraction, but she never got off at the other end. Perhaps she's become the Haunted Mansion's 1,000th happy haunt.

Perhaps, the most enchanted room at the Magic Castle, and one of the most popular, is the music room, or, as it is better known, Invisible Irma's room. The room is occupied by a baby grand piano. The piano bench is supposedly occupied by Invisible Irma, who's invisible. All a visitor has to do is request any song—*any* song—and Invisible Irma immediately plays it! Invisible Irma also has a wicked sense of humor and often answers questions put to her by playing songs with relevant lyrics or song titles.

Needless to say, the Magic Castle has created its own ghost story for Invisible Irma. According to the legend, Irma was a frequent guest at the Lane family mansion back in the early 1900s, and she loved to play the piano whenever she visited. Mr. Lane was not musically inclined, however, and didn't enjoy the piano music. He moved the instrument up to the tower, next to the third-floor guest rooms so that he didn't have to hear it. Invisible Irma took this as a personal insult, so when she died in 1932, she swore she would return to haunt the mansion.

Irma the Invisible Ghost. Though normally invisible, Invisible Irma is captured here on a (promotional) spirit photograph. (Photo by Young & Robin, courtesy of Pamela Young Photography, with permission by the Magic Castle)

When the Magic Castle opened its doors in 1963, the piano was moved from the attic back to the music room. Invisible Irma's ghost returned, along with her phantom bird (which now "lives" in a very real gilded cage next to the piano).

So, that's how magicians have created ghosts and spirits over the years, and how they've put them to work. But what about normal people? Let's see how ghosts, poltergeists, and other paranormal entities and activities have been reflected in popular culture, in literature, on the stage, and on the screen.

The Least You Need to Know

➤ Magic was used in ancient times to convince worshippers of the power of deities and spirits.

➤ The Davenport brothers were the most successful early stage performers to use magic to present séances.

➤ Many magicians have created and performed ghost-themed illusions. Some depend on special lighting, smoke, mirrors, or reflective surfaces to produce the spirits.

➤ Some magicians, like Houdini, made a career out of debunking, or at least demystifying, those claiming to be able to communicate with ghosts.

➤ The Magic Castle, a private club for magicians and their friends located in Hollywood, California, is haunted by friendly ghosts—or is it just an illusion?

Apparitions and the Arts

Quick! Think of a movie or movie about ghosts. Were you able to think of one—or maybe a hundred and one? That's because art, in whatever form, reflects the culture in which it's created. And ghost stories have been a part of the folklore of every civilization as far back as anyone can discover.

It would be impossible to put together a complete list of all of the ghost characters and tales that have appeared in literature, theater and films since *Pliny the Younger* first described a haunted house in a 1st-century letter to a friend. But, let's pause long enough to look at a few notable, typical examples in each of these three genres.

Ghost Writing

As we've seen, people have written and collected ghost stories for thousands of years. Plutarch wrote in the 1st century of the haunted baths in Rome. In Homer's *The Odyssey,* written in the 9th century, Ulysses travels to the underworld where he meets with spirits of the dead. Joseph Glanvill, Richard Bovet, and John Beaumont were noted for their collections of ghost stories in the 17th century.

An early 19th-century American short story, "The Legend of Sleepy Hollow," tells the story of a headless horseman, a phantom rider that haunts a New England roadway. It was written by Washington Irving (1783–1859), who was born in New York to a wealthy British merchant. He adapted a German folk tale into his famous story, which

Ghostbusting

If you like ghost stories, there's no need to spend a fortune on books. You'll find dozens of books filled with ghost stories for readers of all ages at your local public library.

first appeared in *The Sketch Book* (serialized in the United States 1819–1820).

The modern horror novel is often attributed to Edgar Allan Poe. Many of his works had a death theme. Even some of stories in his first collection, *Tales of the Grotesque and Arabesque* (written in 1839 and published in 1840) showed his morbid preoccupation with death. (It included one of his most famous short stories, "The Fall of the House of Usher." A winged death omen [see Chapter 4, "Something Wicked This Way Comes"] appears in "The Raven" [published in *The Raven and Other Poems*, 1845].) By the second half of the 19th century, the gothic horror novel was well entrenched.

God Bless Us Everyone

Charles Dickens (1812–1870) was perhaps the greatest writer of fiction in 19th-century England. His now-classic books include *David Copperfield, Oliver Twist, Nicholas Nickleby, Martin Chuzzlewit, The Old Curiosity Shop, Bleak House, Hard Times, A Tale of Two Cities,* and *Great Expectations*.

Ghostly Pursuits

Partly as a result of the success of *A Christmas Carol,* the Christmas ghost story emerged as a literary genre. After all, in the 19th century, Christmas was a time for the family to gather around the glowing fire in the hearth, and it was a natural time for the telling of stories. And if ghost stories made the listeners lean in closer and snuggle closer together, well, all the better.

By 1860, the ghost story was a regular feature in the *Christmas Annual,* a special holiday issue put out by many British and American magazines. Some people compiled ghost stories or made up their own specifically for telling at the family get-togethers at Christmas. In the late 19th century, Lord Halifax of England was especially known for his collection.

In 1843, Dickens produced *A Christmas Carol* (subtitled *A Ghost Story of Christmas*), the first of a series of Christmas books, which also included *The Chimes, The Battle of Life, The Haunted Man,* and the popular *The Cricket on the Hearth. A Christmas Carol* is a story of redemption, as ghostly spirits try to help Scrooge and change his miserly ways. First, to make amends for his cruelty in the past, Scrooge first receives a visit on Christmas Eve from the ghost of his old partner Jacob Marley, who is bound in chains and dragging the phantom money-chest that does him no good in the afterlife.

Scrooge dismisses the ghost's visit as a "piece of undigested potato." But in the course of one evening, Scrooge is visited by three more spirits: the Ghost of Christmas Past, the Ghost of Christmas Present, and the Ghost of Christmas Yet to Come. The last ghost shows Scrooge what will happen if he doesn't mend his ways. By the end of the novella, Scrooge is a changed man!

A Christmas Carol was an instant and incredible success. In the 150 years since its publication, there have been innumerable stage and film adaptations.

Do You Have a Screw Loose?

Novelist Henry James (1843–1916) was born in New York of Irish and Scotch ancestry. His well-known ghost story *The Turn of the Screw* was published in 1898.

In the tale, a young governess (who acts as narrator) is hired to take charge of two orphaned children, Miles and Flora, at Bly, an English country estate in Essex, owned by the children's handsome uncle. At first, all seems idyllic, but soon the governess senses the presence of two ghosts, those of an ex-valet Peter Quint and her own predecessor Miss Jessel. The governess believes that the children are communicating with the spirits. When she learns that Quint and Jessel had been lovers while alive, she's convinced that the apparitions have returned to steal away the children into their spectral world of sin and evil.

The climax of the story comes when the governess confronts Flora and, she thinks, the spirit of Miss Jessel together; the girl is hurried away to safety by the housekeeper, Mrs. Grose. The governess fights with Quint for Miles's soul, however; and in the course of the attempted exorcism, the boy dies in the governess's arms.

Because no one else but the governess ever sees or feels the presence of the apparitions, it's left to the reader to decide whether the ghosts were real or just the hysterical fantasy of a sensitive and impressionable young woman.

Ghostbusting

It's important to take into account your own physical condition and state of mind at the time of a sighting when you later analyze your ghost-hunt data. Were you wide awake? Were you bored? Were you sober? Your results are much more reliable if you know they were collected when you were totally alert with a clear mind and a comfortable, rested body.

You're Giving Me Goosebumps

If you've looked at children's literature lately, you know there's a phenomenon going on by the name *GOOSEBUMPS*. So far there are more than 50 *GOOSEBUMPS* books in the series, all written by R.L. Stine and published by Scholastic, Inc. GOOSEBUMPS is the best-selling book series for children ever: More than 200 million books, translated into 16 languages, have been sold worldwide.

The first GOOSEBUMPS book, *Welcome to Dead House,* established the fun, tongue-in-cheek but slightly scary tone for the series. The books have featured some of the best-known characters from the horror genre, such as mummies and werewolves, but ghosts and hauntings have been the main characters in several of the books. Among the ghostly titles in the GOOSEBUMPS series are *The Ghost Next Door, The Haunted Mask (I* and *II), Ghost Beach, Phantom of the Auditorium, The Barking Ghost, The Headless Ghost, Ghost Camp, My Best Friend Is Invisible,* and *The Haunted School.*

In addition to the GOOSEBUMPS books, there's been a GOOSEBUMPS television series on the Fox network and shelves full of GOOSEBUMPS toys and products for kids!

The Play's the Thing

As far as anyone can tell, ghosts have always been a part of the theater. And why not? They grab and hold an audience's attention besides being colorful (in a sense) and off-beat.

Ghosts appeared as characters in many of the plays written by Roman philosopher, statesman, and dramatist Seneca (4? B.C.–A.D. 65). Usually, his ghosts offered the prologue, commented on the onstage events, or, if they entered into the action of the play, sought revenge from the protagonist for some wrong they received while alive. Almost all ghosts in plays of this period were revenge-seeking.

A new form of apparition, the whining ghost begging favors from the living, appeared in medieval drama. The moaning-and-complaining ghost was a popular character up to the end of the 16th century.

By the time of Elizabethan England, the theater was depicting ghosts more sympathetically, although the appearance of a spectre was frequently little more than a stage device. In *Doctor Faustus* (1588, possibly 1590), for example, playwright Christopher Marlowe (1564–1593) has Mephistopheles conjure up several spirits of the dead, including that of Helen of Troy. Her beauty prompts Faustus to declare, "What this the face that launched a thousand ships?"

To Be or Not to Be ...

Perhaps the first ghosts that the audience could take seriously appeared in Shakespeare. They were fully

Boo!

Don't be frightened away by the iambic pentameter and some of the weird words no one says anymore. Shakespeare's plays are worth reading, seeing, and enjoying. They must be, or they wouldn't still be hanging around and being produced 400 years after they were written. If you don't know how to start to tackle the Bard of Avon, you might take a peek *at The Complete Idiot's Guide to Shakespeare* (Alpha Books, 1999).

developed human characters; they just happened to be dead. In addition to the ghosts that appear onstage, there's mention of apparitions and the spirit world in Shakespeare's plays.

Although ghosts had appeared in earlier Shakespeare plays, the Ghost of Hamlet's Father in *Hamlet* (1600) raised serious problems for the theatergoer. England at the time was officially a Protestant state, so ghosts were considered to be demonic creatures. Yet, many of the audience members still held their Catholic beliefs regarding apparitions. Thus, the ghost of Hamlet's father created a controversy not usually appreciated in modern day: Was the phantom to be taken literally (that is, was it the ghost of a deceased relative) or was it, in fact, a devil *pretending* to be Hamlet's father in order to lead the Dane into some soul-damning action?

It's a puzzlement. Indeed, the Shakespearean ghost has been the subject for entire books and college theses. Forgive me if I recommend that you put the horse before the cart, but I'd suggest you experience the Shakespearean ghosts for yourself by picking up the scripts to the following masterpieces of the theater. Ghosts appear in them all:

➤ *Richard III.* Populated by "Ghosts of those murdered by Richard III."

➤ *Julius Caesar.* Caesar's ghost visits Marcus Brutus, who was one of Caesar's assassins, on two nighttime occasions. As was popular ghost folklore of Elizabethan times, a candle flickers when there's a spirit present. Brutus notices the flame before seeing the ghost, and cries out:

> How ill this taper burns! Ha! who comes here?
> I think it's the weakness of mine eyes
> That shapes this monstrous apparition.
> It comes upon me. Art thou anything?
> Art thou some god, some angel, or some devil,
> That mak'st my blood cold and my hair to stare?
> Speak to me what thou art.

➤ *Macbeth.* Apparitions attend the Three Witches and Hecate, their unearthly queen and the ghost of Banquo, who was murdered on Macbeth's order, materializes at the King's celebratory banquet.

Any discussion of theater ghosts must include the superstitions surrounding Shakespeare's *Macbeth*. Legend has it that the play is cursed, perhaps because of its underlying theme of witchcraft and sorcery. Misfortune extends to actors who perform the play and the theaters in which it appears. Since *Macbeth*'s first productions, countless accidents and injuries have occurred during rehearsal and performance of the play.

There are so many legends surrounding the spectre of evil associated with Shakespeare's *Macbeth*, that, as we saw in Chapter 19, "All the World's a Stage," actors' superstition forbids saying the actual name of the play, especially within a theater. Those in the theatrical profession simply usually refer to it as "the Scottish play."

Ghostly Pursuits

Even noted actor Sir Laurence Olivier was not immune to the *Macbeth* curse. During the 1937 production that starred Olivier at the Old Vic in London, the director and one of the actresses were injured in a taxicab accident. Oliver lost his voice in rehearsal, postponing the opening for four days. The manager of the theater also fell ill during rehearsals and had a fatal heart attack before opening night. During a preview performance, Olivier's sword broke, the blade flew into the audience, and struck a gentleman who died from fright of a heart attack. Finally, Olivier himself was almost killed when he was nearly hit by a falling sandbag.

Phantom Phrases

A **dybbuk,** found in Jewish legend, is a restless soul that enters the body and takes possession of a still-living human being.

Knock, Knock: I'm Coming In

The concept of spirit possession is explored in the Yiddish play, *The Dybbuk* (1914) by Russian-born Solomon Anski. In Jewish folklore, a *dybbuk* is a restless soul that enters the body of a person, left open to possession because the person is living in sin. The dybbuk's spirit overwhelms the living soul, but it can be driven out by exorcism.

That's the Spirit

Noël Coward's *Blithe Spirit* was written and produced (both in London and New York) in 1941. After *Private Lives,* it's probably his most famous play. It's certainly his most popular, having racked up the most performances and productions of any of his works.

Coward wrote the play in just five straight days and said in his autobiography *Future Indefinite* that "I knew it was witty, I knew it was well constructed, and I also knew that it was going to be a success." He changed only two lines of dialogue from its first draft to the first production, which he directed. In the original London production, Margaret Rutherford created the role of the medium Madame Arcati. It was, perhaps, her most famous stage role in a remarkable theater and film career.

The movie version of *Blithe Spirit* was filmed in 1941. Rex Harrison starred as the haunted husband Charles, Kay Hammond repeated her stage role as the first ghost wife Elvira, Constance Cummings portrayed Ruth (Charles's second wife, who also dies and returns as a ghost), and Rutherford repeated her remarkable portrayal of Madame Arcati.

The "Improbable Farce," as the play is subtitled, involves Charles Condomine and his wife Ruth, both members of the smart society set in Kent, England, who decide to hold a private séance in their home, as was then fashionable. The sitting is led by the somewhat madcap but deliciously over-the-top Madame Arcati. The séance invokes the ghost of Charles's first wife, Elvira, who decides not to leave. In fact, she rigs the brakes on the car so that Charles will have a fatal accident and join her in the spirit world.

Unfortunately, Ruth takes the car, and it's she who dies and meets Elvira in the hereafter. By the third act of the comedy, Charles is heckled by the ghosts of both wives. Finally, Madame Arcati, with the assistance of Edith, a maid whom Arcati puts into a trance, manages to send both wives back to the Other Side.

The play is full of comic references to mediums, séances, ghost sightings, and paranormal activity. Even the Society for Psychical Research doesn't escape a bit of friendly razzing.

High Spirits, a musical version of the play, was produced in London in 1964 and opened at the Alvin Theatre in New York on April 7, 1964. The book and music for the show were by Hugh Martin and Timothy Gray, and Coward himself directed the show. Beatrice Lillie portrayed Madame Arcati and Tammy Grimes was Elvira. The show ran nearly a year, 375 performances, yet it was no *Hello, Dolly!* or *Funny Girl,* both of which also opened the same season.

Dressed to Haunt

Stephen Mallatratt's stage adaptation of Susan Hill's ghost-story novel, *The Woman in Black,* opened at the Lyric Theatre in London's West End in January 1989. Six months later, it moved to the Fortune Theatre, where it's been running ever since. In the play, a young London barrister is sent to settle the affairs of a recently deceased elderly woman in an outlying province, unaware that his client's bog-surrounded mansion and the grounds around it are haunted. A chalk-faced ghost, dressed in a black dress and black hooded cape, appears suddenly and unexpectedly throughout the suspenseful, spine-tingling drama.

A Touch of the Irish

The Weir, the Royal Court Theatre's acclaimed Olivier Award winning play by Conor McPherson, opened on London's West End at the Duke of York's Theatre on October 8, 1998. It was first presented the previous July at the Royal Court Theatre Upstairs. Its New York City premiere, featuring the entire original London cast, took place on April Fool's Day, 1999. In the play, a quiet woman who has just moved to a remote village in Ireland is brought to meet the characters at the local pub. In a transfixing evening, three men share stories of ghosts and fairies. By the end, she tells her own compelling and very personal ghost story. Her heart-breaking tale—and stop reading *here* if you don't want to know how the play—involves a telephone call from the dead: her young daughter who has recently drowned (see Chapter 13, "Urban Legends").

Phantoms on Film

There have been dozens of feature films produced that are either about ghosts or have ghosts as central characters to the story. For some reason, the sets of movies with ghost and spirit themes often seem to be plagued with strange, almost paranormal problems while being shot. For example, during filming of *The Amityville Horror,* actor James Brolin had a series of unpleasant accidents, including a sprained ankle and being trapped in a stalled elevator.

Ghostly Pursuits

Noted mind reader Max Maven reported in "The Supernatural Side of Hollywood," a Halloween 1989 report for the Movietime Channel, that "virtually every major participant in the hit film *The Exorcist* became ill at some point during the shoot. The sets were destroyed by a freak fire and had to be completely rebuilt. One actor, Jack Magowran, died of a heart attack shortly before he was to shoot his death scene. With so many problems, the original two-month shooting schedule stretched to nine months."

Ghostbusting

A ghost film may be the perfect movie for a date. You might be surprised how close your date wants to grab and hold onto you—or vice versa—when something scary comes onto the screen!

For those of you who are *really* into ghost films, on the next page is a more complete, yet still selective, list of ghost films from 75 years of filmmaking. Many are available for rental or purchase on video.

There have been more than a hundred movies that feature ghosts, spirits, or apparitional creatures as major characters in their plots. We've already mentioned quite a few in this book, including:

➤ *Carrie* (1976) (and a new, unrelated sequel, *Carrie II* (1999)

➤ *The Exorcist* (1973), *The Exorcist II: The Heretic* (1977) and *The Exorcist III* (1990)

➤ *The Amityville Horror* (1979), *Amityville II: The Possession* (1982), and *Amityville 3-D* (1983)

100 Phantom Films

Haunted Castle (1921)
The Ghost Walks (1934)
One Frightened Night (1935)
The Ghost Goes West (1935)
The Ghost Comes Home (1940)
The Ghost Breakers (1940)
Hold That Ghost (1941)
The Ghost of Frankenstein (1942)
Ghost on the Loose (1942)
The Ghost and the Guest (1943)
Ghost Ship (1943)
Between Two Worlds (1944)
Ghost Catchers (1944)
The Uninvited (1944)
The Canterville Ghost (1944; 1986, remake)
Blithe Spirit (1945)
The Time of Their Lives (1946)
The Ghosts of Berkeley Square (1947)
Ghost Chasers (1951)
Carousel (1956)
House on Haunted Hill (1958)
Ghost of Dragstrip Hollow (1959)
Ghosts of Rome (1961)
Carnival of Souls (1962)
The Ghost (1963)
Ghost in the Invisible Bikini (1966)
Ghosts Italian Style (1969)
The Other (1973)
The Legend of Hell House (1973)
Don't Look Now (1973)
Ghost in the Noonday Sun (1973)
Madhouse Mansion (1974)
Poor Girl, A Ghost Story (1975)
Burnt Offerings (1976)
Cathy's Curse (1976)
The Evil (1978)
Inferno (1978)
The Changling (1979)
The Hearse (1980)
The Shining (1980)
Somewhere in Time (1980)
House of the Dead (1980)
Oh Heavenly Dog (1980)
The Haunting of Julia (1981)
Kiss Me Goodbye (1982)
Soul Survivor (1982)
The Keep (1983)
Christine (1983)
The Entity (1983)
One Dark Night (1983)

The Haunting Passion (1983, made for TV)
All of Me (1984)
The Ghost Writer (1984)
The Oracle (1985)
House Where Evil Dwells (1985)
The Fog (1985)
The Heavenly Kid (1985)
The Supernaturals (1985)
The Legend of Hell House (1985)
Ghost Fever (1985)
Nomads (1986)
Frenchman's Farm (1986)
The Wraith (1986)
Ghostriders (1987)
Eyes of Fire (1987)
Made in Heaven (1987)
Siesta (1987)
Angel Heart (1987)
Ghost Fever (1987)
Ghost Town (1988)
Sister, Sister (1988)
Gotham (1988, made for TV)
Wings of Desire (1988)
Lady in White (1988)
The Haunting of Sarah Hardy (1989)
Always (1989)
In the Dead of the Night (1989, made for TV)
The Other (1989)
Heart of Midnight (1989)
Turn of the Screw (1989, made for TV)
Field of Dreams (1989)
Flatliners (1990)
Ghosts Can't Do It (1990)
Heart Condition (1990)
In the Spirit (1990)
The Forgotten One (1990)
A Ghost in Monte Carlo (1990)
Ghost Dad (1990)
Jacob's Ladder (1990)
Dead Again (1991)
Defending Your Life (1991)
Switch (1991)
Truly, Madly, Deeply (1992)
Death Becomes Her (1992)
Candyman (1992)
The Green Man (1992)
Hearts and Souls (1993)
The House of Spirits (1993)
The Crow (1994)
Candyman II (1995)

Everyone has their own favorite films. But here are thumbnail sketches of my 13 favorite ghost flicks (and their sequels). They really tickled me, and I think they deserve to haunt us for years to come:

➤ *Topper* (1937). An uptight banker is haunted by the ghosts of the Kirbys, two of his society friends. Needless to say, the spirits are invisible except to him. There were two sequels, *Topper Takes a Trip* (1939) and *Topper Returns* (1941). The films served as the basis for the *Topper* television series (1953–1956), starring Leo G. Carroll as the banker Cosmo Topper, and Robert Sterling and Anne Jeffreys as the Kirbys.

➤ *Here Comes Mr. Jordan* (1941). A prizefighter/saxophone player (Robert Montgomery) dies in a plane crash. The trouble is, he was supposed to live for 40 more years. Someone made a mistake. They try to send the spirit back, but his body's been cremated. So the soul is placed into the body of someone else who has recently died. That person comes back to life, but it's really … well, you get the picture. The movie was remade as *Heaven Can Wait,* starring Warren Beatty (1978).

➤ *The Ghost and Mrs. Muir* (1946). A widow (Gene Tierney) living in a seaside house is haunted by the ghost of a sea captain (Rex Harrison). Before long, they fall in love. This film served as the basis for a television series (1968–1970) of the same name starring Hope Lange and Edward Mulhare.

➤ *House on Haunted Hill* (1958). An eccentric millionaire (Vincent Price) invites several guests to a house where many murders have taken place. The director, William Castle, was known for the outlandish promotional gimmicks he thought up for his horror films. This one featured Emergo: The movie theater was rigged so that at a particular moment in the film, an illuminated skeleton (suspended by a wire) would sail (apparently) off the screen and out over the heads of the screaming audience. During their last years, spook shows frequently showed *House on Haunted Hill* as one of their feature movies (see Chapter 24, "The Magic Connection").

➤ *Thirteen Ghosts* (1960). A down-on-his-luck scholar inherits a house, but it's—surprise!—haunted. During initial release of the William Castle thriller, audience members were given special glasses called "ghost viewers" so that they could see the spirits on the screen. The marketing gimmick was called Illusion-O.

➤ *The Haunting* (1963). An anthropologist, a paranormal skeptic, and a medium decide to spend a weekend together to investigate a haunted house in Boston. (A special-effects-laden remake was released in July 1999.) The film is based on Shirley Jackson's 1959 book, *Haunting of Hill House*.

➤ *Ghost Story* (1981). Four elderly men (Fred Astaire, Melvyn Douglas, John Houseman, and Douglas Fairbanks, Jr.) who share a secret from their past swap ghost stories.

➤ *Poltergeist* (1982). A young girl watching TV inadvertently opens a door to the spirit world. Havoc ensues as avenging spirits and ghouls invade the house and try to capture the family's children. As it turns out, the dead aren't happy because the house was built over the cemetery in which they're buried. Zelda Rubinstein (who provided the foreword to this book) portrayed the medium Tangina Barrons in *Poltergeist* and its two sequels, *Poltergeist II: The Other Side* (1986) and *Poltergeist III*. The first sequel's plot involved phone calls from the dead.

Ghostly Pursuits

Two of the leading actors and the director of *Poltergeist* had personal experiences of spirit activity years before making the film. Ironically, according to Zelda Rubinstein (who portrayed the medium in all three *Poltergeist* movies) no unusual ghost-like activity occurred on the set of the films themselves.

While working in New Hampshire summer stock, JoBeth Williams (who portrayed the mother, Diane Freeling) awoke to feel her bed shaking violently. Also, the air was icy cold. The owner of the house was not surprised: The ghost, which she believed to be the spirit of someone who died there, had caused a ruckus in the room before.

Beatrice Straight (who played parapsychologist Dr. Lesh), her children, and their house-keeper heard unexplained cries and other noises at their farmhouse in Connecticut. The children also felt unseen hands pulling the covers off their beds. A psychic, invited into the home by Straight, used a Ouija board to identify the ghost as that of a Native American who had drowned in a nearby lake. (The tribe had been friendly with the original owners of the farm.)

Director Tobe Hooper experienced poltergeist activity in his home for three days after his father's death. Glass and ceramic objects shattered on their own, or they were found broken, flung far from their shelves. Also, the father's rocking chair began rocking on its own.

➤ *Ghostbusters* (1984). Four out-of-work parapsychologists (Bill Murray, Dan Aykroyd, Harold Ramis, and Rick Moranis) set up shop as ghostbusters to help rid New York of its monstrous apparitions. There was a sequel, *Ghostbusters II* (1989).

➤ *Maxie* (1985). The ghost of a starlet from the 1920s haunts her old apartment and eventually takes possession of the woman living there with her husband (Mandy Patinkin). Glenn Close played the twin role of haunter and hauntee.

➤ *Beetlejuice* (1988). The eccentric ghosts haunting a barn in New England try everything in the book—and then some—to scare off the new owners who live there. Michael Keaton played the title spook.

➤ *Ghost* (1990). A stockbroker (Patrick Swayze) returns from the Other Side to track down his murderers. Whoopi Goldberg won an Oscar for her portrayal of the medium who helps him cross over. Demi Moore played his girlfriend in this tear-jerker.

➤ *Casper* (1995). Carrigan Crittendon (Cathy Moriarty) and her partner Dibs (Eric Idle) hire a "ghost therapist," Dr. James Harvey (Bill Pullman), to exorcise the ghosts from Crittendon Manor. Harvey's daughter Kat (Christina Ricci) becomes friends with Casper. The film's four ghost characters are based on Casper and The Ghostly Trio (Stretch, Stinkie, and Fatso) which appear in Harvey Comics.

Well, I hope you've enjoyed our travels through the world of ghosts, apparitions, spirits, and the paranormal. The next time you hear a strange noise in the dark, or you think you catch a glimpse of something weird fly by, you'll be ready!

Ghost hunters, arise! You know what to look for, and how to search for them. And if you're out there, sitting all alone in some haunted house or ancient graveyard, don't be scared. Remember, it's always darkest before the dawn.

The Least You Need to Know

➤ The treatment of ghosts in popular culture has reflected the beliefs of the civilizations that produced them.

➤ Ghosts have been recorded in letters and manuscripts since the time of the classical Greeks and Romans. Ghost literature came to the forefront with the work of such 18th- and 19th-century authors as Edgar Allen Poe, Charles Dickens, and Henry James.

➤ Ghosts and apparitions have always been important characters in the theater, from Greek tragedies to the works of Shakespeare and the light comedy of Noel Coward.

➤ Movies are able to project terrifying images of ghost phenomena. More than a hundred films have featured apparitional characters.

Phantom Phrases

agent   The apparition, or ghost, seen by a human being (or **percipient**).

amulet   Any object that's thought to have the power to ward off ghosts and evil spirits or to bring good luck.

apparition   Any disembodied spirit that appears visibly.

apport/asport   An apport is a solid object that seemingly appears from nowhere in the presence of a medium. Some apports are assembled from invisible material matter; others are teleported from another often-distant location. An asport is any object the spirits or the medium makes disappear or teleports to another location.

astral projection/astral body   *See* out-of-body experience.

automatic writing   Communication from a spirit in written form. The medium holds a pen or pencil against paper and allows the spirit to take possession or control of his or her hand to write out a message.

automatism   Any unconscious and spontaneous muscular movement caused by the spirits. Automatic writing is one form of automatism.

channeling   A form of spirit communication, mostly popular in the United States during the "New Age" fad of the 1970s. During a channeling session, an unseen entity takes possession of the medium (called a channeler) to impart spiritual guidance or wisdom. The channeled entity was seldom a deceased human; rather it was a spiritual creature such as an angel, demon, the Higher Self, or part of the Universal Mind.

cold reading   A technique using a series of statements, questions, and answers that allows fake mediums, mind-readers, and magicians to obtain previously unknown information about a person.

collective apparition   An unusual type of spirit sighting in which more than one person sees the same phenomenon.

collective unconscious   From the analytical psychology of Carl Jung, the collective unconscious is the collective memory of all of humanity's past, held in an individual's unconscious mind.

control   A control lives in the spirit world and is manifested by a medium, usually in a séance, to act on the mediums behalf as guide among the spirits. A control may appear as a disembodied voice, speaking through the medium's own voice, write with the medium's hand, be materialized visually either partially or full-form, or take full possession of the medium's body.

crisis apparition   A crisis apparition is a specific type of out-of-body experience in which the agent projects his or her astral body at a time of crisis or death to a particular percipient, usually a loved one.

cross-correspondences   Interrelated bits of information received from the spirit world by different mediums at different times and locations. The communications must be joined together to form a complete message from the spirit(s).

direct voice phenomenon (DVP)   A spirit voice, spoken directly to sitters at a séance. The sound usually seems to come from a point near the medium, or through a spirit horn or trumpet, but not from the mouth of the medium.

direct writing   A spectral phenomenon, seen most often in a séance, in which spirit handwriting appears directly on a previously unmarked surface.

drop-in communicator   A drop-in communicator is a spirit or entity that makes its presence known at a séance. Its identity is usually unknown to the medium and the sitters.

dybbuk   A dybbuk, found in Jewish legend, is the restless soul of a deceased human being that enters the body and takes possession of a still-living person.

ectoplasm   Ectoplasm is a solid or vaporous substance, lifelike and moldable, that supposedly exudes from the body of a medium (usually from one of the facial orifices) to form seemingly corporeal limbs, faces, or entire bodies. Ectoplasm is a usually dense but liquidy, milky-white substance with the scent of ozone.

electronic voice phenomena (EVP)   The capture of spirit voices on magnetic tape as an audio recording. Many times, no sound is heard while the tape is recording. It's only upon playback that the harsh, hushed voices can be heard.

exorcism   The expulsion of a ghost, spirit, demon, or other entity/entities thought to be possessing or haunting a human being or location. The ritual, conducted by an exorcist, is usually religious in nature, and calls upon some Higher Power to cast out the evil force(s).

ghost   A form of apparition, usually the visual appearance of a deceased human's spirit soul.

ghost lights   *See* ignis fatuus.

ghost hunt/ghost investigation   A ghost hunt is an informal attempt to simply sight or record a ghost in a location similar to others known to be haunted. A ghost investigation, on the other hand, is a carefully controlled research project, set up to record paranormal activity, usually at a location known or presumed to be haunted.

ghost hunter   A person who searches for, finds, and sometimes is able to identify apparitions or the cause of spirit activity.

ghostbuster   A person who removes a ghost, poltergeist, spirit entity, or spectral activity from a haunted site.

gray lady   A gray lady is the ghost of a woman whose death has been caused by a loved one or who died while waiting for her lover to return or appear.

hallucination   A false or distorted perception of objects or events with a full belief in their reality. Ghosts, as we define them, are not hallucinations, because they have a real, external cause.

haunt   A ghost that returns to the same location is said to haunt it. Ghosts generally haunt places, not people.

ignis fatuus   Literally meaning "foolish fire," ignis fatuus are any of a variety of ghost or spectral lights. According to some folkloric traditions, the lights are souls of the dead; in other legends, they are imp-like spirits.

Kabbalah   A collected way of thinking based primarily on ancient Jewish spiritual writings and their mystic interpretation.

magnetometer   A device to measure the presence of a magnetic field as well as its strength, direction, and fluctuation. Paranormal researchers use the device in an attempt to detect a ghost's magnetic or energy aura.

Marian apparition   The appearance of the ghostlike figure of the Virgin Mary, mother of Jesus.

materialization   The manifestation or production of some physical object or person from the spirit world. The most difficult and impressive materialization is all (or even part of) a human spirit, especially if the ghost's face is recognizable.

medium   Someone who can communicate with spirits on behalf of another living being. The word suggests that the medium acts as a midway point, halfway between the worlds of the living and the dead.

mesmerism   The induction of a sleep or trance state, discovered during the work of Friedrich Anton Mesmer, from whose name the word is derived. Also known as hypnotism.

near-death experience (NDE) A near-death experience is undergone by a person who clinically dies, or comes very close to actual death, and is revived. Often, the person recalls extraordinary, even paranormal, visions of an afterlife. American physician Dr. Raymond Moody coined the phrase in the 1970s.

341

necromancy/necromancer   A form of prophecy, in which the seer or sorcerer/sorceress raises the spirit (though not usually the corporal remains) of the dead in order to have the wraith foretell future events. It was thought that upon entering eternity, the spirit would have full knowledge of the past, present, and future.

objective apparitions   Apparitions or phenomena that appear independent of our minds, thoughts, or feelings. **Subjective apparitions,** on the other hand, are hallucinations created by our minds.

oracle   In ancient Greece, a seeress who is about to communicate with the gods and the deceased to foretell the future.

Ouija board   A board pre-printed with letters, numerals, and words used by mediums to receive spirit communications. Usually a planchette is employed to spell out words or point out numbers or words. A game version of the Ouija board was mass-marketed as OUIJA by Parker Brothers in 1966 and is currently distributed by Hasbro.

out-of-body experience (OBE)   An out-of-body experience (also called astral projection) is the paranormal phenomenon in which a spirit double (also called the astral body) leaves your body and travels to another location.

paranormal   Something that is beyond the range of normal human experience or scientific explanation.

percipient   A person who sees (i.e., perceives) an apparition or ghost.

phantom hitchhiker   *See* phantom traveler.

phantom traveler   A phantom traveler is the ghost of a human or animal that haunts a specific roadway, route, or vehicle. The phantom hitchhiker, who requests a ride, then suddenly disappears from inside the vehicle, is the best-known type of phantom traveler legend.

planchette   A palm-sized triangular platform, usually on wheels, that is used as a pointer during the operation of a Ouija board.

poltergeist   A non-human spirit entity. Although its name is based on Greek roots meaning "noisy ghost," the poltergeist is usually more malicious and destructive than ghosts of dead human beings. Traditional poltergeist activities are thumpings and bangings, levitating and moving objects, stone-throwing, and starting fires.

postcognition   *See* retrocognition.

purgatory   In Roman Catholic doctrine, the place where souls of people who have died in grace must suffer while being cleansed their sins before they can be admitted into heaven.

radio voice phenomenon (RVP)   Receiving the voice of a deceased human being over a regular radio.

reciprocal apparition   An exceedingly rare type of spirit phenomenon in which both the agent and percipient see and respond to each other.

repressed psychokinetic energy   A theoretical psychic force produced, usually unconsciously, by an individual undergoing physical or mental trauma. When released, some think the power causes paranormal occurrences such as poltergeist activity. A classic, though fictional, example would be what *Carrie* (of film and Stephen King novel fame) did at the prom.

retrocognition   A sudden time warp in which you find yourself in the past, seeing or experiencing events of which you had no prior knowledge. Also called *postcognition.*

scrying   A type of prophecy in which the fortune-teller reveals the future while staring into a mirror, onto some other shiny or reflective surface, or into a crystal (such as a gemstone or a crystal ball).

séance   A gathering of individuals, usually led by a medium, for the purpose of receiving spirit manifestations or communication with the dead. Also known as a "sitting," a "spirit circle," or, simply, a "circle."

sensitive   Parapsychology jargon for someone who's aware of or can feel (you know, is sensitive to) paranormal presences that can't be picked up by the regular five senses.

shaman   A wizard in tribal societies who is an intermediary between the living, the dead, and the gods.

spirit cabinet   A spirit cabinet, or simply cabinet, is a solid or curtained enclosure within which the medium sits to allow the spirits to appear unimpeded in darkness. The first spirit cabinet was introduced by the Davenport brothers in the 1850s in New York City. Its use was quickly adopted by many of the leading mediums of the day.

spirit photography   A spirit photograph captures the image of a ghost on film. Many spirit photographs are supposedly intended as a mere portrait of a living human being, but when the film is developed, an ethereal ghostly face or figure can be seen hovering near the subject.

spirit theater   A term used by modern-day magicians to describe shows, acts, or tricks in which ghosts or other spirit activity are apparently produced.

spiritualism   A belief system that spirits of the dead can (and do) communicate with living humans in the material world. Usually this contact is made through an intermediary known as a *medium.*

spook show   Also called a ghost show or spookeroo, a spook show was a magic show, most popular during the 1950s, that featured horror- and ghost-themed magic tricks. Often one or two horror movies were shown as part of the evening's entertainment.

subjective apparitions   *See* objective apparitions.

super-ESP   A powerful form of telepathy that allows a medium to unconsciously pick up information about a deceased person from other living people.

supernatural   Something that exists or occurs through some means other than any known force in nature. As opposed to paranormal, the term "supernatural" often connotes divine or demonic intervention.

telepathic projection   A now-discredited theory first espoused by Frederic W.H. Myers, a 19th-century paranormal investigation suggesting that spirits of the dead sent mental messages to the living rather than physically returning as ghosts.

teleportation   A kind of paranormal transportation in which an object is moved from one distinct location to another, often through a solid object such as a wall.

Wild Hunt   A group of ghost huntsmen, horses, and hounds in procession, always seen at night. Leaders of legendary and mythological Wild Hunts include Herne the Hunter, Sir Francis Drake, the god Odin, and the goddess Holda.

Continuing the Ghost Hunt

Most paranormal researchers recommend that if you wish to undertake a serious investigation, you should contact an organization or individual that can do so professionally and scientifically. This is especially true if you're having problems with a haunting—either by a ghost or poltergeist. You'll need help.

Four Notable Ghost-Hunter Organizations

If you think your case is serious enough to interest one of the long-standing leading paranormal research organizations, such as the SPR or one of its associates, by all means contact one of them. If the society feels it's not the appropriate agency to investigate your haunting, it may recommend other options.

Here are four long-standing organizations of note:

Society for Psychical Research (SPR)
49 Marloes Road
London W86LA
England
Phone: 0171-937-8984

American Society for Psychical Research (ASPR)
Patrice Keane, Executive Director
5 West 73rd Street
New York, NY 10023
Phone: 212-799-5050
Fax: 212-496-2497
Web site: http://www.aspr.com/index.htm

Ghost Research Society (GRS)
Dale Kaczmarek, President
P.O. Box 205
Oak Lawn, IL 60454-0205
Phone: 708-425-5163
Fax: 708-425-3969
Web site: http://www.ghostresearch.org

Committee for the Scientific Investigation of Claims of the Paranormal (CSICOP)
P.O. Box 703
Amherst, NY 14226-0703
Web site: http://www.csicop.com

CSISCOP's investigations are not limited to ghost phenomena. Indeed, their inquiries cover the full range of paranormal activities. They publish *Skeptical Inquirer* magazine. If you have access to the Internet, I'd recommend contacting them there and visiting their many links.

Ghosts on the Internet

Several individuals and organizations have Web pages on the Internet describing their services. Whenever possible, I've listed the group's founder, director, or chief investigator. The following is a very brief list of who and what's out there.

Please note that their mention on this list is not necessarily a recommendation or endorsement of their expertise or success rate. As with any consultant, you'll have to interview a ghost hunter to make sure the two of you are in sync. Nevertheless, all of these people and individuals are seriously interested in ghost phenomena and deal with paranormal activity. A good way to start out finding your spectre-seeking soul mate is by visiting some of these Web sites.

D. Trull, *Enigma* Magazine
Web site: http://www.parascope.com/articles/0397/ghostin.htm
E-mail: dtrull@parascope.com

G.H.O.S.T. (formerly The New York Society of Psychic Research and Paranormal Investigation)
David Umbria, Director
Phone: 718-982-9725
Web site: http://theghosthunters.com
E-mail: ghost@theghosthunters.com

Dave Umbria is a former student of and investigator for Ed and Lorraine Warren of the New England Society for Psychic Research (see their entry coming up).

The Ghost Hunters of Baltimore
Jay McClenahan, Founder
Web site: http://www.angelfire.com/biz/GhostInvestigation
E-mail: GhstHnter@aol.com

The Ghost Hunters group operates in the Maryland, Virginia, and Washington, D.C. areas.

International Ghost Hunters Society
Dave Oester and the Rev. Sharon Gill, co-founders
Web site: http://www.ghostweb.com

International Society for Paranormal Research
Los Angeles, California
Web sites: http://www.hauntings.com; http://www.ISPR.net

Kansas Ghost Hunters
Shawn Barger, Co-founder
Web site: http://home.swbell.net/shawnb/

New England Society for Psychic Research
Ed and Lorraine Warren, Directors
P.O. Box 41
Monroe, CT 06468
Web site: http://www.warrens.net/

Although based in New England, the Warrens or members of their staff conduct research throughout the United States.

North Jersey Society of Paranormal Research
Web sites: http://www.charonpress.com/ghost/ghost.htm;
http://www.prognetsys.com/paranormal;
http://www.prognetsys.com/ep
E-mail: gary@prognetsys.com

Paranormal Investigations
Dave Christensen, President
P.O. Box 1323
Bellevue, NB 68005-1323
Phone: 402-553-1703
Web site: http://www.SwiftSite.com/PARANORMAL_INVESTIGATION/
E-mail: gosthunter@aol.com

Paranormal Research Society of New England
John Zaffis and Mike Roberg, Ghost Investigators
Web site: http://www.prsne.com

Pennsylvania Ghost Hunters Society
Rick Fisher, Director
Web site: http://users.desupernet.net/rfisher/pghs.html

Philadelphia Ghost Hunters Alliance (PGHA)
Lewis Gerew, Webmaster
Web site: http://members.aol.com/Rayd8em/index.html

Richard Senate
Web sites: http://www.charonpress.com/ghost/ghost.htm;
http://www.aim.tj/JAM/ghost/ghstglry.htm

Richard Senate, author and ghost hunter, maintains two Web sites. The first site listed describes his books. The second site provides an ever-changing array of ghost photos, generally submitted by amateur ghost hunters.

Shadowlands
Dave Juliano, Shadow Lord
Web sites: http://theshadowlands.net/ghost/
http://users.aol.com/shadoland2/ghost.html
E-mail: shadowlord@theshadowlands.net; ghosts@theshadowlands.net

In addition to his work as a ghost hunter, Dave Juliano has maintained this superb ghost site since 1995. It includes multiple links to other sites of interest. Various search engines regularly rate this as one of the most popular ghost sites on the Web.

South Jersey Ghost Research
Jonathan Williams, Director
Phone: 609-218-7447
Web site: http://theghosthunters.com/southjersey/
E-mail: sjgr@theghosthunters.com

S.P.I.R.I.T.
Web site: http://www.ghosthunter.org/

This organization, dedicated to ghost hunting and other paranormal research, has local chapters and investigators throughout the United States.

United States Ghost Research (USGR)
Web site: http://member.xoom.com/usgr

The White Crow Society
314 West 231 Street, Suite #465
Riverdale, NY 10463
Phone/fax: 718-543-4183
Web site: http://www.geocities.com/CapeCanaveral/Hangar/1533/
E-mail: white_crow_soc@geocities.com

Sites for Haunted Locations

There are dozens of other Web sites dedicated to ghostly happenings, paranormal activity, and sharing ghost stories. Most are set up by aficionados rather than by professional researchers, but many of the sites are interesting and valuable. Of course, Web sites come and go, and much of what's posted has to be taken with a large grain of salt. Please, don't hold me responsible for the claims made on these sites or for the information provided. That said, here are just a few of the ghost sites that were up and running at the time of publication.

Ghosts of Derby, England
http://www.derbycity.com/ghosts/ghosts.html

Ghosts of Ely, England
http://www.ely.org.uk/ghosts.htm

Ghosts of New Orleans
http://www.parascope.com/articles/1097/neworleans.htm

Ghosts of North Portland, Oregon
http://www.hevanet.com/heberb/ghosts/ghosts.htm

Ghosts of the Prairie (American Ghost Society)
http://www.prairieghosts.com/

Ghosts of Tombstone, Arizona
http://www.clantongang.com/oldwest/ghost.htm

Haunted Maine
http://www.prairieghosts.com/hauntme.html

Hollywood's Most Famous Ghosts
http://www.vaportrails.com/USA/USAFeatures/Ghost/Ghost.html

Micronesian Tales, Ghosts, and Legends
http://members.xoom.com/agana/main.htm

Sites for Ghost Links

Almost every Web site devoted to ghost and ghost hunting also provides some links to similar sites. The sites in this group are very similar, however, in that they provide multiple links, sometimes separating them into subcategories of interest.

GHOOOSTS
http://netmar.com/~alba/ghosts/ghosts.html

A very popular site with lots of ghost links.

GHOST Links
http://cannylink.com/paranormalghosts.htm

Ghost Sites of the Web
http://www.disobey.com/ghostsites/

Hauntings
http://www.webdesignfx.com/nemesis/spirit/index.htm

Lots and lots of links.

Obiwan's UFO-Free Paranormal Page—Links
http://www.ghosts.org/links.html

Multiple links, separated by categories.

Sites for Ghost Stories, Essays, and Chat

Because most ghost sites are maintained by individual ghost hunters or research organizations, their emphasis is on investigation and sightings. Some ghost sites are put up just for fun, to share fictional stories or philosophical theses, or simply to swap ideas with fellow ghost lovers. If you're more interested in the latter, you might want to check out these sites.

Archive X: Ghost Stories and Folklore
http://www.crown.net/X/GhostStories.html

Ghosts, Ghostly Encounters, and Ghost Happenings!
http://members.aol.com/Inside463/ghost.html

How to Create Fake Photos of Ghosts
http://www3.sympatico.ca/roddy/ghost-front-door.html

Obiwan's UFO-Free Paranormal Page
http://www.ghosts.org/

Why Do Some Ghosts Wear Clothes?
http://www.prairieghosts.com/clothes.html

Ghost Tours

Some towns offer Ghost Tours, taking amateur ghost hunters on a sightseeing expedition of area haunted houses and sites. It's worth checking with local tourist offices and the Yellow Pages when you're in a city you think might be haunted. Here are just a few ghost tours that are currently available in the United States and Great Britain:

Cape May, New Jersey

Elaine's Ghost Tours
Phone: 609-88-GHOST

Charleston, South Carolina

"Ghosts of Charleston" walking tour
18 Broad Street, Suite 709
Charleston, SC 29401
Phone: 1-800-854-1670
Web site: www.tourcharleston.com
E-mail: info@tourcharleston.com

Chicago, Illinois

Chicago Supernatural Ghost Tours
There are at least three "ghost hosts" in the Windy City, and Richard Crowe has been conducting various ghostly itineraries for 25 years.
Phone: 708-449-0300

Ghost Tours—Bus and Walking
Howard Heim, guide
7344 S. Talman Avenue
Chicago, IL 60629
Phone: 773-SPOOKY-1 (773-776-6591)

Excursions into the Unknown
Dale Kaczmarek, leader
Phone: 708-425-5163

Fredericksburg, Virginia

"Phantom of Fredericksburg" Ghost Tour
The Living History Company of Fredericksburg
904 Princess Anne Street, Suite C7
Fredericksburg, VA 22401
Phone: 540-899-1776
Toll free: 1-888-214-6384

Gettysburg, Pennsylvania

Ghost Tours of Gettysburg
Phone: 717-337-0445

Harpers Ferry, West Virginia

Ghost Tours of Harpers Ferry
conducted by Shirley Dougherty
Phone: 304-725-8019

Hollywood, California

Grave Line Tours
Although it's not exactly a ghost tour, Grave Line Tours offers a morbidly weird and wonderful tour of Hollywood death sites. Sightseers ride in a hearse to visit murder, suicide, and burial sites of the stars. Grave Line's macabre motto boasts: "Get within six feet of your favorite stars!"
P.O. Box 931694
Los Angeles, CA 90093
Phone: 323-469-4149

Key West, Florida

Ghost Tours
A walking tour of Key West's haunted, historic district.
Phone: 305-294-9255

Historic Hauntings
A re-creation of a turn-of-the-century spirit séance.
Phone: 305-292-2040

Lancaster County, Pennsylvania

Ghost Tours
Departs from Strasburg, Pennsylvania.
Phone: 717-687-6687

New Orleans, Louisiana

Restless Spirit Tours
Phone: 504-895-0895
Web site: http://members.aol.com/vamptour
E-mail: vamptour@aol.com

New York City, New York

"East Village Ghosts"
Street Smarts N.Y.
Phone: 212-969-8262

Philadelphia, Pennsylvania

Ghost Tours
Phone: 215-413-1997
Web site: www.ghosttour.com

Salem, Massachusetts

Better known for its place in the history of witchcraft than for ghosts and apparitions, there are, nevertheless, several haunted sites located in Old Salem, including the Old Jail, the Corwin home, the Ropes Mansion, the Athaeneum Library, and the residence of Susan Ingersoll. Ingersoll's home inspired her cousin, Nathaniel Hawthorne, to write the gothic horror novel *The House of the Seven Gables*. Salem holds an annual 10-day Haunted Happenings with more than 50 events. For information, contact:

Visitor Center
Old Town Hall
32 Derby Square
Salem, MA 01970
Phone: 508-744-0004

San Antonio, Texas

Ghost Hunt
Phone: 210-436-5417

San Francisco, California

Ghost Hunt Walking Tour
Daily guided tours by Fassbinder, a member of the International Ghost Hunters Society.
Phone: 415-922-5590

Savannah, Georgia

Savannah Walks, Inc., Low Country Ghost Tour
Phone: 1-888-SAV-WALK
Web site: www.savannahwalks.com

London, England, and Great Britain

London Walks conducts three different nighttime walking ghost tours of London: "Ghosts of the West End" (Monday, Thursday), "Ghosts of the Old City" (Tuesday, Saturday), "Ghosts, Gaslight, and Guinness" (Wednesday), and "Haunted London" (Friday, Sunday). All four ghost walks are offered on Halloween!

London Walks
P.O. Box 1708
London NW6 4LW
England
Phone: 0171-624-3978, 0171-794-1764, or 0171-911-0285
Fax: 0171-625-1932
Web sites: http://www.walks.com; http://london.walks.com
E-mail: london@walks.com

London Ghost Walk
Nighttime tours, daily except Wednesday.
Web site: http://www.london-ghost-walk.co.uk
E-mail: enquiries@london-ghost-walk.co.uk

Apparition Expeditions
Operated by Shannon O'Hara of Chandler, Arizona, Apparition Expeditions escorts amateur ghost hunters on paranormal safaris to Great Britain and elsewhere. Call for her updated itineraries.
Phone: 877-273-3694

Boo-Boo-Boo, Books!

There are literally hundreds of books out there on ghosts, apparitions, paranormal activity, and psychic societies. There are directories of where to find ghosts and compendiums full of ghost stories—some fictional, and many purporting to be true case histories.

Some of these books are available in major bookstores, but most of them can be found in specialty bookstores or on the shelves of your local library. Most non-fiction books about ghosts can be found at 133.1 under the good old Dewey Decimal system.

Bayless, Raymond. *The Enigma of the Poltergeist*. West Nyack, NY: Parker Publishing Co., 1967.

A scholarly but subjective examination of the nature of poltergeists and how they differ from ghosts, apparitions, other spirits. Many famous poltergeist cases are detailed, especially pre-20th century phenomena.

_____. *Apparitions and Survival of Death*. New York: Citadel Press, 1973.

A discussion of what might possibly survive the body after death. Distinctions are made between the soul, apparitions, and spirits.

Burger, Eugene. *Spirit Theater*. New York: Richard Kaufman and Alan Greenberg, 1986.

Written by a magician and spirit-theater performer, this is a lively discussion chronicling the roots of spiritualism and the movement's most famous mediums. This book includes interviews with modern psychic entertainers as well as the methods for several convincing spirit-themed magical illusions.

Cohen, Daniel. *The Encyclopedia of Ghosts*. New York: Dodd, Mead & Co., 1984.

Despite its title, the book is in chapter format. It's an easy and entertaining introduction to familiarize readers with some of the most famous ghost stories.

Finucane, R.C. *Ghosts: Appearances of the Dead & Cultural Transformation*. Amherst, NY: Prometheus Books, 1996.

An excellent and thoughtful examination of how the belief in and perception of ghosts have changed throughout the ages.

Guiley, Rosemary Ellen. *The Encyclopedia of Ghosts and Spirits*. New York: Facts on File, 1992.

A thorough and entertaining compendium of mostly American and British ghostly lore and legend, plus biographies of luminaries in the fields of spiritualism and paranormal research.

Hauck, Dennis William. *Haunted Places: The National Directory*. New York: Penguin Books, 1996.

This is an indispensable U.S. travel guide for hobbyist ghost hunters. More than 2,000 haunted places are listed state-by-state, along with brief descriptions of the sites and their legends. It also includes a bibliography of more than 200 books on ghosts, spirits, and other supernatural phenomena.

Holzer, Hans. *Haunted Hollywood*. New York: The Bobbs-Merrill Co., 1974.

The best-known survey of phantom encounters in Movieland.

Jacobson, Laurie, and Marc Wanamaker. *Hollywood Haunted: A Ghostly Tour of Filmland*. Santa Monica, CA: Angel City Press, 1994.

An updated overview of the more popular haunted spots and celebrity ghosts of Tinseltown.

Man, Myth & Magic: An Illustrated Encyclopedia of the Supernatural. In 24 volumes. Richard Cavendish, ed. New York: Marshall Cavendish Corporation, 1970.

A comprehensive encyclopedia of articles about supernatural, ghost, psychic, and paranormal phenomena.

Ogden, Tom. *Wizards and Sorcerers*. New York: Facts on File, 1997.

An encyclopedic survey of wizards and sorcerers in legend and literature, and how they're reflected in popular culture.

Tyrrell, G.N.M. *Apparitions*. New York: Collier Books, 1963.

This classic book is the result of Tyrrell's survey of ghost and paranormal investigation up to the mid-20th century. It also expounds his theories on the nature of apparitions. The text was adapted and published posthumously (originally in 1953) from a speech Tyrrell made in 1942 as the Myers Memorial Lecture before the Society of Psychical Research.

Underwood, Peter. *Gazetteer of British, Scottish and Irish Ghosts*. New York: Bell Publishing Company, 1985.

Exactly as the title suggests, this is a listing of hundreds of ghosts and haunted locations throughout Great Britain.

The following books are a representative sampling of some you can find that are specific to a particular location or city. This type is particularly interesting if you're going into that region, because it's often filled with many more examples than more general books on ghost activity.

Alexander, John. *Ghosts: Washington's Most Famous Ghost Stories*. Arlington, VA: Washington Book Trading Co., 1988.

Sloan, David L. *Ghosts of Key West*. Key West, FL: Mirror Lake Press, 1998.

Murray, Earl. *Ghosts of the Old West*. Chicago, Contemporary Books, 1988.

Wlodarski, Robert, Anne Nathan-Wlodarski, and Richard Senate. *A Guide to the Haunted Queen Mary*. West Hills, California: Ghost Publishing, 1998.

Finally, the following three books are written for people who want to create their own haunted houses. Many organizations sponsor haunted houses as fundraisers around Halloween. The first book on this list will give you all the dos and don'ts about setting up your own spooky surroundings. It's a detailed and easy-to-follow directions for those serious about putting together a fundraiser or professional "haunted house" attraction and is highly recommended! The last two books are aimed at young readers who want to rig a gag or two around their own homes to fool or surprise friends and family, but even big kids might pick up a trick or two!

Harkleroad, Tim. *The Complete Haunted House Book*. Bristol, TN: Moonlighting Publications, 1998.

Witkowski, Dan. *How to Haunt a House*. NY: Random House, 1994.

Friedhoffer, Robert. *How to Haunt a House for Halloween*. NY: Franklin Watts, 1995.

Haunted Places in the U.S. and Great Britain

There are literally thousands of sites throughout the world that are allegedly haunted. No single directory can ever hope to give a complete listing.

Most of the more than 300 sites detailed in *The Complete Idiot's Guide to Ghosts and Hauntings* are either privately owned, places of business, or institutions not open for tourism, so only the exterior of the buildings can be viewed. However, a courteous request can sometimes result in a quick look around even these premises.

Here's a list of the most popular sites that *are* open to the public. Even so, some are places of business that require admission for entrance, and even then some areas may not be open to visitors.

Whenever possible, I've included addresses, directions, and a phone number. Admission is charged to enter many of the museums and tourist locations. Opening hours vary and telephone numbers may have changed, so please check with the venue or local tourism boards before setting out on a major journey.

Arizona

Big Nose Kate's (saloon)
Tombstone, AZ 85638
Phone: 502-457-3107

California

Alcatraz Island
Located in San Francisco Bay, San Francisco, CA.
Web site: http://www.nps.gov/alcatraz/welcome.html

Operated as part of the National Park Service. Hours of operation vary seasonally, generally from 9:30 A.M. to 4:30 P.M. (6:30 P.M. in the summer months). Closed on Christmas and New Year's Day. Boats depart from Pier 41 on Fisherman's Wharf in San Francisco. Alcatraz is a very popular tourist attraction, so advance ticket sales are *highly* recommended. For information, contact the Blue & Gold Fleet, which operates the boats to the island, at 415-705-5555, or stop at their booth on Pier 41.

The Comedy Store
(Formerly Ciro's nightclub)
8433 Sunset Boulevard
Los Angeles (West Hollywood), CA 90027
Phone: 323-656-6225 (show information);
323-656-6268 (offices)

Disneyland
1313 Harbor Boulevard
Anaheim, CA 92803
Phone: 714-781-4000

Operating hours vary seasonally.

El Fandango Restaurant
2734 Calhoun Street
San Diego, CA 92110
Phone: 619-298-2860

Hart Mansion
(now the William S. Hart Museum)
24151 San Fernando Road
Newhall, CA 91321
Phone: 805-254-4584

Newhall is a part of Santa Clarita, California, about 20 miles northwest of Los Angeles.

Palace Theater
1735 Vine
Hollywood, CA 90028
Phone: 323-467-4571

Hollywood Roosevelt Hotel
7000 Hollywood Boulevard
Hollywood, CA 90028
Phone: 323-466-7000
Toll free: 1-800-833-3333

The Houdini Mansion
2398 Laurel Canyon Boulevard
(at Willow Glen Road, near the junction of
Lookout Mountain Avenue)
Hollywood, CA 90028

While this is private property and no visitors are permitted, you can view the few original foundations that remain from Laurel Canyon Boulevard.

Los Angeles Pet Cemetery
5068 Old Scandia Lane
Calabasas, CA 91302-2507

Mann's Chinese Theatre
(Formerly Grauman's Chinese Theatre)
6925 Hollywood Boulevard
Hollywood, CA 90028
Phone: 323-464-8111

Victorian Inn on the Park
301 Lyon Street
San Francisco, CA 94117
Phone: 415-931-1830

The Olivas Adobe
The Olivas State Historical Monument
4200 Olivas Park Drive
Ventura, CA 93005
Phone: 805-644-4346

Pantages Theatre
6233 Hollywood Boulevard
Hollywood, CA 90028
Phone: 323-468-1770

Paramount's Great America
(amusement park)
P.O. Box 1776
Santa Clara, CA 95052
Phone: 408-988-1776

Exit Great America Parkway off Highway 101. Operating hours vary seasonally.

The *Queen Mary* (hotel and museum)
Berthed at Pier J in the Port of Long Beach.
Mailing address:
1126 Queens Highway
Long Beach, CA 90802-6390
Tour and event information:
562-435-3511
Information and hotel reservations:
1-800-437-2934

Guided tours take guests to many of the allegedly haunted spots throughout the interior of the ship, and special ghost tours are usually added around Halloween.

The Santa Clara House (restaurant)
211 E. Santa Clara Street
Ventura, CA 93005
Phone: 805-643-3264

Closed Mondays.

The Clifton Webb crypt
Hollywood Forever (formerly the Hollywood Memorial Cemetery)
Tomb located in the Sanctuary of Peace
6000 Santa Monica Boulevard
Hollywood, CA 90028
Phone: 323-469-1181

Mausoleum open to the public. A map to the stars' graves is available at the offices by the cemetery's front gate.

Whaley House
Old Town
2482 San Diego Avenue (at Harney Street)
San Diego, CA 92110
Phone: 619-298-2482

Historic monument open to the public as a museum. Exit I-5 at Old Town Avenue.

Winchester House
525 S. Winchester Boulevard
San Jose, CA 95128
Phone: 408-247-2000
Fax: 408-247-2090

Open daily (except Christmas) for guided tours from 9 A.M. Located on Winchester Boulevard, near the intersection of I-280 and I-880 and State Highway #17.

Georgia

Chickamauga-Chatanooga National Military Park
(especially Snod Grass Hill)
Chickamauga, GA
Phone: 706-866-9241

Battlegrounds open to visitors. Located 10 miles south of Chatanooga, Tennessee, on U.S. Highway 27.

Pirate's House Restaurant
20 East Broad Street (at Bay Street)
Savannah, GA 31404
Phone: 912-233-5757

St. Simon's Island Lighthouse and Museum
St. Simon's Island, GA
Phone: 912-638-4666

The island is 55 miles south of Savannah. The Brunswick toll bridge, 30 miles north of the Florida border on I-95, links the island to the mainland. The lighthouse is located at the eastern tip of the island. An iron walkway surrounds the top of the lighthouse.

Hawaii

State Capitol Building
465 S. King Street
Honolulu, Oahu, Hawaii 96813-2911
Phone: 808-587-0800

Idaho

Loon Creek
(especially Boise Basin, north of town)
Boise, ID

On I-84 in southwestern Idaho.

Wood River Camp
Baker Creek, ID

Hours vary seasonally. Baker Creek is in central Idaho, about six miles south of Wood River.

Illinois

Bachelor Grove Cemetery
(one-acre plot near the Rubio Woods Forest Preserve)
Midlothian, IL

Located west of Midlothian, a southern suburb of Chicago, in the Rubio Woods Forest Preserve. From Chicago, travel I-294 south to Cicero Avenue, then go west on the Midlothian Turnpike to the Rubio Woods exit. Visitation may be restricted due to recent vandalism.

361

Beverly Unitarian Church
(also called the Irish Castle)
10244 South Longwood Drive (at 103rd)
Chicago, IL 60643
Phone: 773-233-7080

Evergreen Cemetery
87th Street and Kedzie Avenue
Chicago, IL
Phone: 773-794-0707

Graceland Cemetery
4001 North Clark Street (at Irving Park Road)
Chicago, IL 60613
Phone: 773-525-1105

From downtown Chicago, travel north on Lakeshore Drive, then exit at Irving Park Road.

Holy Family Church
1019 South May Street
Chicago, IL 60607
Phone: 312-492-8442

Hull House
800 South Halsted Street
Chicago, IL 60607
Phone: 312-413-5353

Now operated as a museum. At the corner of Halsted and Polk streets.

Indian Head Park
Chicago and Hayes streets
Willow Springs, IL60480
Phone: 708-246-3137

Hours vary seasonally. Willow Springs is southwest of Chicago. Take I-294 toward Justice, then exit at Archer Avenue.

Jewish Waldheim Cemetery
North Riverside, IL 60546
Phone: 708-366-4100

Located across from Woodlawn Cemetery. The ghost has been seen at the gates and along Des Plaines Avenue between the cemetery and Melody Hill Ballroom.

Lincoln Tomb State Historic Site
Springfield, IL
For more information, contact the State Historical Sites Division
313 6th Street North
Springfield, IL 62701
Phone: 217-785-1584

Resurrection Cemetery
7600 South Archer Avenue
Justice, IL 60458
Phone: 708-458-4770

Resurrection Mary's ghost appears on stretches of Archer Avenue in Justice, south of Chicago. Take I-294, exit at 95th Street, and travel west to Roberts Road, then head north to Archer.

St. Turbius Church
56th Street and Karlow Avenue
Chicago, IL 60646

Indiana

Willard Library
21 First Avenue
Evansville, IN 47710
Phone: 812-425-4309

Iowa

Grand Opera House
135 Eighth Street
Dubuque, IA 52001
Phone: 319-588-4356

Ham House
(also known as Mathias Ham House)
2241 Lincoln Street
Dubuque, IA 52001
Phone: 319-583-2812

The Gothic mansion is now a museum, administered by the Dubuque Historical Society.

Kentucky

Liberty Hall
218 Wilkinson Street
Frankfort, KY 40501
Phone: 502-227-2560

Now a museum, operated by the Society of Colonial Dames of America.

Louisiana

Beauregard House and Garden Museum
(also known as LeCarpentier House)
1113 Charles Street
New Orleans, LA 70116
Phone: 504-523-7257

Open for tourism.

Hermann-Grima Historical House
820 St. Louis Street
New Orleans, LA 70116
Phone: 504-525-5661

Open for tourism.

Laveau House
1020 St. Ann Street
New Orleans, LA 70116
Phone: 504-568-5661

Open for tourism.

St. Louis Cemetery
400 Basin Street
New Orleans, LA 70116
Phone: 504-482-5065

The first grave of Marie Laveau is in St. Louis Cemetery No. 1, 25 feet to the left of the entrance. The other grave of Marie Laveau is in St. Louis Cemetery No. 2.

Maine

Boothbay Opera House
Boothbay Harbor, ME 04538
Phone: 207-633-6855

Located on Maine's southwestern coast, on Highway 27, 10 miles south of U.S. Highway 1.

Maryland

Fort McHenry
Baltimore, MD

Open for visitors as part of the National Park Service (since 1933). Tours are also conducted.

Point Lookout State Park
Point Lookout, MD
Phone: 410-592-2897

At the end of Highway 5 in southern Maryland. The park's mailing address is Star Route 48, Scotland, MD 20687. The converted Point Lookout Lighthouse and Fort Lincoln are located here. In October, park rangers conduct a ghost tour.

Edgar Allan Poe House
203 North Amity Street
Baltimore, MD 21202
Phone: 410-396-7932

Since 1949 (exactly 100 years since Poe's death), the house has been open as a public museum.

Westminster Church
Fayette and Greene streets
Baltimore, MD

For information on Edgar Allan Poe's grave, located in the churchyard, contact 410-706-7228.

Massachusetts

Fort Warren Historical Site
George's Island
Boston Harbor
Boston, MA

Ferries depart from Long Wharf and Rowes Wharf in Boston. Information on the site (including a pamphlet about the ghost) is available from the Metropolitan District Commission, 20 Somerset Street, Boston, MA 02108; information: 617-698-1802; public relations: 617-727-5114.

363

The Mount
Highway 20 and Plunkett Street
Lenox, MA 01240
Phone: 413-637-1899

The Mount is currently a theater.

Minnesota

Guthrie Theater
725 Vineland Place
Minneapolis, MN 55403
Phone: 612-377-2224

Public areas open to patrons.

Missouri

Joplin Lights
Near Joplin, MO

The lights are best seen along a two-mile stretch of Devil's Promenade Road, outside the village of Hornet, about 11 miles southwest of Joplin. From Joplin, take I-44 west, then turn south on State Line Road just before entering Oklahoma. Travel about four miles to Devil's Promenade.

Montana

Bonanza Inn
Virginia City, MT 59755

Located in southwestern Montana.

The Custer House
Fort Abraham Lincoln
Crow Indian Reservation, MT

The historic fort is located on the Crow Indian Reservation, southeast of Billings in southern Montana.

Little Bighorn National Battlefield
Crow Indian Reservation
Crow Agency, MT
Phone: 406-638-2621

The battleground is on reservation lands, on I-90 15 miles from Hardin. The haunted stone house, formerly the park guard headquarters, is near the cemetery. Reno Crossing is located about five miles from the battlefield.

Nebraska

State Capitol Building
10th Street and Lincoln Parkway
Lincoln, NE 68501
Phone: 402-471-2311

Nevada

Fourth Ward School
At the corner of B and C streets
Virginia City, NV 89440
Phone: 775-847-0975

For information, contact the Virginia City Chamber of Commerce, Box 464, C Street, Virginia City, NV 89440; 775-847-0311.

St. Paul's Episcopal Church
Upstairs window
South F and Taylor streets
Virginia City, NV

Not open for tourism. The ghost appears at the upstairs window.

New Hampshire

Country Tavern
452 Amherst Street
Nashua, NH 03063
Phone: 603-889-5871

New Jersey

The Spy House Museum
119 Port Monmouth Road
Port Monmouth, NJ 07758

New Mexico

St. James Hotel
Room 17 and "Mary's Room"
17th and Collinson streets
Cimarron, NM 87714

Located near the junction of U.S. Highway 64 and Highway 21. The hotel's mailing address is Route 1 Box 2, Cimarron, NM 87714; or call 505-376-2664.

New York

Durand Eastman Park
(along Lake Ontario)
Rochester, NY

Eamonn's (restaurant)
(also known as Eamonn-Loudon House; formerly Loudon Cottage)
151 Menands Road
Loudonville, NY 12211
Phone: 518-463-7440

Open to restaurant patrons. Current building greatly enlarged from original cottage. Loudonville, just north of Albany, is located at U.S. Highway 9 and Osborne Road.

Fort Ticonderoga
Fort Road, Box 390
Ticonderoga, NY 12883
Phone: 518-585-2821

On Lake Champlain at the Vermont border.

State Capitol Building
Albany, NY 12223
Phone: 518-455-4100

Storm King Pass
Stony Point, NY

Located along the Hudson River between Storm King Mountain and Stony Point.

North Carolina

Brown Mountain lights
Linville Gorge
Brown Mountains
Morganton, NC

The lights are best seen along Highway 181 between Morganton and Lenoir in western North Carolina.

Maco light
Along the tracks near the Atlantic Coast Railroad Crossing
(formerly the Wilmington-Florence-Augusta tracks)
Outside Maco, NC

For more information, contact the Southeastern North Carolina Beach Association, Wilmington, NC 28401.

North Dakota

Fort Abercrombie
Abercrombie, ND 58001
Phone: 701-553-8513

Northeast of downtown Abercrombie, which is located in southeast North Dakota.

The George Custer House
Fort Abraham Lincoln
401 W. Main
Mandan, ND 58554-3164
Phone: 701-663-4758
E-mail: falf@tic.bisman.com

Ohio

Hinckley Library
Ridge and Center roads
Hinckley, OH 44233
Phone: 330-278-4271

Near Akron in northeast Ohio.

Oregon

Barclay House
719 Center Street
Oregon City, OR 97045
Phone: 503-557-6261

Operated as a museum. Located on a hill overlooking the city. From McLoughlin Street in the center of town, follow 10th Street to the top of the hill, turn left at 7th Street, then left again at Center Street.

McLoughlin House
713 Center Street
Oregon City, OR 97045
Phone: 503-656-5146

Operated as a museum since the 1930s. Located next to Barclay House.

Pennsylvania

Baleroy
111 West Mermaid Lane
Philadelphia, PA 19118

In Chestnut Hill section of the city. Tours available upon special arrangement.

Gettysburg National Military Park
Business Route 15
Gettysburg, PA
Phone: 717-334-1124

Battlegrounds are open to visitors.

Margaret Grundy Memorial Library
Radcliffe Street
Bristol, PA 19007
Phone: 215-788-7891

Rhode Island

The Palantine lights (phantom ship)
(off Block Island)
Block Island, RI

Block Island is in the Rhode Island Sound off the south coast of Rhode Island, about 11 miles from Montauk, Long Island.

Ferry service is available from Galilee, Rhode Island. For a schedule, contact Interstate Navigation Co., Box 482, New London, CT 06320; 860-442-9553. The lights, when seen, are most visible from the State Beach or Settler's Rock Grove. For visitor information, contact the Chamber of Commerce, Drawer D, Block Island, RI 02807; 401-466-2982.

South Carolina

The Old Lighthouse and Baynard Plantation
Hilton Head Island, SC

From I-95, take Highway 462 to Highway 278, which heads onto the island.

Yeoman's Hall
Charleston, SC

On the site of the old Goose Creek Plantation, just south of Charleston.

Tennessee

Carnton Mansion
1345 Carnton Lane
Franklin, TN 37064
Phone: 615-794-0903

Orpheum Theatre
203 South Main Street
Memphis, TN 38173
Phone: 901-525-7800

Texas

The Alamo
Alamo Plaza
San Antonio, TX 78201
Phone: 210-225-1391

Open for tourism. For more information, contact The Alamo Visitor Center at 210-225-8587.

Marfa lights
Marfa, TX

Marfa is located 26 miles west of Alpine, Texas, on U.S. Highway 67/90. One of the best viewing spots is about eight miles east of Marfa on Highway 90, where there's a plaque that describes the ghost lights. Other good viewing areas are on Mitchell Flat southwest of Marfa and on the plateau between Marfa and Alpine.

Houston Public Library
500 McKinney
Houston, TX 77002
Phone: 717-236-1313
Web site: http://www.hpl.lib.tx.us

Utah

Utah State Historical Society
300 Rio Grande Street
Salt Lake City, UT 84101
Phone: 801-533-3500

Vermont

Lake Memphremagog
Newport, Vermont

The lake is along the Quebec-Vermont border at Newport, at I-91.

Virginia

Aquia Episcopal Church
2938 Jefferson Davis Highway
Stafford, VA 22554
Phone: 540-659-4007
Web site: http://www.illuminet.net/aquiachurch/

Located in Stafford County, 20 miles north of Fredericksburg.

West Virginia

Harpers Ferry National Park
P.O. Box 65
Harpers Ferry, WV 25425
Phone: 304-535-6205

Wisconsin

Majestic Theater
12th and Mitchell streets
Milwaukee, WI 53204
Phone: 414-299-0021
Recorded information: 414-383-1880

Wyoming

Fort Laramie National Historic Site
Laramie, WY
Phone: 307-837-2221

Located three miles west of Ft. Laramie on Highway 160.

Old Faithful Inn
Yellowstone National Park
Wyoming
Information: 307-344-7901
Reservations: 307-344-7311

Open for patrons. The park, in northwest Wyoming, can be entered from U.S. Highways 14 and 89/287.

St. Mark's Episcopal Church
19th Street and Central Avenue
Cheyenne, WY 82001
Phone: 307-634-7709

Washington, District of Columbia

U.S. Capitol Building
Washington, D.C. 20006
Phone: 202-224-3121

For general information about touring Washington sites, contact the Washington Visitors Association, 1212 New York Avenue, Northwest, Suite 600, Washington, D.C. 20005; 202-789-7000.

Decatur House
748 Jackson Place, Northwest
Washington D.C 20006
Phone: 202-842-0920

367

The house, currently occupied by National Trust for Historic Preservation, is maintained as a museum and open to visitors. Located at the corner of Jefferson Place and H Street in Lafayette Square.

Ford's Theatre
511 10th Street, Northwest
Washington, D.C. 20066
Phone: 202-426-6927

Maintained by the National Park Service as a museum. Open seven days a week, 9 A.M. to 5 P.M. Ford's Theatre is also a working playhouse, operated by the Theatre Society. The auditorium of the theatre is closed when there are matinee performances (Thursday and Sunday afternoons, in season).

The Octagon
1799 New York Avenue, Northwest
Washington, D.C., 20006-5291
Recorded information: 202-638-3105
Administration: 202-638-3221

Located at the intersection of New York Avenue, 18th Street, and E Street, The Octagon is open to the public as a museum Tuesday through Sunday, 10 A.M. to 4 P.M. $3 for adults, $1.50 for students and seniors.

The Petersen House
516 10th Street, Northwest
Washington, D.C. 20006
Phone: 202-426-6830

Owned by the National Park Service. The second floor, the site of Abraham Lincoln's death, has been renovated with furnishings of the Lincoln period and is open as a museum seven days a week, 9 A.M. to 5 P.M.

The White House (the Executive Mansion)
1600 Pennsylvania Avenue, Northwest
Washington, D.C. 20500

For tour information, contact the White House Visitor Center, 1450 Pennsylvania Avenue, Northwest, Washington, D.C. 20004; 202-208-1631, or for 24-hour recorded information, 202-456-7041.

Woodrow Wilson House
2340 S Street, Northwest
Washington, D.C. 20008
Phone: 202-387-4062

Maintained as a museum by the National Trust for Historical Preservation. On Embassy Row.

England

British Museum
Great Russell Street
Bloomsbury, London, WC1B 3DG
Phone: 0171-635-1555
Recorded information: 0171-580-1788
Fax: 0171-323-8118

Open daily, Monday through Saturday 10 A.M. to 5 P.M., Sunday 2.30 to 6 P.M., except January 1, Good Friday, the first Monday in May, and December 24 to 26, when the museum is closed. Self-guided tours by cassette/headsets are available. Admission is free.

Chingle Hall
760 Whittingham Lane
Goosnargh, Preston
Lancashire PR3 2JJ
Phone: 01772-861-082

Located six miles north of Preston. Open to visitors and overnight guests from April to October.

Theatre Royal, Drury Lane
Catherine Street
Covent Garden
London, WC2B 5JF
Phone: 0171-494-5000

Public areas open to patrons. Backstage tours available daily. Call 0171-494-5091 for advance booking.

Hampton Court Palace
East Molesey, Surrey
Phone: 0181-781-9500

The splendid parks surrounding the palace are open daily. Visiting hours of the palace and other buildings on the grounds vary considerably, though usually from 9:30 or 10:15 A.M. to 4:30 or 6 P.M.

The Haymarket, Theatre Royal
Located between Piccadilly Circus and Buckingham Palace
London SW1Y 4HT
Phone: 0171-930-8800

Public areas open to patrons. A theatre and backstage tour is also available to groups.

The Tower of London
Tower Hill EC3M 4AB
London
Phone: 0171-709-0765

Open daily March through October, Monday through Saturday 9 A.M. to 6 P.M. and Sunday 10 A.M. to 6 P.M. From November through February, the Tower is open Monday to Saturday 9 A.M. to 5 P.M. and Sunday 10 A.M. to 5 P.M. Closed on January 1 and December 24 to 26.

Windsor Castle
Windsor, Berkshire
Phone: 01753-831-118

Twenty miles west of London on the south bank of the Thames River. Visiting times to Windsor Castle vary seasonally, generally from 10 A.M. to late afternoon or, in the summer, into the early evening. Hours are further limited to the State Apartments and the Albert Memorial Chapel, both of which are located on the castle grounds. The State Apartments cannot be visited when the Queen is in residence at Windsor.

Scotland

Glamis Castle
Glamis
Angus DD8 1RQ
Phone: 030-784-242/243
Fax: 0307-84257

Open daily, noon until 5:30 P.M. The last tour departs at 4:45 P.M. on Easter weekend, then the last Saturday in April to mid-October.

Index

A

Academy of Religion and Psychical Research, 122
activities of poltergeists, 50-51
  phantom drummers, 53-54
  stone-throwing and falling stones, 52-53
actors and actresses, *see* Hollywood
Adelphi Theatre, 232
afterlife, belief in, 7-8
  locations of spirit world, 9-10
agents (apparitions), 6
airplanes, *see* planes and airships
Akron Civic Theatre, 236
aku aku, 155
Alabama, haunted schools, 263
Alamo, 227
Alcatraz, 297
All Hallows Eve, 11
Allerton Mansion, 174
Amityville Horror, 59-60
amulets (protection from evil), 45-47
amusement parks, 294-296
  Disneyland, 295-296
  King's Island, 294-295
  Paramount's Great America, 294
Angelo State University, 264
Angels of Mons, 223-224
Antrim Castle, 204
apparitions
  agents, 6
  collective, 31
  crisis, 32-33
  objective vs. subjective, 140
  percipients, 6
  reciprocal, 31
  vs. ghosts, 4-6
apports, 96-98
Arkansas, haunted schools, 264
armies (phantom), 222-224
  Angels of Mons, 223-224
  Dieppe Raid Case, 222-223
  Legend of the Legionaries, 223
Ash Manor House, 188
Ashley Place levitation, 103-104
astral bodies, 26

astral projection, 30-31
  arrival cases, 32
  crisis apparitions, 32-33
  Wilmot apparition, 31-32
Athens State College, 263
Atlas Theatre, 241
automatic writing, 68
automobiles (James Dean's), 251-252

B

Bachelor Grove Cemetery, 215-216
Baleroy Mansion, 168
Ballechin House, 188-189
Barclay House, 170
Battle Abbey (England), 211-212
battlefields, 229-230
  Alamo, 227
  Civil War, 227-229
  Custer's Last Stand, 226-227
Beaulieu Abbey (England), 210
Beauregard House, 177
Belcourt Castle (Newport, RI), 213-214
Bell House, 175-176
Bertrand, Alexandre, 70-71
Bettiscombe Manor (screaming skulls), 162
birds (death omens), 40
Black Shucks (death omens), 40
Blithe Spirit, 332-333
boats, *see* ships
Bolton Mansion, 168
Bolton Priory (England), 210-211
Bonanza Inn (Virginia City, MT), 214-216
Boothbay Opera House, 239
Borley Rectory, 183-187
  Harry Price investigation, 184-87
Boston University, 259
Bow Head, 189
British College of Psychic Science, 122, 213
British dirigible R-101, 252-254
British Museum, 300
Brown Mountain lights, 161
Browning circle, 103
  home circles, 83-84

C

Cagney, James, 280
California, haunted houses and schools, 170-173, 271-272
Caligula, 19
Capitol Building, 180-181
castles, haunted, *see* haunted castles
Catholicism, 63-64
  phantom monks and nuns, 209-216
celebrities, 273
  Cagney, James, 280
  Harlow, Jean, 273-275
  Nelson, Ozzie, 275-276
  Novarro, Ramon, 276
  Reeves, George, 276-277
  Savalas, Telly, 280-281
  Sommer, Elke, 281
  Wayne, John, 277
  Webb, Clifton, 277-280
  see also Hollywood
cemeteries, 216-217
  Bachelor Grove Cemetery, 216
  Graceland Cemetery, 216
  Jewish Waldheim Cemetery, 217
  St. Louis Cemetery, 217
chalcedony, 45
channeling, 111
charms, 45-47
Chase Home, 167-168
Chicago, haunted houses, 174-175
  Allerton Mansion, 174
  Beverly Unitarian Church, 174
  Hull House, 174
  Schweppe Mansion, 174-175
Chingle Hall, 189-190
Christianity, 21-22
Christopher, Milbourne, 317
Civil War, 227-229
clairvoyance, 4